CONFLICT
BEHAVIOR
& LINKAGE
POLITICS

Comparative Studies of Political Life

Series Editor: MARTIN O. HEISLER

CARL BECK, FREDERIC J. FLERON, JR., MILTON LODGE, DEREK J. WALLER, WILLIAM A. WELSH, M. GEORGE ZANINOVICH, *Comparative Communist Political Leadership*

ROGER W. BENJAMIN (with Alan Arian, Richard N. Blue, and Stephen Coleman), *Patterns of Political Development: Japan, India, Israel*

WOLFRAM F. HANRIEDER, ed., *Comparative Foreign Policy: Theoretical Essays*

ALLAN KORNBERG, ed., *Legislatures in Comparative Perspective*

STEIN ROKKAN (with Angus Campbell, Per Torsvik, and Henry Valen), *Citizens, Elections, Parties: Approaches to the Comparative Study of the Processes of Development*

JONATHAN WILKENFELD, ed., *Conflict Behavior and Linkage Politics*

CONFLICT BEHAVIOR & LINKAGE POLITICS

EDITED BY

JONATHAN WILKENFELD

University of Maryland

DAVID McKAY COMPANY, INC.

NEW YORK

1973

CONFLICT BEHAVIOR AND LINKAGE POLITICS

For Judy

Contributors

Robert Burrowes: Associate professor and director of graduate studies, Department of Politics, New York University; articles in *World Politics, Journal of Conflict Resolution,* and *Comparative Political Studies.*

John N. Collins: Assistant professor, Department of Political Science, University of Missouri-St. Louis; currently working in the field of Public Administration and Urban Policy.

Lewis A. Coser: Distinguished professor of sociology, State University of New York at Stony Brook; books include *The Functions of Social Conflict* (1957), *Men of Ideas* (1965), *Political Sociology* (1967), and *Continuities in the Study of Social Conflict* (1967); articles in the *American Journal of Sociology, Social Problems, American Sociological Review,* and *Journal of Social Issues,* among others.

Michael Haas: Professor of political science and chairman of the Committee on Peace Research, University of Hawaii; author of *Approaches to the Study of Political Science* and two forthcoming books—*Behavioral Political Science* and *International Conflict*; articles in *American Political Science Review, Comparative Political Studies,* and *Journal of Peace Research,* among others.

Leo A. Hazlewood: Assistant professor, Department of Government, Florida State University; has contributed to *New Directions in Comparative Politics* (ed. James N. Rosenau).

Warren R. Phillips: Associate professor, Department of Political Science, Ohio State University; articles in *Journal of Conflict Resolution, Papers of the Peace Research Society,* and *Comparative Political Studies.*

James N. Rosenau: Professor of political science, Ohio State University; books include *Domestic Sources of Foreign Policy* (1967), *Contending Approaches to International Politics* (1969), *Linkage Politics* (1969), *International Politics and Foreign Policy* (1969), *The Scientific Study of Foreign Policy* (1971); articles in *American Political Science Review, World Politics, Journal of Politics, Journal of Conflict Resolution,* among others.

R. J. Rummel: Professor of political science and director of the Dimensionality of Nations Project, University of Hawaii; author of *Applied Factor Analysis* and *Dimensions of Nations*; articles in *American Political Science Review, World Politics, Journal of Conflict Resolution, Journal of Peace Research,* among others.

Bertram Spector: Ph.D. candidate, Department of Politics, New York University.

Richard H. Van Atta: Assistant professor, School of International Service, The American University; article in *Papers of the Peace Research Society*.

Jonathan Wilkenfeld: Associate professor of government and politics, University of Maryland; articles in *Journal of Peace Research*, and *Journal of Conflict Resolution*.

Dina A. Zinnes: Associate professor, Department of Political Science, Indiana University; Co-author of *Content Analysis* (1963); articles in *Journal of Conflict Resolution*, *Journal of Peace Research*, and *World Politics*.

Contents

PART III   Domestic Conflict Behavior Linkages

CONFLICT
BEHAVIOR
& LINKAGE
POLITICS

Introduction

The term "linkage politics" was first used by James N. Rosenau to describe a relatively new approach within the discipline of political science.[1] Rosenau developed the concept to apply to the linkage between any two political systems, but the linkage referred to in the present context is that which apparently exists between the two traditional subfields of comparative and international politics. Implicit in the linkage concept is the notion that these are in fact two distinct areas of concern. Implied also is that they overlap under certain circumstances, at least in the sense that events in one sphere influence and are in turn influenced by events in the other.

Rosenau defines linkage as "any recurrent sequence of behavior that originates in one system and is reacted to in another."[2] While there remains little doubt that such linkages exist, it has nevertheless been convenient for scholars of comparative and international politics to disregard or, to use the more contemporary term, to hold constant, factors in the other sphere. Thus, for the student of international politics, the nation functions in the international environment on the basis of the givens of that system, unrestrained by any domestic considerations. Differences existing between national systems are not considered crucial to an understanding of a nation's international behavior. This approach to international politics has been referred to as the "realist school," and among its leading proponents is Hans J. Morgenthau.[3] From the other perspective, the student of comparative politics feels that the international system is virtually irrelevant for purposes of explaining domestic political events. In both cases, this has led to a rather stultified approach. Situations arose in which the actions of a nation appeared to be "irrational," in that they could not be explained adequately on the basis of the conceptual tools of either of the two approaches.

It is to these types of problems that the emerging linkage politics approach addresses itself. The purpose of studying linkage politics is to gain a more complete understanding of events by taking account of a large number of variables that have a bearing on the ultimate behavior of a nation, whether this behavior be manifested in the domestic or international spheres. The adoption of such an approach does not imply that all previously unexplained phenomena now come within our grasp. It merely adds a new dimension to those phenomena already accounted for.

While linkage politics as a concept is meant to encompass all areas of

[1]James N. Rosenau, ed., *Linkage Politics* (New York: Free Press, 1969).
[2]Ibid., p. 44.
[3]Hans J. Morgenthau, *Politics Among Nations* (New York: Alfred A. Knopf, 1967).

domestic and international behavior, it is not possible within the confines of the present volume to use the idea in its broadest sense. The scope of the present endeavor is limited to studies concerned with domestic and/or foreign conflict behavior. Thus, conflict behavior in one sphere is treated as a dependent variable, and an effort is made to isolate those variables in the other sphere that appear to be related to this phenomenon.

In no way should the endeavor undertaken in the following pages be considered a quest for a general theory by which we will be able to predict and/or explain the actions of nations. A theory of domestic and foreign conflict behavior will emerge only in the doubtful eventuality that we are able to isolate and measure properly virtually all variables operating in a given situation. In a sense, then, the present purpose will be to examine the feasibility of adding several new variables to the list. In this way, through the work of many independent scholars, we will begin to reach the theory that has been so long anticipated by social scientists.

A LINKAGE APPROACH TO CONFLICT BEHAVIOR

In 1963 R. J. Rummel published a study that dealt with the relationship between the domestic and foreign conflict behavior of nations. His major finding, based on data for seventy-seven nations in the mid-1950s, was that "foreign conflict behavior is generally completely unrelated to domestic conflict behavior."[4] This initial finding was further substantiated in two subsequent studies. Utilizing slightly different methods of analysis, Rummel found "a positive association, albeit small, between domestic conflict behavior and the more belligerent forms of foreign conflict behavior on the part of a country."[5] Raymond Tanter, in a work that essentially replicated the first Rummel study for a later period, concluded "there is a small relationship between . . . domestic and foreign conflict behavior which increases with a time lag."[6]

These findings appear to run counter to well-accepted notions of the relationship between domestic and foreign conflict behavior patterns of nations. It is commonly supposed that the leadership of a nation, under conditions of a deteriorating position at home, will seek to divert the attention of the population by engaging in some form of foreign conflict behavior. Thus, a nation can unite a divided people behind the banner of a common cause. R. Barry Farrell, for example, speaks of political leaders of constitutional democracies who find it useful to take attention away from internal

[4]R. J. Rummel, "Dimensions of Conflict Behavior Within and Between Nations," chap. 3, this volume.

[5]R. J. Rummel, "Testing Some Possible Predictors of Conflict Behavior Within and Between Nations," *Peace Research Society Papers* 1(1963): 101–2.

[6]Raymond Tanter, "Dimensions of Conflict Behavior Within and Between Nations, 1958–1960," *Journal of Conflict Resolution* 10 (March 1966): 41–64.

political problems by stressing international affairs.[7] Quincy Wright, in his monumental work on the study of war, mentions with prominence the possibility of linkages between conflict occurring in the domestic and foreign spheres.[8] Richard N. Rosecrance, in his systemic study of world politics, feels that a correlation may exist between international instability and the domestic insecurity of elites. Although he contends that war may occur in the absence of internal instability and that internal frictions may occur in the absence of war, he also argues that the two factors appear to be associated in the chaotic international patterns of modern times.[9] F. H. Denton, while not committing himself either way in this regard, has suggested that civil wars that precede and contribute to international wars, and international wars that cause and contribute to civil wars, are both "intuitively satisfying hypotheses."[10] Finally, Ernst B. Haas and Allen S. Whiting have stated:

Groups seeking self-preservation and no more may be driven to a foreign policy of conflict—if not open war—in order to defend themselves against the onslaught of domestic rather than foreign enemies. In times of extreme domestic tensions among elites, a policy of uniting a badly divided nation against some real or alleged outside threat frequently seems useful to a ruling group.[11]

The apparent contradiction between the findings of Rummel and Tanter and this commonly accepted theory provided the stimulus for the present study. Whether linkages exist between conflict behavior in the domestic and foreign spheres is too important a question to be relegated to this limbo. If Rummel and Tanter are correct, then we can finally put to rest the whole notion that foreign conflict behavior is related to domestic conflict behavior, a theory that has been popular both among political scientists and among political analysts in general. On the other hand, if it can be established that Rummel's and Tanter's conclusions were incomplete because their analyses did not account for certain relevant factors, then we will have significantly advanced knowledge in this area. In either case, it is important that the question of the relationship between domestic and foreign conflict behavior be reopened.

Beginning with this focus on the relationship between conflict behavior in the two spheres, the present volume has been expanded to include other

[7]R. Barry Farrell, "Foreign Politics of Open and Closed Political Societies," in *Approaches to Comparative and International Politics*, ed. R. Barry Farrell (Evanston: Northwestern University Press, 1966), p. 185.

[8]Quincy Wright, *A Study of War* (Chicago: University of Chicago Press, 1942).

[9]Richard N. Rosecrance, *Action and Reaction in World Politics* (Boston: Little, Brown and Co., 1963), pp. 304–5.

[10]F. H. Denton, "Some Regularities in International Conflict, 1820–1949" (Rand Corporation, 1965), p. 20.

[11]Ernest B. Haas and Allen S. Whiting, *Dynamics of International Relations* (New York: McGraw-Hill, 1956), p. 62.

domestic and foreign factors as well. Here again, an initial impetus was partially provided by Rummel. In a recent study, Rummel attempted to investigate the possible relationships between various national attributes and foreign conflict behavior, using data for 1955.[12] Specifically, he tested hypotheses relating foreign conflict behavior to such domestic attributes as the level of economic and technological development, the level of international communications, the totalitarianism of a nation's government, the power of a nation, and the instability of a nation. As was the case with his earlier studies, he once again failed to confirm any of his hypotheses relating foreign conflict behavior to societal attributes.

With these findings in mind, the first premise around which the present volume is organized is that the Rummel and Tanter approach may have tended to obscure more specific trends in the interests of reaching conclusions that could be generalized across all nations. It is these trends in domestic and foreign conflict linkages that are assessed in the various studies presented here. It is proposed that conflict linkages do in fact exist, and that they take on various forms, depending upon (1) the type of nation under consideration, (2) the type of conflict behavior involved, (3) the type of temporal relationship, and (4) the conflict situation and context.

Type of Nation

There is evidence in the literature that the governmental structure of a nation is crucial to an understanding of both the process and the nature of domestic and foreign policy decision making. Some types of governmental structures may be able to withstand large amounts of domestic disorders without resorting to attention-diverting devices such as foreign violence. Under some conditions, nations may be unable to resort to foreign violence because of the severity of the domestic violence they are undergoing. However, the literature does not speak with one voice concerning the way in which type of nation influences relationships between the domestic and foreign spheres.

Several recent studies have attempted to show that, with regard to general linkages between the two spheres, the supposed differences between democratic and totalitarian systems are not as great as would be imagined. Thus, Farrell observes that in constitutional democracies, it is fairly common for decision makers seeking reelection to espouse foreign policy decisions with an eye to the ballot box rather than in accordance with environmental realities. He indicates that in a totalitarian system, while the circumstances are not quite equivalent, it is nevertheless the case that

---

[12]R. J. Rummel, "The Relationship Between National Attributes and Foreign Conflict Behavior," in *Quantitative International Politics*, ed. J. David Singer (New York: Free Press, 1968).

decision makers perceive international policy as manipulable to serve domestic intents.[13] Milton J. Rosenberg contends that given the general anti-Communist trend of public opinion in the United States, conciliatory moves on the part of the government would be considered gross violations of the public trust. These dynamics are present in the Soviet Union as well. With its lack of institutions guaranteeing high office for fixed terms, the leadership must remain sensitive to public opinion among the subelite, the military, and provincial functionaries in the party system.[14]

The more conventionally expressed view is that differences in nation type do influence the extent to which the domestic and foreign spheres are linked. Joseph Frankel has maintained:

One of the most significant relationships within the environment is the interaction between domestic and foreign affairs. On the basis of relative security and isolation from foreign affairs, it has been customary for British and American thinkers and statesmen to believe that the two domains are separate and that domestic affairs prevail. Very different is the tradition of the continental countries where such separation has never taken place.[15]

It is in the area of conflict linkages that we find the greatest tendency among scholars to argue for the importance of differentiating among types of nations. Farrell observes that the use of international crises to divert attention away from internal problems is a device most commonly found in the totalitarian system. Nevertheless, he warns against assuming that the democratic system is completely immune from this type of linkage.[16] Differentiation of nations according to level of economic development has also been cited as having a bearing on the relationship between domestic and foreign conflict. James N. Rosenau contends that the literature on economic and political development often refers to the ways in which foreign policies of modernizing societies are shaped by their internal needs, such as the sustaining of charismatic leadership, the need for elite identity and prestige, and the needs of in-groups to divert the attention away from domestic problems and thereby to placate their opposition.[17] Elsewhere, Rosenau has stated:

[An] example . . . is provided by the leaders of underdeveloped countries who often seem to be better able to overcome domestic strife and inertia by citing the hostility of the external environment than by stressing the need for hard work and

[13]Farrell, "Foreign Politics," p. 185.
[14]Milton J. Rosenberg, "Attitude Change and Foreign Policy in the Cold War Era," in *Domestic Sources of Foreign Policy*, ed. James N. Rosenau (New York: Free Press, 1967), pp. 128,130.
[15]Joseph Frankel, *International Relations* (New York: Oxford University Press, 1964), p. 54.
[16]Farrell, "Foreign Politics" p. 186.
[17]James N. Rosenau, "Pre-Theories and Theories of Foreign Policy," in Farrell, ed., *Approaches to Comparative and International Politics*, p. 33.

patience at home. In effect, they attempt to solve domestic issues by redefining them as falling in the foreign policy area.[18]

Finally, in this regard, Pablo Gonzales Casanova speaks of the need for national unity within developing nations. He feels that the policy best suited for development is that provided by national unity and a "nationalist anti-imperialist front." This policy of nationalism is least understood in the developed world, and most directly binds the problems of internal and external politics.[19]

In the above discussion, the concern has been with establishing the importance of nation type in the consideration of domestic and foreign conflict behavior. It is contended that Rummel's and Tanter's failure to discover relationships between conflict behavior in the two spheres may have come about primarily due to their failure to consider type of nation as an important mediating factor. In a sense, we may find it necessary to pull back at least partially from the current cross-national studies which assert that certain generalizations apply across *all* nations. Still, it will not be necessary to argue that the individual nation is the only appropriate level of analysis at which we can formulate valid generalizations.[20] This would be moving too far in the other direction. There is a point, however, at which we must introduce some limiting factor and still be engaged in cross-national research. It is noteworthy that Rummel, in his article in *General Systems Yearbook*, allows for the possibility that the lack of relationship in his findings, while constituting a cross-national generalization, may be misleading. Thus he states:

This is not to say that there are not particular cases in which domestic and foreign conflict behavior are related. There may well be situations in which the domestic political elite of a nation will foment foreign conflict as a means of quieting internal squabbling. Moreover, if one were to take a longitudinal slice out of the history of many nations, a very close relation in the fluctuations of domestic and foreign conflict might be found.[21]

Tanter also makes an effort to explain the rather small relationship between the two types of conflict behavior. He writes:

There may be no "simple" relationship between domestic and foreign conflict behavior, but there may be a causal relationship which is being obscured by other

[18]Rosenau, *Domestic Sources*, p. 25.

[19]Pablo Gonzales Casanova, "Internal and External Politics of Underdeveloped Countries," in Farrell, ed., *Approaches to Comparative and International Politics*, p. 144.

[20]For a discussion of the level-of-analysis problem, see J. David Singer, "The Level-of-Analysis Problem in International Relations," *World Politics* 14 (October 1961); and Wolfram F. Hanrieder, "Actor Objectives and International Systems," *Journal of Politics* 27 (February 1965).

[21]Rummel, "Dimensions of Conflict Behavior," p. 92.

phenomena. That is, the relationship may be mediated by a third variable such as the personality characteristics of the national decision-makers.[22]

Type of Conflict Behavior

A second major assumption underlying the studies assembled here is that conflict linkages differ, depending upon the *type* of conflict behavior under consideration. While type of conflict was taken into account in the Rummel and Tanter studies, its effect was obscured by their failure to consider the type of nation involved. It is the contention here that certain types of foreign conflict behavior may be related to domestic violence or other domestic attributes. In other cases, foreign attributes and behavior may engender domestic conflict responses.

It is appropriate at this point to deal briefly with the concept of conflict behavior itself. Definitions of "conflict" abound in the literature of political science, sociology, and social psychology.[23] For the most part, these definitions are concerned with conflict situations involving two or more parties. In that sense, we can speak of situations that exhibit zero-sum or nonzerosum characteristics, two-person or *n*-person situations, and the relative payoffs for participants in conflict situations. In the present content, many of these notions are of little use, since the major concern is with a particular and rather limited aspect of conflict behavior. Thus, the limiting assumption made here is that conflict behavior in the international sphere is not necessarily the outcome of the nation's interactions with other nations, but rather the outcome of behavior patterns and attributes within the nation. We are assuming that a nation's conflict behavior can be explained in part on the basis of its own national attributes. For the moment, then, we are not considering any connection between the activities of one party and the conflict behavior aroused in the other.

The actual operational measures of conflict behavior are discussed more fully in the individual studies. For present purposes, domestic conflict behavior is conceived as manifestations of internal disorders within a society. These manifestations vary in intensity from strikes and demonstrations to guerrilla wars and revolutions. Similarly, foreign conflict behavior is conceived as manifestations of foreign violence engaged in by a nation. These may vary in intensity from protests and accusations to mobilizations and wars.

It is perhaps appropriate to deal briefly with the limiting factor imposed on this analysis by the notion of conflict adopted here. In order to determine what portion of a nation's foreign conflict can be explained by its domestic attributes and behavior, it is assumed that *all* foreign conflict of a nation can

---

[22]Tanter, "Dimensions of Conflict Behavior," p. 60.
[23]See Clinton F. Fink, "Some Conceptual Difficulties in the Theory of Social Conflict," *Journal of Conflict Resolution* 12 (December 1968): 412–60.

be explained by these domestic variables. Likewise, it is assumed that *all* domestic conflict of a nation can be explained by external factors. While these determinants are useful in carrying out the research proposed in this volume, it must be borne in mind that we are thereby neglecting other very important determinants of conflict behavior. The positing of linkages between phenomena in the two spheres does not deny the possibility of conflict behavior in one sphere resulting from other conflict behavior in that same sphere.

Hopefully, the type of research strategy adopted here will eventually lead to a more balanced approach to the analysis of the determinants of national behavior. We are thus seeking something close to what Rosenau has referred to as "adaptive politics"[24] or "linkage politics."[25] The distinctive subject matter of this approach is the interaction between the political actor and the external environment. It does not necessarily deny that certain national actions are products of events in only one sphere, nor does it contend that actions are shaped totally by the effects of linkages between spheres.

Temporal Relationships

The third element to be introduced into the present analysis of conflict behavior is a temporal, or lagged, relationship. In this sense, we are bringing in the notion of a directed relationship, which heretofore has been treated merely as an association. Thus, for example, we can investigate the possibility that the occurrence of one type of conflict behavior systematically precedes the occurrence of the other. If in fact conflict in one sphere is viewed as a reaction to conflict in the other, then we can note and differentiate those types of conflict that engender immediate reactions from those that involve a time lag. As was the case with the concept of type of conflict, the notion of temporal relationships is considered by both Rummel and Tanter. However, its effects are again obscured by their failure to differentiate types of nations.

With the introduction of lagged relationships into the analysis, we can investigate directed relationships between domestic and foreign conflict behavior. The more popular notion in the literature is that domestic conflict precedes foreign conflict. Sociologists such as Georg Simmel have noted this sort of relationship in dealing with conditions under which conflict with an external enemy may actually be functional to a group. In this situation, conflict heightens the concentration of a group and eliminates elements

[24]James N. Rosenau, "Compatibility, Consensus, and an Emerging Political Science of Adaptation," *American Political Science Review* 61 (December 1967): 985.
[25]James N. Rosenau, "Toward the Study of National-International Linkages," in Rosenau, ed., *Linkage Politics*, pp. 44–63.

that might blur the group's boundaries.[26] The unity that may result from conflict with an outside enemy is most pointed when it brings together elements which at best are usually indifferent to each other and at worst are actually hostile toward one another.[27] Lewis A. Coser states, "Conflict with another group leads to the mobilization of the energies of the group members and hence to increased cohesion of the group."[28] Coser goes one step further by stating that, in some cases, enemies may actually be sought in order to bring about unity within the group.[29] Finally, Peter M. Blau, in his work on exchange theory, states the following:

Opposition activates conflict by giving overt social expression to latent disagreements and hostilities, but it also helps to remove the sources of these conflicts. It is a disturbing and divisive force that ultimately contributes to social stability and cohesion. For minor cleavages that fundamentally disrupt society are most likely to occur precisely when recurrent oppositions have been suppressed and conflicts have smouldered.[30]

Within the literature of political science, we have already noted writers such as Farrell, Wright, Rosenau, Rosecrance, and Denton postulating relationships between prior domestic conflict and subsequent foreign conflict. In fact, social thinkers as far back as Thucydides have been aware of the implicit link between domestic disorders and the extent to which nations engage in foreign conflict behavior. In more recent times, the press, particularly in analyses of the behavior of non-Western, underdeveloped nations, has frequently attributed the propensity to engage in foreign conflict to the effects of domestic insecurity on leadership groups.

Thus far, we have dealt with a lagged relationship between the occurrence of domestic conflict and the subsequent occurrence of foreign conflict. The study of time lags also allows us to postulate a lagged relationship between the occurrence of foreign conflict and the subsequent occurrence of domestic conflict. In general, the notion of a directed relationship of this sort between the two spheres has been neglected in political science literature. This is not to say that this relationship is any less important than the previously discussed one, but that it has been a much more difficult concept to grasp. In this regard, Wolfram F. Hanrieder has stated:

Not only are domestic allocations of values strongly affected by the international environment, but national decision-makers have become very conscious of the

[26]Georg Simmel, *Conflict and the Web of Group-Affiliations* (Glencoe, Ill.: Free Press, 1955), pp. 98–99.
[27]Ibid., p. 102.
[28]Lewis A. Coser, *The Functions of Social Conflict* (New York: Free Press, 1956), p. 95. Reprinted as chap. 1, this volume, p. 18.
[29]Ibid., p. 19.
[30]Peter M. Blau, *Exchange and Power in Social Life* (New York: John Wiley and Sons, 1964), p. 304.

fact that many external events have a more or less direct impact on the allocation of values that traditionally has taken place largely within the national in-
stitutional structures.[31]

Karl W. Deutsch has also dealt with the relative impact of external events
on various types of nations. It is his contention that the impact of international affairs on the internal affairs of a nation declines with the stability
and autonomy of the internal decision-making system. He goes on to state:

A national [political] system that is likely to collapse or to go to pieces will
make the country remarkably sensitive to foreign impacts. This is sometimes
the case in civil wars. On the other hand, the highly cohesive national community, with a high capacity for adjustment and learning, may be able to absorb the
impact of foreign changes, to retain the linkage groups with partial autonomy
but still within the national community, and simply go on by a series of adjust-
ments.[32]

Conflict Situation and Context

The final factor to be discussed is the type of conflict situation or the
context in which conflict linkages are examined. Here we are stepping back
from the cross-national level of analysis in order to investigate conflict
linkages occurring in a regional or situational context.

It is commonly supposed that nations involved in a specific conflict situation are compelled into actions based on the dictates of the situation itself.
There is little doubt that this is true in the case of a war between two or
more nations. There are, however, cases in which nations are involved in
conflict situations that flare up into full-scale wars only infrequently, but
in which the antagonists are in a constant state of hostility toward each
other. This type of conflict situation is of particular interest.

The group of studies included in the present volume constitutes a sampling of the more significant recent work dealing with conflict linkages.
With the exception of chapters 1, 3, 4, and 7, all essays are published here
for the first time. All of the studies constitute empirical research into the
question of conflict linkages between the domestic and foreign spheres.
That is, they all employ data in order to test hypotheses relating conflict
behavior in one sphere to attributes or behavior in the other sphere.

Part I includes two selections of a theoretical nature which deal with the
notion of linkages between behavior in the two spheres of human activity.

[31]Wolfram F. Hanrieder, "Compatibility and Consensus: A Proposal for the Conceptual
Linkage of External and Internal Dimensions of Foreign Policy," *The American Political Science Review* 61 (December 1967): 973.

[32]Karl W. Deutsch, "External Influences on the Internal Behavior of States," in
Farrell, ed., *Approaches to Comparative and International Politics,* p. 8.

Chapter 1, reprinted from Lewis Coser's *The Functions of Social Conflict*, deals with the notion that groups experiencing problems of internal dissension may be more likely to engage in aggressive behavior externally than would internally cohesive groups. His work, along with that of Georg Simmel, constitutes the major social-psychological basis for the notion of conflict linkages at the national and international levels. The essay that is chapter 2 is by James N. Rosenau, and in it he compares the concept of linkage politics to other cross-system concepts, such as intervention, integration, and adaptation. He also presents the general linkage politics framework, and reviews some of the more significant studies that have utilized the concept.

Part II reports on data-based studies dealing with conflict linkages. These studies deal specifically with foreign conflict behavior as a dependent variable. That is, an attempt is made in each of the essays to explain various aspects of foreign conflict behavior on the basis of domestic or systemic considerations. The selections fall into two broad classes: (1) cross-national, and (2) case studies.

Chapter 3 sets the tone for this section; it is an essay by R. J. Rummel in which the major finding shows that domestic and foreign conflict behavior of nations are unrelated. This conclusion is based on data from seventy-seven nations for the period between 1955 and 1957. As we have noted, this finding is in sharp contrast with well-accepted notions as to the possible linkages between conflict behavior in the two spheres. Since its original publication in 1963, the Rummel finding has stimulated a great deal of reaction on the part of other researchers in the field. Efforts have been made by these researchers to specify those conditions under which relationships that Rummel did not find actually do appear. The chapters by Wilkenfeld, Phillips, Hazlewood, Haas, and Van Atta reflect this general research.

Several recent works, also stimulated by the original Rummel study, examine conflict linkages through a case study approach. That is, they attempt to establish a relationship between domestic attributes and behavior and foreign conflict within specific sets of nations. Burrowes and Spector's essay on the Middle East, and that by Collins on Africa fall into this group. Finally, Part III of this volume reverses the process, in that domestic conflict behavior becomes the dependent variable, and we seek to explain its occurrence on the basis of external factors. The lone study in this section is by Wilkenfeld and Zinnes; in it they construct a Markov chain model to explain the occurrence of domestic conflict behavior on the basis of prior domestic and foreign conflict levels.

PART I
A THEORETICAL PERSPECTIVE ON LINKAGES

.1. Conflict with Out-Groups and Group Structure*

LEWIS A. COSER

CONFLICT WITH OUT-GROUPS INCREASES INTERNAL COHESION

The group in a state of peace can permit antagonistic members within it to live with one another in an undecided situation because each of them can go his own way and can avoid collisions. A state of conflict, however, pulls the members so tightly together and subjects them to such uniform impulse that they either must get completely along with, or completely repel, one another. This is the reason why war with the outside is sometimes the last chance for a state ridden with inner antagonisms to overcome these antagonisms, or else to break up definitely. . . .

The fighter must "pull himself together." That is, all his energies must be, as it were, concentrated in one point so that they can be employed at any moment in any required direction. . . .

The well-known reciprocal relation between a despotic orientation and the war-like tendencies of a group rests on this informal basis: war needs a centralistic intensification of the group form, and this is guaranteed best by despotism.[1]

This and the following propositions attempt a more detailed discussion of the impact of conflict with another group upon group structure.

It was suggested earlier that group boundaries are established through conflict with the outside, so that a group defines itself by struggling with other groups. Simmel goes on to suggest that outside conflict will strengthen the internal cohesion of the group and increase centralization. . . .

Outside conflict unites the group and heightens morale, but whether it will also result in centralization depends on the structure of the group it-

*Reprinted, with permission of The Macmillan Company, from Lewis A. Coser, *The Functions of Social Conflict* (New York: Free Press, 1956), pp. 87–110. © by the Free Press, a Corporation, 1956.

[1]Georg Simmel, *Conflict*, trans. Kurt H. Wolff (Glencoe, Ill.: Free Press, 1955), pp. 87, 88, 92, 93.

self as well as on the nature of the conflict.[2] Internal cohesion is likely to be increased in the group that engages in outside conflict. The occurrence of despotism, however, is inversely related to the strength of internal cohesion; despotism will occur where there is insufficient cohesion at the outset of the conflict and where the conflict situation fails to bring about the cohesion necessary for concerted action.

However, conflict between groups or nations has often led to anomie rather than to an increase in internal cohesion. This alternative sequence to which Simmel alludes needs to be incorporated in the present discussion.

The degree of group consensus prior to the outbreak of the conflict seems to be the most important factor affecting cohesion. If a group is lacking in basic consensus, outside threat leads not to increased cohesion, but to general apathy, and the group is consequently threatened with disintegration. Research on the impact of the depression on the family has shown, for example, that families lacking internal solidarity before the depression responded apathetically and were broken, whereas solidary families actually were strengthened.[3]

Lack of consensus or lack of solidarity is not synonymous with divergencies and conflicts within the group. If the group reacts to outside threat by inner divergencies over the conduct of the conflict, it indicates that the issue at stake is important enough for the group members to fight about among themselves. This is quite different from the situation in which the

[2]For recent discussions of the control function of the primary group, see especially Edward Shils, as well as Robert K. Merton and Alice S. Kitt in *Studies in the Scope and Method of "The American Soldier,"* ed. Robert K. Merton and Paul Lazarsfeld (Glencoe, Ill.: Free Press, 1950). As to the relation between centralization and conflict in large-scale organizations, Robert Michels *Political Parties* (Glencoe, Ill.: Free Press, 1949). remains the classic statement. See also Philip Selznick, "Foundations of the Theory of Organizations," *American Journal of Sociology* 13 (1948): 25–35.

What has been said here with regard to the relation between centralization and group structure in the face of outside conflict is not to be construed as a complete acceptance of what Michels calls "the iron law of oligarchy." There is agreement with Michels that centralizing tendencies in large-scale organizations, especially if they are engaged in continuous struggle with outside groups, are neither artibrary nor accidental nor temporary, but inherent in the nature of the organization and in the nature of its conflict relations. Yet recognition of the existence and relevance of centralizing tendencies does not commit one to the view that "the majority of human beings, in a condition of eternal tutelage, are predestined by tragic necessity to submit to the dominion of a small minoirty, and must be content to constitute the pedestal of an oligarchy." Michels, *Political Parties*, p. 390. A number of recent studies, such as Seymour M. Lipset, *Agrarian Socialism* (Berkeley: University of California Press, 1950), and Rose Laub, "An Analysis of the Early German Socialist Movement" (Master's thesis, Columbia University, 1951), suggest that countervailing tendencies such as the ideology of the group and the interest of the membership are crucial intervening variables.

[3]Cf. Robert K. Merton's contribution to the restudy of Robert Angell's *The Family Encounters the Depression: A Re-Analysis of Documents Bearing on the Family Encountering the Depression* (New York: Social Science Research Council, 1942). Merton used estimates of family solidarity before the depression in order to predict the probable impact of the depression on family stability.

members simply do not care about and remain indifferent to the outside threat.

Here a distinction introduced by Robin Williams seems to be most helpful:

Given a social group which is a "going concern," a sensed outside threat *to the group as a whole* will result in heightened internal cohesion. . . . However [this general principle] holds true only under very specific conditions: (a) the group must be a "going concern," i.e., there must be a minimal consensus among the constituent individuals that the aggregate is a group, and that its preservation as an entity is worthwhile; (b) there must be recognition of an outside threat which is thought to menace the group as a whole, not just some part of it.[4]

The relation between outer conflict and inner cohesion does not hold true where internal cohesion before the outbreak of the conflict is so low that the group members have ceased to regard preservation of the group as worthwhile, or actually see the outside threat to concern "them" rather than "us." In such cases disintegration of the group, rather than increase in cohesion, will be the result of outside conflict.

The contrasting effects of the recent war on the French and on the British social structure provide a convenient illustration. The Nazi attack appreciably increased the internal cohesion of the British social system, temporarily narrowing the various political, social, and economic fissures that existed in British society. In France, on the other hand, these fissures were widened to the point of a breakdown in consensus even concerning the most basic question of all: whether France was to continue as an independent national unit.

In discussing Simmel's proposition that internal conflict may be taken as an index of the stability of a relation, we made the distinction between conflicts that take place within a structure of consensual agreement and conflicts in which no such agreement exists. We concluded that only in the former case may internal conflict be said to be functional for the relation. We can now make the same point regarding the effect of outside conflict on inner structure: during World War II, attempts at centralization by the French government were unavailing and could not mend the basic cleavages nor remedy the lack of social solidarity. The only alternative to disintegration then came to be the "despotism" of the Pétain regime.

As long as the outside threat is perceived to concern the entire group (or society), internal conflicts do not hinder concerted action against the outside enemy. Negro-white relations in America exemplify this situation. The fact that the Negro minority, despite its exclusion from important rights and privileges of American society, showed no willingness during

[4]Robin M. Williams, Jr., *The Reduction of Intergroup Tensions*, SSRC Bulletin No. 57 (New York: 1947), p. 58.

the Second World War to follow Japanese propaganda for "solidarity between the dark and yellow races" indicates that on the whole the Negro group did not abandon its identification with American values. On the contrary, one result of the war seems to have been an increase in Negro-white solidarity. External conflict had an integrative rather than a disruptive effect. On the other hand, enemy attack against British and Dutch colonies in Southeast Asia resulted in disintegration of the social structure; a majority of the members of these societies perceived the threat as directed against "them," i.e., against the British or Dutch overlords, rather than as directed against "us," the natives. Because they did not define the situation as threatening to themselves, they were unresponsive to attempts to overcome the menace.

We may now reformulate Simmel's proposition:

Conflict with another group leads to the mobilization of the energies of group members and hence to increased cohesion of the group. Whether increase in centralization accompanies this increase in cohesion depends upon both the character of the conflict and the type of group. Centralization will be more likely to occur in the event of warlike conflict and in differentiated structures requiring marked division of labor.

Despotism seems to be related to lack of cohesion; it is required for carrying out hostilities where there is insufficient group solidarity to mobilize energies of group members.

In groups engaged in struggle with an external enemy, the occurrence of both centralization and of despotism depends upon the system of common values and upon the group structure prior to the outbreak of the conflict.

Social systems lacking social solidarity are likely to disintegrate in the face of outside conflict, although some unity may be despotically enforced.

Remembering a previous proposition which stated that the closer the relationship, the more intense the conflict, we are now led to ask whether outside conflict, given that it forces the group to pull itself together, does not thereby increase the possibility of the emergence of hostile feelings within the struggling group itself, and does not affect, consequently, the way in which this group deals with internal conflict. This relation will be examined presently. . . .

THE SEARCH FOR ENEMIES

Groups, and especially minorities, which live in conflict and persecution, often reject approaches or tolerance from the other side. The closed nature of their opposition without which they cannot fight on would be blurred. . . . A group's complete victory over its enemies is thus not always fortunate. . . . Victory lowers the energy which guarantees the unity of the group; and the dissolving forces, which are always at work, gain hold. . . . Within certain groups, it may even be a piece of political wisdom to see to it that there be some enemies in order for the unity of the members to remain effective and for the group to remain conscious of this unity as its vital interest.[5]

Following up the idea that outside conflict increases group cohesion, Simmel now claims that struggle groups may actually "attract" enemies in order to help maintain and increase group cohesion. Continued conflict being a condition of survival for struggle groups, they must perpetually provoke it.

Moreover, he implies, outside conflict need not even be objectively present in order to foster in-group cohesion; all that is necessary is for the members to perceive or be made to perceive an outside threat in order to "pull themselves together."[6] Threats may or may not exist in objective reality, but the group must feel that they do. Social perception of an outside threat may be distorted, but its effect on the in-group may be the same as that of undistorted perception of objective threat.

A struggle group's search for new enemies resembles the process that Gordon W. Allport has called "the functional autonomy of motives."[7] Allport contends that motives which have arisen originally in pursuit of a specific goal may continue to operate although the original goal no longer exists. Robert K. Merton uses a similar conceptual framework to explain bureaucratic ritualism with its characteristic displacement of goals, whereby "an instrumental value becomes a terminal value."[8] Likewise, conflict,

[5]Simmel, *Conflict*, pp. 97–98.

[6]In suggesting that conscious distortion of the social perception of group members may be "political sagacity," Simmel introduces the role of group leaders in the manipulation of the membership's reactions. In all previous discussions, as well as in those that follow, he limits his analysis almost entirely to the impact of conflict on total group structures without differentiating between leaders and followers (although this distinction is the subject matter of other parts of his sociology; see especially *The Sociology of Georg Simmel*, trans. and ed. Kurt H. Wolff (Glencoe, Ill.: Free Press, 1948), pp. 181–306). For the time being, this distinction will be omitted in the discussion, since it would involve a new and exceedingly complex field of analysis. At this point we should, however, acknowledge that leaders may have a vested interest in conflict as a unity-producing mechanism so that they may (1) accentuate already existing conflict (e.g., the leaders of the Gironde in the French Revolution or the Southern War Party in the Mexican War of 1846) if internal dissension and dissatisfaction threaten their leadership; (2) actually "search for an enemy whenever the esprit de corps threatens to become slack," (Grace Coyle, *Social Process in Organized Groups* [New York: Richard R. Smith, 1930], p. 161), as the totalitarian leadership did in Germany, Italy, and Russia, and as the Czarist police knew well when they invented the "Protocols of the Wise Men of Zion."

[7]Gordon W. Allport, *Personality* (New York: Henry Holt and Co., 1937), chap. 7. Max Weber was the first sociologist to suggest these developments, e.g., in his distinction between those who live "off" politics and those who live "for" politics; the former are organizationally conservative. In order to maintain the structure, they may be led to advocate radical changes of the organization's functions. Cf. *From Max Weber*, trans, Hans Gerth and C. Wright Mills (New York: Oxford University Press, 1946), pp. 77–128.

[8]Robert K. Merton, *Social Theory and Social Structure* (Glencoe, Ill.: Free Press, 1949), chap. 5.

which the group originally engaged in as a means to a stated end, now becomes an end in itself.

This recalls our earlier discussion of nonrealistic conflict. Just as such a conflict is governed not by the desire to obtain results, but by a need to release tension in order to maintain the structure of the personality, so the group's search for enemies is aimed not at obtaining results for its members, but merely at maintaining its own structure as a going concern.

Even after the initial conflict situation which brought them into being no longer prevails, struggle groups continue to act according to the "law upon which they originally entered the scene." As Chester Barnard says, "An organization must disintegrate if it cannot accomplish its purpose. It also destroys itself by accomplishing its purpose."[9] Thus new purposes must be found in order to avoid dissolution. The history of the Populist and Progressive farm movements in the United States show many instances when farmers' organizations originally set up to combat railroad or elevator interests moved on, once this battle was won, to raise new demands and tackle other antagonists in the political sphere. In his study of the Canadian Commonwealth Federation in Saskatchewan, Seymour Lipset shows that the farmers' victory over a particular antagonist, far from leading to the disappearance of the struggle organization, led it to extend its field of operation against other antagonists.[10] Labor history also affords many similar examples.

Disappearance of the original enemy leads to a search for new enemies so that the group may continue to engage in conflict, thereby maintaining a structure that it would be in danger of losing were there no longer an enemy.[11]

We should stress here that the "new enemy" which these groups actually evoke, or whose threat they exaggerate, really exists, unlike the "invented" enemy we shall deal with later. Moreover, provoking the enemy by proclaiming his "dangerous intentions" may have the effect of a "self-fulfilling prophecy": the "enemy" will "respond" and in this way actually become as dangerous to the group as it accused him of being in the first place.

It would be rewarding to study the evolution of conflict groups from this point of view. Attention would focus on groups that have accomplished their original objective either through their own victory or because social change has brought about, without their intervention, the objective for which they originally struggled. The task would be to discover why some of

---

[9]Chester Barnard, *The Functions of the Executive* (Cambridge, Mass.: Harvard University Press, 1950), p. 91.

[10]Lipset, *Agrarian Socialism.*

[11]One is reminded here of the finding of psychoanalysis that the loss of a hate object may have as serious consequences for the personality as the loss of a love object.

these groups disappeared while others succeeded in finding other "hate objects" to maintain them.

Such "searching for the outside enemy" (or exaggeration of the danger which an actual enemy represents) serves not only to maintain the structure of the group, but also to strengthen its cohesion when threatened by a relaxation of energies or by internal dissension. Sharpness of outside conflict revives the alertness of the membership, and either reconciles divergent tendencies or leads to concerted group action against the dissenter.

The corollary of the "search for the outer enemy" is the search for the inner enemy when these rigid structures encounter defeat or an unexpected increased external danger.

Groups tend to deny that reverses in conflict with out-groups can be attributed to the strength of the adversary, for this would be an admission of their own weakness. Hence they look in their own ranks for a "dissenter" who hampered unity and the concerted action against the enemy. (Note the reaction against Menshevists, Trotskyists, and Bucharinists in the Bolshevik party.) So in societies, where the rigidity of structure inhibits realistic conflict, a perennial tendency exists to account for defeat in war in terms of "treason" within. The "stab-in-the-back" myth was used by German nationalists after the First World War; it appeared again in Vichy's explanations for the defeat of France in the Second World War. This is a variant of the scapegoating mechanism: though defeat was due to outsiders, the violence of the reaction aroused looks for hate objects among insiders. Those group members who must bear the burden of being the scapegoats, through their sacrifice, cleanse the group of its own failings, and in this way reestablish its solidarity: the loyal members are reassured that the group as a whole has not failed, but only some "traitors"; moreover, they can now reaffirm their righteousness by uniting in action against the "traitors." In struggle groups the same mechanism is at work in the perennial drives for purification, namely, the "pulling together" of the group against an inner "threat."

The inner enemy who is looked for, like the outer enemy who is evoked, may actually exist: he may be a dissenter who has opposed certain aspects of group life or group action and who is considered a potential renegade or heretic. But the inner enemy also may be "found," he may be simply invented, in order to bring about through a common hostility toward him the social solidarity which the group so badly needs.

This mechanism may also operate in the search for the outer enemy: he may be invented to bring about social solidarity. W. I. Thomas's theorem that "if men define their situations as real, they are real in their consequences," would apply to the invention of enemies even more directly than to the search for a real enemy. If men define a threat as real, although there may be little or nothing in reality to justify this belief, the threat is real in its consequences—and among these consequences is the increase of group cohesion.

But the aspect of the scapegoating mechanism that concerns us more particularly here is the type of imaginary threat that the scapegoat represents. The anti-Semite justifies his persecution of the Jew in terms of the Jew's power, aggression, and vengefulness. "He sees in the Jew everything which brings him misery—not only his social oppressor but also his unconscious instincts."[12] Mingled fear and dread of the Jew is one of the key elements of the complex anti-Semitic syndrome. This imaginary threat leads to a "regrouping" of the anti-Semite by his joining, as in Germany, the real community of like-minded men, or by his joining, as in America, an imaginary pseudo-community of likewise threatened individuals. There comes about a kind of illusory collectivity of all those who are similarly "threatened" by the Jew and who have lost everything but their common "danger" in the face of the expected aggressive actions of Jews.

Some types of anti-Semitism, as do other forms of prejudice, have important functions for those who suffer from "degrouping," that is, from a loss of cohesion in the society of which they are a part. Anti-Semitism provides "a means for pseudo-orientation in an estranged world.[13] "The [Jew's] alienness seems to provide the handiest formula for dealing with the alienation of society."[14] The degrouped man, by directing his diffuse hostility upon a specific target and then attributing his sense of menace to this target group, attempts to find a solid point of repair in a world that otherwise makes no sense to him.

The "inner enemy" may be provided by the social system insofar as target selection is group-sustained and institutionalized. "Prejudice," as Talcott Parsons pointed out, "is not only directed by individuals against scapegoat groups, but can readily become a phenomenon of group attitude, that is, become partly institutionalized. Then instead of being disapproved by members of one's own group for being prejudiced, one is punished for not being prejudiced."[15] "Discrimination is sustained not only by the direct gains to those who discriminate, but also by cultural norms which legiti-

[12]Otto Fenichel, "Elements of a Psychoanalytic Theory of Antisemitism," in *Antisemitism, A Social Disease*, ed. Ernst Simmel (New York: International Universities Press, 1946), p. 29.

[13]T. W. Adorno et al., *The Authoritarian Personality* (New York: Harper & Bros., 1950), p. 622.

[14]Ibid., p. 619.

[15]Talcott Parsons, *Religious Perspectives of College Teaching in Sociology and Social Psychology* (New Haven: Edward W. Hagen Foundation, n.d.), p. 40. Psychoanalytically oriented observers (cf. Leo Lowenthal and Norbert Guterman, *Prophets of Deceit*, vol. 5 of *Studies of Prejudice* [New York: Harper & Bros., 1950–51]) have commented upon the similarity of fear of the Jew and the Negro to the well-known parasitophobia symptoms. Yet, anti-Semitism can lead to group formation and identification while parasitophobia cannot. Hence, "fear of Negroes" or "fear of Jews" is more functional than parasitophobia for those who suffer from degrouping.

mize discrimination."[16] There are indications that the degree of rigidity of the social structure may help determine the degree to which the acting out of prejudice (discriminatory behavior) against inner enemies is institutionalized. A few examples will clarify this point.

Writing just before the First World War, Thomas P. Bailey, a Mississippi professor, said of the association between fear of the Negro and the social status system of the south:

The veriest slavery of the spirit is to be found in the deep-seated anxiety of the South. Southerners are afraid for the safety of their wives and daughters and sisters; Southern parents are afraid for the purity of their boys; Southern publicists are afraid that the time will come when large numbers of Negroes will try to vote and thus precipitate race war.... Southern businessmen are afraid that agitation of the Negro question will interfere with business or demoralize the labor market. Southern officials are afraid of race riots, lynchings, savage atrocities, paying not only for Negro fiendishness but also for the anxiety caused by fear of what might be.[17]

More recent investigators have confirmed this early diagnosis. Frank Tannenbaum writes: "The South gives indications of being afraid of the Negro. I do not mean physical fear. It is not a matter of cowardice or bravery; it is something deeper and more fundamental. It is fear of losing grip upon the world."[18]

This pervasive fear among many southerners of the Negro's aggressive violence serves an important function in maintaining the rigid southern status system. If the Negro is dangerous, if he is a perennial threat to the most intimate possessions of the white southerner, it is crucially important to "keep him in his place"; in other words, to maintain the position and the cohesion of the dominant white status group. If the Negro is dangerous, then all those in the white group who attempt to befriend him can be effectively characterized as "renegades" endangering the very existence of the white group.

Regarding fear of intermarriage and miscegenation, Myrdal remarks:

What white people really want is to keep the Negroes in a lower status. "Intermarriage" itself is resented because it would be a supreme indication of "social equality," while the rationalization is that "social equality" is opposed because it would bring about "intermarriage."[19]

Fear of the Negro, far from deriving from the Negro's actual behavior, is a

---

[16]Robert K. Merton, "Discrimination and the American Creed," in *Discrimination and National Welfare,* ed. Robert K. Merton (New York: Harper & Bros., 1948), pp. 112–13.

[17]Thomas P. Bailey, *Race Orthodoxy in the South,* pp. 346–47, quoted by Gunnar Myrdal, *An American Dilemma* (New York: Harper & Bros., 1944), p. 1356.

[18]Frank Tannenbaum, *Darker Phases of the South* (New York: G. P. Putnam's Sons, 1924), pp. 8–9.

[19]Myrdal, *An American Dilemma,* p. 591.

means of keeping the status system intact, of rallying all members of the white group around its standards.[20]

To our knowledge, what we have said here about the relation between rigidity of structure and the search for the enemy still remains to be strictly verified, except on the level of small-group research.[21] But it seems to be a hypothesis well worth testing.

Thus, a study of the Communist party would try to determine to what extent external threats to the group are objectively real and to what extent, on the contrary, the membership must perpetually "create" external threats (or internal scapegoats) in order to maintain internal loyalty.

Similarly, it would be rewarding to study the internal cohesiveness of the Jewish and other religious minority groups from this point of view. It appears that anti-Semitism ordinarily increases the internal solidarity of the Jewish group,[22] but it may also be that social solidarity.is strengthened by constant emphasis on the dangers of anti-Semitism whether or not it is actually present or objectively threatening at any particular time.

In line with the present discussion, we may reformulate Simmel's proposition:

Rigidly organized struggle groups may actually search for enemies with the deliberate purpose or the unwitting result of maintaining unity and internal cohesion. Such groups may actually perceive an outside threat although no threat is present. Under conditions yet to be discovered, imaginary threats have the same group-integrating function as real threats.

The evocation of an outer enemy or the invention of such an enemy strengthens social cohesion that is threatened from within. Similarly, search for or invention of a dissenter within may serve to maintain a structure which is threatened from the outside. Such scapegoating mechanisms will occur particularly in those groups whose structure inhibits realistic conflict within.

There are shifting gradations between the exaggeration of a real danger, the attraction of a real enemy, and the complete invention of a threatening agent.

[20]That this fear of the Negro is one of the favored manipulative devices of the southern demagogue hardly needs any elaboration here.

[21]See the citations of Kurt Lewin and R. Lippitt, "An Experimental Study of The Effect of Democratic and Authoritarian Group Atmospheres," *University of Iowa Studies in Child Welfare* 16, no. 3 (1940): 45–198.

[22]Cf. the highly stimulating observations of J. P. Sartre in *Commentary* 5 (1946): 306–16, 389–97, 522–31.

.2. Theorizing Across Systems: Linkage Politics Revisited*

JAMES N. ROSENAU

ALTHOUGH THE great breakthroughs in empirical political theory have yet to occur, the last decade of theoretical effort has been marked by forward movement. At least it is now possible to discern what the nature and shape of the great breakthroughs will be. Stated succinctly, breakthroughs will be characterized by theoretical constructs which specify how and under what conditions political behavior at one level of aggregation affects political behavior at another level. Recent years have witnessed substantial clarification of the dynamics that underlie political behavior at the individual, local, national, and international levels, but the capacity to move predictively back and forth among two or more of these levels is presently lacking. Yet, the rapid advances at the several levels have revealed that more theorizing is needed, that across-systems-level theory has much greater explanatory power than within-systems-level theory.

So it is a good time to take stock. Having taken great strides, we can usefully pause to assess the problems that may hinder progress toward the bright theoretical future that is now in sight. The across-systems breakthroughs may still be decades away, but it is not too early to consider what conceptual and methodological equipment they may require.

I

It must quickly be stressed that we are interested in middle-range theory and not in across-systems breakthroughs which can be applied to any two system levels. While the sense of forward movement is evident at all levels

*An earlier version of this paper was presented at the annual meeting of the American Political Science Association, Chicago, September 7, 1971. In preparing it I have benefited greatly from the assistance of Norah Rosenau. The support of the National Science Foundation through its Grant GS-3117 to the Research Foundation of The Ohio State University is also gratefully acknowledged.

25

of analysis, our concern here is confined primarily to the strides that have and will be taken in theorizing about the interaction of national and international systems. No doubt some future Einstein of political science will eventually break through to across-systems theory that is applicable to any two levels, but my knowledge of recent progress is limited mainly to the national-international realm, thus restraining the impulse to move beyond the middle range.

It is possible, however, to state the nature of across-systems theory in general terms. Consider figure 1 as outlining four levels of aggregation at which political behavior occurs. The least aggregated level is represented by the Xs. The organization and analysis of clusters of Xs leads to the A level of aggregation and a similar process gives rise to the B level. The latter in turn may be aggregated in such a way as to create the C level. Depending on the perspective of the analyst, of course, a virtually endless number of levels can be used as the basis for inquiry. Whatever the number of levels regarded as relevant, the actors at each level—the Xs, As, Bs, and C in figure 1—are viewed as having some common attributes and as engaging in behavior that is to some extent recurrent. In terms of empirical theory, therefore, their actions and interactions are posited as possessing lawful properties that the researchers seek to uncover and explain. Within-systems theory presumes that these properties can be adequately explained by examining the similarities and differences that characterize the actors at each level. Whether his data base is a case (say, an A in figure 1) or a comparative sample (say an A, A_1, A_2 and A_3), the within-systems theorist thus limits his efforts to predicting to the behavior of the actors in the system and/or explaining why they behave as they do. He may well take note of the antecedents of their behavior, but the scope of his theoretical concerns extends neither to the systems in which the antecedents are located nor to the systems into which the behavior of the actors is projected. In explaining the actions of voters, for example, the within-systems theorist may specify the factors which predispose them to vote in one way or another, but he will not be interested in either the personality systems through which their predispositions were shaped or the policy-making systems created by the outcome of their vote. Similarly, the within-systems theorist who focuses on public policies at the national level may identify the private groups that press for and are affected by the policies, but he does not theorize about the variations in the dynamics that sustain or transform the groups and that may be systematically linked to variations in public policy.

The across-systems theorist, on the other hand, aspires to explanations in which actions and interactions at one level are at least partially accounted for by attributes and behavior at another level. He is not content to presume that the properties that are lawful at the level of aggregation

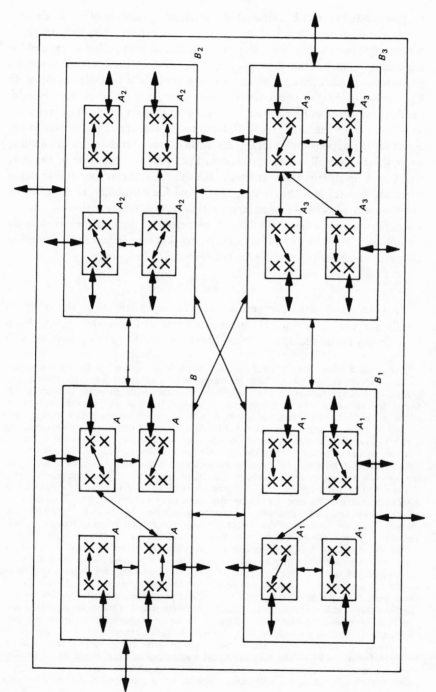

Figure 1. Four Levels of Aggregation

that interests him can be adequately explained by holding other levels constant. He is so impressed by the number and variety of system levels in which individuals and groups occupy roles that he is impelled to expand his explanatory net beyond the dynamics operative at the level to which his hypotheses predict. Stated differently, the dependent variables comprising his theory all concern phenomena at the same systemic level, but his independent variables will be drawn from lesser or greater levels of aggregation as well as from the same level. Put in terms of figure 1, his efforts to account for the actions and interactions of, say, the A-level actors will include propositions that allow for variation in the nature or behavior of those at the X or B levels (the thick arrows in the figure). Conceivably, if his talents are truly Einsteinian, they might also allow for variability at the C level, but it seems reasonable to anticipate that across-systems theory will develop first across adjacent levels of aggregation. Such theory is difficult enough to formulate without attempting to skip over levels and accounting for phenomena greatly removed in time, space, or function.[1]

II

That across-systems theoretical breakthroughs still lie in the future is hardly surprising. Formidable problems confront those who seek to build such theory in the realm of politics. Most notably, the analyst is faced with

[1]The question arises as to whether across-systems theory is likely to develop in one particular direction, either that in which the independent variables predict to phenomena at a greater level of aggregation or to a level involving smaller units. In terms of figure 1, will theory development move from explanation of the As in terms of the Xs, to the Bs in terms of the As, and to the Cs in terms of the Bs, or will the progression move from the Cs to the Bs, the Bs to the As, and the As to the Xs? It might be argued that since empirical theorists aspire to ever more encompassing constructs, they will primarily follow the first course. Such an argument, however, misreads the nature of scientific parsimony. The effort to develop theory that embraces ever more encompassing bodies of data does not necessarily require moving to new, more comprehensive levels of aggregation. To be parsimonious as a theorist is to reduce the number of independent variables needed to account for variation in a set of phenomena. Parsimony need not also entail adding to the range of phenomena encompassed by the dwindling number of explanatory variables. To search for "master" variables that account for most of the variation in the As of figure 1 is not to require exploration of the impact of the Bs upon them. As long as the across-systems theorist is able to move toward the replacement of many independent variables with a few "master" ones, he remains true to his aspiration for parsimony, and it does not matter whether some of the master variables are located in less aggregated systems or whether they are dimensions of more aggregated systems. The choice as to which direction an across-systems theorist should move depends, in the final analysis, on the kinds of phenomena that interest him and the questions they lead him to ask. If, for example, his focus is that of the national political system, a variety of considerations can lead him to search for master variables among the subsystems that comprise the national polity and equally varied concerns can lead him to look to international systems for constraints that shape behavior at the national level. Indeed, his temperament and curiosity may encourage him to look in both directions, albeit Einsteinian talents may be required to develop viable theory which spans the levels of aggregation immediately adjacent to both sides of the level that encompasses the phenomena he is trying to explain.

the need to comprehend the dynamics of actors at two levels of aggregation so well that he can trace variations at one level to variations at the other. Such a task is awesome because few among us ever feel that our comprehension at one level is sufficient and thorough enough to identify the master variables that account for varying phenomena at that level. A lifetime of concentrated inquiry often seems necessary to the acquisition of parsimonious theory at a single level, so that to achieve such competence at two levels looms as a fine but unobtainable aspiration. More concretely, across-systems theory at the national and international levels appears to require the knowledge and conceptual equipment of both the area specialist and the discipline generalist. More accurately, if the theory involves the behavior of actors in several geographic or cultural areas, it requires the knowledge of several types of area specialists as well as that of the generalist.

The problem of acquiring adequate skills at two levels of aggregation is further compounded by the seemingly endless variety of actors and actions that sustain the processes of politics. The variety is so great that the political analyst, unlike the economist, cannot readily presume that certain attributes or behavioral predispositions predominate at one level and thus concentrate his efforts at the other level. Rather he must allow for wide variability at both levels, with the result that time and energy must be devoted to probing a multiplicity of actors. This important difference between economics and politics has been succinctly summarized by Susan Strange, who notes that

... the study of politics—whether local, national, or international, whether ancient, Renaissance, revolutionary, or contemporary—impresses the student with the unlikeness of the actors involved, with the variety of generative ideas by which they are influenced, by the quirks and oddities of the systems within which they act. The study of economics impresses the student with the likeness to one another of consumers, or of producers, or of markets and mechanisms from Toledo to Timbuctoo. The units along the economic scales are essentially equivalent and undifferentiated.[2]

In view of this difference, it is hardly surprising that across-systems theory has been abundantly developed in economics but has yet to appear in political science. Compared to the political scientist, the economist simply does not have to probe as many variations at one level in order to make statements about how they may be systematically linked to variations at another level.

Stated differently, most political systems are subsystem dominant, whereas economic systems tend to be system dominant. That is, the behavior of two or more actors in most political systems can substantially

[2]"The Politics of International Currencies," *World Politics* 22 (January 1971): 224.

alter the structure and dynamics of the system in which they act, but such is not the case in many economic systems. The United States, for example, can alter world politics unilaterally by changing its diplomatic positions, but few of its postwar efforts to cope with world monetary crises prevented continuous upheavals in the world's financial structure.

In short, the problem of variability in politics becomes more acute the greater the levels of aggregation at which across-systems theory is sought. Students of elections or legislatures who seek partial explanations of public policy through variations in the distribution of votes do not need to examine every voter or every legislator because these actors are known to share attributes and predispositions that can be subdivided into relatively few categories. Thus relieved of the task of probing the nature of many of his independent variables, the analyst can devote most of his efforts to examining variations in the dependent variables. Students of national and international systems, on the other hand, cannot proceed to the dependent variables so readily. Each of the actors treated as independent variables must be carefully examined to determine the extent to which they are similar to each other, and these similarities, along with the differences among them, must then be taken into account in any across-systems theory that is developed.

III

Despite these obstacles to across-systems theory, recent years have been marked by intellectual stirrings that may well be the prelude to theoretical breakthroughs that sweep them aside. The signs of forward movement are still faint, but they are unmistakable and, more importantly, they are characterized by one element essential to any breakthrough, namely, a readiness to ignore long-standing conceptual boundaries and think anew about interaction across different levels of aggregation. Insofar as the interaction of national and international systems is concerned, forward movement is manifest in an emerging preoccupation with a host of concepts that denote such interaction.[3] Interdependence, penetration, linkage, intervention, emulation, integration, adaptation—these are typical of the concepts that some students of national and international politics have begun to take seriously. As discussed below, these are not different labels for the same phenomena, but concepts that are differentiated by important nuances of meaning and, in some instances, even by inconsistent empirical referents. Yet common to all of these concepts is a focus on some form of

---

[3]An empirical indication that this preoccupation has become widely shared can be seen in the survey finding that more than three-fourths of a sample of 101 distinguished students of international phenomena believe that more research designs ought to be characterized by across-systems analysis in the future. Cf. James N. Rosenau, *International Studies and the Social Sciences* (Minneapolis: International Studies Association, 1971), p. 106.

interaction between national and international political processes. The emergence of this shared focus is certainly a significant development, especially as it has evolved less than a decade after students of the two fields were impressively warned that efforts to conduct research simultaneously at both levels were bound to fail.[4]

The reasons for this growing preoccupation with concepts that facilitate across-systems analysis are varied, ranging from a concern in the case of the linkage concept to bring two fields of inquiry closer together,[5] to an effort in the case of the concept of integration to give meaning to idealism,[6] to an attempt in the case of the concept of intervention to clarify immediate policy questions.[7] One source of this emerging focus, however, stands out. Technology is rendering the world smaller and smaller, so that the interaction of national and international systems is becoming increasingly intense and pervasive. The conceptual tidiness achieved through analyzing the two types of systems separately is thus no longer compelling. There is simply too much evidence of overlap between them for analysts to conduct research at one level blissfully ignoring developments at the other.

The various concepts which may become elements of eventual theoretical breakthroughs can be differentiated in a number of ways. They can be distinguished in terms of the scope of the phenomena they encompass, with the concepts of interdependence and linkage having the widest scope and intervention and emulation the narrowest. They differ in terms of whether an event, an actor, or a process serves as the central analytic focus, with intervention, adaptation, and linkage exemplifying, respectively, these three foci. They vary substantially in the degree to which specific relationships are hypothesized or assumed at different system levels, with the concept of integration being perhaps the most, and that of interdependence the least, theoretically developed. They diverge considerably in the extent to which violence and hierarchy are treated as central dimensions, intervention and penetration being the concepts most pervaded by these dimensions and linkage and adaptation the least. They vary in terms of the amount of planning posited as antecedents to the across-systems processes, intervention and linkage being the two extremes in this regard. They are also marked by differences in the extent to which attitudinal or

[4]J. David Singer, "The Level-of-Analysis Problem in International Relations," *World Politics* 14 (October 1961): 77–92.

[5]See, for example, James N. Rosenau, *Of Bridges and Boundaries: A Report on a Conference on the Interdependencies of National and International Political Systems*, Research Monograph No. 27 (Princeton, N.J.: Center of International Studies, 1967).

[6]Stanley Hoffmann, "International Organization and the International System," *International Organization* 24 (Summer 1970): 389.

[7]Symposium, "Intervention and World Politics," *Journal of International Affairs* 22 (1968): esp. 198–207, 217–46.

behavioral phenomena are the organizing focus, with emulation and adaptation more illustrative of the former and penetration and integration more reflective of the latter. Finally, the various concepts differ in terms of whether the posited dependent variables are located in a more or less aggregated system than the one which contains the independent variables. The concepts of adaptation, intervention, and penetration, for example, are concerned with the nation-state as the site of the dependent variable, while integration models posit international systems as the arenas in which outcomes are to be observed and measured. In the case of the linkage concept, on the other hand, both national and international systems are treated as levels at which outcomes are located.

Notwithstanding all these differences, however, it bears repeating that the several concepts are all parallel in that they all share a concern with across-systems phenomena. While none of them may ever actually serve as the basis of the breakthroughs that lie ahead, they are guiding us down the right road. Nothing in the ensuing analysis of the insufficiencies of the concepts should be permitted to obscure this common and crucial quality.

IV

While the main purpose here is to assess theory and research associated with the linkage concept, it is useful to look briefly at the uses and limits of the other concepts concerned with across-systems phenomena. In each case several criteria of evaluation can fruitfully be applied: Has consensus developed with respect to the precise nature and scope of the phenomena delimited by the concept? Has the concept been formulated in such a way that variations at one level of aggregation are systematically associated with variations at another level? If not, does it readily lend itself to the derivation of such associations? Has the concept served as a tool of empirical inquiry? If so, do the operational definitions of it allow for quantitative analysis or have its applications been tailored to particular case histories? In short, have theoretical and empirical efforts based on the concept yielded any generalizations and findings that can serve as building blocks for further inquiry?

These questions are most easily answered for the concept of interdependence. In each case clear-cut negative answers are in order. Interdependence is perhaps the most generic of all the concepts in the growing lexicon of across-systems theory and, as such, it is used in an extremely loose fashion, with little effort being made either to give it precise meaning or to specify empirical referents which distinguish phenomena that are interdependent from those that are not. Indeed, so general is the concept that it is rarely defined and is instead usually presumed simply to refer to any phenomena in one system, the functioning of which cannot occur without some events or processes occurring in one or more other systems. Interdependence does not necessarily connote direction, regularity, purpose, or even interaction insofar as across-systems processes are concerned. Interdependencies can originate or culminate in international organizations or in nation-states; they can occur spasmodically or continuously; they can be intended or unintended; they can sustain desirable tendencies or regretted ones; they can involve specific transactions or simply perceived dependence. It follows that no variables are widely regarded as signifying the presence of interdependent phenomena and, consequently, that uses of the concept rarely, if ever, involve the specification of associations between independent and dependent variables. In itself, in fact, interdependence is not usually posited as being causal, but is rather treated as the context in which phenomena at one level may be posited as fostering outcomes at another level.

Plainly, the concept of interdependence, as it is presently construed, does not hold out much promise as a foundation of across-systems theory. To identify an interdependence between national and international systems is to begin to account for the shrinkage of social and geographic distance, but it is not otherwise to differentiate among phenomena or to provide guidance for further theory and research. Since analysts do not tend to attribute great explanatory power to it, it is not a concept which can be said to hinder inquiry, but neither can it be viewed as an especially useful tool in the storehouse of across-systems analysis.

In sharp contrast to the minimal utility that attaches to the concept of interdependence, work on the concept of integration has advanced rapidly and yielded an extensive body of theoretical and empirical materials. Those collected over the past fifteen years with respect to regional integration have recently been succinctly summarized[8] and, relative to the other concepts analyzed here, the summary depicts an impressive array of hypotheses and findings pertinent to a wide variety of across-systems phenomena. Not only have "enormous quantities of information . . . been uncovered about common markets, parliamentarians, regional interest groups, trade and mail flows, attitudes of masses, self-definitions of interest by elites, career patterns of civil servants, role perceptions, relations between various kinds of economic tasks, links between economic, political, and military tasks, and the influence of extrasystemic actors," but close analysis of these data reveals that they are "by no means randomly collected information."[9] On the contrary, it proved possible to identify thirteen "empirical generalizations," six of which are "global" in their appli-

---

[8]Ernst B. Haas, "The Study of Regional Integration: Reflections on the Joy and Anguish of Pretheorizing," in Leon N. Lindberg and Stuart A. Scheingold, eds., "Regional Integration: Theory and Research," *International Organization* 24 (Autumn 1970): 607–46.

[9]Ibid., p. 613.

cation to regional groupings of nation-states, while "socialist groupings," West European nations, African nations, and Latin American nations are each the subject of one generalization (consisting of several parts) and "the external world" of the regional groupings is the focus of three generalizations (each consisting of two parts).[10]

This is not the place to enumerate these findings, but suffice it to note that they all involve interaction between attributes or behavior of units at one level of aggregation (usually the nation-state) and outcomes for units at another level (usually the regional grouping). To be sure, in summarizing the findings Haas finds cause for concern about their limitations as well as satisfaction in the progress they represent. He notes that important definitional differences still prevail among students of integration,[11] that "only a few" of the generalizations "rise above the level of verifying simple hypotheses based on readily observed behavior,"[12] and that therefore many gaps remain and much needs to be done to move work on regional integration into and beyond a pretheoretical stage.[13] In particular, Haas is uneasy about "the indefinite nature of the end state or the terminal condition to which regional integration is supposed to lead." He sees work on the concept as sometimes positing a process and sometimes an outcome as the end state, a distinction which is "appealing . . . because it sidesteps the definitional problem," but which at the same time holds back the development of theory:

It is not only a question of whether we wish to explain the process, necessarily stressing a time dimension, whereby relationships change between nations and actors or to describe the terminal condition (which could be conceived in static terms) to which the process is likely to lead. The job is to do both; but the task of selecting and justifying variables and explaining their hypothesized interdependence cannot be accomplished without an agreement as to possible conditions to which the process is expected to lead. In short, we need a dependent variable.[14]

While the lack of clarity and consensus on the dependent variables embraced by the concept certainly indicates that its full potential has still to be realized, there is good reason to believe that this problem will not resist solution for long and that students of regional integration will continue to contribute to across-systems theory. The concept lends itself to such progress because, unlike interdependence, it is precise in specifying the kind of phenomena at the national and international levels which have either been conceived or found to be systematically associated with each other. The fact that theory-building is plagued by definitional differences

[10]Ibid., pp. 614–21.
[11]Ibid., pp. 610–11.
[12]Ibid., p. 621.
[13]Ibid., p. 622.
[14]Ibid.

and confusion over the identity of the dependent variables is not a cause for serious concern, since the progress toward specification of empirical referents has been so pronounced and continuous for well over a decade. One need only peruse the essays comprising the symposium for which the aforementioned summary serves as an introduction to know that the concept of integration will long operate as a stimulus to across-systems theory and research.[15]

Notwithstanding this potential, however, it must be noted that the concept of integration can never make more than a limited contribution to across-systems analysis. This is so because its scope is restricted to a particular set of phenomena, namely, those encompassed by noncoercive efforts to create "new types of human communities at a very high level of organization."[16] Stated more succinctly, "the main reason for studying regional integration is . . . normative."[17] This means that while a wide variety of actors, attitudes, and behaviors are of interest to students of integration, they will nevertheless ignore the many phenomena which are important aspects or determinants of across-systems processes but which are unrelated to the norms that sustain their inquiries. To be sure, their models are not so naive as to be confined only to processes which promote integration. Most students of the subject allow for a full range of variation in their key variables, including those which operate to hinder integration or foster disintegration. More than a few studies have straightforwardly (albeit regretfully) interpreted data as indicating tendencies away from integrationist attitudes and patterns.[18] To allow for a wide range of variation in the variables of a model, however, is not necessarily to probe a wide range of variables. And in this respect the integration theorists operate within narrow limits and can be counted on to enrich only a small proportion of the dimensions of across-systems processes that mark present-day world politics. Most notably, in addition to eschewing coercive phenomena in their formulations, their foci are such that they are unlikely to contribute to across-systems processes that culminate at the national level of aggregation. The attributes and dynamics of national actors are crucial to their research, but only as independent variables and what happens to the nation-state as a consequence of the role it does or does not play in regional integrative or disintegrative processes is essentially be-

[15]For especially provocative analyses that demonstrate the stimulating character of the concept, see part 2 of the symposium (Lindberg and Scheingold, "Regional Integration, pp. 649–916) and, in particular, Leon N. Lindberg, "Political Integration as a Multidimensional Phenomenon Requiring Multivariate Measurement," pp. 649–731.

[16]Haas, "Study of Regional Integration," p. 608.

[17]Ibid.

[18]For example, see Leon N. Lindberg and Stuart A. Scheingold, *Europe's Would-Be Polity: Patterns of Change in the European Community* (Englewood Cliffs, N.J.: Prentice-Hall, 1970).

yond the pale of their concerns. For all of the abstract models founded on it, in short, the concept of integration would seem to be capable of producing only partial understanding and limited breakthroughs in across-systems theory.

Researchers who have sought to tailor the concept of adaptation to the needs of across-systems analysis have to a large extent avoided the foregoing limitations inherent in the concept of integration. More accurately, the foci and purposes that guide inquiry into adaptive phenomena are quite different from those that direct integration research. Stated succinctly, adaptation focuses on the national level of aggregation; it is not limited to noncoercive phenomena; and it is not a concept that arises out of normative concerns.

To the extent that it has been developed for the analysis of phenomena aggregated at the national level, adaptation refers to the efforts and processes whereby national societies keep their essential social, economic, and political structures within acceptable limits. It posits fluctuations in the essential structures as stemming from changes and demands that arise both within and external to the adapting society. All the factors, coercive as well as noncoercive, which keep (or fail to keep) these fluctuations within a given set of acceptable limits are considered to be adaptive (or maladaptive) phenomena, as are those which underlie alterations in these limits and which thus give rise to what are called adaptive transformations. Four basic modes of keeping the fluctuations within acceptable limits have been posited as available to societies and any of the twelve possible shifts from one of these modes to any of the others are viewed as adaptive transformations.[19] Since both the adaptive modes and transformations involve the nature of the balance that is achieved between conflicting internal and external needs, the concept readily lends itself to across-systems analysis. Indeed, it facilitates analysis across three levels of aggregation, the subnational level at which internal demands arise, the international level from which external demands emanate, and the national level at which the demands are or are not reconciled. To comprehend either a nation's capacity for adaptation or its actual persistence through time, therefore, the analyst must probe phenomena at several levels of aggregation and his theories must account for the interaction between at least two of the levels. Inescapably, in short, the concept of adaptation forces across-systems analysis.

Although frequently misinterpreted as reflecting a concern for the preservation of the status quo at any moment in time, the main reason for studying national adaptation is not normative. Interest in adaptive phe-

---

[19]For an elaboration of these major components of the adaptation concept, see James N. Rosenau, *The Adaptation of National Societies: A Theory of Political System Behavior and Transformation* (New York: McCaleb-Seiler, 1970).

nomena does not require the analyst to posit end states or anticipate terminal conditions. It can be as appropriate to investigate national actors which fail to adapt as those which successfully cope with their environment. As long as an adapting entity manages to persist, adaptation is conceived to be a never-ending process, one which can include military aggression, revolutionary upheavals, dictatorial repressions, or integration into larger federations as well as rational calculations, democratic elections, peaceful transitions, or policies of intransigent isolation. Life in an adaptive national society can be restless or content, static or dynamic, stable or chaotic; but whatever the prevailing conditions, the study of national adaptation concerns itself with the fluctuations in the society's essential structures to which both internal and external demands give rise. The researcher who focuses on the phenomena of adaptation is led to do so not by normative concerns, but by an intellectual fascination with the question of why and how most national societies adjust to a rapidly changing world and why some fail to make it. Thus, unlike his counterparts who focus on integration, the student of national adaptation is not constrained by his central concept to ignore any phenomena which may operate as important aspects or determinants of across-systems phenomena. Admittedly, analysts or policy makers who venerate the nation-state may be inclined to view adaptive phenomena in a normative context and use the concept as a guide to efforts to maintain a desired status quo. Such an approach, however, is not inherent in the way the concept has been formulated. It is essentially a tool of basic research, whatever the applied purposes to which it might be put.

On the other hand, this is not to say that the concept of adaptation stands up well against all the evaluative criteria set forth above. In the first place, work on it is only a couple of years old and is thus not nearly as advanced or cumulative as that which has been done on integration. Virtually no empirical case studies, much less any quantitative analyses, have been undertaken,[20] so that presently the literature consists primarily of two main theoretical formulations,[21] both of which have been rigorously criticized.[22] Thus it is too early to reach any conclusions as to

[20]W. Scott Thompson of Tufts, however, is presently undertaking a comparative analysis of the Philippines and Thailand in the context of the adaptation model.

[21]Rosenau, *The Adaptation of National Societies*, and Patrick J. McGowan, "Toward a Dynamic Theory of Foreign Policy," mimeographed (Syracuse, 1971). Also see an earlier paper of McGowan's, "A Formal Theory of Foreign Policy as Adaptive Behavior," mimeographed (Paper presented at the annual meeting of the American Political Science Association, Los Angeles, 1970).

[22]Peter A. Corning, "Toward an Evolutionary-Adaptive Theory of Politics," mimeographed (Paper presented at the annual meeting of the Midwest Political Science Association, Chicago, 1971). For an elaborate presentation of Corning's own use of the adaptation concept, see Peter A. Corning, "The Biological Bases of Behavior and Some Implications for Political Science," *World Politics* 23 (April 1971): 321–70.

whether the apparent theoretical utility of the concept will in fact pay off. It would seem, unlike the concept of interdependence, to provide the basis for observing how variables at two or more levels of aggregation vary in relation to each other, but the observations have yet to be made and unforeseen methodological difficulties may well lie ahead.

A second limitation of the concept of adaptation is that it is exclusively centered on the nation-state. That is, just as the integration concept is limited by the fact that all its dependent variables are posited as operative at the international level, so are all the dependent variables in the study of national adaptation confined to measures of change or constancy within the national society whose adaptive behavior is the focus of attention. Subnational and extranational factors, to the extent that they are the sources of demands made upon the adapting society, are treated as independent variables. They may even be manipulated as intervening variables if the adaptive model allows for feedback processes whereby the adapting society's domestic and foreign policies foster responses abroad and at home that in turn produce demands that cause fluctuations in its essential structures. In the end, however, the student of national adaptation concentrates on the fluctuations and his interest in phenomena at the subnational and extranational levels ends once he ascertains the way they operate in relation to the various modes of adaptation. To be sure, the concept of adaptation could readily be applied to regional groupings or subnational entities. But such applications have yet to occur (perhaps in the case of the former because their essential structures are still so unformed), and thus the concept's potential contribution to across-systems analysis is presently limited to a narrow (though important) set of phenomena.

Although it has been the focus of numerous inquiries, the concept of intervention is narrower in scope than either adaptation or integration.[23] In its most common usage it refers to an action and not a process—to a single sequence of behavior, the initiation and termination of which is easily discernible and the characteristics of which are dependent on the use or threat of force. An intervention begins when one national society explicitly, purposefully, and abruptly undertakes to alter or preserve one or more essential structures of another national society through military means, and it ends when the effort is either successful, abandoned, or routinized.[24] Some analysts prefer to conceive of intervention in much wider terms and posit any sequence of behavior, military or nonmilitary, as interventionary if it involves one actor's intentional efforts to affect the domestic affairs of another. In effect, these broad formulations equate intervention with influ-

[23]Indeed, in one formulation intervention is seen as but one form of adaptation. See James N. Rosenau, "Foreign Intervention as Adaptive Behavior," in *Law and Civil War in the Modern World*, John Norton Moore (forthcoming).

[24]For a lengthy discussion of this and other conceptions of intervention, see James N. Rosenau, "Intervention as a Scientific Concept," *Journal of Conflict Resolution* 13 (June 1969): 149-71.

ence. While the lack of definitional consensus in this regard has proved troublesome and is likely to persist,[25] the tendency to use military phenomena as the empirical referents for the concept is becoming increasingly pronounced. Agreement on the precise nature of interventionary phenomena may never be unanimous, but such widespread concurrence has emerged with respect to the military formulation that it is reasonable to confine the ensuing discussion to it.[26]

Two reasons for the growing readiness to focus on the narrow, military conception of interventionary behavior are worthy of note. One is that increasing attention to across-systems phenomena has led to greater definitional specificity and, in turn, to a proliferation of concepts designed to account for what were once regarded as simply the nuances of a single concept. Thus, in the case of intervention, those phenomena associated with the prolonged and routinized processes whereby one society is consistently involved in the domestic affairs of another are increasingly brought under the rubric of the concept of penetration (see below), leaving abrupt, overt, and coercive efforts to affect domestic affairs abroad to analysis by students of interventionary phenomena.

The second reason for equating interventionary and coercive phenomena is that threatened or actual military interventions seem increasingly likely to mark world politics as rapid social change within national societies intensifies the extent and frequency of internal violence and as shrinking social and geographic distance between societies intensifies the degree and frequency of outside involvement in domestic upheavals. Or, if the actual number of interventions is no greater than in the past, these factors make their importance and consequences seem greater, with the result that the attention of both students of national and international systems has been attracted to them. Students of national systems are not so much concerned with across-systems phenomena as they are with the applied problem of how to improve the quality of foreign policy to the point where the need for interventionary behavior can either be avoided or made more effective. These policy analysts are primarily, if not exclusively, preoccupied with phenomena at the national level, either those that underlie the intervening nation's behavior or those that shape the outcome in the intervened nation. To be sure, some theoretical insights and considerable data relevant to across-systems phenomena have been generated by the policy analysts,[27] but these consist largely of uncoordinated case his-

[25]The reasons why definitional differences are likely to persist can be found in James N. Rosenau, "The Concept of Intervention," *Journal of International Affairs* 22, no. 2 (1968): 165–76.

[26]For evidence of this emerging consensus, see Rosenau, "Foreign Intervention as Adaptive Behavior," pp. 2–6.

[27]For example, see Alexander L. George, David K. Hall, William R. Simons, *The Limits of Coercive Diplomacy: Laos-Cuba-Vietnam* (Boston: Little, Brown & Co., 1971); Graham Allison, Ernest May, and Adam Yarmolinsky, "Limits to Intervention," *Foreign Affairs* 48

tories and do not systematically posit patterns of association between variations at two levels of aggregation.

The analysts who have approached interventionary phenomena from an international perspective, on the other hand, have developed the concept in such a way that it does lend itself to the derivation of across-systems propositions. Their perspective leads them to pose the problem in terms of the interplay between internal and external violence—that is, the conditions in the international system that conduce to interventions and those aspects of domestic upheaval that attract interventions—and once posed in this way, they are led to prove how variations at one of the levels interact with those at the other. Stated differently, once internal war and domestic violence came to be recognized as pervasive phenomena of crucial relevance to the study of politics,[28] the processes by which such phenomena become internationalized quickly became a major focus of analytic attention.[29] It did so both for those in the field of international law with an applied interest in the creation of a more stable world order[30] and for those interested in basic research into the dynamics of international politics and foreign policy.[31] Indeed, the interaction between internal and external violence has proved so stimulating to theory-building that those interested in this dimension of interventionary behavior have been able to generate quantitative data and test hypotheses which depict across-systems processes that both originate and culminate in both national and international

---

(January 1970): 245–61; Max Beloff, "Reflections on Intervention," *Journal of International Affairs* 22, no. 2 (1968): 198–207.

[28]Perhaps with the publication of Harry Eckstein, ed., *Internal War* (New York: Free Press, 1964).

[29]See, for example, James N. Rosenau, ed., *International Aspects of Civil Strife* (Princeton, N.J.: Princeton University Press, 1964).

[30]Cf. John Norton Moore, "The Control of Foreign Intervention in Internal Conflict," *Virginia Journal of International Law* 9 (May 1969): 209–342; and Symposium, "Foreign Intervention in Civil Strife," *Stanford Journal of International Studies* 3 (June 1968): 1–122.

[31]For example, see C. R. Mitchell, "Civil Strife and the Involvement of External Parties," *International Studies Quarterly* 14 (June 1970): 166–94; John W. Eley, "Intervention as Transnational Behavior: A Critique and a Proposal," *International Studies Quarterly*, forthcoming; Metin Tamkoc, *International Civil War* (Ankara: Middle East Technical University, 1967); Charles Tilly, "Research on the Relations Between Conflict Within Polities and Conflict Among Polities," mimeographed (Ann Arbor, 1970); Andrew M. Scott, "Military Intervention by the Great Powers: The Rules of the Game," mimeographed (New York, 1968); David W. Paul, "Soviet Foreign Policy and the Invasion of Czechoslovakia: A Theory and a Case Study," *International Studies Quarterly* 15 (June 1971): 159–202. George A. Kelly and Linda B. Miller, *Internal War and International Systems: Perspectives on Method*, Occasional Paper No. 21 (Cambridge: Center for International Affairs, Harvard University, 1969); George A. Kelly and Clifford W. Brown, eds., *Struggles in the State: Sources and Patterns of World Revolution* (New York: John Wiley and Sons, 1970); Frank J. Popper, "Internal War as a Stimulant of Political Development," *Comparative Political Studies* 3 (January 1971):413–24; and John W. Eley, "Internal Wars and International Events: An Analysis of the Internationalization of Internal Wars" (Ph.D. diss., University of Maryland, 1969).

systems. In this sense, of course, the concept of intervention is actually broader than those of integration and adaptation (which, it will be re-called, focus only on dependent variables that are located, respectively, at the international and national levels). It is much narrower, however, in the sense that it is limited to single sequences of coercive behavior.

That curiosity about the dynamics and consequences of internal wars led students of intervention to derive findings and generalizations that may contribute to across-systems analysis can be readily demonstrated. In the first place, as will be seen below, such a focus has encouraged the develop-ment of models in which the concept of intervention is treated, in the larger context of linkage politics, as one form of penetration. The interest in across-systems phenomena has led not only to a proliferation of concepts designed to differentiate among them, but, even more significantly, it has resulted in the proliferation of concepts that bear close relation to or sub-sume each other. Second, at least a few quantitative studies have become available in recent years. In a cross-national survey Sullivan used a num-ber of indicators of national attributes to probe the "international conse-quences of domestic violence."[32] Hazlewood has used a factor analysis of a series of variables to probe the interaction of domestic violence and at-tributes of the international system.[33] Collins has used the same tech-nique to explore similar interactions for thirty-three independent coun-tries in Africa.[34] And Eley has collected data on thirty internal wars as a means of investigating the dynamics whereby such conflicts become inter-nationalized.[35] Third, these empirical inquiries have resulted in a number of hypotheses, some tested by the data and some derived from them, that posit variations at the two levels as systematically associated with each other. Eley, for example, tested some twenty-nine preliminary hypoth-eses, from which ten emerged as more advanced propositions. The follow-ing are illustrative of his derivations:

1. There is a significant positive relationship between the type of responses stimu-lated by internal wars and the type of internal war involved.
1.1 Any internal war is more likely to be marked by at least material support for one of the belligerents if it is a revolutionary war or a political civil war than if it is a war of independence.

[32]John D. Sullivan, "International Consequences of Domestic Violence," mimeographed (Paper presented at the annual meeting of the American Political Science Association. New York, 1969).

[33]Leo A. Hazlewood, "Informal Penetration, Systemic Constraints, and Political Vio-lence," mimeographed (1971).

[34]John N. Collins, "Foreign Conflict Behavior and Domestic Disorder in Africa," chap. 9, this volume.

[35]John W. Eley, "The International Dimensions of Internal Wars: A Preliminary Anal-ysis," mimeographed (Paper presented at the annual meeting of the Southern Political Sci-ence Association, 1970).

2. There is a significant negative relationship between the type of responses stimulated by internal wars and the power rankings of the responding actors.

2.1 Small or medium power actors are more likely to intervene in internal wars than are great power actors.[36]

Notwithstanding its potential for across-systems analysis, however, the concept of intervention cannot in itself provide the basis for major theoretical breakthroughs. The exclusive concern with coercive phenomena is a severe constraint on theory-building. What is needed is a more generic concept which allows for both coercive and noncoercive phenomena as well as for across-systems processes that originate and culminate at both the national and international levels.

Although below we conclude that it is too early to reach a judgment about the theoretical utility of the linkage concept,[37] it may meet the test of a generic concept. At least it seems especially free of the deficiencies of the concepts examined thus far. Moreover, despite early doubts and even an attempt to dismiss it as incapable of generating research,[38] it has evoked some interest and exploration. Thus it is to the efforts along this line that our attention now turns.

V

As previously noted, the linkage concept was not developed in response to either normative pressures or sheer intellectual curiosity. Rather its initial formulation arose out of a conviction that students of comparative and international politics were needlessly and harmfully ignoring each other's work. The world had become so small, it was argued, that specialists in comparative (i.e., national and subnational) politics could no longer hold international variables constant in their models and, conversely, those who specialized in international politics could no longer afford to treat domestic variables as constant features of the world scene.

To facilitate the convergence of the two fields, it was proposed that a "linkage" serve as the basic unit of analysis, "defining it as any recurrent sequence of behavior that originates in one system and is reacted to in an-

---

[36]Ibid., pp. 19–20.

[37]The original formulation of the linkage concept in which its components were specified in considerable detail was first presented at the 1966 annual meeting of the American Political Science Association and later published in James N. Rosenau, ed., *Linkage Politics: Essays on the Convergence of National and International Systems* (New York: Free Press, 1969), pp. 44–63. For an earlier, less elaborate formulation, see Karl W. Deutsch, "External Influences on the Internal Behavior of States," in *Approaches to Comparative and International Politics*, ed. R. Barry Farrell (Evanston, Ill.: Northwestern University Press, 1966), pp. 5–26.

[38]James N. Rosenau, "Adaptive Strategies for Research and Practice in Foreign Policy," in *A Design for International Studies: Scope, Objectives, and Methods*, ed. Fred Riggs (Philadelphia: American Academy of Political and Social Science, 1971), pp. 218–45.

other."[39] The original formulation stressed that a single reaction did not constitute a linkage. Only those sequences of behavior in one system that, in the process of unfolding, are recurrently linked to phenomena in another system were so defined. Since boundary-crossing sequences could occur through "processes of perception and emulation as well as . . . direct interaction,"[40] allowance was made for intermittent as well as continuous linkages. No operational definition of intermittency was offered, but it was plainly emphasized that the scheme was designed to uncover the more enduring dimensions of politics and not to analyze isolated historical events.[41]

The original formulation also posited the initial and terminal stages of a linkage as, respectively, outputs and inputs for the national or international system in which the sequence of behavior either originated or culminated. In this way, across-systems analysis that could be undertaken from either a national or international perspective was made possible. Indeed, analysis based simultaneously on both perspectives was built into the framework by identifying the existence of a "fused" linkage—one which

arises out of the possibility that certain outputs and inputs continuously reinforce each other and are thus best viewed as forming a reciprocal relationship. In other words, a fused linkage is one in which the patterned sequence of behavior does not terminate with the input. Stated in positive terms, a fused linkage is conceived to be a sequence in which an output fosters an input that in turn fosters an output in such a way that they cannot meaningfully be analyzed separately.[42]

Three basic processes were posited as providing the means by which outputs and inputs get linked together. A *"penetrative process* occurs when members of one polity serve as participants in the political processes of another."[43] A *"reactive process* is the contrary of a penetrative one: It is brought into being by recurrent and similar boundary-crossing reactions rather than by the sharing of authority." The third process is in turn a special form of the reactive one. Referred to as an *"emulative process,"* it "is established when the input is not only a response to the output but takes essentially the same form as the output."[44]

In order to make the ensuing analysis clear, one final component of the original framework should be noted here. It consists of a 24 by 6 matrix

---

[39]Rosenau, *Linkage Politics*, p. 45.
[40]Ibid.
[41]Ibid., p. 48.
[42]Ibid., p. 49.
[43]For a more elaborate development of the concept of a penetrated political system than is provided in the original linkage framework, see James N. Rosenau, "Pre-Theories and Theories of Foreign Policy," in Farrell, ed., *Approaches to Comparative and International Politics*, pp. 65–92. For another, slightly different elaboration of the nature of penetrative processes, see Andrew M. Scott, *The Revolution in Statecraft: Informal Penetration* (New York: Macmillan Co., 1967).
[44]Rosenau, *Linkage Politics*, p. 46.

compiled out of "twenty-four aspects of polities that might serve as or give rise to outputs and inputs . . . [and] six aspects or (from a polity perspective) subenvironments of the international system that might generate or receive outputs and inputs."[45] The derivation of the components of the matrix was admittedly arbitrary:

In the case of the twenty-four polity subcategories, we have merely listed some of the more obvious determinants of outputs and inputs, trusting that their general characteristics are self-evident. The listing includes phenomena that sustain behavior at different levels (actors, attitudes, institutions, and processes) and that unfold in different settings (the government, the polity, and the society). Likewise, in the case of the environmental categories, we have proceeded on an equally simple and impressionistic basis. The only rationale for the categorization is the impression that both actors and observers tend, often unknowingly, to think about international phenomena in terms of the units represented by the six subenvironments. Again no claim is made that these six are exhaustive or mutually exclusive. Further inquiry may well reveal that other output or input phenomena, such as those of a legal, technological, and military kind, are so important as to justify the establishment of additional categories. We do contend, however, that these six environments are operative in the minds of actors and that they are thus at least a meaningful sample for our purposes here.[46]

The six proposed categories of the international system are the "Contiguous Environment," the "Regional Environment," the "Cold War Environment," the "Racial Environment," the "Resource Environment," and the "Organizational Environment."[47]

While it was readily conceded that the 144-cell matrix was crude and that not all of the cells would yield interesting or important findings, it was argued that the scheme offered a number of possible advantages as an agenda for research. It was suggested that students of linkage phenomena had a variety of options open to them: they could undertake comparisons of different societies within any cell; they could engage in comparative analysis of one or many societies across one or more of the rows (i.e., how the same or different aspects of the same society or different ones are linked to the various polity attributes); and they could pursue any one of multitudes of other combinations and permutations of these options. Moreover, through the listing of a series of substantive questions, it was asserted that any or all of these options seemed likely to pay off in intriguing insights, and perhaps solid findings, about the interaction of phenomena at the national and international levels.[48]

[45]Ibid., p. 49. The matrix itself can be found on p. 52.
[46]Ibid., pp. 51–53.
[47]For an elaboration of the boundaries and nature of each subenvironment, see ibid., pp. 60–63.
[48]For the case made for the linkage framework, see ibid., pp. 53–60.

The initial effort to apply this framework systematically to empirical materials fell far short of the claims made for it. Twelve scholars spent two full days in January 1966 discussing the main features of the framework, clarifying the components of the matrix, and reaching agreement on which of its dimensions they would all use in applying the approach to the comparison of two or more national societies. Despite these self-conscious efforts at coordination, however, the resulting essays[49] failed to yield comparable findings. The linkage dimensions they were all to investigate turned out to have different meanings for each of them. Indeed, the task of actually applying the original formulation apparently proved so vexing that a few of the participants in the initial discussions abandoned it entirely in their essays. Taken as a whole, moreover, the resulting essays proved to be a methodological hodgepodge, with some founded on quantitative data, some on journalists' observations, and some on overall impressions. Some tested hypotheses and others provided historical narrative. All in all, the editor of the essays was compelled to conclude that the provision of a loosely designed, atheoretical typology was a failure as a research strategy.[50] The resulting volume did contain useful descriptions of the interaction of national and international systems, but as an instance of comparative inquiry into such phenomena it was painfully unproductive.

The editor, however, also made clear his conviction that the lack of comparability was the fault of the research strategy and not of the participants in the project. Reflection on the reasons for the failure to achieve a coordinated set of essays led to the recognition that the original framework —and especially the 144-cell matrix—was simply a typology that was totally lacking in theory.[51] The cells were created by the convergence of national and international variables, but there was no specification of the phenomena that might be found in them. In the absence of any guidance along these lines, it is hardly surprising that the essays were marked by variability rather than comparability. At the time, therefore, it seemed clear that a different research strategy ought to have been used:

If some predictions about the phenomena embraced by each cell of the matrix had been hazarded, those using it would have at least had some guidance as to the kinds of questions to explore and the kinds of data to gather. Comparisons might have then revealed that the predictions were erroneous or far-fetched, but at least extensive analysis would have been undertaken and a clearer picture thereby ob-

[49]Ibid., chaps. 4–12.
[50]This conclusion is elaborated in ibid., pp. 15–17. For a similar assessment, see the cogent book review by Dina A. Zinnes, *Midwest Journal of Political Science* 14 (May 1970): 344–47.
[51]It is thus no accident that in recounting here the development of the linkage concept, it has been labeled as constituting a "framework" or a "formulation"; the label of "model" or "theory" has been carefully avoided.

tained of the conditions under which linkage processes are inoperative. Bad theory, in other words, would have been better than no theory—both as a means of achieving coordinated effort and as a way of extending comprehension.[52]

In sum, the noncomparability of the original essays suggested that the strategy used would prove counterproductive, that the massive framework intended to stimulate a variety of across-systems analyses would in fact stifle investigation, demonstrating through its very massiveness and lack of direction the wisdom of continuing to confine theory and research to a single analytic level. Indeed, without going so far as to agree with one critic who contended that circulating an atheoretical matrix known to lack mutually exclusive categories is irresponsible and a "scandal,"[53] the desirability of burying the framework was publicly asserted.[54]

VI

Yet the linkage concept did not die. The original prognosis may prove correct, but a variety of researchers have pursued it in a variety of directions. Indeed, five years later the concept was still regarded as sufficiently viable to justify devoting a panel at the annual meeting of the American Political Science Association to an evaluation of the problems, progress, and potential of national-international linkages as foci and tools of inquiry.[55]

Perhaps most of the investigations into linkage phenomena have been nation-state centered, with one or another external environment being treated as the source of outputs and the national society as the locus of inputs. That is, many researchers have employed the concept in an effort to explain behavior at the national level. In some instances single countries have served as the analytic focus. For example, Manley has concentrated on Guyana,[56] Clark on Venezuela,[57] Hodnett and Potichnyj on the

[52]Rosenau, *Linkage Politics*, p. 16.

[53]Marion J. Levy, " 'Does It Matter if He's Naked' Bawled the Child," in *Contending Approaches to International Politics*, ed. Klaus Knorr and James N. Rosenau (Princeton, N.J.: Princeton University Press, 1969), p. 105.

[54]See note 38.

[55]The panel was organized by Albert F. Eldridge, Jr., of Duke University and, in addition to an earlier version of this chapter, included presentation of the following papers: Sheldon W. Simon, "Further Reflections on a Systems Approach to Security in the Indian Ocean Arc"; Terry L. McCoy, "External Outputs and Population Policy Making in Latin America"; and Curtis E. Huff, Jr., "Regional Patterns and Changes After Military Coups D'Etat: The Foreign Relations of African States."

[56]Robert H. Manley, "Linkage Politics: The Organizational Environment for Guyanese Nation-Building," mimeographed (Paper presented at the annual meeting of the International Studies Association, San Juan, 1971).

[57]Robert P. Clark, Jr., "Economic Integration and the Political Process: Linkage Politics in Venezuela," mimeographed (1969).

Ukraine,[58] Bunker on Peru,[59] and Couloumbis on Greece.[60] In other instances one or two nations have been intensively examined or contrasted with a view to generalizing beyond the single case. Wahlbeck has examined Finland in such a context[61] and Meadows has contrasted Indonesia and the Philippines for the same purpose.[62] In still other cases linkage phenomena involving types of nation-states have served as the basis of comparative analysis. Reid is looking at micro-states,[63] Sonneberg at "pariah" states,[64] Lewis at small states,[65] Grundy at the black states of Southern Africa,[66] and Blong at "political systems exhibiting high versus low levels of external penetration."[67]

Although a minority, some analysts have centered their inquiries at the international level. Hoadley and Hasegawa have investigated the postwar linkages between two proximate nations, China and Japan.[68] McCoy has probed international population programs, with a variety of international, national, and subnational agencies external to Latin America being treated as the sources of outputs and the twenty-one nation-states of that region as the loci of inputs.[69] Hazlewood, as previously noted, has similarly treated outputs and inputs in order to investigate "the impact of certain kinds of international behavior as predictors of domestic political violence."[70]

[58]Grey Hodnett and Peter J. Potichnyj, *The Ukraine and the Czechoslovak Crisis* (Canberra: Australian National University, 1970).

[59]Rod Bunker, "Linkages and the Foreign Policy of Peru, 1958–1966," *Western Political Quarterly* 22 (June 1969): 280–97.

[60]Theodore A. Couloumbis, "The Foreign Factor in Greek Politics," mimeographed (1971); also see idem, *Greek Political Reaction to American and NATO Influences* (New Haven: Yale University Press, 1966).

[61]Krister Wahlbach, "Finnish Foreign Policy: Some Comparative Perspectives," *Cooperation and Conflict* 4 (1969): 282–98.

[62]Martin Meadows, "Theories of External-Internal Political Relationships: A Case Study of Indonesia and the Philippines," *Asian Studies* 6 (December 1968): 297–324.

[63]George L. Reid, "Linkage Theory in Application to Micro-States," mimeographed (Ph.D. diss. prospectus, Southampton, N.Y., 1970).

[64]Milton Sonneberg, mimeographed paper (Ph.D. diss. prospectus, Cleveland, 1971).

[65]Vaughan A. Lewis, "The Structure of Small State Behavior in Contemporary International Politics" (Ph.D. diss., Jamaica, W.I., 1971).

[66]Kenneth W. Grundy, "The Foreign Policies of Black Southern Africa," mimeographed (Paper presented at the Symposium on International Law and National Development in Southern Africa, Los Angeles, 1970). Also see idem, "Host States and the Southern African Liberation Struggle," *Africa Quarterly* 10 (April–June 1970): 15–24.

[67]Clair Karl Blong, "A Comparative Study of the Foreign Policy Behavior of Political Systems Exhibiting High Versus Low Levels of External Penetration," mimeographed (Ph.D. diss. prospectus, College Park, Md., 1971).

[68]J. Stephen Hoadley and Sukehiro Hasegawa, "Sino-Japanese Relations 1950–1970: An Application of the Linkage Model of International Politics," *International Studies Quarterly* 15 (June 1971): 131–57.

[69]Terry L. McCoy, "A Functional Taxonomy of International Population Programs," mimeographed (Paper presented at the American Society of International Law Regional Meeting, Charlottesville, 1971).

[70]"Informal Penetration," p. 1.

Edmondson, Feld, Korbonski, and Domínguez, on the other hand, have compared across international levels (i.e., across subenvironments, in the terminology of the linkage framework), with the outputs and inputs they treat being located at different levels of international aggregation: Edmondson confines his attention to transnational racial phenomena;[71] Feld focuses on the links between the national societies of Eastern Europe and the European Economic Community (EEC);[72] Korbonski probes the links between roughly the same East European societies and the Council of Mutual Economic Assistance (COMECON);[73] and Domínguez explores the interaction among the central international system, international organizations, and (especially) international subsystems on the peripheries of world politics.[74]

Doubtless other inquiries into linkage phenomena have been completed or are underway,[75] but the foregoing sample is sufficient to suggest some major trends in the development of the concept. In the first place, one is struck by the extent to which the various studies, each in its own way, are concerned with hierarchical phenomena. Both the case studies and the comparative analyses focus on linkages between superiors and subordinates. It would seem to be no accident that Latin American and East European societies are predominant among the case studies, since many of the linkages discussed therein involve outputs originating with nearby superpowers. The same emphasis pervades the comparison of micro-, pariah, and small states. Even the studies cast at the international level, especially Domínguez's, focuses on hierarchical links between the strong and the weak. Conspicuously missing are analyses of linkages in which,

[71]Locksley Edmondson, "Africa and the African Diaspora: Interactions, Linkages, and Racial Challenges in the Future World Order," mimeographed (n.d.).

[72]Werner J. Feld, "National-International Linkage Theory: The East European Communist System and the EEC," *Journal of International Affairs* 22, no. 1 (1968): 107–20.

[73]Andrzej Korbonski, "Theory and Practice of Regional Integration: The Case of Comecon," *International Organization* 24 (Autumn 1970): 942–77.

[74]Jorge I. Dominguez, "Mice That Do Not Roar: Some Aspects of International Politics in the World's Peripheries," *International Organization* 25 (Spring 1971): 175–208.

[75]And surely the growing sensitivity to such phenomena can also be found in many studies that are not explicitly cast in a linkage framework. Such a sensitivity, for example, is plainly evident in the finding that" . . . the major explanatory variable in understanding the new Romanian conception of bloc relations and conflict resolution is party institutionalization." Kenneth Jowitt, "The Romanian Communist Party and the World Socialist System: A Redefinition," *World Politics* 43 (October 1970): 38–60. For other recent inquiries sensitive to linkage phenomena that were received too late to incorporate into the text of this essay, see Frank C. Darling, "The Traditional Polities of Asia: A Macro-Analytical Approach," *Pacific Community* (Winter 1971): 52–76; Albert F. Eldridge, "Foreign Policy and Discrimination: The Politics of Indigenization," mimeographed (1971); Martin and Joan Krye, "Experimental Application of the Linkage Concept to Military Occupation: The Okinawan Case," mimeographed (1972); and R. K. C. Tung, "External Dependence and Internal Underdevelopment: Politics of Penetration and Permeability," mimeographed (Paper presented at the Fifth Nordic Conference on Peace Research, Norway, 1972).

say, the twenty major national actors in world politics are loci of inputs.[76] Topdog-underdog comparisons appear to pervade use of the linkage concept, perhaps because they involve more immediately self-evident phenomena. While such a trend is not necessarily regrettable, since world politics is surely marked by significant hierarchical differences, neither is it entirely welcome. It indicates that those who study only the major national and international actors presume that the foci of their inquiries have somehow remained outside of the linkages that have grown with the decrease in the world's social and geographic distances.[77] Such a presumption seems exceedingly risky and, accordingly, it is regrettable that the linkage concept may come to be seen as primarily a tool for the analysis of hierarchical links across national and international levels of aggregation. It is certainly no less reasonable to presume that linkage processes are as dynamic, if not more so, in situations of relative equality as they are in those where hierarchical considerations are crucial.

The amenability of the linkage concept to topdog-underdog relationships would appear to underlie another tendency in the aforementioned studies, particularly those in which the inputs occur at the national level. This is the fact that most of them focus mainly on the penetrative process and ignore the reactive and emulative processes. Bunker starts from the "primary assumption" that "Peru is a thoroughly penetrated society,"[78] just as Couloumbis's first paragraph asserts that "Greece has been, is and probably will continue to be 'a penetrated political system.' "[79] Likewise, Lewis argues that penetrative processes are "the *base* elements from which internal and external linkages can be derived"[80] and Grundy posits them as a central strategy which black South African states could employ toward each other or toward the white South African states (Portugal, Rhodesia, and South Africa).[81] Indeed, the concern for penetrative processes has even led one student of linkage phenomena to investigate on a comparative basis the foreign policy behavior of polities differentiated by the degree to which they are penetrated systems.[82] To a large extent, in short, linkage and penetration have come to be used synonymously.

Another characteristic of many of the linkage studies is the readiness of their authors to tailor the original framework to the specific foci of

[76]A partial exception here is the Hoadley-Hasegawa inquiry into Sino-Japanese linkages. See Hoadley and Hasegawa, "Sino-Japanese Relations."

[77]A possible exception here is Bruce M. Russett, "Indicators for America's Linkages with the Changing World Environment," *The Annals* 388 (March 1970): 82–96. However, Russett used the notion of linkage more as a means of measuring relationships than as a concept for analyzing the processes on which relationships are founded.

[78]"Linkages and Foreign Policy of Peru," p. 281.

[79]"Foreign Factor in Greek Politics," p. 1.

[80]"Structure of Small State Behavior," p. 263.

[81]"Foreign Politics of Black Southern Africa," pp. 37–38.

[82]Blong, "Comparative Study of Foreign Policy Behavior."

their research. Clark, for example, broadened the "Cold War" environment into a "center-periphery" category,[83] while Manley found the need to retitle it as the "East-West" environment and to add two other external environments, the "ideological" and the "North-South."[84] Similarly, Reid found good reasons to identify a special type of insular polity, "the archipelagic,"[85] and to differentiate between the "emulative" process of linkage and one he calls the "imitative" process.[86] In a like manner Domínguez's concern with international subsystems led him to delineate a particular kind of fused linkage process.[87] Conceptual innovations of this kind are, of course, welcome. The original framework was admittedly crude and arbitrary, and it is hardly surprising that its application generated revision. Furthermore, the innovations themselves would seem— at least in the case of those identifying new linkage processes—to be creative and to enlarge the explanatory capacity of the linkage concept.

Unfortunately, the empirical data thus far generated by the linkage framework have not been as innovative as the conceptual revisions. As previously implied, most of the data that have become available describe specific historical developments in particular countries and are not readily usable in contexts other than those in which the authors used them. Bunker's detailed, almost month-by-month account of how events internal and external to Peru got linked[88] is typical of the linkage data that comprise the presently available literature. There are exceptions, as the aforemen-

[83]"Economic Integration," p. 5.

[84]"Linkage Politics," p. 1.

[85]Consisting of islands "which form a chain," such as those found in the Caribbean, and which "may experience linkage phenomena which emanate from outside the geographical area but which are transmitted through the chain by being received first in that island which is more receptive to the phenomena and subsequently dispersed among the others through the channels of social communication which are relatively more intense between members of the chain than between members and nonmembers" ("Linkage Theory," p. 9).

[86] "Some states may be appropriately regarded as being affected by emulative processes in the sense that they undertake activity with the objective of seeking to equal or excel in the attainment of some end state which is seen to be possessed by actors of similar resource capabilities. Other states may, then, be regarded as being involved in imitative behavior if they seek to achieve similar conditions as are perceived to be possessed by actors whose resources are significantly greater" (ibid., p. 3).

[87]"Fusion occurs when there is a rise in simultaneous violent conflict in geographically contiguous subsystems previously indifferent toward each other. A precondition for fusion is that the local subsystems must already be relatively autonomous from the international center at least in the issue areas to be fused. Linkage through fusion takes place through local centers. A linkage through the center (whether systemic or subsystemic) means: (1) significant direct relations between the linked countries are few; (2) these countries are now relevant to each other primarily because they are significantly affected by the friendly or hostile actions of a given center power in their competition for resources which can be used in the local subsystem or in the countries themselves; and (3) only the linking center is a member of the two or more linked subsystems" (p. 187).

[88]"Linkages and Foreign Policy of Peru," esp. pp. 285-95.

tioned studies by Hazlewood and Eley demonstrate,[89] but for the most part the concept has yet to yield a rich data base that can be used to explore the interaction of the many variables through which linkages get formed and sustained. Indeed, since the comparative inquiries noted above are still largely conceptual and have yet to move into an empirical phase, one is compelled to note that not even faint traces of such a data base have become discernible and that, after all, it may be that the linkage concept will prove incapable of serving as a building block for further across-systems theory.

On the other hand, it can be argued that it is premature to anticipate an outpouring of linkage data, that the concept is too new and the phenomena it depicts too elusive for abundant quantifiable materials to have already become available. At least, such an argument would stress, the linkage framework has stimulated the consideration of phenomena, processes, or problems that had not previously been investigated. If this is so, then a clue as to the long-run utility of the linkage concept is to be found in the kinds of theoretical insights that the several years of inquiry have yielded. Even if the case histories do not provide data for further analysis, they and the more conceptual efforts that together comprise the presently available literature on linkages ought at least to have resulted in a series of generalizations about across-systems phenomena which will eventually stimulate the generation of appropriate data and the subsequent development of across-systems theory. Here the record is a mixed one. Some of the studies have not yielded anything resembling a generalization or hypothesis susceptible to empirical refinement. Their authors may have been led by the 24 by 6 matrix to investigate factors that might otherwise have been ignored—as Bunker did in Peru, Hodnett and Potichnyj in the Ukraine, and Clark in Venezuela—but the results were nonetheless bound by time and place. Bunker, for example, examined generally overlooked aspects of Peru, but his conclusions that "Peru has a penetrated political system," that "there are instances when Peru has an effective foreign policy," that "interest groups in Peru do influence its foreign policy," that "national economic growth is often the issue that initiates a foreign policy response," and that "international actors other than nation-states have important

---

[89]Another exception is the data creatively generated by McCoy, "A Functional Taxonomy." These are derived from tables in which each column represents one of the 21 Latin American countries and each row one of the international, national, and subnational agencies that support family planning programs somewhere in Latin America. The data consist of entries in the relevant cells of the tables indicating the fact or kind of support which the various agencies give to the various countries. A horizontal examination of the tables gives a clear picture of which are the most active agencies, whereas a vertical perusal provides a quick insight into which countries are likely to be the site of the most extensive national-international linkages in the population issue area.

roles in the formation of the foreign policies of Peru"[90] hardly exert pressure for further research. Similarly, Hodnett and Potichnyj were led by the framework to probe the attitudes, communications, institutions, and actors operative in the role played by the Ukraine in the Czechoslovak crisis of 1968, but their interpretation of this role as amounting to a fused linkage process[91] is not likely to serve as the basis for additional inquiry. Nor is the fact that Clark uncovered support for his hypotheses that "the configuration of linkage components" in Venezuela were such as to prevent or render meaningless that country's "participation in multi-national economic integration in Latin America"[92] likely to serve as an element of future across-systems theory. No less discouraging are those studies employing the linkage framework which derive generalizations that are so broad as to be irrefutable, and thus useless as a building block. Manley's derivation from his work on Guyana of the proposition that "external factors can have either a positive or negative impact on the nation-building process"[93] is an example of this failing.

In short, it would appear that to some extent the linkage framework has merely provided a new rhetoric with which to analyze old problems and, to the extent that this becomes its predominant use, it can hardly be counted on as a route to future theoretical breakthroughs. To repeat, however, the record is a mixed one. Some of the studies subjected to scrutiny were laden with interesting propositions, as a result either of examining data or readying the concept for the collection of data. The hypotheses derived by Eley cited above (p. 41), are indicative of the former process and the work of Blong and Reid is illustrative of the latter process. Blong deduced from his reasoning three challenging and general hypotheses relative to the dynamics of penetration that he plans to test on empirical data.[94] Reid's prospectus, although it does not formally identify any propositions, is pervaded with general expectations about the linkages that will be found to sustain the politics of microstates. Noting that the prime ministers of such societies tend to hold several cabinet posts, for instance, Reid observes that this can give rise to important role conflicts, an observation which leads him to hypothesize that "Where domestic issues are highly salient, and where the decision-maker has little previous experience in formulating purposive strategies of response to external phenomena, there will be an increased probability that foreign policy considerations will be dealt with in the context of more longstanding domestic issues, and foreign policy

---

[90]"Linkages and Foreign Policy of Peru," pp. 295–96.

[91]*Ukraine and the Czechoslovak Crisis*, pp. 115–25.

[92]"Economic Integration," pp. 2–3 (for the hypotheses) and 38–40 (for a summary of the findings).

[93]"Linkage Politics," p. 3.

[94]"Comparative Study of Foreign Policy Behavior," pp. 13–15.

may thus play a subordinate role in the total policy matrix."[95] Similarly, while indicating the many ways in which oceanic microstates are especially weak, Reid's reasoning also leads him to hypothesize about important ways in which the insularity of such societies enhances their strength: ". . . for even weak insular polities there is a delay in the transmission of linkage phenomena across the national boundary which will provide the decision-makers with a greater degree of time to contrive a response than would be available to leaders in even relatively larger continental polities."[96] Plainly, propositions such as these are sufficiently intriguing and specific to stimulate types of inquiries that might not otherwise be undertaken.

VII

So it is really too soon to reach a firm judgment about the theoretical utility of the linkage concept. It appears to have surmounted the major problem inherent in an atheoretical framework, that of failing to spark and guide further inquiry. In addition, it seems to offer advantages over a number of other concepts that have across-systems connotations. At the same time there has yet to develop convincing evidence that it lends itself to the derivation of interrelated propositions that systematically link variations at one level of aggregation with variations at another level. Some hypotheses and data do exist, but these are unrelated to each other and are a long way from comprising an integrated across-systems theory. Whether they will eventually prove to be building blocks of such a theory or merely isolated insights based on a common terminology is as yet unde-termined. Either outcome seems possible on the basis of progress thus far.

Lest the aspiration to an integrated linkage theory be abandoned be-cause it was not defined clearly enough, it is perhaps useful to outline briefly what such a theory might look like if it were to develop. The en-suing effort does not purport to be other than merely suggestive and is offered only as an example of the kinds of interrelationships that may be used to break through to the construction of across-systems theory. What follows is exceedingly crude and simplified, partly because clarity is best served through simplicity, but mainly because the conceptual and em-pirical equipment necessary to frame incisive linkage theory has still to be developed.

To illustrate the possible contours of viable linkage theory, we will use East Asia and the behavior of four national societies toward it as an ex-ample.[97] China, Japan, the United States, and the Soviet Union are the

---

[95]"Linkage Theory," p. 14.

[96]Ibid., pp. 16–17.

[97]The idea for this example originated with a reading of Robert E. Bedeski, "The Pros-pects of Crisis in East Asia: Dimensions and Approaches," mineographed (Columbus, Ohio, 1971).

four societies, and each is assumed to have a main goal in East Asia, the pursuit of which is presumed to be measurable on a five-point intensity scale ranging from "vigorous" to "halfhearted." The primary goals ascribed to the four countries are as follows:

Intensity Scale
1 2 3 4 5

China: vigorous maintenance   . . . . .   halfhearted mainte-
            of sovereignty   nance of sovereignty
Japan: vigorous securing of   . . . . .   halfhearted securing of
            markets and resources   markets and resources
U.S.:   vigorous maintenance   . . . . .   halfhearted mainte-
            of balance of power   nance of balance of
                                                     power
U.S.S.R.:   vigorous defense of   . . . . .   halfhearted defense of
            eastern border areas   eastern border areas

In addition, the theory assumes that the domestic life and structure of each society can be summarized in terms of fluctuations along one central dimension, which in turn is one of the two prime determinants of the degree to which the main goal in East Asia is being pursued vigorously or halfheartedly. The central domestic dimension is also assumed to be measurable on a five-point scale, referred to as a structural scale, and is listed below for each society, with the characteristic at the left being the one that tends to foster vigorous pursuit of the main East Asian goal and the one at the right being the basis of halfhearted pursuit:

Structural Scale
1 2 3 4 5

China: centralized   . . . . .   decentralized
            leadership   leadership
Japan: economic   . . . . .   economic
            growth   stagnation
U.S.:   interventionist   . . . . .   isolationist
            tendencies   tendencies
U.S.S.R.:   singular   . . . . .   collective
            leadership   leadership

The other major determinant of the degree to which each society's East Asian goal is pursued vigorously or halfheartedly is the interaction pattern that results from the way in which all four pursue their respective goals at any moment in time. That is, different combinations of vigorous or halfhearted pursuit of the four goals are presumed to give rise to different degrees and forms of stability and instability in the East Asian international system, and these are in turn likely to encourage increased or decreased vigor in the pursuits of the goals by each power.

Linkage theory becomes relevant when one attempts to develop propositions about how the degree of stability of the East Asian system will affect each society's location on the structural scale and how location on the structural scale will affect the degree of vigor with which each society pursues its external goals, thus affecting the nature and structure of the East Asian system. Given five-point scales, the possible permutations and combinations in this regard are too numerous to record here. They can readily be calculated with the aid of a computer, however, so that the only obstacle to viable linkage theory is the obvious inadequacy of the assumption that societal goals and structures can be reduced to single dimensions. Leaving this inadequacy aside, the example is pervaded with linkages. First, there are the linkages in which the outputs are found in the various domestic structures and the inputs in the East Asian system. The Cultural Revolution in China, for instance, moved that country toward the decentralization extreme, with the result that international politics in East Asia entered a new era of stability. Second, there are the linkages in which the outputs are located in the East Asian international system and the inputs in the domestic structures of the major powers. One can readily imagine, for example, how instability in that region would foster movement toward the interventionist extreme of the U.S.'s structure and the singular leadership extreme of the Soviet Union's structure. Third, there are the linkages in which the vigor of each society's effort to achieve its East Asian goal operates as the output and the locations on the structural scale of the other three societies are viewed as inputs. That is, not only may one or another aspect of the domestic structures of each of the four be systematically linked to East Asian systemic factors, but they may also vary systematically with changes in the vigor with which each of the other societies pursues its external goals.

In short, an integrated linkage theory posits a vast feedback system. Variations at each level are seen to be systematically linked to variations at the other levels in such a way as to feed back into and become part of the behavioral sequences at the original level. The links and the feedbacks are not the only—or even the most important—determinants of behavior at any level (there are other determinants of East Asian stability besides the vigor with which the major powers in the region pursue their East Asian goals). Yet, if theory along these lines could ever be developed, it ought to be possible to anticipate and trace the global repercussions of events and trends in an ever smaller world. Another cultural revolution in China, the ouster or death of another Khrushchev in Russia, another racial flareup in the United States, another resurgence of the birth rate in Japan, another exacerbation of tension in East Asia—such developments would be data that fit readily into, rather than undermine, the across-systems theories toward which our emerging conceptual tools are inexorably leading us.

PART II

FOREIGN CONFLICT BEHAVIOR LINKAGES

.3. Dimensions of Conflict Behavior Within and Between Nations*

R. J. RUMMEL

". . . unless our statements are in terms so precise that it would be impossible in them to make a definite mistake, it will be impossible in them to make a definite advance in science."

—Lewis Fry Richardson

THIS STUDY has been undertaken with the conviction that to understand war and other forms of violent international behavior is the first step to avoiding them, and with the belief that the road to understanding such conflict is through systematic scientific research.

This study has three goals: (1) to find the dimensions of variation among nations with respect to their domestic and foreign conflict behavior during a period of contemporary history; (2) to determine the approximate position of each nation along these dimensions; and (3) to ascertain what relationship exists between the dimensions of foreign conflict behavior on the one hand, and the domestic conflict behavior dimensions on the other.

Data have been collected on twenty-two measures of foreign and domestic conflict behavior for seventy-seven nations for the years 1955, 1956, and 1957. These data will be intercorrelated and factor-analyzed. Factor scores for each country will be calculated to determine the position of each nation along the foreign and domestic conflict dimensions found. These scores will then be used in a multiple regression analysis of the relationship between domestic and foreign conflict behavior.

COMPARATIVE CONFLICT

Domestic Conflict

Surprisingly little comparative conflict research[1] in English has been done in the social sciences. Those published studies that have come

*Prepared in connection with research sponsored by the National Science Foundation, Contract NSF-G24827. Reprinted in slightly abridged form from *General Systems Yearbook* 8 (1963): 1–50, by permission of the author and the publisher. Copyright 1963 Society for General Systems Research.

[1]By "comparative conflict," I mean the study or speculation about conflict in two or more countries or politically independent systems.

to my attention and that have appeared during 1945–61 are shown in table 1. Most of these studies deal with a particular kind of violence, such as riots or assassinations, and the overwhelming number (eleven out of fifteen) of these are interested in revolutions and rebellions alone. There is only one study concerned with guerrilla and underground conflict,[2] and that is a proposal of research to be done; there is only one study[3] which examines riots qua riots. No work has been done on comparative religious or political conflict per se and there is only one work on economic conflict.[4]

The nature of this research is much more cosmopolitan than one might suppose. Seven of these studies are concerned with conflict only in the West[5] while eight deal with exclusively non-Western conflict;[6] the remainder are studies not limited to any one region.[7]

When one considers these studies from a methodological point of view,

[2]J. K. Zawodny, "Unexplained Realms of Underground Strife," *American Behavioral Scientist* 4 (1960): 3–5.

[3]H. O. Dahlke, "Race and Minority Riots: A Study in the Typology of Violence," *Social Forces* 30 (1952): 419–25.

[4]A. Kornhauser, R. Dubin, and A. M. Ross, eds., *Industrial Conflict* (New York: McGraw-Hill Book Co., 1954).

[5]P. Meadows, "Town and Country in Revolution," *Sociology and Social Research* 31 (1947): 273–78; T. Parsons, "Certain Primary Sources of Aggression in the Social Structure of the Western World," in *Conflicts of Power in Modern Culture*, ed. L. Bryson et al., (1947), pp. 29–48; F. Tannenbaum, "On Political Stability," *Political Science Quarterly* 75 (1960): 161–80; A. M. Ross and D. Irwin, "Strike Experience in Five Countries 1927–1947: An Interpretation," *Industrial and Labor Relations Review* 4 (1951): 323–42; C. Kerr and A. Siegel, "The Isolated Mass and the Integrated Individual—An International Analysis of the Inter-Industry Propensity to Strike," in Kornhauser et al., *Industrial Conflict*; E. J. Hobsbawm, *Primitive Rebels* (Glencoe, Ill.: Free Press, 1960).

[6]J. A. Benda, "Revolutions and Nationalism in the Non-Western World," in *New Era in the Non-Western World*, ed. W. S. Hunsberger (Ithaca, N.Y.: Cornell University Press, 1957); R. B. Pike, "Sources of Revolution: Their Impact on Freedom and Reform in Latin America," in *Freedom and Reform in Latin America*, ed. R. B. Pike (South Bend, Ind.: Notre Dame Press, 1959), pp. 28–58; R. H. Fitzgibbon, "Revolutions: Western Hemisphere," *South Atlantic Quarterly* 55 (1956): 263–79; A. Tischendorf, "Assassination of Chief Executives in Latin America," *South Atlantic Quarterly* 60 (1961): 80–88; St. Clair Drake, "Some Observations in Interethnic Conflict as One Type of Intergroup Conflict," *Journal of Conflict Resolution* 1 (1957): 155–78; Max Gluckman, *Custom and Conflict in Africa* (Oxford: Blackwell, 1955); P. H. Gulliver, "Land Shortage, Social Change, and Social Conflict in East Africa," *Journal of Conflict Resolution* 5 (1961): 16–26; Robert A. LeVine, "Anti-European Violence in Africa: A Comparative Analysis," *Journal of Conflict Resolution* 3 (1959): 420–29.

[7]D. Pierson, "Race Prejudice as Revealed in the Study of Racial Situations," *International Social Science Bulletin* 2 (1950): 467–78; Denis William Brogan, *The Price of Revolution* (New York: Harper & Bros., 1952); Brian Crozier, *The Rebels: A Study of Post-War Insurrections* (Boston: Beacon Press, 1960); Feliks Gross, *The Seizure of Political Power* (New York: Philosophical Library, 1958), R. D. Hopper, "Revolutionary Process, A Frame of Reference for the Study of Revolutionary Movements," *Social Forces* 28 (1950): 270–79; H. Seton-Watson, "Twentieth Century Revolutions," *Political Quarterly* 22 (1951): 251–65; Joseph Bornstein, *The Politics of Murder* (New York: Sloane, 1958).

one finds that eight of the twenty-four studies (Crozier, Dahlke, Tischendorf, LeVine, Pierson, Gulliver, Kerr, and Ross) are concerned with the analysis of conflict data. Of the remainder, the works of Hopper, Meadows, and Drake may be considered theoretical formulations—the rest are speculative or historical narrative in approach.

On the systematic side, the statistical method has been used twice by the sociologists Kerr and Ross, who were concerned with strikes. Their technique was to analyze their data in terms of frequency of strikes by industry, which enabled them to determine those industries that were most strike-bound, thus giving them a clue to the conditions underlying strikes. Refined statistical tools of comparison were not used. Nor do I know of any other study using mathematical or statistical techniques that has made a comparison between nations of domestic conflict.

The propositions resulting from these twenty-four studies show little similarity. If one were to abstract their propositions and try to order them, almost no convergence toward any one condition or group of conditions of conflict would be found. This point is illustrated by some propositions on revolution chosen from these studies:

Non-Western revolution is a revolt against poverty, inequality, and imposed inferiority (Benda).

The common denominator of revolution in Latin America is awakening nationalism and quickened communications (Fitzgibbon).

Table 1.   Comparative Conflict Studies, 1945–61

Conflict	Studies	Total
Type of conflict		
economic	Kornhauser	1
general social	Hobsbawm; Gluckman; Gulliver	3
racial	Drake; LeVine; Pierson	3
Type of conflict behavior		
revolution and rebellion	Benda; Brogan; Crozier; Fitzgibbon; Gross; Hopper; Meadows; Parsons; Pike; Seton-Watson; Tannenbaum	11
guerrilla and underground activity	Zawodny	1
riots[a]	Dahlke; Kerr; Ross	3
assassinations	Tischendorf; Bornstein	2
	Total	24

[a] Includes strikes.

Rebellion is usually a symptom of misgovernment (Crozier).

Sources of revolution in Latin America are the colonial tradition, religion, individualism, economic inequalities, and foreign influences (Pike).

Political revolution cannot take place where political strength is dispersed among the organs of government and the political parties, and where there is a multiplicity of overlapping groups (Tannenbaum).

This lack of convergence may be the result of different approaches to different types of conflict and conflict behavior over different regions by these twenty-four studies. On the other hand, this lack of convergence may mean that there is no dimension common to conflict in and by itself. If this latter possibility is true, then conflict is not an empirical dimension along which groups can be compared, but a conceptual category mixing up quite different and possibly independent phenomena. Whether this be the case is a question which this study, in part, is designed to answer.

Foreign Conflict

When one shifts his attention to conflict between nations rather than within them, one is confronted with an almost overwhelming amount of material. In my own file of material on international conflict, I can count about 230 titles containing the word war. If I were to include in the count subjects related to war, such as tensions, hostility, conflict, armaments, peace, etc., the number would be increased many fold.

The study of international conflict is limited to no one discipline. Rather, scholars of almost every discipline have written on international conflict. To my mind, for example, come such studies as those by the sociologist, Janowitz;[8] the economist, Boulding;[9] the political scientists, Snyder and Paige;[10] the international relations specialist, Wright;[11] the social psychologist, Pear;[12] the anthropologist, Turney-High;[13] the historian, Nef;[14] the mathematician, Rapoport;[15] and the physicist, Richardson.[16]

[8]Morris Janowitz, "Military Elites and The Study of War," *Journal of Conflict Resolution* 1 (1957): 9–18.

[9]Kenneth E. Boulding, *Conflict and Defense* (New York: Harper & Row, 1962).

[10]Richard C. Snyder and Glenn D. Paige, "The United States Decision to Resist Aggression in Korea," *Administrative Science Quarterly* 3 (1958): 341–78.

[11]Quincy Wright, *A Study of War*, vols. 1 and 2 (Chicago: University of Chicago Press, 1942).

[12]T. H. Pear, *Psychological Factors of Peace and War* (New York: Philosophical Library, 1950).

[13]Harry Holbert Turney-High, *Primitive War, Its Practices and Concepts* (Columbia: University of South Carolina Press, 1949).

[14]John U. Nef, *War and Human Progress* (Cambridge, Mass.: Harvard University Press, 1950).

[15]Anatol Rapoport, *Fights, Games and Debates* (Ann Arbor: University of Michigan Press, 1960).

[16]Lewis Fry Richardson, *Arms and Insecurity* (Pittsburgh: Boxwood Press, 1960); idem, "Contiguity and Deadly Quarrels: The Local Pacifying Influence," *Journal of the Royal*

The various approaches used in studying international conflict reflect this general interest. It is not difficult to find almost all possible methods being applied, such as the case study[17] and the comparative study,[18] the theoretical[19] and the empirical,[20] the statistical[21] and the mathematical,[22] the speculative[23] and the systematic,[24] the experimental[25] and the field,[26] and certainly, the polemical.[27]

When one considers these studies as a whole, three methodological points stand out. First, there appears to be little concern with aspects of conflict behavior other than the most violent form—war. The nature of threats, diplomatic protests, mobilizations, severance of diplomatic relations, expulsion of ambassadors, etc., the relationship between such acts, and their general relation to war apparently has been little studied. Lewis Fry Richardson, for example, concentrated the latter part of his life on the statistical and mathematical study of war, and in that regard was one of the most persistent students of the subject. Yet, in none of his works[28] can

Statistical Society 115 (1952): 219–31; idem, *Statistics of Deadly Quarrels* (Pittsburgh: Boxwood Press, 1960).

[17]Allen S. Whiting, *China Crosses the Yalu* (New York: Macmillan Co., 1960); Jacques Freymond, *The Saar Conflict 1945-1955* (New York: Frederick A. Praeger, 1960).

[18]T. Abel, "The Element of Decision in the Pattern of War," *American Sociological Review* 6 (1941): 853–59; Wright, *Study of War.*

[19]Boulding, *Conflict and Defense*; Alex Strachey, *The Unconscious Motives of War: A Psycho-Analytical Contribution* (London: Allen and Urwin, 1957).

[20]Dina A. Zinnes, "Hostility in International Decision-Making," *Journal of Conflict Resolution* 6 (1962): 236–43; Hornell Hart, "Depression, War, and Logistic Trends," *American Journal of Sociology* (September 1946): 112–22.

[21]Richardson, *Arms and Insecurity*; idem, "Contiguity and Deadly Quarrels"; idem, *Statistics of Deadly Quarrels*; Rapoport, *Fights, Games and Debates.*

[22]N. Rashevsky, *Mathematical Theory and Human Relations, An Approach to a Mathematical Biology of Social Phenomena* (Bloomington, Ind.: Principia Press, 1947); idem, *Mathematical Biology of Social Behavior* (Chicago: University of Chicago Press, 1951); Karl W. Deutsch, *Nationalism and Social Communication* (Cambridge, Mass.: Technology Press, MIT, 1953).

[23]Victor H. Wallace, *Paths to Peace* (New York: Cambridge University Press, 1957); Walter Millis, "A World Without War," in *A World Without War,* ed. Walter Millis et al. (New York: Washington Square Press, 1961), pp. 53–106.

[24]Pitirim A. Sorokin, *Social and Cultural Dynamics*, vol. 3 (New York: American Book Co., 1937); T. C. Schelling, *The Strategy of Conflict* (Cambridge, Mass.: Harvard University Press, 1960).

[25]H. A. Grace and J. O. Neuhaus, "Information and Social Distance as Predictors of Hostility Toward Nations," *Journal of Abnormal and Social Psychology* 47 (1952): 540–45; Muzafer Sherif et al., *Intergroup Conflict and Cooperation* (Norman: University of Oklahoma, Institute of Group Relations, 1961).

[26]H. Cantril and W. Buchanan, *How Nations See Each Other: A Study of Public Opinion* (Urbana: University of Illinois Press, 1953); Snyder and Paige, "U.S. Decision to Resist Aggression in Korea."

[27]C. Wright Mills, *The Causes of World War Three* (New York: Simon and Schuster, 1958); Emery Reves, *The Anatomy of Peace* (New York: Harper & Bros., 1946).

[28]See the bibliography at the end of Rapoport's excellent analysis and critique of Richardson's work ("Lewis Fry Richardson's Mathematical Theory of War," *Journal of Conflict Resolution* 1 (1957): 249–99).

one find a concern for other manifestations of international conflict than those involving deaths.

This concentration on war may have led to disregarding some important questions. For example, does increasing conflict between countries manifest itself in increasingly hostile and violent acts, with war as the extreme act? That is, do such acts as expelling an ambassador or an economic boycott measure the degree of international conflict, with war being the highest degree—the result of increasingly hostile behavior? Or, on the other hand, do many of these conflict acts constitute different dimensions of international conflict, such that the occurrence or non-occurrence of war appears independently of the prior existence of less violent behavior? This study, in part, may approach an answer to these questions.

A second methodological point is that the literature shows a general lack of concern with replication—with taking the propositions resulting from previous studies and subjecting them to further test.[29] As a case in point, the hypothesis that the decision to go to war is the result of emotions, sentimental tensions, or other irrational motives was subjected to test by Theodore Abel[30] against the occurrence of twenty-five wars and found no confirmation. Rather, the proposition emerged that the decision to go to war is the result of rational calculation. To my knowledge this most significant finding has not been subjected to further test,[31] although both the proposition that lacked confirmation and the one that emerged are assumptions of many studies.[32] If, however, our knowledge of international conflict is to be built on a reliable foundation, such hypotheses must continually be subjected to verifications using different techniques and different data.

And third, few works on international conflict are concerned with developing a pool of conflict data, systematically organized and with explicit criteria for inclusion or exclusion of data. I can think of only six works in

[29]According to Murray Sidman, *Tactics of Scientific Research* (New York: Basis Books, 1960), "The maturity of a science may be judged in part, by the extent to which systematic replication establishes the reliability and generality of its data."

[30]"Element of Decision."

[31]While not explicitly testing the hypothesis, however, some of the content analysis findings of the North group at Stanford are relevant to it and point to emotion as playing an important role in such decisions. See for example, Zinnes, "Hostility in International Decision-Making."

[32]For example, the assumption that emotional drives play a significant role in decisions to go to war is basic to the approach in the following works: Erskine B. Childers, *The Road to Suez* (London: Macgibbon and Kee, 1962); Otto Klineberg, *Tensions Affecting International Understanding* (New York: Social Science Research Council, 1950), Fredrick S. Dunn, *War and the Minds of Men* (New York: Harper & Bros., 1950); Alex Strachey, *Unconscious Motives.* On the other hand, the assumption that emotional drives are minimal seems to underlay the work of Snyder and Paige, "U.S. Decision to Resist Aggression in Korea"; and Whiting, *China Crosses the Yalu.*

which such data can be found.[33] Yet if the theoretical propositions of a Boulding and the experimental findings of a Sherif and his colleagues are to be tested in the real world, real world data must be readily available.

Factor Analytic Studies of Cross-National Variables

Although factor analysis has been formulated and developed within the discipline of psychology,[34] as a purely statistical method for determining the patterns of relationships among a collection of variables, the method is of great potential value outside of psychology. This can be seen from its increasingly wide use. Factor analysis has been applied to the value scores of foreign students to determine the factor patterns of the values of Americans, Indians, Japanese, Chinese, and Norwegians,[35] to locate the dimensions of interaction among people within groups,[36] to test a hypothesis about the voting behavior of justices of the Supreme Court,[37] to study the factors making for the success of thirty-two businesses,[38] to determine the dimensions of eighty-eight community (county) systems[39] and the dimensions of American local governments,[40] to determine the factors of cerebral disease,[41] and for determining the weights to apply to indices that might be used to predict the course of a stock market.[42]

But, so far, the method has found little use in trying to make sense out of the innumerable and ever-shifting constellations of variables with which the student of cross-national behavior is confronted. I know of only three scholars who have published applications of factor analysis to such sub-

[33]G. Bodurt, *Losses of Life in Modern Wars* (Oxford: Clarenden Press, 1916); Samuel Dumas and K. O. Vedel-Petersen, *Losses of Life Caused by War* (Oxford: Clarenden Press, 1923); L. E. Tsao, "Chronological Table of Major Wars in Europe and Asia in the Last One Hundred and Fifty Years," *Chinese Social and Political Science Review* 20 (1936): 393; Richardson, *Statistics of Deadly Quarrels;* Sorokin, *Social and Cultural Dynamics;* Wright, *Study of War.*

[34]For a concise but clear history of factor analysis, see Harry H. Harman, *Modern Factor Analysis* (Chicago: University of Chicago Press, 1960), pp. 3-6.

[35]Charles Morris, *Varieties of Human Value* (Chicago: University of Chicago Press, 1956).

[36]E. F. Borgatta and L. S. Cottrell, Jr., "On the Classificiation of Groups," *Sociometry* 18 (1955): 665-78; Borgatta, Cottrell, and H. J. Meyer, "On the Dimensions of Group Behavior," *Sociometry* 19 (1956): 223-40.

[37]Glendon Schubert, "The 1960 Term of The Supreme Court: A Psychological Analysis," *American Political Science Review* 56 (1962): 90-113.

[38]E. P. Godfrey, Fred E. Fiedler, and D. M. Hall, *Boards, Management, and Company Success* (Danville, Va.: Interstate Printers and Publishers, 1959).

[39]Christen T. Jonassen and Sherwood H. Peres, *Interrelationships of Dimensions of Community Systems* (Columbus: Ohio State University Press, 1960).

[40]Robert C. Wood, *1400 Governments* (Cambridge, Mass: Harvard University Press, 1961).

[41]Harold P. Bechtoldt, Arthur L. Benton, and Max L. Fogel, "An Application of Factor Analysis in Neuropsychology," *The Psychological Record* 12 (1962): 147-56.

[42]E. C. Rhodes, "Construction of an Index of Business Activity," *Journal of the Royal Statistical Society* 100 (1937): 18-39.

ject matter. The most encompassing of them is Raymond Cattell's set of three articles[43] that were published within a space of three years, and that were the result of a factor analysis of seventy-two variables. The first of these studies involved a population of sixty-nine countries, which because of difficulties with his data, he later reduced in his more "refined" study to forty countries.[44] His other study was an attempt to group nations according to similar cultural patterns as derived from his seventy-two-variable, sixty-nine-nation analysis. With the possible exception of Hofstaetter,[45] who did his factor analysis using American states as his population, there is apparently no published research whose aim has been to follow up and replicate Cattell's work.[46]

Another application of factor analysis to cross-national variables has been made separately by Brian Berry[47] who, using Norton Ginsburg's data,[48] did a factor analysis of forty-three variables on a population of ninety-five countries. His analysis resulted in the variation between nations on his variables being accounted for by four factors: technology, demographic, contrast in income and external relations, and large vs. small nations. The only other published factor analysis of cross-national variables that I know about is Leo Schnore's[49] analysis of eleven variables in an effort to see if urbanization forms a cluster with indices to economic development. A factor common to urbanization and economic development emerged from his study.

[43]Raymond Cattell, H. Breul, and H. Parker Hartman, "An Attempt at More Refined Definition of the Cultural Dimensions of Syntality in Modern Nations," *American Sociological Review* 17 (1951): 408–21; Raymond Cattell, "The Dimensions of Culture Patterns of Factorization of National Characters," *Journal of Abnormal and Social Psychology* 44 (1949): 443–69; idem, "The Principal Culture Patterns Discoverable in the Syntal Dimensions of Existing Nations," *Journal of Social Psychology* 32 (1950): 215–53.

[44]The factors he extracted from his two studies differ slightly. From each he got twelve factors, which, with respect to the more refined work, are enlightened affluence vs. narrow poverty, vigorous order vs. unadopted rigidity; cultural pressure and complexity vs. direct ergic expression, size, emancipated rationalism vs. unchanged stability; classical patriarchalism vs. uncontrolled ferment, oriental patter, metropolitan laxity vs. rural austerity, bourgeois philistinism vs. improvident bohemianism, mechanics culture, morality vs. poor integration and morale, and a residual factor.

[45]P. R. Hofstaetter, "A Factorial Study of Culture Patterns in the U.S.," *Journal of Psychology* 32 (1951): 99–113.

[46]One of the primary aims of the National Science Foundation's Dimensionality of Nations Project at Northwestern University, and under which data for this study were collected, is to do such a replication of Cattell's work.

[47]Brian J. L. Berry, "An Inductive Approach to the Regionalization of Economic Development," in *Essays on Geography and Economic Development*, ed. Norton Ginsburg (Chicago: University of Chicago Press, 1960); idem, "Basic Patterns of Economic Development," in *Atlas of Economic Development*, ed. Norton Ginsburg (Chicago: University of Chicago Press, 1961), pp. 110–19.

[48]Ginsburg, *Atlas of Economic Development.*

[49]Leo F. Schnore, "The Statistical Measurement of Urbanization and Economic Development," *Land Economics* 37 (1961): 229–45.

The research here, then, certainly is beating no new path in applying factor analysis to nonpsychological data, nor is it essentially unique in using the method on cross-national data. What is different about this study, however, is that it is trying to apply factor analysis for the first time to delineate the dimensions of inter- and intranation conflict behavior.

CONFLICT BEHAVIOR AND ITS MEASURES

Conflict Behavior

Interpersonal and intergroup conflict have variously been defined as "a test of power between antagonistic parties,"[50] the existence of "incompatible or mutually exclusive goals or aims or values espoused by human beings,"[51] "opposition among social entities directed against one another,"[52] or "an adjustment process in which, as opposing energy-systems meet, the energies of each are directed against the other to remove, dominate, or destroy it."[53] The common components of these and other definitions of conflict appear to be that of *a situation* in which *two or more* parties direct their energies *at each other* in order *to achieve goals* that can only be *gained at each other's expense.*

The key to identifying a conflict situation, therefore, may be to look for the *actions* which those involved in conflict are directing toward each other. Since "conflictful behaviors are those designed to destroy, injure, thwart, or otherwise control another party or other parties,"[54] one should be able to measure such conflict behavior in terms of specific acts (e.g., assassinations, threats), or occurrences reflecting an aggregation of such acts (e.g., revolution, war).

Measures of Conflict Behavior

With respect to the methods and goals of this study, any act or occurrence chosen to index conflict behavior must:

1. be capable of empirical delimitation;
2. be an act or occurrence of sufficient interest to be generally reported— that is, data must be available;
3. be applicable to all countries (e.g., "colonial violence," if made a mea-

---

[50]Lewis A. Coser, *The Functions of Social Conflict*, (Glencoe, Ill.: Free Press, 1956), p. 137.

[51]Jessie Bernard, "The Sociological Study of Conflict," in *The Nature of Conflict* (UNESCO, 1957), p. 38.

[52]Quincy Wright, *Problems of Stability and Progress in International Relations* (Berkeley and Los Angeles: University of California Press, 1954), p. 146.

[53]L. J. Carr, "A Situational Approach to Conflict and War," *Social Forces* 24 (1946): 301.

[54]Raymond W. Mack and Richard C. Snyder, "The Analysis of Social Conflict—Toward an Overview and Synthesis," *Journal of Conflict Resolution* 1 (1957): 218.

sure, would not be applicable to those countries without colonies) if spurious factors are not to result;

4. be as diverse as possible to cover the greatest possible range of conflict behavior;

5. be an act of or within, or an occurrence with respect to, seven or more countries (this is to prevent the correlations from being dependent on too few such happenings and, therefore, to reduce the role of aberrations on what are meant to be general conclusions).

On the basis of these criteria, nine measures of domestic and thirteen measures of foreign conflict were chosen for this study.[55] The domestic conflict measures and a brief definition of the conflict act or occurrence are as follows:

1. *Number of assassinations:* any politically motivated murder or attempted murder of a high government official or politician.

2. *Number of general strikes:* any strike of 1,000 or more industrial or service workers that involves more than one employer and that is aimed at national government policies or authority.

3. *Presence or absence of guerrilla warfare:* any armed activity, sabotage, or bombings carried on by independent bands of citizens or irregular forces and aimed at the overthrow of the present regime.

4. *Number of major government crises:* any rapidly developing situation that threatens to bring the downfall of the present regime—excluding situations of revolt aimed at such an overthrow.

5. *Number of purges:* any systematic elimination by jailing or execution of political opposition within the ranks of the regime or the opposition.

6. *Number of riots:* any violent demonstration or clash of more than 100 citizens involving the use of physical force.

7. *Number of revolutions:* any illegal or forced change in the top governmental elite, any attempt at such a change, or any successful or unsuccessful armed rebellion whose aim is independence from the central government.

8. *Number of antigovernment demonstrations:* any peaceful public gathering of at least 100 people for the primary purpose of displaying or voic-

---

[55]Data have been collected on more measures than are used in the study. These measures—number of disputes, number of civil wars, number of social revolutions, number of demands, number of reprisals, presence or absence of banditry, presence or absence of colonial violence, presence or absence of political strife—did not conform to one or another of the criteria above. The occurrence of civil war and social revolution were too infrequent for criterion 5, and were consequently merged with data on palace revolutions into a more general measure called "number of revolutions." And data on reprisals were merged with the data on boycotts into a measure called "number of negative sanctions" since the two categories could not be kept empirically distinct.

ing their opposition to government policies or authority, excluding those demonstrations of a distinctly antiforeign nature.

9. *Number of people killed in all forms of domestic violence:* any deaths resulting directly from violence of an intergroup nature, thus excluding deaths by murder and execution.

And the measures of foreign conflict and definitions are as follows:

1. *Number of antiforeign demonstrations:* any demonstration or riot by more than 100 people directed at a particular foreign country (or group of countries) or its policies.
2. *Number of negative sanctions:* any nonviolent act against another country—such as boycott, withdrawal of aid—the purpose of which is to punish or threaten that country.
3. *Number of protests:* any official diplomatic communication or governmental statement, the purpose of which is to complain about or object to the policies of another country.
4. *Number of countries with which diplomatic relations severed:* the complete withdrawal from all official contact with a particular country.
5. *Number of ambassadors expelled or recalled:* any expelling of an ambassador from, or recalling for other than administrative reasons an ambassador to, a particular country—this does not involve expulsion or recall resulting from the severance of diplomatic relations.
6. *Number of diplomatic officials of lesser than ambassador's rank expelled or recalled:* replace "ambassador" by "officials of lesser . . . rank" in above definition.
7. *Number of threats:* any official diplomatic communication or governmental statement asserting that if a particular country does or does not do a particular thing it will incur negative sanctions.
8. *Presence or absence of military action:* any military clash of a particular country with another and involving gunfire, but short of war as defined below.
9. *Number of wars:* any military clash for a particular country with another and in which more than .02 per cent of its population are militarily involved in the clash.
10. *Number of troop movements:* any rapid movement of large bodies of troops, naval units, or air squadrons to a particular area for the purpose of deterring the military action of another country, gaining concessions, or as a show of strength.
11. *Number of mobilizations:* any rapid increase in military strength through the calling up of reserves, activation of additional military units, or the demothballing of military equipment.
12. *Number of accusations:* any official diplomatic or governmental state-

ment involving charges and allegations of a derogatory nature against another country.

13. *Number of people killed in all forms of foreign conflict behavior:* the total number of deaths resulting directly from any violent interchange between countries.

In order to avoid logically necessary correlations and factors, each of these measures is defined in a way to make them mutually exclusive and each datum is used only once. A logical connection might be made between threats and accusations, for example, if threats were defined as "any accusations that contained an implied or stated sanction that would result from the recipient doing or not doing a certain thing," then accusations would be a necessary condition for the occurrence of threats, and the two would be found correlated together in the results of the analysis.

More extensive definitions of some of these measures as well as examples are given in appendix 1.

Sources of Data

Five sources—*The New York Times Index, New International Yearbook, Keesing's Contemporary Archives*,[56] *Facts on File*, and *Britannica Book of The Year*—were combed for data with respect to these measures. Each datum was recorded on a separate card, some 3,500 cards in all being collected; where the sources differed with respect to an event—say, the number of killed or number of riots—the mean value between them was used.

Measures of Error

Random Error.   The kinds of error that might affect the results of this study can be divided into two types: random error and systematic error. If random error were present, it would mean that there was an equal probability that the values on a particular measure for a certain country are under or overstated—that the direction of error as well as its magnitude is not correlated with any attributes of the countries of concern, nor with the other measures for which data are taken.

Some random error resulting from clerical mistakes and ambiguous descriptions in the sources probably exists in the data of this study. Assuming for the moment that the data are highly affected by such error, what would be its influence upon the results? Its effect on the correlations between the measures would be to reduce the value of the correlations below what they would be without such error. That is, a significant correla-

---

[56]*Keesing's Contemporary Archives* was found least productive of data, and, therefore, was used only in the very beginning of the data collection.

tion between data that one suspects have a lot of random "noise" can be considered even more significant than if one were dealing with uncontaminated data.[57] And the impact of such error on the results of the factor analysis would apparently be to lower somewhat the loadings that the variables have on the factors,[58] but not to distort the factor structure as a whole. With or without random error, one would likely extract the same factors, but with slightly lower loadings if random errors are present.[59] The possible existence of random error, then, should not unduly affect one's confidence in the results. But the situation is different with respect to systematic error.

Systematic Error. Errors which cause the data to consistently over or understate that being measured and which are correlated with the other measures of concern may bias the analysis to a degree that the outcome is highly distorted. That is, the result may be overly high or low correlations, and factors with little existential validity.

It would be unwise to assume that such errors do not exist in the data. In fact, the contrary assumption that such errors contaminate the data to a high degree appears more plausible. Also warranted appears to be the assumption that this systematic error is in the direction of causing the data to consistently understate the actual occurrence of conflict behavior. Except in the case of random error, I cannot imagine any influence that would cause a country systematically to be reported as having more riots, more troop movements, more assassinations, etc. than it really does have.

Three elements may influence the systematic understating of conflict behavior for a particular country. Censorship may prevent news of such behavior from being disseminated. Or if such news is disseminated, it may not get into the sources used because the country of concern is of little interest to the world at large (e.g., a demonstration in Nepal or Uruguay), or the news goes unreported because it happened concurrently with an occurrence considered important enough to be reported in great depth. Two measures will be used to index the possibility that systematic error in the form of censorship and/or lack of world interest is influencing the results.

The first measure will be a three-point censorship scale based on data from a 1955 Associated Press survey of the world's press[60] and from

[57]See Mordecai Ezekiel and Karl A. Fox, *Methods of Correlation and Regression Analysis*, 3rd ed. (New York: John Wiley and Sons, 1959), chap. 18, on the effect of random error.

[58]When the factors are uncorrelated (orthogonal) among themselves, a "loading" is the correlation of each measure with each factor.

[59]See Mosier's experimental findings on this point and Cattell's comments. Charles I. Mosier, "Influence of Chance Error on Sample Structure: An Empirical Investigation of the Effect of Chance Error and Estimated Communalities on Simple Structure in Factorial Analysis," *Psychometrika* 4 (1939): 33–44; Raymond Cattell, *Factor Analysis* (New York: Harper & Bros., 1952), p. 293.

[60]*New York Times*, 9 January 1955.

the *Worldmark Encyclopedia of Nations* (1960). World interest in a particular nation will be measured by the number of countries with foreign embassies and legations in that nation.[61] The assumption here, of course, is that the number of resident embassies and legations in a country reflects the interest the world has in that nation's affairs.

The correlation between each of these systematic error measures and each of the domestic and foreign conflict behavior measures will be assessed, and these measures will also be included in the factor analysis of the conflict measures. If there is no correlation between the measures of systematic error and the measures of conflict behavior, then one can conclude that systematic error as tapped by the two measures are not seriously affecting the results. The same conclusion will be valid if high positive correlations between the two measures and other measures are found. This is because we can assume the direction of systematic error to be under rather than overstatement. For example, if censorship is positively correlated with riots and if censorship is acting to suppress information about the actual number of riots, then even in the case that the actual number of riots were known, such knowledge would not alter the rank of this nation relative to other nations on this measure sufficiently to distort the correlations. Censorship would then act much like random error—making the correlations lower than they really are. If, however, these two measures are negatively correlated with the others then the interpretation of the results should be made with the utmost care. For then the suppression of information, for example, could cause a nation's rank relative to others to be completely reversed on the measures.

In the event that there is no correlation between the measures of systematic error and the data on conflict behavior, however, there is still no certainty that such errors have not affected the conclusions—as is true in any scientific study. Only replication and independent confirmation can give one confidence enough to assert that the effect of systematic error is nil. As Sidman suggests, the "soundest empirical test of the reliability of data is provided by replication,"[62] and as McClelland counsels, as "independent studies continue to confirm the general hypothesis, it becomes less and less likely that some nonrandom error of measurement could have created the relationship under investigation."[63]

[61]I had thought originally of using the number of AP and UP reporters in a particular country as an index to interest in its affairs, but research in the library, contact with the journalism department, and communication with AP and UP have convinced me that the idea is impractical. Each wire service, evidently, has a large number of part-time employees of the nationality of the country in which its bureau is located. The number of such employees is increased or decreased according to current events within the country, and the records as to the number of such employees at any time are kept by each foreign bureau.

[62]Sidman, *Tactics of Scientific Research*, p. 70.

[63]David C. McClelland, *The Achieving Society* (Princeton, N.J.: D. Van Nostrand Co., 1961), p. 24.

Population

Data have been collected on all nations for the period 1955, 1956, and 1957 which meet the following criteria:

1. sovereign statehood for at least two years,[64] as evidenced by diplomatic relations with other countries and the existence of a foreign ministry or its equivalent;[65]
2. a minimum population of a 800,000, which eliminates aberrations within the nation-state system like Monaco and Liechtenstein.

The number of nations thus considered is seventy-seven, the names of which can be found in appendix 2.

Each measure used in this study is a summation of the data for the three years, 1955–57. The years were chosen with future studies in mind, some of which will attempt to relate factors resulting from a factor analysis of the structural characteristics and nonconflict behavior of nations to the dimensions of conflict behavior resulting from this study. The nonconflict factors will be extracted from data for 1955, the year for which the most data are available.[66] Since the conflict behavior data are generally subsequent in occurrence to the nonconflict data, it will be easier to infer direction of causation from what relations are found.

Stability of the Data

Since the data were collected for only three years, one might justifiably ask whether the data are unique to this period, and whether or not generalizations thus derived are only specific to this particular span of history. After all, during this period the Mideast War and the Hungarian Revolution occurred.

The stability of the data—how well the data reflect general conflict behavior over extended periods of time—was checked in three ways. First, the data on three measures—war, war and military action, and number of people killed in all foreign conflict—were checked for their correlation with Lewis F. Richardson's data on war from 1825–1945 inclusive. The results are given in table 2. These are extremely high correlations and

[64]The time period of two years is to allow domestic behavior to adjust to independence after what may have been a period of nationalistic and, perhaps, violent agitation for independence.

[65]This is similar to the definition employed by Haas and Whiting: "the *pro forma* capacity to enter into diplomatic relations with other states through the existence of a foreign ministry, regardless of whether the ministry is *in fact* able to make independent decisions." Ernst B. Haas and Allen S. Whiting, *Dynamics of International Relations* (New York: McGraw-Hill, 1956), p. 61*n*.

[66]This will be done by the Dimensionality of Nations Project.

Table 2.   Correlations of 1955–57 Data with Richardson's Data[a]

Richardson's Data	1955–57 Conflict Data		
	War	War + Military Action	$\log_{10}$ (No. Killed)
War, 1825–1945	.86[b]	.81[b]	.83[b]

[a] Lewis Fry Richardson, *Statistics of Deadly Quarrels* (Pittsburgh: Boxwood Press, 1960). This is a count of the number of wars in which a nation was involved which resulted in more than 3,163 deaths, i.e., more than $\log_{10}$ (deaths) = 3.5.
[b] Product moment $r, p < .01$ (nonnormal distributions); $N = 30$.

imply that the frequency of war for each of the thirty nations is predictive of the amount of war each will have from 1955 to 1957. Of the thirty, those countries that depart most from this prediction are the U.S.S.R., which had far more war (Hungary), and China, which had far more military action (Formosa), than could be predicted on the basis of their past history of warfare.

Second, the data on domestic conflict were compared with data collected by Harry Eckstein for similar measures for seventy nations for 1945–59.[67] The product moment correlations are given in table 3. Since the number of riots and other forms of domestic violence may be a function, in part, of the number of people there are that can be involved in such violence, the correlations were calculated a second time, holding population constant.

Third, the correlations between Raymond Cattell's five measures of conflict behavior, which he included in his factor analysis of seventy-two variables for sixty-nine countries, were calculated from his unrotated fac-

Table 3.   Correlations of 1955–57 Data with Eckstein's Data[a]

1946–59	Number Killed in Domestic Violence	Total Violence[b]	Guerrilla War and Revolution	Rioting
Total violence[b]	.55[c] (.52)[d]	.71[c] (.70)[d]		
Internal warfare and coup			.50[c] (.52)[d]	
Rioting				.67[c] (.66)[d]

[a] Harry Eckstein, "The Incidence of Internal Wars, 1946–1959," Appendix I of *Internal War: The Problem of Anticipation* Report submitted to the Research Group in Psychology and the Social Sciences, Smithsonian Institution, Washington, D.C., 15 January 1962.
[b] Derived by summing all occurrences of domestic conflict behavior.
[c] Product moment $r, p < .01$ (nonnormal distributions); $N = 70$.
[d] Partial correlation, holding 1955 population constant.

[67] Since his data are not broken down into separate years, a reliability check of my data against his data for 1955–57 cannot be made.

tor structure and compared with the intercorrelations among similar measures for the 1955–57 data of this study. Table 4 shows the results. A comparison of ten intercorrelations shows that only one for the 1955–57 data differs significantly from that for the 1837–1937 data. As a matter of fact, the correlations from the different data for war-revolution, revolution–foreign clashes, and foreign clashes–assassinations are surprisingly close.

Table 4. Comparison of Correlations Between 1955–57 Data and Correlations Between Cattell's Data[a]

Measures[b]	Cattell's Correlations 1837–1937	Conflict Data Correlations 1955–57
1. War-revolution	.06	−.04[c]
2. War-riots	.41	.12[c]
3. War-foreign clashes	.58	.38[c]
4. War-assassinations	.08	.19[c]
5. Revolution-riots	.14	.32[c]
6. Revolution-foreign clashes	.13	.12[c]
7. Revolution-assassinations	.06	.19[c]
8. Riots-foreign clashes	.54	.08[d]
9. Riots-assassinations	.36	.45[c]
10. Foreign clashes-assassinations	.14	.15[c]

[a] Calculated from Cattell's unrotated factor structure, "The Dimensions of Culture Patterns of Factorization of National Characters," *Journal of Abnormal and Social Psychology* 44 (1949): 443–69.

[b] Cattell defines foreign clashes as "fighting incidents and political clashes not accompanied by or immediately followed by war."

[c] Correlations are not significantly different from Cattell's, $p > .05$.

[d] Correlations significantly different, $p = .002$.

These three comparisons—with the Richardson and with the Eckstein data, and with the Cattell correlations—point to the conclusion that the 1955–57 data are probably not unique, but instead may mirror the long-run conflict behavior within and between nations.

Transformations

In order to reduce the effect on the correlations of aberrant data—data, say, with a standard score of ten or twenty—transformations were applied to most nondichotomous distributions. In the case of the two number-of-killed measures and the accusations measure, a log transformation was used. For the other measures, where generally one, and not more than two, digit values are present, data were grouped on a 0, 1–3, 4–7, 8–15, . . . basis with the common ratio of the geometric progression after zero being two.

FACTOR ANALYSIS

The Method

Factor analysis seems ideally suited to determining the nature of inter-relationships between a large number of variables. Applied to a collection of variables, factor analysis delineates those which cluster together—which covary more with each other than they do with any of the other variables included in the analysis.[68] If, for example, one were to factor analyze an aggregation of cross-national variables, like GNP, number of vehicles, electrical production, number of religious groups, size of country, population, and trade, it would probably be found that GNP, vehicles, and electricity covary together quite closely in comparison with the other variables—that is, they are a dimension of variation among all those cross-national variables.

Principal Components

One may choose among many factor *techniques* for determining the clusters of relationships—the dimensions—among the conflict behavior measures.[69] The technique chosen here is called principal components (or principal factor), and is chosen from among competing techniques because it yields a mathematically unique solution and because the first factor extracts the maximum of variance from the original data while each succeeding factor extracts the maximum of remaining variance.

Assumptions. The application of factor analysis to any set of data assumes certain characteristics of the data that should be made explicit.[70] First, the data for each country are assumed to be of equal importance, and are thus given equal weight. That is, the number of riots for the United States is considered just as important as the number of riots for Yemen and each is thus given equal weight in the results. For a study like this, which is trying to determine the general characteristics of conflict for all countries, such an assumption appears warranted.

A second assumption is that all the interrelationships between the variables are linear. "The one scale condition which destroys the effectiveness of factorization is that in which true curvilinear relations exist in the correlation plots."[71] As a check on this assumption, the twenty-four trans-

---

[68]For a conceptual introduction to the nature of factor analysis see Benjamin Fruchter, *Introduction to Factor Analysis* (Princeton, N.J.: D. Van Nostrand Co., 1954), pp. 1–11. For a discussion of many of the nontechnical methodological aspects of factor analysis, see Sten Henrysson, *Applicability of Factor Analysis in the Behavior Studies: A Methodological Study* (Stockholm: Almquist and Wiksell, 1957), p. 56.

[69]See Harman, *Modern Factor Analysis*, p. 115, for a tabular breakdown of the different factor techniques, their assumptions and properties and distinguishing characteristics.

[70]For an outline of the assumptions concerning the nature of the data, see Henrysson, *Applicability of Factor Analysis*, pp. 29–30.

[71]Cattell, *Factor Analysis*, p. 328.

formed measures were plotted against each other, with the result that no significant curvilinear relationships were found.

If one wishes to test the significance of the correlations each of the measures has on the factors extracted, then a third assumption is that the data are distributed normally. However, the data used here do not meet this assumption, and because often more than half the nations are tied at the minimum value, the distributions are generally such that they cannot be transformed to a normal distribution. No tests of significance will be made, therefore, of the relationships between the variables and the factors. With respect to the factors themselves, however, the same basic factors most probably would emerge, regardless of the underlying distribution of the data.[72]

Problem of the Correlation Coefficient. For assessing the intercorrelation among the measures, there are several correlation coefficients one can choose such as the product moment, rank, tetrachoric, and phi-over-phi-max. Since the factors are extracted on the basis of the interrelationships among the data determined by the correlation coefficient, the choice of the coefficient is basic to the analysis. Because the distributions of the conflict data are nonnormal, generally *J* distributions, and because some of the data are dichotomous, thought was given to which correlation coefficient would give the most meaningful results.[73] The rank correlation coefficient was ruled out because of the large number of tied ranks (about 80 percent of the nations tied for the minimum rank for some of the measures). Tetrachoric and phi-over-phi-max were ruled out because of the extreme splits on some of the measures (the most extreme being a 91–9 percent split in the case of the war measure), and because of the continuous nature of many of the distributions. The product moment coefficient (which becomes the phi coefficient where dichotomous data are concerned) on the other hand, is applicable to both continuous and dichotomous data. Moreover, not only does it appear to make more use of the information in the data and to give more meaningful and less distorted results than the other coefficients, but it is also the coefficient upon which the factor analytic model is based. The product moment, therefore, was chosen for this study.

Problem of Communality. A further problem confronts the factor analyst with regard to what value to put in the principal diagonal of the

[72]Ibid. This point is strongly made by Cattell and with less vehemence by L. L. Thurstone, *Multiple Factor Analysis* (Chicago: University of Chicago Press), pp. 66–67.

[73]On this point, see also Cattell, *Factor Analysis*, p. 326, Fruchter, *Introduction to Factor Analysis*, p. 201, and J. B. Carroll, "The Nature of the Data, or How to Choose a Correlation Coefficient," *Psychometrika* 26 (1961): 347–71. For a comparison of the results using the tetrachoric, phi-over-phi max, and the phi coefficient on the same dichotomous data, see Andrew L. Comrey and E. Levonian, "A Comparison of Three Point Coefficients in Factor Analysis of MMPI Items," *Educational and Psychological Measurements* 18 (1958): 739–55.

correlation matrix to be factor analyzed. This value determines the portion of the total variance of the measures that will be factored.

If one wants to analyze only the variance common to more than one of the measures, then one might insert in the diagonal for that measure its squared multiple correlations with all the other measures—squared multiple correlation thus being inserted for all the measures. If one is concerned with reliable variance, including that unique to single measures, then reliabilities may be inserted (if they are available), and if one wants to analyze all the variance—common, specific, and error—then unities are appropriate.[74]

In this study I am interested in accounting for as much of the total variance of my measures as possible, and in having an indication of how much of this total variance has been extracted by the factors. Unities, therefore, will be inserted in the principal diagonal.

Problem of Number of Significant Factors. Regardless of what is put in the principal diagonal, there is still the problem of determining the number of factors that will be extracted. For, if all the factors possible were extracted, one would end up with as many factors as there are measures—hardly a parsimonious solution. One possibility is to specify the minimum amount of variance a factor must account for in order to be extracted, which specification can be made on the basis of an estimate as to the amount of error the data contain. Since the actual amount of error in my data is a large unknown and will largely be indicated by the results of the factor analysis itself, possibly a more analytic solution is called for. The one that will be used here is that suggested by Kaiser,[75] who says, "allow me to suggest a 'best' answer to the question of the number of factors: it is the number of latent roots greater than one of the observed correlation matrix. This conclusion is based on the relatively independent criteria of algebraic necessity, psychometric reliability, and psychological meaningfulness."

Rotation

Whatever the factor technique chosen, the factor analyst is faced with the problem of whether he will be satisfied with the factor solution as given, or whether he wishes to *rotate* the factors to a more desirous solution. The difficulty with an unrotated factor solution is that the correlations of the measures with the factors are dependent on the whole set of measures included in the analysis, and will thus vary from analysis to analysis as new measures are included or old ones omitted.[76] If one wants to de-

---

[74]See Fruchter, *Introduction to Factor Analysis*, pp. 51–52.

[75]Henry F. Kaiser, "The Application of Electronic Computers to Factor Analysis," *Educational and Psychological Measurements* 20 (1960): 141–51.

[76]Cattell, *Factor Analysis*, p. 249.

limit the dimensions that reflect recurring patterns of relationships among the measures, that is, to be able to identify recurring factors in subsequent studies, then rotation is necessary.

Problem of the Criteria of Rotation. The decision to rotate presents one with numerous alternatives. The factors can be rotated to an a priori solution by making the first factor colinear with a particular measure. For example, if one were interested in what kind of factors would emerge independent of a war factor and how the other measures would correlate with this dimension, then the first factor might be rotated to make it perfectly correlated—colinear—with the war measure.

Another possibility is to rotate to an oblique solution, where the factors can be correlated with each other and thus may give the best possible fit to the clusters of measures. This is the solution most favored by Cattell.[77] If one, however, is exploring a field for the first time, it may be best to rotate to a solution in which the factors give the best possible orthogonal fit to the clusters. This gives one a parsimonious solution with which to work. And, if after visual inspection of the orthogonally rotated solution a more meaningful oblique solution appears feasible, such can then be done.

A decision to use orthogonal rotation, at least initially, still does not exhaust the alternatives. There are several possible criteria for orthogonal rotation which could be used.[78] The one chosen for use here is an analytic criterion that has gained wide recognition for yielding a meaningful and invariant solution—Thurstone's simple structure[79] criterion as determined by Kaiser's Varimax analytic solution.[80]

RESULTS

Domestic Conflict Behavior Measures

Table 5 gives the unrotated and orthogonally rotated factor matrices for the domestic conflict measures. The triangular correlation matrix is given in the upper left portion of table 10 below. The unrotated matrix shows the typical principal component general dimension, and two bipolar

[77]Ibid., pp. 116–17, 123.
[78]See Harman, *Modern Factor Analysis*, chap. 14.
[79]See Thurstone, *Multiple Factor Analysis*, chap. 14.
[80]See Henry F. Kaiser, "Computer Program for Varimax Rotation in Factor Analysis," *Educational and Psychological Measurement* 19 (1959): 413–20. One should not, however, accept unqualified the Varimax solution. John R. Hurley and Raymond B. Cattell, "The Procrustes Program: Producing Direct Rotation to Test a Hypothesized Factor Structure," *Behavioral Science* 7 (1962): 260, warn that "the extreme facility of application of Varimax, plus a lack of forewarnings in its publication, has led to a great number of man hours of research ending in nothing—or worse—when the factor analytically unqualified psychologist or editor *accepts*, as uniquely meaningful, the machine given answer." To avoid this danger, the Varimax solution will be checked manually to make sure that orthogonal simple structure is compatible with the data.

Table 5.   **Factor Analysis of Domestic Conflict Measures**[a]

Measures	Factor Matrix[b]			Orthogonally Rotated Factor Matrix[b]			h^2
	D_1	D_2	D_3	Turmoil	Revolutionary[c]	Subversive[c]	
1. Assassinations	(62)	17	(61)	(59)	−03	(66)	78
2. General strikes	(75)	05	−24	(52)	(60)	05	63
3. Guerrilla warfare	48	(−57)	(59)	−04	28	(90)	90
4. Major government crisis	(52)	35	−10	(60)	21	−04	41
5. Purges	(67)	−14	−34	32	(71)	03	60
6. Riots	(76)	38	−03	(79)	31	09	73
7. Revolutions	(66)	−43	−36	09	(85)	13	75
8. Antigovernment demonstrations	(74)	46	14	(85)	17	19	79
9. Domestic number killed	(80)	−40	−05	23	(75)	42	79
Percent Common Variance	65.0	18.0	16.0	39.0	37.6	23.4	100.0
Percent Total Variance	45.8	13.3	11.7	27.7	26.7	16.6	70.8

[a] Decimals omitted from loadings.
[b] Parentheses indicate loadings ≥ .50.
[c] Signs reversed.

dimensions. That a general dimension should come out with as high loadings as it has (the lowest loading is .48 for guerrilla warfare) and accounting for as much of the common variance—65 percent—and total variance—45.8 percent—is a good indication that the domestic conflict measures used are reflecting a general conflict situation, or the existence of domestic conflict societies, one might say.[81] One might note the high communalities (h^2) for the measures and the fact that 70.8 percent of the total variance of the measures is being accounted for by the three factors. This implies that there is a great deal of relationship between all the measures and that the dimensions are reflecting a good deal of meaning. If the data were infused with considerable *random* error and arbitrariness due to ambiguous and meaningless definitions, the communalities should be quite low.

When the dimensions are rotated to a more invariant position, the first rotated dimension comes out as a nonorganizational, spontaneous conflict behavior dimension—a *turmoil* dimension.[82] Antigovernment demonstra-

[81] This is also evidenced by all the correlations between the measures being positive.

[82] There are possibly two approaches to naming a factor or dimension. One may try to label a factor with what one considers is the underlying source of the clustering of measures

tions, riots, and major government crises, are highest on this dimension with assassinations, and general strikes having lower but respectable loadings. Assassinations and general strikes, which are not always of a spontaneous nature, and general strikes, which generally are organized, are not wholly of this dimension. General strikes have a higher correlation with the second dimension, and assassinations are also higher on the third dimension.

The second and third dimensions appear to represent organized conflict behavior, i.e., behavior that is planned with definite objectives and methods in mind. This type of behavior is the most violent, as shown by the high correlations of number killed with these two dimensions. Since revolutions, purges, and general strikes are highly correlated with the second dimension while the correlation of assassinations and guerrilla warfare is low, the second dimension might be an overt, organized conflict behavior dimension—or, for short, a *revolutionary* dimension.[83] The third dimension, which is almost specific to guerrilla war, and which also has assassinations highly correlated with it, is a kind of covert, organized conflict behavior dimension—a *subversion* dimension.

Hence, one can divide domestic conflict into three independent continua: a disorganized, spontaneous conflict behavior, or *turmoil* dimension; an overt, organized conflict behavior, or *revolutionary* dimension; and a covert, organized conflict behavior, or *subversion* dimension. In terms of accounting for the relationships among the measures, the turmoil and revolutionary dimensions, respectively, account for 39 percent and 37.6 percent of the common variance, as opposed to 23.4 percent for the subversive dimension, and, therefore, may be considered the most important dimensions of domestic conflict behavior.

Foreign Conflict Behavior Measures

Table 6 shows the unrotated and rotated factor matrices of the foreign conflict behavior measures, and the bottom right of table 10 gives the tri-

---

(or variables). Hence, I might call the first rotated factor a "rapid industrial growth factor," implying that in those countries in which rapid economic growth is taking place, one finds many riots, demonstrations, etc. This I call *source labeling*, and it is with respect to source labeling that the term "factor" appears to me most appropriate. On the other hand, one might label the factor in terms of the measures entering into the cluster and what they may represent in terms of a typology. This kind of labeling I call *type labeling*, and it is the approach used here. I prefer to leave source labeling to the future, when systematic analysis of the relationship between the dimensions of this study and such things as rapid industrial growth, technological change, political system, etc. will indicate some of the possible sources of such a cluster of conflict behavior as indicated by the turmoil dimension. When type labeling is used, "dimension" may more aptly describe the different types emerging from the factor analysis. The methodology of factor analysis, however, is so deeply infused with "factor" as to require its use in describing the operations performed.

[83] "Revolutionary" is chosen over "revolution," since the latter implies an event or act, whereas the former stands more for a situation or atmosphere. This is more in accord with purges and general strikes being highly correlated with this dimension.

Table 6.   Factor Analysis of Foreign Conflict Measures[a]

Measures	Factor Matrix[b]			Orthogonally Rotated Factor Matrix[b]			h^2
	F_1^c	F_2	F_3	F_1^c	F_2	F_3	
1. Antiforeign demonstrations	(59)	14	48	13	42	(63)	60
2. Negative sanctions	(65)	11	44	20	41	(64)	62
3. Protests	(78)	22	−13	(62)	49	22	67
4. Severance of diplomatic relations	45	−46	(54)	13	−17	(82)	71
5. Expulsions or recalls—ambassadors	10	(67)	12	−16	(66)	−08	47
6. Expulsions or recalls—lesser officials	(53)	44	−06	33	(60)	08	48
7. Threats	(91)	07	05	(65)	43	48	84
8. Military action	(73)	−48	04	(65)	−14	(57)	77
9. Wars	(65)	−04	(−57)	(85)	15	−10	75
10. Troop movements	(73)	33	01	47	(59)	28	64
11. Mobilizations	(61)	−34	−10	(60)	−08	35	49
12. Accusations	(89)	01	−05	(70)	35	41	79
13. Number killed—foreign	(80)	−19	−36	(87)	10	19	80
Percent Common Variance	69.2	16.6	14.2	46.2	24.6	29.1	100.0
Percent Total Variance	46.0	11.0	9.4	30.7	16.3	19.3	66.4

[a] Decimals omitted from loadings.
[b] Parentheses indicate loadings, $\geq$ .50.
[c] Signs reversed.

angular correlation matrix. The unrotated general and two bipolar dimensions emerge again, although the general dimension in the case of foreign conflict behavior is not as strong as is the general dimension for domestic behavior. Expulsion or recall of ambassadors is quite low on the general dimension; severance of diplomatic relations has a much higher loading but still below the lowest on the general domestic conflict behavior dimension.

The first dimension accounts for a high 69.2 percent of common and 46 percent of total variance, with the amount of variance being extracted by the second dimension dropping off sharply. Like the domestic dimensions, the first foreign conflict behavior dimension is accounting for most of the conflict behavior. The communalities are also generally high, and in conjunction with the high variance being accounted for, imply that here also something of meaning is being extracted.

The first dimension of the rotated factor matrix defines a cluster containing war, number killed, mobilizations, accusations, threats, military actions, and protests. When one disregards those measures which are also highly correlated ±.4 or better with other dimensions, mobilizations, war, and number killed remain. These are measures which represent the preparation for war, the actual act of war, and the consequences of war. Therefore, it appears reasonable to call the first rotated dimension a *war* dimension. As can be seen from table 6, this dimension accounts for much more of the relationship among foreign conflict behavior—46.2 percent of common variance—than either of the other dimensions. That a war continuum accounting for the most variance in conflict behavior should emerge may not perhaps appear strange to students of international relations, who look upon war as a prime mechanism through which the international system adjusts to changes within the system.[84]

The second dimension appears to represent a nonviolent form of foreign conflict behavior. The measures that are mainly correlated with this dimension—expelling or recalling ambassadors, expelling or recalling officials of lesser than ambassadorial rank, and troop movements—are forms of nonviolent behavior—military action, war, and number killed have very low loadings. Consequently, this dimension seems to pull together that conflict behavior which stops short of violence—which may only be designed as diplomatic moves or counters with respect to minor or ephemeral issues. The second factor might, therefore, be named a *diplomatic* dimension.

The third dimension apparently characterizes an actively hostile mood represented by the tendency to sever diplomatic relations, antiforeign demonstrations, military action of a limited nature, and negative sanctions, and may accordingly be called a *belligerency* dimension. The extraction of a belligerency dimension independent from war and a diplomatic dimension is not unreasonable. War and diplomatic conflict behavior both may be calculated coldly rational at one time and at another be underlain with considerable belligerency. The emergence of the cluster of measures defined by the third dimension indicates, however, that there are kinds of foreign conflict behavior that one may identify as being particularly of a belligerent nature.

Three independent continua of foreign conflict behavior can now be identified: a *war* dimension; a nonviolent foreign conflict behavior, *diplomatic* dimension; and an actively hostile, *belligerent* dimension.

Other information also can be extracted from this factor analysis. If one looks at the rotated domestic conflict dimensions, it can be seen that no one measure has loadings greater than ±.35 for all three dimensions—

[84]Millis, "World Without War."

that is, no one measure is general to these continua. However, for the foreign conflict behavior rotated factor matrix, one notices that "threats" (.65; .43; .48) and "accusations" (.70; .35; .41) are such general measures. This reflects their high values on the first unrotated dimension (.91 and .89 respectively), which in turn reflects their high correlations with all the other measures. These product moment correlations are shown in table 7 and imply that threats, and to a slightly lesser extent, accusations are fairly

Table 7. Correlations of Threats and Accusations with Other Foreign Conflict Measures

Foreign Conflict Measures	Number of Threats	Number of Accusations
1. Number of antiforeign demonstrations	.50[a]	.46[a]
2. Number of negative sanctions	.64[a]	.48[a]
3. Number of protests	.66[a]	.69[a]
4. Number of countries with which relations severed	.38[a]	.39[a]
5. Number of ambassadors expelled or recalled	.12[b]	.11[b]
6. Number of nonambassador officials expelled or recalled	.50[a]	.45[a]
7. Number of threats	—	.81[a]
8. Presence or absence of military action	.62[a]	.65[a]
9. Number of wars	.55[a]	.56[a]
10. Number of troop movements	.68[a]	.62[a]
11. Number of mobilizations	.55[a]	.46[a]
12. Number of accusations	.81[a]	—
13. Number of people killed in all foreign conflict	.63[a]	.70[a]

[a] $p < .01$ (nonnormal distributions); $N = 77$.
[b] $p > .05$ (nonnormal distributions); $N = 77$.

good indices to the existence of general foreign conflict behavior. This suggests that a simple summation of standard scores for threats and accusations may be an index to the state of relations between countries—a sort of thermometer for measuring the extent of their conflict behavior or the severity of a crisis.

Factor Scores

With respect to this study, the factor scores are the values each country has on each of the dimensions extracted. They indicate, for instance, whether a country is high or low on the *turmoil and war* dimensions. Only nations with standard scores on each dimension equal to or greater than 1.0 are given in table 8. Due to the skewness of the factor score distributions, there are no standardized negative factor scores less than or equal to -1.00.

The factor scores for each dimension are calculated by adding together

Table 8. Standardized Factor Scores, by Rank[a]

Domestic Dimensions			Foreign Dimensions		
Turmoil	Revolutionary	Subversive	War	Diplomatic	Belligerent
France (3.16)	Argentina (4.07)	Cuba (4.08)	Israel (3.20)	U.S.S.R. (3.85)	Egypt (3.80)
Argentina (3.00)	China (2.69)	Burma (4.08)	Egypt (3.19)	U.S. (2.73)	Jordan (3.80)
India (2.25)	India (2.69)	Philippines (4.08)	France (3.18)	Dom. Rep. (2.65)	Pakistan (3.80)
Pakistan (1.72)	Guatemala (2.16)	Argentina (2.61)	U.K. (3.18)	Argentina (2.31)	Afghanistan (1.71)
Guatemala (1.71)	Brazil (1.85)	Indonesia (2.61)	Hungary (2.27)	Venezuela (2.31)	Chile (1.71)
Haiti (1.71)	Paraguay (1.85)	Columbia (1.14)	U.S.S.R. (2.27)	Hungary (1.61)	Rep. of China (1.71)
South Africa (1.68)	Hungary (1.62)	Costa Rica (1.14)	Syria (2.24)	Sweden (1.61)	W. Germany (1.71)
Iraq (1.54)	Syria (1.62)	India (1.14)	Yemen (1.31)	Iraq (1.19)	India (1.71)
Italy (1.44)	Haiti (1.54)	Lebanon (1.14)	Nicaragua (1.09)	Yugoslavia (1.19)	Iraq (1.71)
Jordan (1.44)	Egypt (1.09)				Peru (1.71)
Cuba (1.41)	Burma (1.00)				Syria (1.71)
Indonesia (1.30)	Honduras (1.00)				
Poland (1.14)	Indonesia (1.00)				
Chile (1.11)					

[a]Only countries with standardized factor scores ≥ ± 1.00 are shown; where countries are tied for the same rank, they are ranked in alphabetical order.

the standard scores for those measures on the particular dimension which have a correlation greater than or equal to .50, and no correlation on another dimension within the matrix equal to or greater than .40. Hence, the factor score is a composite of those measures which are most strongly associated with that dimension.

RELATIONSHIP BETWEEN DOMESTIC AND FOREIGN CONFLICT BEHAVIOR

Two approaches will be used here in determining what relationship exists between domestic and foreign conflict behavior. First, a factor analysis of domestic and foreign conflict behavior measures together will be calculated. This should help determine whether there are any common conflict behavior dimensions general to both the domestic and foreign domains, e.g., whether the turmoil dimension extends into international behavior or is specific to domestic relations; whether the war or belligerency dimensions will merge with the subversion dimension.

And, second, a multiple regression analysis will be done to see how well each of the foreign conflict behavior dimensions separately can be predicted by all the domestic conflict behavior dimensions, and vice versa. While the factor analysis should tell us how specific the domestic and foreign conflict behavior dimensions are to their respective domains, the multiple regression should tell us to what degree foreign (or domestic) conflict behavior can be predicted from such domestic (or foreign) behavior.

Domestic and Foreign Conflict Measures

The results of factor analyzing the domestic and foreign conflict measures together are given in table 9. The upper right block of table 10 gives the correlation between the domestic and foreign measures. The first thing one might note from table 9 is that the first unrotated dimension is not general to all the measures, thus indicating a lack of commonness among them. What this lack of commonness might be is suggested by the rotated dimensions, which show the clear separation of domestic and foreign conflict into distinct dimensions. This suggests that there may be little relationship between domestic and foreign conflict behavior. More precise evidence of this lack of relationship is given below with the results of the multiple regression.

The first rotated dimension, accounting for 31.2 percent of the common and 22 percent of the total variance, appears strongly as an *aggressive* dimension, delimiting a cluster of measures including those of a violent (war, .83; number killed in foreign conflict, .89; military action, .70), menacing (mobilizations, .63; troop movements, .62; threats, .78), and assertive (protests, .69; accusations, .80) nature. The second dimension, in contrast, is wholly a domestic conflict behavior continuum, with high correlations for all domestic measures, excepting guerrilla war and assassinations. On this dimension one finds a merging of those measures which previously had delimited the turmoil and revolutionary dimensions, and one might, therefore, call this continuum an *instability* dimension—representing a general conflict atmosphere reflected by a wide range of conflict behavior.

Table 9. Factor Analysis of Domestic and Foreign Conflict Measures[a]

Measures	Factor Matrix[b]						Orthogonally Rotated Factor Matrix[b]						
	F_1	F_2	F_3	F_4	F_5	F_6	F_1	F_2^c	F_3	F_4^c	F_5^c	F_6^c	h^2
1. Assassinations	38	-48	20	30	(-51)	-16	19	35	30	00	(72)	13	78
2. General strikes	25	(-72)	-05	03	25	17	-11	(81)	04	00	00	07	67
3. Guerrilla warfare	01	(-57)	-04	-03	-49	-35	-12	28	-09	21	(73)	-10	69
4. Major government crisis	32	-41	13	45	20	21	02	(54)	30	-29	02	32	57
5. Purges	(50)	-49	-31	-07	15	06	24	(70)	-21	10	02	14	62
6. Riots	45	(-61)	20	06	13	11	06	(72)	29	11	09	17	66
7. Revolutions	19	(-66)	-31	-04	01	13	-02	(71)	-22	-03	17	-09	59
8. Antigovernment demonstrations	(59)	(-51)	28	01	06	04	21	(63)	36	22	13	21	69
9. Number killed—domestic	33	(-73)	-20	-33	-11	03	09	(76)	-16	30	26	-19	81
10. Antiforeign demonstrations	(62)	-04	20	17	22	-26	29	21	20	22	02	(59)	57
11. Negative sanctions	(63)	17	31	26	07	-32	38	-04	32	19	10	(64)	70
12. Protests	(71)	35	18	-15	05	11	(69)	-01	25	23	-25	20	70
13. Severance diplomatic relations	44	06	-33	45	45	-22	19	19	-27	-20	-15	(75)	76
14. Expulsions/recalls ambassadors	19	-28	20	(-50)	-01	-42	-05	17	01	(72)	16	01	58
15. Expulsions/recalls lesser officials	(52)	17	20	-44	30	13	41	14	18	44	-46	06	63
16. Threats	(86)	32	01	-05	-02	-13	(78)	01	06	27	-05	41	86
17. Military action	(66)	25	-43	30	-09	-04	(70)	06	-27	-22	09	41	78
18. Wars	(61)	24	-04	-10	-35	46	(83)	09	17	-10	-04	-21	78
19. Troop movements	(69)	25	11	-33	-01	-15	(62)	-01	08	49	-09	20	68
20. Mobilizations	(54)	31	-12	24	-29	-07	(63)	-13	-01	-11	21	27	55
21. Accusations	(84)	24	-15	-07	-02	-05	(80)	12	-06	20	-06	33	80
22. Number killed—foreign	(77)	19	-30	-03	-25	28	(89)	20	-09	-08	01	02	85
23. Censorship	-19	-02	(51)	44	-18	17	-20	-13	(59)	-33	18	01	55
24. Embassies and legations	31	02	(74)	-05	-01	20	17	05	(78)	21	-09	02	69
Percent Common Variance	40.9	23.1	11.5	9.9	7.9	6.6	31.2	23.3	11.5	10.6	9.7	13.5	100.0
Percent Total Variance	28.2	16.0	8.0	6.8	5.5	4.6	22.0	16.1	8.0	7.3	6.7	9.3	69.0

[a] Decimals omitted from all loadings. [b] Parenthesis indicates loadings ≥ .50. [c] Signs reversed.

The third dimension represents the two error measures (which intercorrelate .28), and may be called an error dimension. The reason that these error measures formed an independent dimension can be seen from the correlations of these measures with the conflict behavior measures as shown along the margin of table 10. The highest correlation of censorship with any of the conflict behavior measures is – .27, with most of the other correlations being very nearly zero. The correlations for the other measure of error are higher, but with the highest being .34, and with many of the correlations being also close to zero. The lowness of these correlations and the extraction of an error dimension are good evidence that systematic error *as tapped by these measures*, has little effect on the results.

The fourth dimension—expulsion or recall of ambassador (.72)—is like the *diplomatic* dimension extracted from the factor analysis of the foreign conflict behavior measures. And the fifth dimension—guerrilla warfare (.73) and assassinations (.72)— is similar to the *subversion* dimensions found in the domestic analysis.

The sixth dimension, with severance of diplomatic relations (.75), antiforeign demonstrations (.59), and military action (.41) correlated with it, is much the same dimension found in the separate factor analysis of the foreign conflict measures—the *belligerent* dimension.[85]

When domestic and foreign conflict behavior measures, then, are factor analyzed together, foreign and domestic conflict behavior per se retain their distinctiveness, but the results of the separate analyses are altered slightly. The domestic turmoil and revolutionary dimensions combine into a more general instability dimension. And the war dimension changes into the more general aggressive dimension. The subversive, diplomatic, and belligerent dimensions, however, retain their identity. It is not surprising that the first dimensions of the separate analysis should thus be changed when all the measures are combined. Amalgamating the measures has the effect of making what factors emerge more relevant to general conflict behavior. One might expect, therefore, that factors specific to a particular area of conflict behavior would become broader in interpretation when other kinds of behavior are brought into comparison. What is surprising is the virtually complete specificity of the dimensions extracted from the separate factor analysis. When all the measures are factor analyzed together no two domestic and foreign conflict measures have correlations greater than ±.46 with the same factor. That is, the dimensions remain common to their domains.

[85]"Belligerency" implies both attitude and action—an attitude of hostility, enmity, or hatred, and overt acts following from such hostility. "Aggressive," in terms of which the first dimension is named, implies only overt action. A nation may have assertive, nonpassive foreign policies, which may or may not have their source in hostility, hatred, or the balancing of alternatives.

Table 10. Correlation Matrix[a]

	1	2	3	4	5	6	7	8	9	10	11	12	13	14	15	16	17	18	19	20	21	22	23	24
1. Assassinations		28	45	35	31	45	19	51	33	23	28	01	03	16	-09	15	15	19	06	28	20	18	08	21
2. General strikes			24	29	46	56	50	57	51	20	-01	-01	14	13	07	-04	01	-01	-10	-09	07	04	-03	00
3. Guerrilla warfare				09	17	13	33	20	52	00	-00	-23	-08	17	-11	-10	-10	-10	-11	-11	-09	-04	05	-07
4. Major government crisis					30	36	38	41	20	21	29	10	28	-01	05	09	11	09	-05	05	11	13	05	22
5. Purges						42	49	36	57	24	13	08	32	18	24	26	30	17	24	13	27	34	-21	03
6. Riots							32	69	53	36	16	19	18	26	08	15	08	12	13	02	21	19	05	19
7. Revolutions								23	62	05	-04	-11	03	12	-11	-04	12	-04	07	-12	04	12	-08	-06
8. Demonstrations									45	38	26	29	14	26	28	36	16	20	23	21	35	21	-07	30
9. Domestic killed										16	-04	-00	-03	25	16	05	02	07	14	-06	12	22	-22	-01
10. Antiforeign demonstrations											53	39	36	14	29	50	33	25	39	22	46	35	05	18
11. Negative sanctions												47	33	05	33	64	35	24	45	38	49	30	03	33
12. Protests													19	09	47	66	39	51	63	46	69	52	-10	29
13. Severance diplomatic relations														-08	12	38	54	07	15	23	39	31	-15	-08
14. Expulsions/recalls—ambassadors															10	12	-08	01	24	-10	11	02	-14	13
15. Expulsions/recalls—lesser officials																50	13	33	43	15	45	32	-23	34
16. Threats																	62	55	68	55	81	63	-19	25
17. Military action																		38	45	54	65	72	-09	07
18. War																			32	37	56	77	-10	20
19. Troop movements																				30	62	53	-13	33
20. Mobilizations																					46	41	-17	07
21. Accusations																						70	-27	09
22. Foreign killed																							-16	08
23. Censorship																								28
24. Embassies and legations																								

[a]Correlations rounded off and multiplied by 100.

The dimensions that have been extracted from the merged analysis are orthogonal to each other—an orthogonality which is forced on the dimensions by the varimax criteria used for rotation. This separation of foreign and domestic conflict behavior on the most general first two dimensions, therefore, may be an artifact of the forced independence of the dimensions. Figure 1 displays the result of manually rotating the previously rotated

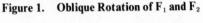

Figure 1.   Oblique Rotation of F_1 and F_2

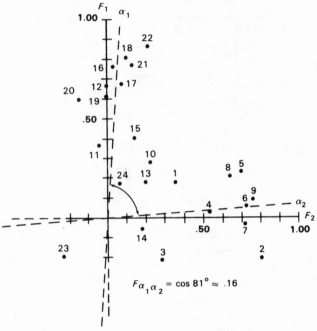

first factors to a better fitting oblique solution. The war dimension is rotated to α_1, and the turmoil dimension to α_2. The result is little different. The correlation between the two dimensions is increased from .00 to .16, a very low correlation, and an indication that the orthogonal results are hardly artifactual.

Multiple Regression

The results of the factor analysis of the amalgamated domestic and foreign conflict measures, where the domestic and foreign conflict measures were separated into different dimensions, suggests that there may be no relationship between the two domains. This lack of relationship can be more precisely investigated through the use of multiple regression.

Factor analysis is relevant when one is concerned with determining the nature of the interrelationships among a collection of measures, or when prior to multiple regression one wants to reduce a set of highly related measures to a smaller number of uncorrelated dimensions that can serve as independent variables in the multiple regression. If highly interrelated variables are used as independent variables in a multiple regression, the reliability of the regression coefficients is decreased considerably[86] and the results may accordingly be distorted. Therefore, in the case that one suspects high intercorrelations among his independent variables, a two-step approach might be warranted—factor analysis of the measures to get uncorrelated dimensions, and the use of such dimensions in place of the measures in the multiple regression.[87]

Table 11 gives the most relevant results of multiple regression of the three domestic conflict behavior dimensions on each of the three foreign conflict behavior dimensions separately.

Table 11. Predictions of Foreign Conflict Behavior—Independent Variables: Turmoil, Revolutionary, Subversion

Dependent Variable	Standard Deviation	Standard Error	Multiple R	Proportion Variance R^2
War	2.40	2.36	.26[a]	.07
Diplomacy	1.49	1.46	.26[a]	.07
Belligerency	1.00	.97	.31[a]	.10

[a] $p > .05$ (nonnormal distributions); $N = 77$.

An important thing to note in the table is that domestic conflict behavior accounts for very little of the variance R of foreign conflict behavior along the three foreign dimensions. This is reflected in the very small change from standard deviation to standard error. The standard error is the standard deviation of the residuals—the difference between the value predicted on the basis of the multiple regression and the actual value for a country on the dependent variable. The standard error indicates the degree to which the prediction equation fits the dependent variable. The slight change between the standard deviation of the dependent variable and the standard error shows that the variation in the dependent variable is not being predicted by the independent variables.

Therefore, multiple regression of the domestic dimensions on each of the foreign conflict behavior dimensions, in turn, leads to the conclusion that domestic conflict cannot predict foreign conflict behavior.

The foreign conflict dimensions together, however, might still predict

---

[86]Ezekiel and Fox, *Methods of Correlation*, pp. 295–98.

[87]See E. J. Buchatzsch, "The Influence of Social Conditions on Mortality Rates," *Population Studies* 1 (1947): 229–48, as a research example of such an approach.

the position of a country on any one of the domestic conflict behavior dimensions. The results of checking this possibility are given in table 12.

Table 12. Predictions of Foreign Conflict Behavior—Independent Variables: War, Diplomacy, Belligerency

Dependent Variable	Standard Deviation	Standard Error	Multiple R	Proportion Variance R^2
Turmoil	2.43	2.31	.37[a]	.14
Revolutionary	1.73	1.70	.27[b]	.07
Subversive	1.00	1.01	.14[b]	.02

[a] $.01 < p < .05$ (nonnormal distribution).
[b] $p > .05$ (nonnormal distributions); $N = 77$.

Here, also, the lack of relationship appears, with the possible exception of the prediction of turmoil, which would be significant at the .05 level if the factor scores for the dimensions involved would have been distributed normally. Since the distributions are not distributed normally, however, one cannot gauge the precise significance of the correlation. Nevertheless, one can still see from R that all but a small part—14 percent—of the variance of turmoil is unaccounted for by the foreign conflict behavior dimensions and that the standard error (2.31) of the prediction of turmoil by these dimensions is only slightly different from the standard deviation (2.43).

As suggested strongly by the merged factor analysis, and reinforced by the multiple regressions, then, foreign and domestic conflict behavior are not generally related to and generally cannot be predictors of each other. This finding is justified in regard to conflict behavior as tapped by my measures, and in regard to sovereign nations for the middle 1950s.[88] This is not to say that there are no particular cases in which domestic and foreign conflict behavior are related. There well may be situations in which the domestic political elite of a nation will foment foreign conflict as a means of quieting internal squabbling.[89] Moreover, if one were to take a longitudinal slice out of the history of many nations, a very close relation in the fluctuations of domestic and foreign conflict behavior might be found. What the conclusion does say, however, is that taking sovereign nations as a whole for the same period of time, foreign and domestic conflict behavior generally vary independently of each other.

[88]Although the above test of stability of the measures would argue that the findings are valid for a much longer period.
[89]As Haas and Whiting suggest, "groups seeking self-preservation and no more may be driven to a foreign policy of conflict—if not open war—in order to defend themselves against the onslaught of domestic rather than foreign enemies. In times of extreme domestic tension among elites, a policy of uniting a badly divided nation against some real or alleged outside threat frequently seems useful to a ruling group." From Haas and Whiting, *Dynamics of International Relations*, p. 62.

POSSIBLE ERRORS OF COMMISSION OR OMISSION

No one is closer to a particular piece of research than the one who actually has done the investigation and analysis. And although the more methodologically sophisticated might point out many errors of commission or omission and the substantively oriented many assumptions, factual errors, sources not considered, and data omitted, the researcher is in a position to know many possible errors of commission or omission in his own work.

Possible Errors of Commission

Nontheoretical Choice of Measures. The measures used here were chosen on definitional, practical, and statistical criteria. Theoretical relevance within the context of conflict theory was not made a criterion. Possibly, if such were done, the overall results would be more theoretically relevant, and would help to choose between competing theories in conflict. Such a criterion is not used here, however, because of my belief that such comprehensive theories of conflict *capable of test* do not yet exist.

Number of Years. Resources did not permit collecting data on more than three years. The evident stability of the 1955–57 data notwithstanding, the collection of data for a longer period would have considerably added to the methodological soundness of this study and the persuasiveness of its conclusions. If data had been collected for a longer period, say ten years, many of the distributions probably would have lost their *J* shapes and would have been normal or capable of normalization—thus allowing the use of many statistical tests and increasing the reliability of the conclusions.

Static Approach. This study does not take change into consideration. The findings, therefore, are relevant to only the *absolute* amount of conflict behavior. It is possible, for example, that a high rate of increase in domestic conflict behavior may be strongly related to the increase in amount of foreign conflict behavior. Such a relationship, however, would be missed by this study. The static rather than dynamic approach was used as a "best" first step to map the relationships between the amounts of conflict behavior. Later, it was thought these findings could be used as stepping stones for moving into the far more complex area of change.

Correlation Coefficient. The product-moment coefficient has been used here, and was chosen over several other possible coefficients. The question as to which coefficients are best under given conditions is still moot. Possibly, although not likely, the use of another coefficient, such as the tetrachoric, might have given more reliable and invariant results. An approach to an answer to this question could be made by doing the factor analysis using different coefficients, but such is beyond the resources of this study.

Reliability Test.   No direct test of the reliability of the definitions was made. Indirectly, however, their reliability was indicated by the high correlations of the data collected with similar data collected by others and by the high communalities of the measures in the factor analyses. If the definitions were unreliable, then considerable random error should contaminate the data, lowering considerably or making nonsignificant their correlations with data from other studies and also reducing the amount of common variance that will be associated with the other measures included in the factor analyses.

Measures of Error.   Two measures of error were used to get at systematic bias. Neither of these measures, however, indexes the possibility of conflict behavior news being squeezed out of our sources by the occurrence of events of great importance and interest. Hence, a good deal of systematic error from this source, as well as other unknown sources, may have contaminated the results without one knowing it. Only replication may lessen the probability of this having happened.

Factor Scores.   The factor scores were calculated by adding the standard scores of each nation on those measures high on the particular dimension and low on the others. The result is probably a very close approximation to the actual factor scores a country would have if one were to use more precise techniques involving the data, correlation, and factor matrices. The additional accuracy one would thus gain, however, did not seem worth the expenditure in time and resources.

Possible Errors of Omission

Lack of Cooperation Measures.   Conceptually, conflict is generally considered as one end of a cooperation-conflict continuum. The dimensions of conflict behavior found here might very well, then, be only parts of continua which would also involve cooperation behavior. As implied by Richardson,[90] for example, war and trade might well form a bipolar dimension. It would be interesting and important, therefore, to find out whether and what cooperation measures lie at the opposite ends of the various dimensions of conflict extracted. This possibility was recognized from the beginning, but a decision had to be made as to whether to limit the collection of data to half of the conflict behavior measures in order to collect data on an equal number of cooperation measures, or try to cover the conflict behavior field as best as possible first. Because the former approach would assume knowledge about the relationships among conflict behavior data—the very knowledge the study was supposed to uncover—in order to decide which measures to omit, the latter approach, as a first step, was thought advisable.

[90]Richardson, *Arms and Insecurity.*

Pairs of Nations. The results of this study are a comparison of each nation with all other nations. It might have been more relevant, however, to have done the analysis with respect to pairs of nations. An analysis across pairs of nations, for example, would have yielded information on the relationship between the measures of conflict behavior of Syria and Israel, and the U.S. and U.S.S.R., with such relationships generalized across all possible pairs. Such information might be of more immediate foreign policy import than that resulting from a comparison of each nation with all others. It was felt, however, as in the case of the static versus the dynamic alternative, that the approach used here should come first, as a necessary prior step, and that the information derived from this study can then be used in a future study of these dyadic relationships.

Oblique Rotation. Some factor analysts, such as Raymond Cattell, argue that oblique rotation is to be preferred over the orthogonal solution this study employs. Quite possibly he is right, but these things should be judged relevant to the area of concern. In a field where little prior factor exploration has taken place to serve as a guide as to what to expect, the more parsimonious and conceptually simpler solution might be better as a first approximation. This was the reasoning behind the orthogonal rotation decided upon, although others might weigh the alternatives differently.

Political, Economic, Sociological Measures. No multiple regression of nonconflict measures on the conflict-behavior factors has been done. Certainly, this is a most important step and will enable us to get some leverage on some of the significant conditions underlying both domestic and foreign conflict behavior. Rather than use measures such as size of population, GNP, extent of party competition, and so forth, it was felt that a more reliable study of the conditions underlying conflict could be made later using the results to come out of the Dimensionality of Nations Project, which is attempting to determine the dimensions of the political, economic, social, cultural, and value characteristics and behavior of nations around 1955. The orthogonal factors resulting from the Project's analysis of such data may then be used as independent variables in a multiple regression study of conflict behavior.

DISCUSSION, SUMMARY, AND PROPOSITIONS

Discussion

One of the significant findings of this study is perhaps the apparent lack of relationship between domestic and foreign conflict behavior. That they vary independently of each other was brought out both by the factor analysis and the multiple regression. This lack of relationship between them may be seen in the results of two other studies.

In Cattell's seventy-two-variable, sixty-nine-nation study,[91] his three domestic conflict variables and two foreign conflict variables remained separated both in the unrotated and oblique rotation cases. His rotation leads to equivocal results, however, since the two foreign conflict variables load highly on a factor correlated $-.44$ with the factor upon which two of the domestic conflict variables are highly loaded. What would happen in the case of orthogonal rotation is not clear. Still, the unrotated matrix, the continual separation of the variables on different factors after rotation, and the fact that his data are taken from the period 1837-1937, point to a certain historical generality to the lack of relationship between domestic and foreign conflict.

Richardson also found a difference between domestic and foreign conflict behavior, but of a different kind. He found that domestic violence occurred less often in comparison to foreign violence than one should expect— that there must be some kind of "pacifying" influence at work in domestic affairs.[92] Although Richardson felt he had proved the existence of a pacifier, he could not determine its nature. For some reason, as one crosses from the domestic to the international system the frequency of violent conflict behavior increases—as though we were crossing between two worlds.

The general independence between domestic and foreign conflict behavior indicates that different necessary and sufficient conditions for both must be sought—that rapid industrialization, or underdevelopment, or dictatorships, or unstable political systems, or technological changes cannot be general conditions of both domestic and foreign conflict behavior as is often asserted. This is not to say that such conditions may not be generally *necessary*—producing the required atmosphere for conflict behavior—but that the general condition setting off the behavior must differ between the two worlds.

Also indicated by the general independence between foreign and domestic conflict behavior, is the conclusion that foreign conflict behavior is not a necessary and sufficient condition of domestic peace. The idea that brothers will squabble unless faced by a common enemy appeals to common sense and is enshrined in public mythology. The results of this study, however, show that domestic conflict behavior and domestic peace occur whether or not foreign conflict is present. Throwing this lack of relationship between domestic and foreign conflict into sharp relief is the fact that within the domestic and foreign domains conflict behavior is highly related. These high within domain correlations can be seen from the intercorrelations of the domestic measures given in the upper left triangular matrix and the intercorrelation of the foreign measures in the lower right matrix in table 10 above.

[91]Cattell, "Dimensions of Culture Patterns."
[92]Richardson, "Contiguity and Deadly Quarrels."

Another finding of interest emerging from the 1955–57 data is the great significance of threats and accusations, which were found highly related to almost all the measures of foreign conflict. With regard to this study, one may only conjecture about the mechanism at work here. Perhaps threats and accusations are a form of communication which takes place only after a certain threshold of unfriendliness has been passed. Protests, a communication measure which was found not so generally related to international conflict behavior, may operate above or below this threshold. A country may protest routinely to another about some incident, but probably will not openly charge another with an unfriendly act or threaten that country unless strained relations already exist. Then, accusations may function to state the case, both domestically and internationally, and threats to draw the line and make explicit the commitment or the consequences.

While serving as communications devices, threats and accusations may also feed back into the conflict situation, acting to strongly increase tension and stimulate greater involvement. A charge-countercharge, threat-counterthreat nexus may occur, feeding onto itself, and transcending the original issue. This is speculation, of course, but the possibility is strongly suggested by their being the most highly correlated among the foreign conflict behavior measures with the general dimension of the unrotated factor matrix in table 6.

If such be the case, it poses a dilemma for the study of deterrence. Threats appear necessary to state the conditions under which nuclear weapons will be used—to prevent miscalculation on the part of the enemy. Threats, however, must be repeated to show that national resolve has not slipped and to reinforce the deterrent ability of one's weapons. Yet the use of such threats by both sides—their reiteration and accentuation—might escalate a current crisis beyond control.

Whether or not such a dilemma exists in reality, whether or not threats do act as both stimulus and response, threats and accusations together may enable the systematically oriented student of international conflict to get some purchase on measuring crisis. An index that is a linear composite of threats and accusations may well serve as a thermometer for measuring and comparing the heat—the intensity—of crises so that hypotheses about crisis may be both tested and generated.

While threats and accusations are so generally related to international conflict, war is not. Accounting for 46.2 percent of the common variance, the war dimension is the most important of the international conflict dimensions. Still, the occurrence or nonoccurrence of many kinds of conflict behavior seem to operate independently of war. This is reflected by the other orthogonal dimensions, the diplomacy and belligerent, which account for low, but still respectable amounts of variance. International conflict behavior is not, therefore, unidimensional—a sort of Guttman scale of behavior, with each act becoming more severe until war is reached—but tridimensional. This multidimensional quality of international conflict behavior has been noted elsewhere. With respect to tensions and disputes Morgenthau says, for example, that: "Between two nations there is sometimes no tension at all, yet there are disputes. Or sometimes, despite the existence of a tension, the dispute has no relation to the tension."[93]

A particular conflict act, then, need not presage war. It may instead be an almost automatic diplomatic reaction to a relatively minor situation—expelling an official for spying, applying pressure on a country by recalling one's ambassador, or discontinuing aid shipments, and so forth. Or a conflict act may be evidence of contained hostility—enmity sufficient to bring the people to the streets condemning the other country, to cause diplomatic relations to be severed, boycotts to be imposed, and perhaps frequent and spontaneous border clashes—but "contained" hostility in that mobilization does not occur, war is not declared, and the lid is kept on. War may indeed escalate out of such a situation, but the finding here is that war generally occurs independently of them.

In addition to the three foreign conflict behavior and three domestic conflict behavior dimensions, five dimensions of domestic and foreign conflict behavior taken together have also been extracted. The main value of this merged analysis is in indicating the lack of relationship between the measures of domestic and foreign conflict behavior and the relationship of systematic error to the measures. Since the measures are so generally unrelated across domestic and foreign domains, the dimensions resulting from the separate factor analyses should be used as input into future research.

These three domestic and three foreign dimensions of conflict behavior may now serve as independent variables in other studies or, in particular, they can be used to test various propositions as to the causes of conflict behavior. As dimensions of conflict behavior, they may also serve as guides for constructing the conflict structure of computer or human simulations of international relations. Less obvious, perhaps, is their value in pointing out the measures upon which one might concentrate data collection. If several measures are highly correlated with the same dimension, then one need only collect data on possibly one or two of them in order to represent the dimensions with respect to the period of concern.

Summary

The goals of this study were to determine the dimensions of variation in the domestic and foreign conflict behavior of nations, to locate the position of each nation on these dimensions, and to use these dimensions to ascer-

[93]Hans Morgenthau, *Politics Among Nations*, 2nd ed. (New York: Alfred A. Knopf, 1954), p. 404.

tain the relationship between domestic conflict behavior and that in the international area.

Data were collected for seventy-seven nations on nine measures of domestic conflict behavior and thirteen measures of foreign conflict behavior for the years 1955, 1956, and 1957. The data were intercorrelated using the product moment coefficient, and with unities in the diagonal of the correlation matrix, a principal component factor analysis was calculated separately for the domestic and for the foreign conflict behavior data.

Factors whose eigenvalues were greater than unity were extracted and these solutions were rotated orthogonally to simple structure using the varimax criterion. In this manner, three dimensions of domestic conflict behavior—*turmoil, revolutionary,* and *subversive* dimensions—and three dimensions of foreign conflict behavior—*war, diplomatic,* and *belligerent* dimensions—were determined. Factor scores for each of the seventy-seven nations were computed to locate these nations on the six dimensions.

The relationship between domestic and foreign conflict behavior was investigated in two ways. First, a factor analysis along the above lines was calculated for all the conflict behavior measures together. The result was that the measures of domestic conflict behavior completely separated themselves onto dimensions different from those upon which the foreign conflict measures were loaded, thus indicating a general lack of relationship across the two domains of conflict behavior within them. This lack of relationship was defined further by doing a multiple regression analysis of the domestic conflict behavior dimensions on each of the dimensions of foreign conflict behavior in turn, and, similarly, by doing a multiple regression of the foreign conflict behavior dimensions on each of the domestic ones.

The stability of the data was checked by assessing its correlation with similar domestic data for 1946–59 collected by Harry Eckstein, with war data for 1825–1945 collected by Lewis F. Richardson, and by comparing the intercorrelations among the 1955–57 data with intercorrelations calculated by Raymond Cattell for similar data on five like measures, 1837–1937. As a consequence, the data were found highly stable. The possibility of systematic error distorting the results was tested by including in the factor analysis measures relating to the amount of censorship in and world importance of a country. An independent error factor was extracted and is a good indication that systematic error as tapped by these measures of error did not affect unduly the results.

Propositions

With respect to a comparison across nations for the same period of time, the following propositions emerge from this study:[94]

---

[94]It is important to note that because these propositions were derived from a spatial study across nations, they are not relevant to the conflict behavior and relationships between such behavior of a nation over a period of time.

1. The domestic conflict behavior of nations varies along three uncorrelated dimensions: *turmoil, revolutionary, subversive.*
2. The foreign conflict behavior of nations varies along three uncorrelated dimensions: *war, diplomatic, belligerent.*
3. A *war* dimension is more important than any other dimension of foreign conflict behavior in accounting for the variation in conflict behavior between nations.
4. The variation in acts or occurrences of domestic conflict behavior are generally highly related to each other.
5. The variation in acts or occurrences of foreign conflict behavior are generally highly related to each other.
6. Foreign conflict behavior is generally completely unrelated to domestic conflict behavior.
7. Foreign conflict behavior is not a necessary and sufficient condition for domestic peace.
8. The acts or occurrences of conflict behavior within and between nations are not sporadic—unpredictable—but are patterned and can be predicted on the basis of their history of such conflict behavior.
9. General international conflict behavior and the intensity of the underlying conflict may be indexed through a summation of the standard scores of the number of threats and number of accusations made.
10. Systematic error resulting from censorship or the lack of interest in a nation will not unduly affect the conclusions derived from domestic and foreign conflict behavior data.

APPENDIX 1.
Definitions of Conflict Behavior Measures

Domestic Conflict Behavior

1. *Assassination:* the politically motivated murder or attempted murder of a high governmental official or politician. Among high governmental officials are included the governors of states or provinces, the mayors of large cities, members of the cabinet, and members of the national legislature. Among high politicians are included members of the inner core of the ruling party or group and leaders of the opposition. An example of an assassination is the "politically motivated" murder of the governor of Eva Peron Province, Argentina, February 1, 1955.

2. *General Strike:* any strike of industrial or service workers which involves more than one employer and that is aimed against national governmental policies or authority. A strike is not considered general unless at

least 1,000 workers are involved. General strikes do not include those strikes whose nature is to force the government or private industry to grant wage or working concessions. An example of a general strike is the strike of 14,500 African clothing workers in Johannesburg, Union of South Africa, November 19, 1957, in protest against a law requiring certain jobs be held by whites.

3. *Guerrilla War:*   armed activity on the part of bands of citizens or irregular forces aimed at the overthrow of the existing government. Such activity may take the form of sporadic attacks on police posts, small villages, government patrols, or military barracks. A country is also considered to have guerrilla war when sporadic bombing, sabotage, or terrorism occurs. As defined here, guerrilla warfare was present in Cuba during the three years, 1955–57, of interest.

4. *Major Government Crisis:*   any rapidly developing situation which threatens (excluding revolution) to bring the immediate downfall of the present government. Such situations are usually evidenced by the declaration of military law, state of siege, or the suspension or abrogation of the constitution. A vote of no confidence by a parliamentary majority, or the forced resignation or impeachment of top officials are also considered major government crises. A new major government crisis is not counted unless at least three months of stability have intervened since the previous crisis. A major government crisis is exemplified by the situation leading up to the abdication of the king of Cambodia, March 2, 1955, in protest against Nationalist "politicians" who were trying to alter his policies.

5. *Purge:*   the systematic elimination by the political elite either of opposition within their ranks or of opposition within the country by jailing or execution. "Elimination of opposition" refers to the arrest, jailing, exiling, or execution of the opposition leaders. The arrest or execution of nonleader members of opposition groups does not constitute a purge. If the elimination of opposition continues over a period of time without a relaxation of more than three months, then it is one purge. An elimination of opposition incident upon the take over of the government by a new political elite, regardless of whether a purge had been carried on by the old elite up to the take over, is to be considered a new purge only if the opposition purged includes elite politically and/or ideologically associated with the previous regime—if the elite taking over continues to eliminate the same leaders without adding a new category of opposition (e.g., Catholic leaders who were untouched during previous regime) then it is not a new purge as here defined. "Arrest" is considered synonymous with "jailing" and carries no idea of time detained—the fact of arrest per se is sufficient to indicate a purge. An example of a purge is the arrest by Jordanian police of more than fifty "leftist" leaders, civil employees, government members, and army officers thought to be hostile to the regime, April–May 1957.

6. *Riot:*   any violent demonstration or clash of a large group of citizens. The term "violence" refers to the use of physical force, and "large" means at least one hundred people involved. The existence of a riot is generally evidenced by the destruction of property, people being wounded or killed, or by the use of the police of riot control equipment such as clubs, guns, or water cannons. Arrests per se do not indicate a riot. Riots of a distinct antiforeign nature are categorized as antiforeign demonstrations. A riot as here defined occurred in Turkey, October 24, 1957, when five hundred university students clashed with police after a rally in support of former President Inonu.

7. *Antigovernment Demonstration:*   any unorganized peaceful, public gathering of at least one hundred people for the primary purpose of displaying or voicing their opposition to governmental policies or authority. This does not include political party rallies or general strikes. Student strikes aimed at the government are considered antigovernment demonstrations. A demonstration which involves the use of force is categorized as a riot. An illustration of a demonstration is the gathering of 100,000 Belgians to protest against a proposed cut in governmental subsidies to Roman Catholic schools, Belgium, March 26, 1955.

8. *Revolution:*   any armed successful or unsuccessful attempt on the part of a group of citizenry to form an independent government (not including colonial rebellions), or any illegal or forced change in the top governmental elites or any attempt at such a change. This may be in the nature of a coup d'état, or an attempted take over on a grand scale, involving pitched battles between opposing forces. When an attempt to overthrow the government, however, involves only scattered and irregular forces who attack from hiding, it is categorized as a guerrilla war. A revolution occurred in Ecuador, August 1–8, 1956, when a two-hundred man army led by a lieutenant colonel and a senator attempted to overthrow the government.

9. *Number Killed in Domestic Violence:*   this is a summation of the number killed as a direct consequence of any domestic intergroup violence in the nature of riots, strikes, revolutions, guerrilla war, banditry, and tribal warfare. This does not include murders, executions, and suicides. The number of killed for Indonesia in 1955, for example, is 4,176 and is the result of guerrilla war and revolution.

Foreign Conflict Behavior

1. *Antiforeign Demonstration:*   any demonstration or riot by more than one-hundred people directed at a particular foreign country (or group of countries) or its policies. This includes attacking an embassy, legation, or information office of another country, or attacking for political reasons either foreign nationals on the street or their property (e.g., plantations).

This also includes the gathering of more than one hundred people to hear speeches and to march in protest against the policy of another country. Demonstrations and riots against the foreign occupying authority in the occupied part of a country are considered antiforeign demonstrations. Also included in this category are strikes against the goods of another nation, either by dock workers or consumers, and attacks on border posts by unofficial irregular groups (e.g., the Irish Republican Army). An instance of a demonstration is the gathering of 2,000 Warsaw students to publicly protest against the U.S.S.R. and to accuse her of the World War II massacre of Polish officers, Poland, October 25, 1956.

2. *Negative Sanction:* any act on the part of a government which has as its purpose the punishment of another country for its behavior. This includes such acts as boycotts, withdrawal of military or economic aid, freezing of assets, embargo, or limitation of movement of the other's nationals within the country. Negative sanctions do not include expulsion or recall of diplomats, severance of diplomatic relations, military action and war. An example of a negative sanction is the stopping of all oil shipments to France and England by Saudi Arabia, November 8, 1956, in protest against their actions in the Mideast War.

3. *Protest:* any official diplomatic communication or governmental statement by the executive leaders of a country which has as its primary purpose to protest against the actions of another nation. Diplomatic notes of protest are counted as are editorials of protest appearing in a leading government newspaper of totalitarian countries. For example, Bulgaria protested to the U.S. on February 4, 1956, over propaganda balloons being sent over her territory.

4. *Severance of Diplomatic Relations:* the complete withdrawal from all formal diplomatic relations with another country. Such was the case with the Republic of China, for example, when she severed relations with Egypt when the latter recognized the mainland Chinese government.

5. *Expulsion or Recall of Ambassador:* any expulsion of an ambassador from another country, or any recalling for other than administrative reasons an ambassador to another country. This does not include any expulsion or recall involved during the severance of diplomatic relations. An instance of this measure is Venezuela's recall of her ambassador to Argentina in a dispute over rules of asylum, July 6, 1957.

6. *Expulsion or Recall of Lesser Officials:* any expulsion of diplomatic officials from another country of lesser than diplomatic rank, or any recalling for other than administrative reasons, such officials. This does not include any expulsion or recall involved in the severance of diplomatic relations. Each act of expulsion or recall is counted rather than the number of officials expelled or recalled. For example, if three diplomats from the same country are expelled at the same time for spying, this is counted as

one act. An expulsion of a lesser official was made by the Netherlands, for example, in January 22, 1957, when she expelled a U.S.S.R. embassy official and charged him with spying.

7. *Threat:* any official diplomatic communication or government statement by the executive leaders of a country which states or implies that a particular country (or group of countries) will incur certain negative sanctions if it acts in a certain way. Such negative sanctions may not only include those mentioned under "negative sanctions" above, but also severance of diplomatic relations or the use of force. Editorials containing such threats appearing in the leading government newspapers of totalitarian countries are counted. An example of a threat is the statement made by the American Secretary of State, October 17, 1957, when he warned the U.S.S.R. that an attack by her on the territory of Turkey "will bring U.S. retaliation against the territory of the U.S.S.R."

8. *Military Action:* any action by members of the regular forces of a nation which are directed against the property or citizens of another country and in which fire power is used. When the number of soldiers of a nation involved in the action equals or exceeds in number .02 percent of the population of the country, then that action is categorized as a war for that country. Military action includes any attack on coastal shipping by gunboats, any attack on a foreign plane by one's own planes or antiaircraft batteries, shelling of another's territory, or exchange of gunfire between border patrols. Such military action in terms of border clashes, for example, occurred between Afghanistan and Pakistan, 1956.

9. *War:* any military action for a particular country in which the number of its soldiers involved equals or exceeds .02 percent of its population. This number need not be actually involved in the shooting, but must be involved at the front logistically or as reserves. With respect to this definition, the Mideast War was a war for France, England, Egypt, and Israel.

10. *Troop Movement:* any rapid movement to or massing of large bodies of troops, naval units, or air squadrons in a particular area for the purpose of deterring the military action of another nation, gaining concessions, or as a show of strength. Such movement may take place within a nation, or to or between overseas bases or positions. A troop movement occurred during October 19–24, 1956, when Soviet armored units moved into Poland, Soviet troops moved to the East German border with Poland, and two Soviet cruisers stationed themselves off Danzig harbor.

11. *Mobilization:* any rapid increase in military strength through the calling up of reserves, the activation of additional military units, or the demothballing of military equipment, which is directed at another country (or group of countries). A rapid increase which is due to a change in policy consequent on the change of governments is not counted. The declaration of a state of emergency with respect to another country is categorized as

mobilization. An example of mobilization is the general activation of the Nicaraguan reserves by presidential order on May 1, 1957, with respect to a dispute with Honduras.

12. *Accusation:* any official diplomatic or governmental statement by the executive leaders of a country which makes a charge or allegation against another country (or group of countries). Denunciations are included as are derogatory statements about the character of another nation, its people, or leaders. Editorials containing such accusations appearing in the leading government newspapers of totalitarian countries are counted. An example of an accusation is Yemen's September 17, 1957 charge against England that she had attacked several Yemeni towns.

13. *Number Killed in Foreign Violence:* this is the total number of persons killed as a direct consequence of any foreign violence in which the country is involved. If Yemen and the United Kingdom, for example, are involved in military action against each other, and the total number killed in the action is 1,000, then the value on the number of killed in foreign violence for each country is 1,000. Deaths resulting from colonial violence are not counted.

APPENDIX 2.
Nations Included in Study

Afghanistan	Denmark	Irish Republic
Albania	Dominican Republic	Israel
Argentina	Ecuador	Italy
Australia	Egypt	Japan
Belgium	El Salvador	Jordan
Bolivia	Ethiopia	North Korea
Brazil	Finland	South Korea
Bulgaria	France	Lebanon
Burma	East Germany	Liberia
Cambodia	West Germany	Mexico
Canada	Greece	Nepal
Ceylon	Guatemala	Netherlands
Chile	Haiti	New Zealand
China	Honduras	Nicaragua
Republic of China	Hungary	Norway
Colombia	India	Outer Mongolia
Costa Rica	Indonesia	Pakistan
Cuba	Iran	Panama
Czechoslovakia	Iraq	Paraguay

Peru	Sweden	U.K.
Philippines	Switzerland	U.S.A.
Poland	Syria	Uruguary
Portugal	Thailand	Venezuela
Romania	Turkey	Yemen
Saudi Arabia	Union of South Africa	Yugoslavia
Spain	U.S.S.R.	

.4. *Domestic and Foreign Conflict**

JONATHAN WILKENFELD

ONE OF the most intriguing questions recently raised in the literature of international politics concerns the relationship between the domestic and foreign conflict behavior of nations. In an article written in 1963, Rummel reported the results of a factor analytic study of seventy-seven nations. One of the major findings was that "Foreign conflict behavior is generally completely unrelated to domestic conflict behavior."[1]

This initial result was further substantiated in two succeeding studies. In another study, utilizing slightly different methods of analysis, Rummel found that there was "a positive association, *albeit small*, between domestic conflict behavior and the more belligerent forms of foreign conflict behavior on the part of a country" (emphasis added).[2] Subsequently, Raymond Tanter, in a study which essentially replicated the original Rummel study for a later period, concluded: "There is a *small* relationship between 1958–1960 domestic and foreign conflict behavior which increases with a time lag" (emphasis added).[3] The significant aspect of these latter two studies is that although a relationship was found between internal and external conflict behavior, in both cases the relationship was found to be small.

These findings, particularly those of the first Rummel study, appear to run counter to well-accepted notions about the internal and external be-

*This paper combines the findings of two recent papers: Jonathan Wilkenfeld, "Domestic and Foreign Conflict Behavior of Nations," *Journal of Peace Research*, no. 1 (1968): 56–69; and idem, "Some Further Findings Regarding the Domestic and Foreign Conflict Behavior of Nations," *Journal of Peace Research*, no. 2 (1969): 147–56.

[1] R. J. Rummel, "Dimensions of Conflict Behavior Within and Between Nations," chap. 3, this volume.
[2] R. J. Rummel, "Testing Some Possible Predictors of Conflict Behavior Within and Between Nations," *Peace Research Society Papers* 1 (1963): 101–2.
[3] Raymond Tanter, "Dimensions of Conflict Behavior Within and Between Nations, 1958–1960," *Journal of Conflict Resolution* 10 (March 1966): 61–62.

havior patterns of nations. Specifically, the most widely held notion is that a nation experiencing internal disorders will tend to engage in external conflict behavior in order to divert the attention of the population from internal problems. Thus, the notion of uniting a divided people behind the banner of a common cause. For example, Richard Rosecrance in his systemic study of world politics found:

> There tends to be a correlation between international instability and the domestic insecurity of elites. This correlation does not hold in all instances. War may occur in the absence of internal instability; internal friction may occur in the absence of war. In many of the chaotic international patterns of modern times, however, the two factors were associated.[4]

In this regard, Denton has written "Civil wars preceding and contributing to international wars and international wars causing internal instability and contributing to civil wars both are intuitively satisfying hypotheses."[5]

Thus, there would appear to be some contradiction between the Rummel and Tanter findings and those of such writers as Rosecrance and Denton. This conflict, however, may be more apparent than real. It is not proposed that the mere fact that contradictory examples exist constitutes a negation of the Rummel and Tanter conclusions. Rather, it is suggested that Rummel's arrival at this conclusion was facilitated by the fact that he did not (nor was it his intention to) differentiate between the nations under consideration. Rummel's approach, therefore, in the interests of reaching generalized conclusions, may have tended to obscure any trends in the opposite direction. It is these trends, which were not of primary importance to Rummel and Tanter, which are of particular interest here.

The purpose of the present study is the reevaluation of Rummel's data in an effort both to retain and properly identify any relationships previously obscured by the method Rummel used to analyze his data. The method adopted in the present study is the rearrangement of the nations under consideration into groups, according to type of nation, in an effort to determine whether type of nation has any bearing on the relationship between internal and external conflict.

DATA AND STUDY DESIGN

The study proposed above suggests the following hypotheses:

1. Within certain groups of nations, classified according to type of nation, there tends to be a relationship between internal (domestic) conflict behavior and external (foreign) conflict behavior.

---

[4]Richard Rosecrance, *Action and Reaction in World Politics* (Boston: Little, Brown and Co., 1963), pp. 304–5.

[5]F. H. Denton, "Some Regularities in International Conflict, 1820–1949" (Santa Monica, Calif.: Rand Corporation, 1965), p. 20.

2. Within certain groups of nations, classified according to type of nation, there is a tendency for internal (domestic) conflict and external (foreign) conflict behavior to occur simultaneously, or for the occurrence of one to be followed in time by the occurrence of the other.

The two hypotheses are parallel to two stages in the research proposed. Hypothesis 1 merely infers a relationship, depending on the type of nation, between certain types of internal and external conflict behavior. Hypothesis 2 goes a good deal further, in that it postulates a temporal relationship between elements of internal and external conflict behavior, again depending on the type of nation under consideration and the nature of the conflict behavior.

The literature suggests at least two classificatory schemes that could be used to distinguish between types of nations: one suggested by Morton A. Kaplan[6] and the other by Arthur S. Banks and Phillip M. Gregg.[7] Initially, Kaplan's schema of dividing nations into four groups was considered (1) nondirective, subsystem dominant: (2) nondirective, system dominant; (3) directive, subsystem dominant; and (4) directive, system dominant.[8] However, this proved difficult to operationalize, and so the Banks-Gregg schema was adopted.

Banks and Gregg performed a Q-factor analysis of the political component of *A Cross-Polity Survey.*[9] This technique of factor analysis results in the grouping of nations according to similarities across certain political variables.[10] The actual groupings which emerged from this factor analysis were labeled *polyarchic, elitist, centrist, personalist,* and *traditional.* These groupings, with some modifications, will be adopted for purposes of re-evaluating the data collected for the original Rummel and Tanter studies.

The specific data used in the present study were collected in connection with the Dimensionality of Nations Project. Specifically, Rummel and Tanter collected extensive data on nine measures of domestic conflict behavior and thirteen measures of foreign conflict behavior for all nations in the system during the period 1955-60.[11] These domestic and foreign conflict data were separately factor analyzed in order to identify the distinctive clusters of variables. Prior to the analysis, variables underwent transformations, as reported in table 1. In addition, factor scores were calculated

---

[6]Morton A. Kaplan, *System and Process in International Politics* (New York: John Wiley and Sons, 1957).

[7]Arthur S. Banks and Phillip M. Gregg, "Grouping Political Systems: Q-Factor Analysis of *A Cross Polity Survey*," *The American Behavioral Scientist* 9 (November 1965): 3-6.

[8]Kaplan, *System and Process*, pp. 54-55.

[9]Arthur S. Banks and Robert B. Textor, *A Cross Polity Survey* (Cambridge, Mass: MIT Press, 1963).

[10]Banks and Gregg, "Grouping Political Systems," p. 3.

[11]Rummel, "Dimensions of Conflict Behavior"; Tanter, "Dimensions of Conflict Behavior."

Table 1.   Key to Raw Data Transformations

Domestic Conflict Measures

Class 1	*Class 2*	*Class 3*
Assassinations	General strikes	Number killed in domestic
Guerrilla wars	Purges	violence
Major government crises	Riots	
Revolutions	Demonstrations	

Foreign Conflict Measures

Class 1	*Class 2*	*Class 3*
Severance of diplomatic	Antiforeign	Accusations
relations	demonstrations	Number killed in foreign
Expulsions or recalls—	Negative sanctions	violence
ambassadors	Protests	
Military actions	Expulsions or recalls—	
Wars	lesser officials	
Troop movements	Threats	
Mobilizations		

Class 1—data unchanged

Class 2—data transformed by grouping according to geometric progesssion:

Raw Data	Group Value
0	0
1	1
2–3	2
4–7	3
8–15	4
16–32	5
33–64	6

Class 3—data transformed according to the following:

$$\log_{10} (\text{number} + 1)$$

for the nations on a yearly basis. It is these factor scores, one per dimension per nation per year, that will be used as the data in computing correlations between the dimensions of domestic and foreign conflict behavior.

Tables 2 and 3 summarize the results of the factor analyses performed. These results are also compared with the results obtained by Rummel and Tanter in the earlier analyses.[12] With regard to domestic conflict, it was decided, using the eigenvalue-one criterion, to extract two factors on the orthogonal rotation. These factors are very similar to those found by Tanter in his analysis of the 1958–60 portion of the data.

[12]The factor analyses performed here used the Biomedical Computer Programs BMD03M. To keep this analysis parallel to the earlier Rummel and Tanter analyses, communalities of 1.00 were used for the diagonal elements.

Table 2. Factor Analysis of Domestic Conflict Behavior Data, 1955–60
(Orthogonal rotation; Comparison with Rummel and Tanter solutions)

		Internal War			Turmoil				h^2	
	T2	W1	R2	R3	T1	W2	R1	T	W	R
Assassinations	.41	.30	-.03	(.66)	(.59)	.47	(.59)	.52	.31	.78
Guerrilla wars	(.74)	(.72)	.28	(.90)	.35	.09	-.04	.66	.52	.90
Government crises	.47	(.53)	.21	-.04	(.53)	.35	(.60)	.50	.40	.41
Revolutions	(.89)	(.80)	(.85)	.13	.09	.12	.09	.80	.65	.75
Strikes	.06	.25	(.60)	.05	(.79)	(.62)	(.52)	.63	.44	.63
Purges	(.68)	(.53)	(.71)	.03	.01	.15	.32	.46	.30	.60
Riots	.21	.23	.31	.09	(.83)	(.81)	(.79)	.73	.71	.73
Demonstrations	.10	.02	.17	.19	(.86)	(.85)	(.85)	.75	.72	.79
Domestic killed	(.78)	(.67)	(.75)	.42	.37	.42	.23	.74	.63	.79
Percent Common Variance	49.2	50.5	37.6	23.4	50.8	49.5	39.0	100.0	100.0	100.0
Percent Total Variance	31.7	26.3	26.7	16.6	32.7	25.8	27.7	64.4	52.0	70.8

Parenthesis indicates loading ≥ .50.
Factors labeled W are Wilkenfeld's factors. Factors labeled R are Rummel's 1955–57 factors. Factors labeled T are Tanter's 1958–60 factors.

Table 3. Factor Analysis of Foreign Conflict Behavior Data, 1955–60
(Orthogonal rotation; Comparison with Rummel and Tanter solutions)

	War			Belligerency			Diplomatic			h^2		
	T2	W1	R1	T3	W2	R3	T1	W3	R2	T	W	R
Severance relations	.09	.14	.13	(.82)	(.64)	(.82)	−.06	−.32	−.17	.68	.54	.71
Expelled/recalled— ambassadors	.18	.09	−.16	−.05	−.03	−.08	(.67)	(.55)	(.66)	.49	.31	.47
Military action	(.74)	(.62)	(.65)	.02	.17	(.57)	.28	.18	−.14	.63	.45	.77
War	(.83)	(.80)	(.85)	−.09	−.04	−.10	.02	.16	.15	.70	.67	.75
Troop movements	.32	.08	.47	.26	.09	.28	.46	(.62)	(.59)	.38	.40	.64
Mobilizations	(.58)	(.56)	(.60)	.19	.25	.35	.34	−.05	−.08	.48	.38	.49
F.-demonstrations	.03	.21	.13	(.64)	(.56)	(.63)	.34	.13	.42	.52	.38	.60
Negative sanctions	.22	.16	.20	.26	(.64)	(.64)	(.58)	.21	.41	.46	.48	.62
Protests	.26	.34	(.62)	−.06	.26	.22	(.79)	(.66)	.49	.70	.62	.67
Expelled/recalled—lesser	−.29	−.23	.33	.21	(.56)	.08	(.59)	.38	(.60)	.47	.52	.48
Threats	.35	.40	(.65)	.23	.48	.48	(.70)	(.51)	.43	.66	.66	.84
Accusations	.46	.47	(.70)	.09	.42	.41	(.67)	(.50)	.35	.66	.65	.79
Foreign killed	(.76)	(.77)	(.87)	.23	.09	.19	.21	.21	.10	.67	.65	.80
Percent Common Variance	37.7	38.4	46.2	18.9	30.2	29.1	43.3	30.0	24.6	100.0	100.0	100.0
Percent Total Variance	21.8	19.8	30.7	10.1	15.6	19.3	25.2	15.5	16.3	57.9	51.6	66.4

Parenthesis indicates loading ≥ .50.
Factors labeled W are Wilkenfeld's factors. Factor labeled R are Rummel's 1955–57 factors. Factors labeled T are Tanter's 1958–60 factors.

The first factor, turmoil, contains demonstrations, riots, strikes, and assassinations. Demonstrations have the highest loading on this factor, as was the case with the earlier analyses. As both Rummel and Tanter have pointed out, the turmoil factor represents an unorganized, spontaneous type of conflict behavior.[13] In general, these are the least violent of the domestic conflict variables. Both the Tanter turmoil factor and the present one account for 50 percent of the common variance, while this factor accounts for 39 percent of the common variance on the Rummel three-factor solution.

The second domestic factor, internal war, is quite similar to the second factor extracted by Tanter, and combines the revolutionary and subversive dimensions found by Rummel. This factor groups revolutions, number killed in domestic conflict, guerrilla warfare, purges, and major government crises. This represents an organized, violent type of domestic conflict behavior. Once again, this factor accounts for 50 percent of the common variance on both the Tanter solution and the present one. The two Rummel factors which are combined in internal war account for a total of 61 percent of the common variance.

Table 3 presents the factor analysis of the foreign conflict behavior variables. For the diplomatic factor, there appears to be a fairly close correspondence between the present solution and that reported by Tanter. The overlapping variables are expulsions and recalls of ambassadors, protests, threats, and accusations. In both analyses, the protest variable had the highest loading.

A comparison of the present diplomatic factor with that extracted by Rummel produces some interesting observations. Rummel's diplomatic factor includes only expulsions and recalls of ambassadors and lesser officials, and troop movements. In the present factor, three additional variables are included: protests, threats, and accusations. An intuitive argument can be made for the fact that these three variables, which had been part of Rummel's war dimension, measure foreign conflict behavior less violent in nature than the other four variables loading on the war dimension, and are indeed more characteristic of diplomatic conflict behavior.

Turning now to the war dimension, we note a perfect correspondence between the present factor and Tanter's. These factors include wars, number killed in foreign conflict, military actions, and mobilizations. The order of loadings of these variables on both factors is preserved, with wars still the highest loading variable. Furthermore, these are the same four variables that remain in the Rummel war dimension, after protests, threats, and accusations (the three variables moved over to the diplomatic factor) have

[13]Rummel, "Dimensions of Conflict Behavior," p. 80; Tanter, "Dimensions of Conflict Behavior," p. 50.

been excluded. With the slight exception of wars and number killed in foreign conflict, the order of the loadings has been preserved. This new war factor has some intuitive appeal, since it now includes only those variables characteristic of violent, warlike conflict behavior.

The belligerency factor extracted here includes severence of diplomatic relations, negative sanctions, antiforeign demonstrations, and expulsions and recalls of lesser officials. With the exception of the latter variable, the factor corresponds to the belligerency dimension extracted by Rummel. The Tanter belligerency factor includes only severence of diplomatic relations and antiforeign demonstrations, both of which are included in the Rummel factor as well as the present one.

Some of the differences between the present analyses and those performed by Rummel and Tanter may be partly explained by differences in data compilation. In the Rummel analysis, data on each variable were summed for 1955–57, for each nation, after appropriate transformations had been performed. Thus, Rummel had one composite score for each variable, for a three-year period. This same procedure was followed by Tanter in his analysis of the 1958–60 data. In the present case, the primary interest was in yearly data, so that a time-lag analysis could be performed. Thus, the data were compiled on a yearly basis, after transformations, and a score for each nation on each variable for each of the six years was obtained. In effect, each nation was treated as six separate cases, so that while Rummel and Tanter used 77 and 83 nations and cases,[14] the present analysis includes 74 × 6 or 444 cases.

Since the Rummel-Tanter and the Banks-Gregg studies were undertaken independently and for much different purposes, combining the categories from one with the data compiled from the other could only be done after certain modifications were introduced. First, the periods covered by the studies do not completely coincide. The Rummel and Tanter data cover the six years between 1955 and 1960, while *A Cross-Polity Survey* utilized data through March 1963.[15] This in part accounts for the fact that Rummel's study included 77 nations, Tanter's 83 nations, Banks and Gregg's 115 nations.

Since it was decided to use only the nations originally included in the Rummel study, the discrepancy in number of nations in the two studies necessitated a modification in the groupings. From the polyarchic group, 9 of the original 44 nations included by Banks and Gregg had to be dropped,

---

[14]For the period 1955–57, 77 nations met Rummel's definition of a nation (Rummel "Dimensions of Conflict Behavior," p. 73); for 1958–60, 83 nations met this definition. Of the original 77 nations in the Rummel study, three nations were excluded in the Banks and Gregg study; Syria and Yemen were excluded, since Tanter included them together with Egypt in the U.A.R., and did not collect data on them individually.

[15]No beginning date for the data collection is given, and it is safe to conclude that the date varied from nation to nation.

since they had not been included in the Rummel study. Similarly, 2 of the 24 centrist nations were dropped. The personalist group remained intact. In the elitist group, however, composed in the main of African nations newly emerged in the late 1950s and 1960s, only 4 of 30 remained. Finally,

Table 4.   Nation Groupings

Personalist		Iran	.48[b]
Guatemala	.78	Pakistan	.48[a]
El Salvador	.68	Cambodia	.47[a]
Panama	.68	Burma	.41[a]
Peru	.68		
Honduras	.67	Polyarchic	
Argentina	.66	Norway	−.92
Korea Republic	.65	Ireland	−.92
Nicaragua	.64	West Germany	−.92
Ecuador	.59	Sweden	−.92
Lebanon	.59	Australia	−.92
Paraguay	.58	Netherlands	−.91
Iraq	.57	Denmark	−.91
Haiti	.53	New Zealand	−.91
Thailand	.50	Finland	−.90
Indonesia	.35[a]	Switzerland	−.87
		Italy	−.86
Centrist		U.K.	−.86
Bulgaria	.90	U.S.	−.86
Albania	.89	Canada	−.85
East Germany	.88	Belgium	−.84
Hungary	.86	Costa Rica	−.81
Mongolia	.86	Uruguay	−.81
Czechoslovakia	.86	Japan	−.79
North Korea	.85	Greece	−.77
U.S.S.R.	.85	Israel	−.75
Rumania	.84	France	−.75
Poland	.83	Chile	−.74
Yugoslavia	.82	Dominican Republic	−.74
Spain	.80	Philippines	−.73
Portugal	.77	Turkey	−.72
China	.76	Colombia	−.66
Cuba	.69	Mexico	−.65
Afghanistan	.64	Venezuela	−.63
Saudi Arabia	.63	India	−.62
U.A.R.	.62	Brazil	−.62
Liberia	.58	Bolivia	−.57
Jordan	.58	South Africa	−.55
Nepal	.53	Ceylon	−.50
Ethiopia	.52		

[a] Transferred from elitist group.
[b] Transferred from traditional group.

2 of the 4 traditional nations had to be dropped. In order to overcome this difficulty, what remained of the elitist and traditional groups were collapsed into the other three groups, on the basis of their next highest loadings (see notes to table 4). The final groupings and their loadings are given in table 4.

Stage 1

At this point it was determined to analyze the data in two slightly different forms, corresponding to tests of the two hypotheses suggested earlier. These two steps will be referred to hereafter as stages 1 and 2. In the nature of a pretest of hypothesis 1, it was determined that a test would be performed using the factor scores that emerged from the factor analysis performed by Rummel on the 1955–57 data. A factor score is the value each nation has on each of the dimensions extracted. It may be thought of as a composite of those measures most strongly associated with a particular factor.[16] The calculations performed in the present study were the correlations between the factor scores of all nine possible pairs of three domestic and three foreign conflict behavior dimensions. The results of this analysis are presented in table 5.

Table 5.   Analysis of Rummel Factor Scores, 1955–57

Domestic Conflict Dimension	Foreign Conflict Dimension	Personalist ($N = 15$)	Centrist ($N = 26$)	Polyarchic ($N = 33$)
Turmoil	War	−.29	.28	.39[a]
Turmoil	Diplomatic	.66[c]	.40[a]	−.02
Turmoil	Belligerency	.10	.43[a]	.27
Revolutionary	War	−.20	.55[c]	−.09
Revolutionary	Diplomatic	.49	.21	−.10
Revolutionary	Belligerency	−.27	.33	.45[b]
Subversive	War	−.16	−.08	−.08
Subversive	Diplomatic	.55[a]	−.04	−.10
Subversive	Belligerency	−.19	−.12	.08

[a]$p < .05$.
[b]$p < .01$.
[c]$p < .005$.

The results indicate that for the personalist group, composed primarily of Latin American nations, any kind of internal conflict behavior appears to be related to the "diplomatic" external conflict dimension. For the centrist group, composed primarily of socialist nations, the important relationships mostly involve the "turmoil" type of domestic conflict behavior.

[16]Rummel, "Dimensions of Conflict Behavior," pp. 84–85.

Finally, for the polyarchic group, consisting for the most part of economically developed Western nations, the relationships are between "turmoil" and "war" and "revolutionary" and "belligerency."

A preliminary conclusion seems to be warranted on the basis of the above results. It appears that the grouping of nations in the manner attempted here does in fact isolate relationships that were present but obscured in both the Rummel and Tanter analyses. This may be seen from the fact that pairs of dimensions for which relationships were found between internal and external conflict behavior do not repeat themselves across all other groups. Thus, for the centrist group, in the "revolutionary" and "war" pairing a high correlation was obtained. However, low negative correlations for this pair were obtained for the other two groups. When the nations are taken together, it is easily seen how this important relationship was obscured.

The above results may be viewed as those of a preliminary and exploratory study. The main function of this initial stage was to determine whether, by breaking down the nations studied by Rummel and Tanter into groups, any relationships were found. Having determined this, we now feel justified in going one step further, both in the data used and in the methods of analysis, to develop the theoretical implications of the results. To this stage we now turn.

Stage 2

While stage 1 proposed a correlation analysis of the factor scores which emerged from the Rummel study of the years 1955–57, stage 2, which specifically tests hypothesis 2, proposes the use of yearly factor scores. Furthermore, the data now incorporates the three years added by Tanter, and thus spans the entire period between 1955 and 1960.

The use of yearly data in this stage facilitated the specific testing of hypothesis 2. Thus, it was now possible to investigate the possibility of time lags as a factor in the relation between the occurrence of internal conflict behavior and the occurrence of external conflict behavior. The data were tested not only in order to determine whether there was a relationship between the two for the same year, but also in an effort to determine whether one- and two-year time lags were appropriate in certain cases. Furthermore, time lags of one and two years both from the occurrence of internal to the occurrence of external, and vice versa, were attempted. This possibility was suggested by Denton, in the passage quoted earlier.[17] As will be noted from tables, 6, 7, and 8, negative lags (-1 and -2) indicate that the lag was from foreign conflict in year n to domestic conflict in year $n + 1$ or $n + 2$. Similarly, positive lags ($+1$ and $+2$) indicate lags from internal in year n to external in year $n + 1$ and $n + 2$. A zero lag

[17]Denton, "Some Regularities in International Conflict."

indicates the analysis in which both occurred in the same year. The case of the zero lag is roughly equivalent to the analysis performed in stage 1.

Finally, a specific statistical device was employed in order to deal with a large number of cases for each correlation. For example, for the poly-archic group, composed of 33 nations, when investigating the occurrence of both internal and external conflict behavior in the same year, not only 1955 internal to 1955 external were taken, but also 1956–56 . . . 1960–60. Thus, rather than having only 33 cases for one year, we now have 198 cases for six years. This method contributed greatly to the significance levels of the re-sults obtained, as well as to their reliability. The results for stage 2 are presented in tables 6, 7, and 8.

Personalist Group. This group is composed of 15 nations. Table 4 indicated that this group is composed primarily of Latin American nations (10 out of 15). To a large degree, the nations that make up this group are dictatorships, but they differ from the centrist group of dictatorships in degree of centralization.

Table 6. Personalist Group

	lag = −2 (N = 60)	lag = −1 (N = 75)	lag = 0 (N = 90)	lag = +1 (N = 75)	lag = +2 (N = 60)
Tur–War	.17	−.14	−.18	−.03	−.02
Tur–Dip	−.05	.26[a]	.24[a]	−.02	−.05
Tur–Bel	.11	.14	.11	.05	.17
Int–War	.15	−.08	−.08	−.15	−.30[a]
Int–Dip	.00	−.14	.18	.10	.00
Int–Bel	.29[a]	.37[b]	.16	.28[a]	.29[a]

Negative lags indicate the occurrence of foreign before domestic, and positive lags indi-cate the occurrence of domestic before foreign. Lag = 0 measures both indicators for the same year.

[a] $p < .05$.
[b] $p < .01$.

The results for the personalist group are presented in table 5. This table exhibits a rather interesting relationship between the domestic factor in-ternal war (revolutions, guerrilla warfare, number killed in domestic conflict, major government crises, and purges), and the foreign factor bel-ligerency (severence of diplomatic relations, negative sanctions, antifor-eign demonstrations, and expulsion and recall of lesser officials). A peculiar aspect of this relationship is that, with the exception of the lag = 0 case, all lags from domestic to foreign and from foreign to domestic pro-duce significant correlations, and varying from 8 to 13 percent of the vari-ance explained. While these results are not particularly spectacular, they do indicate an interesting interaction between these two types of conflict behavior in that the internal and external conflict behavior patterns involved here are mutually reinforcing in some way.

The only case in which a significant correlation appears for the lag = 0 case is that between the domestic factor turmoil, i.e. demonstrations, riots, general strikes, and assassinations, and the foreign factor diplomatic, which includes protests, troop movements, expulsion and recall of ambassadors, threats, and accusations. For the lag = − 1 case, where diplomatic conflict behavior precedes by one year the occurrence of turmoil, a significant correlation is also found.

A final result of some interest is the negative relationship found between the domestic factor internal war and the foreign factor war, i.e., wars, number killed in foreign conflict, military actions, and mobilizations. This occurs in the case of a two-year lag between the occurrence of domestic conflict and the occurrence of foreign conflict. Aside from this one negative correlation, war is apparently unrelated to either the turmoil or internal war factors. In part this may be so because in the case of the personalist nations, none was involved in a war during the six-year period under consideration. That wars were the highest loading variable in the war factor may account in part for this lack of relationship. Perhaps a more fundamental conclusion is that for the personalist group, the type of conflict behavior included in the war factor is of such a serious nature that it is rarely systematically related to any sort of domestic conflict behavior which may be occurring within these nations. This sort of pattern involving the war factor does not reappear in either the centrist or the polyarchic groups.

Centrist Group. This group is composed of 26 nations. Twelve of the 26 were socialist during the years under consideration, while an additional 4 are Middle Eastern. The nations exhibit both dictatorial and highly centralized patterns of leadership.

Perhaps the most interesting feature of the results obtained for the centrist group (table 7) concerns the time lags. Thus, in terms of hypothesis 2, for the centrist group it appears never to be the case that the occurrence of external conflict behavior of any sort will be accompanied by the occurrence of internal conflict behavior in a later period. On the other hand, the results clearly indicate that both types of domestic conflict behavior tend to be associated with the subsequent occurrence of foreign conflict behavior.

If in fact we can isolate what appears to be a trend in the centrist group, from the occurrence of internal conflict behavior to the occurrence of external conflict behavior, how can we account for the fact that in some cases a two-year lag occurs, while in others a one-year lag occurs, while in still others no time lag at all is apparent? A centrist nation experiencing internal conflict behavior may not be able to respond in full force and immediately with external conflict behavior. Thus, although an initial re-

Table 7.   Centrist Group

	lag = −2 (N = 104)	lag = −1 (N = 130)	lag = 0 (N = 156)	lag = +1 (N = 130)	lag = +2 (N = 104)
Tur–War	−.08	.02	.05	−.16	−.14
Tur–Dip	−.05	.08	.03	.03	.04
Tur–Bel	.06	.03	.12	.28[b]	.14
Int–War	.11	.15	.31[c]	.32[c]	.43[c]
Int–Dip	−.07	−.17	−.13	−.01	.00
Int–Bel	−.11	.02	.12	.09	.15

Negative lags indicate the occurrence of foreign before domestic, and positive lags indicate the occurrence of domestic before foreign. Lag = 0 measures both indicators for the same year.

[a] $p < .05$.
[b] $p < .01$.
[c] $p < .001$.

sponse appears to be made in some cases, it is really only one or two years later that the nation is in a position, in a sense, to act out its internal problems externally. During the two-year period, although some response is made, it may be postulated that the main attention of the leadership is focused on the task of quelling domestic unrest. Only after this has been accomplished to some degree may the regime attempt to divert the attention of the population from its domestic problems. In this sense, we may have isolated some relevant findings regarding the ability of a centrist nation to respond to internal stress.

The contention that within the centrist group external conflict behavior is a tool in the hands of the leadership for diverting attention from internal disorders is further substantiated by the results obtained for the − 1 and − 2 lags. Since it is apparently never the case that external conflict behavior can lead to domestic unrest, the use of foreign conflict behavior as an "attention-diverter" can never endanger the regime in terms of its corresponding effect on domestic factors, as it did in the case of the personalist group and as will be seen in the polyarchic group. If foreign conflict behavior apparently never leads to domestic conflict behavior, then it may be engaged in without the fear of domestic repercussions.

Polyarchic Group.   This group is composed of 33 nations. It will be noted from table 3 that virtually all of the nations correlating above .80 with this group are economically developed Western nations. Furthermore, those nations with low loadings (below .80) usually exhibit at least one of the above characteristics.

The results for the polyarchic group are presented in table 8. The first thing to be noted here is that the domestic conflict factor internal war is unrelated to any sort of foreign conflict. The only exception here is between internal war and diplomatic, for the lag = 0 case, in which a rather low

Table 8. Polyarchic Group

	lag = −2 (N = 132)	lag = −1 (N = 165)	lag = 0 (N = 198)	lag = +1 (N = 165)	lag = +2 (N = 132)
Tur–War	.17	.12	.21[b]	.13	.32[c]
Tur–Dip	.19[a]	.21[b]	.23[b]	.13	.19[a]
Tur–Bel	.16	.18[a]	.23[b]	.19[a]	.07
Int–War	.00	−.05	−.04	.00	.00
Int–Dip	−.11	−.08	−.16[a]	−.13	−.08
Int–Bel	−.15	−.03	.02	.00	−.09

Negative lags indicate the occurrence of foreign before domestic, and positive lags indicate the occurrence of domestic before foreign. Lag = 0 measures both indicators for the same year.
[a] $p < .05$.
[b] $p < .01$.
[c] $p < .001$.

negative correlation was found. A possible explanation for this may be found in the variables loading on the internal war factor, i.e., revolutions, guerrilla warfare, number killed in domestic conflict, major government crises, and purges. Perhaps for the nations classified as polyarchic, these manifestations of domestic conflict behavior, when they occur at all, are not conducive to producing a foreign conflict reaction. Similarly, this type of domestic conflict is not employed as a reaction to the types of foreign conflict in which these nations may be engaged.

The domestic conflict factor turmoil appears to be related in various ways to all three of the foreign conflict factors. Regarding the relationship between turmoil and war, the negative lags do not produce any significant relationships, while the lag = 0 case and the lag = + 2 case are statistically significant. In the case of the turmoil–belligerency pairs, both positive and negative lags, as well as the lag = 0 case, appear to produce significant results, although the correlation coefficients are quite small.

CONCLUSION

The results obtained in the analysis performed here indicate confirmation of both hypotheses 1 and 2. Thus, not only was a relationship between internal and external conflict behavior found, but the indication is that in some cases a time lag is involved. This statement should now be qualified by indicating the degree of interaction between the two key variables, i.e., type of nation and dimension of conflict. Clearly, as we shift our attention from the personalist, to the centrist, and finally to the polyarchic group, the particular dimensions of conflict behavior that are related change. Indeed, no one particular relationship exists between any pair of internal and external conflict dimensions which holds for all groups equally well.

In the section devoted to the centrist group, we have already examined some possible explanations for the outstanding characteristic of this group, i.e., that a significant relationship is virtually never found when external conflict behavior occurs before internal. In this connection, it was felt that in centrist type nations, in which centralized control of most aspects of life is the primary characteristic, the leadership does not have to concern itself with internal repercussions of external acts.

In the personalist and polyarchic groups, the pattern of relationships is less clear-cut. Here we find some significant relationships for virtually every time lag, from internal to external and from external to internal. Perhaps even more significant was the finding that in several cases a pattern of mutual reinforcement appears in which for a certain pair of internal and external conflict measures, internal appears to precede external while at the same time external appears to precede internal. This is of course in sharp contrast to the finding for the centrist group.

These findings may lead us to some interesting conclusions regarding the types of nations with which we are dealing and their basic decision-making processes. On the one hand, we have highly centralized nations, in which decisions concerning foreign conflict behavior are in some cases generated by the types of internal conflict behavior the nation is experiencing, but in which these external conflict decisions are made in relative isolation from possible internal reactions. On the other hand, in the polyarchic nations, and to a lesser extent in the personalist nations, neither internal nor external actions are taken in isolation from each other.

An additional factor analytic study by Gregg and Banks[18] may help us gain some insights into the phenomena isolated here. In that study, the same variables used in the Q-factor analysis were employed, but the 68 Cross Polity Survey variables were grouped. The first factor, which accounted for 24.6 percent of the variance, was labeled "access." Gregg and Banks note that in the access factor, the following dichotomies are apparent, based on high positive vs. low negative loadings: hierarchical as opposed to competitive bargaining processes; consolidated as opposed to distributed authority and force; executive and single-party politics as opposed to legislative and group politics; totalitarian restrictions as opposed to institutionalized openness of political channels.[19] Table 9 presents the factor loadings of the various areal groupings on this factor. As we would expect, given the nature of the variables concerned, and with particular reference to the types of dichotomies noted above, the East European areal group has the highest negative loading on this factor, followed

[18]Phillip M. Gregg and Arthur S. Banks, "Dimensions of Political Systems: Factor Analysis of *A Cross Polity Survey*," *American Political Science Review* 59 (September 1965): 602–14.
[19]Ibid, p. 607.

Table 9. Distribution of Areal Groupings on Access Factor

Areal Group	Loading
Advanced Western areal group	.45
Latin American areal group	.21
African areal group	−.05
North African, Middle Eastern areal group	−.06
Asian areal group	−.16
East European areal group	−.58

by the Asian and North African–Middle Eastern areal groups. Virtually all the nations loading on the centrist group fall into these areal groupings. On the other hand, the Advanced Western areal group and the Latin American areal group load positively on this factor. These groups are similar in makeup to the polyarchic and personalist groups, respectively.

The results of the Gregg and Banks analysis may give us some clue as to the possible explanation for some of our results. We have noted that the centrist nations exhibit certain patterns that are quite different from those of the personalist and polyarchic groups. The differing factor loadings on the access factor may explain this difference. This is particularly true when we keep in mind the types of variables from which the access factor was created.

Building upon the base provided by the findings obtained here, one area clearly indicated as potentially fruitful for further research is the investigation of the behavior of particular nations involved as participants in particular international conflict situations. Specifically, the confirmation of hypotheses 1 and 2 for certain groups and certain dimensions should give us additional information on which to judge the behavior of nations. What is being proposed here is that nations in the international system do not behave solely on the basis of the givens of the international situation. Depending upon the type of nation, we must look beyond the international sphere to the internal situation in the participating nation in order to determine that nations's reactions.

What we are in essence suggesting is a new look at the notion of "rational" behavior on the part of a nation engaged in conflict. It would appear that the idea of a nation making a correct or an incorrect choice, given the international situation, must be expanded to include the whole sphere of internal politics. Only when we possess all the facts that contribute to a particular response on the part of a nation may we make judgments pertaining to the correctness or rationality of the choice. The hypotheses proposed and tested in this study may contribute to formulating a more comprehensive theory of international conflict.

.5. The Conflict Environment of Nations: A Study of Conflict Inputs To Nations in 1963*

WARREN R. PHILLIPS

THIS RESEARCH was designed to answer three specific questions about the conflict behavior of nations:

1. What are the dimensions of variation in conflict received by nations from the international environment?

2. To what degree is a nation's conflict activity a response to conflict it receives from the environment?

3. Which characteristics of nations explain deviations from a simple stimulus-response model of conflict behavior?

The work reported here is designed to produce systematic information about contemporary patterns of conflict behavior. It is based upon the belief that behavior begets behavior. To this end, data have been collected on several measures of foreign conflict behavior for all nations exhibiting conflict in 1963. These data were organized into two matrices. The first is an input matrix in which each observation represents the total amount of conflict behavior received by a nation regardless of sender. The second is an output matrix in which each observation is a record of a nation's total conflict behavior. The data in each matrix were intercorrelated and factor-analyzed. The factors derived were then compared by use of canonical regression techniques to assess the degree of correlation between inputs and outputs of nations. The residuals (conflict variance independent of this relationship) from the analysis of conflict sent and received were then regressed

*An earlier version of this paper was presented at the annual meeting of the American Political Science Association, Los Angeles, California, September 1970. The author wishes to thank R. J. Rummel, Richard Van Atta, and Jonathan Wilkenfeld for comments on an earlier draft. This paper was prepared in connection with research supported in part by the Advanced Research Projects Agency, ARPA Order No. 1063, monitored by the Office of Naval Research, Contract No. N00014-67-A0387-0003, and by a University of Hawaii Intramural Research Grant.

on a set of twenty-two variables of national characteristics representing the basic patterns of attributes found for 1963.

CONFLICT INTERACTION

The focus of my interest in conflict is on interaction—the interplay of conduct—and, therefore, on conflict processes. In the current terminology of the international relations field, as exemplified by the works of McClelland, Rosenau, Singer, Snyder, and Sondermann, the emphasis is on the *workings* of the international conflict system more than on the analysis of foreign policies.[1] I wish to bring into focus a large number of the aspects, modes and functions of diplomatic-military exchanges between nations.

Other research efforts have concentrated quite heavily on conflict behavior. Previous work has provided a good deal of information about conflict in the international system over time,[2] between select pairs of nations over time,[3] or for all nations at a single point in time.[4] The latter works have considered the behavior of nations toward the environment (bynation behavior), the behavior of nations aimed at specific opponents (dyadic be-

[1]Charles A. McClelland, *Theory and the International System* (New York: Macmillan Co., 1966); James N. Rosenau, *Calculated Control as a Unifying Concept in the Study of International Politics and Foreign Policy*, Research Report No. 15, (Princeton, N.J.: Center of International Studies, 1963); J. David Singer, "The Level of Analysis Problem in International Relations," *World Politics* 14 (1961): 77–92; Richard C. Snyder, *Decision-Making as an Approach to the Study of International Relations* (Princeton, N.J.: Foreign Policy Analysis Project, 1964); Fred A. Sondermann, "The Linkage Between Foreign Policy and International Politics," in *International Politics and Foreign Policy*, ed. James N. Rosenau (New York: Free Press, 1961).

[2]J. David Singer and Melvin Small, "Alliance Aggregation and the Onset of War, 1815–1945," in *Quantitative International Politics: Insights and Evidence*, ed. J. David Singer (New York: Free Press, 1968), pp. 247–86; Frank H. Denton and Warren R. Phillips, "Some Patterns in the History of Violence," *Journal of Conflict Resolution* 12 (June 1968): 182–95; Quincy Wright, *A Study of War* (Chicago: University of Chicago Press, 1942); Lewis F. Richardson, *Arms and Insecurity* (Homewood, Ill.: Boxwood Press, 1960); J. E. Moyal, "The Distribution of Wars in Time," *Journal of the Royal Statistical Society* 112 (1949): 446–49; and Richard Rosecrance, *Action and Reaction in World Politics: International Systems in Perspective* (Boston: Little, Brown and Co., 1963).

[3]Charles A. McClelland et al., "The Communist Chinese Performance in Crisis and Non-Crisis: Quantitative Studies of the Taiwan Straits Confrontation," (China Lake, Calif.: Behavioral Sciences Group, Naval Ordinance Test Station, 1965); Charles A. McClelland, "Access to Berlin: The Quantity and Variety of Events, 1948–1963," in Singer, ed., *Quantitative International Politics*, pp. 159–86; Allen S. Whiting, *China Crosses the Yalu* (Santa Monica, Calif.: Rand Corporation R-356-PR, 1960); Paul Smoker, "A Time Series Analysis of Sino-Indian Relations," *Journal of Conflict Resolution* 8 (June 1969): 172–91; Ole R. Holsti, Robert C. North, and Richard A. Brody, "Perception and Action in the 1914 Crisis," in Singer, ed., *Quantitative International Politics*, pp. 123–58.

[4]R. J. Rummel, "Some Attributes and Behavioral Patterns of Nations," *Journal of Peace Research* 2 (1967): 196–206; idem, "Field Theory and Indicators of International Behavior" (Paper presented at the annual meeting of the American Political Science Association, New York, September 1969); Raymond Tanter, "Dimensions of Conflict Behavior Within and Between Nations, 1958–1960," *Journal of Conflict Resolution* 10 (1966): 41–64.

havior), or the total behavior of all nations for a given time period (systemic behavior). In contrast, I will investigate the conflict inputs to each nation (by object behavior). I will do this by making each observation the total conflict behavior received by a specific object nation.

Recently a conceptual framework which incorporates the concerns of this analysis into a larger milieu has been gaining acceptance in international relations. Rosenau[5] suggests that we look at the environmental linkages with the internal processes of nation states. For Rosenau the "environment of a polity is conceived to be equivalent to the same phenomena as comprise any international system of which the polity is a component part."[6] For the purpose of this study, the relevant environment is the international conflict system. For simplicity, consider a three-nation system as in figure 1. Each pair of actors is engaging in interaction. The conflict ex-

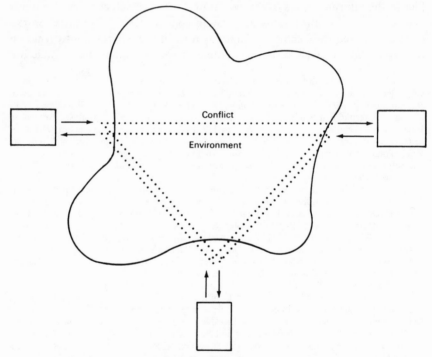

Figure 1.   Three-Nation System

changed between nations is the conflict environment of nations and the total conflict behavior received by a specific nation is the conflict it receives from the international environment.

[5]James Rosenau, ed., *Linkage Politics* (New York: Free Press, 1968).
[6]Ibid., p. 45.

Karl Deutsch has suggested that the highest of a nation's basic functions is its ability for self-transformation, "to respond to events in its environment in new ways, or at least in different and more rewarding ways."[7] It is assumed in this paper that nations, attempting to cope with the conflict received, will pattern their responses in ways they believe most rewarding. Thus, changes in the conflict environment of nations influence either the foreign policy decision-making process within nations or the nation's conflict behavior with specific opponents.[8]

But international relations is more than a tennis match in which each player responds to his opponent's service. There are forces at work within a nation which explain that nation's over-or underreaction to specific conflict experiences. These forces are considered to be a function of the national attributes of these nations. Exactly which combinations of attributes influence overreaction to a specific conflict strategy will be investigated in this report.

Rosenau asserts that we should consider the environment as a set of variables rather than as constraints in the functioning of polities. This approach would seem to call for the delineation of specific patterns of conflict. The development of a series of variables, each independent of the other, would provide a means of testing linkages between environmental inputs and national responses. The present study will consider these environmental inputs as influences acting upon the normal demand-response sequences of nations involved in conflict. Thus, the amount and type of conflict a nation is receiving from the international system should influence its readiness to initiate new conflict behavior. The linkage between conflict sent and received on the part of specific nations will be made by comparing the total conflict behavior aimed at a specific nation with the conflict that a nation initiates to the system.

The existence of a relationship between simple stimulus-response theories and the concept of linkage suggested by Rosenau is supported by arguments from psychology. Charles Osgood,[9] in a review of analytical approaches to psychology, pointed out that all of psychology is a study of what goes into an organism or organization (stimulus) and what comes out (response). The task for all social scientists is the explanation and prediction of relationships among these two sets of observables, stimuli and responses, and to do this they must make certain assumptions about what

[7]Karl W. Deutsch, *The Analysis of International Relations* (Englewood Cliffs, N.J.: Prentice-Hall, 1968), p. 17.

[8]"States are political systems operating within an environment of other systems to which they are adapting and responding." John W. Burton, *Conflict and Communication: The Use of Controlled Communication in International Relations* (New York: Free Press, 1969), p. 10.

[9]Charles Osgood, "Behavior Theory and the Social Sciences," in *Approaches to the Study of Politics*, ed. Roland Young (Evanston, Ill.: Northwestern University Press, 1958).

goes on in "the little black box" between stimulus and response. Osgood warns about the tendency to collect a different explanatory device for every event—this process of adding a new explanation for findings results in what he termed "junk box psychology." This mass conglomeration of ad hoc explanations can be prevented in a number of ways. One way is to delineate separate patterns of conflict sent and conflict received, the stimulus and response of conflict, by designating a set of independent patterns (factors) through factor analysis for each set. After this is done, relationships between conflict sent and received will be analyzed. Subsequently, unexplained conflict in this simple stimulus-response model will be treated as a function of national attribute patterns delineated in a factor analysis of 190 attribute variables. The next sections will specify the conflict received, the conflict sent, and the national characteristics of nations employed in this study.

THE CONFLICT ENVIRONMENT OF NATIONS

Conflict Behavior

The data used in this analysis have been collected from the *New York Times*, using the foreign conflict code sheet developed by Rummel.[10] The data collected include actors, objects, date, and type of conflict act or action. The information in the code sheets for 1963 was reorganized into a set of twenty-three conflict variables presented in table 1. The variables represent combinations of coded information in the code sheet.

The data were originally organized in a "who did what to whom" format. For the purposes of this study, two collections of data are needed. The first collection organizes the data into a *conflict received* matrix which includes the total amount of conflict behavior *sent to* a specific object, regardless of the sender. Thus, for instance, if the United States received two negative communications from the Soviet Union, one from Hungary, and three from China, the United States would be the object of six negative communications. In the second, *conflict sent*, matrix the total number of *conflict* acts for each conflict variable are recorded in nation actor rows. For example, the United States might have sent three negative communications to Cuba, one each to the Soviet Union, China, and Hungary. If so, the total number of negative communications would be six. The total sent may be the same or different than the total received and the nations conflict acts are sent to, do not have to be the same as the nations from whom an object receives conflict. The analysis here is of the total of conflict sent

[10]R. J. Rummel, "A Foreign Conflict Behavior Code Sheet," *World Politics* 18 (January 1966). The use of the *New York Times* has been justified in ibid., and in McClelland, "Access to Berlin"; Warren R. Phillips, *"Dynamic Patterns of International Conflict"* (Ph.D. diss., University of Hawaii, October 1969). While reliability problems may exist in using a single newspaper, it is currently the best data set available.

Table 1.   Dyadic Foreign Conflict Variable List with Codes[a]

Primary Category	Variable No.	Code	Variable
Warning and defensive acts	1	WARNDF	warning or defensive acts
	2	ALRTMB	alerts and mobilizations or military maneuvers
Official acts of violence	3	PLNVIL	planned violent acts
	4	WARACT	incidents of military conflict (0, 1)
	5	DISCMA	discrete military actions
	6	DAYVIL	days of violence
Negative sanctions	7	NEGACT	negative behavior acts
	8	UNCNEG	unclassified negative acts
	9	SEVDPR	severence of diplomatic relations
	10	EXPREC	expulsion or recall
	11	BCOTEM	boycott or embargo
	12	AIDREB	aid to rebels
Negative communications	13	NEGCOM	negative communications
	14	WRTCOM	written negative communication
	15	ORLCOM	oral negative communication
	16	ACCUSN	accusations
	17	PROTST	protests
	18	MINTHM	minor themes
Unofficial violence	19	UNOFVL	unofficial violence
	20	ATKEMB	attacks on embassy
	21	ATKPER	attacks on other official property
	22	ATKFLG	attacks on persons or flag
Nonviolent demonstrations	23	NVIOLB	nonviolent behavior (protest demonstrations, etc.)

[a]These primary categories represent an intuitive classification of action into as broad a conflict spectrum as possible. They do not represent an a priori attempt to delineate patterns, however. One variable in the original code sheet, clashes, is automatically coded for both actor and object. It is part of variables 3 and 4. These are the only variables in the code sheet which are, in part, automatically coded for both actor and object. Variables 1–19 are official acts; variables 20–23 are unofficial acts.

and received and no attempt will be made to speak about dyadic relationships.

Conflict Received

From the 23 variables of conflict received, it will be necessary to reduce the variables to a basic set of patterns of conflict behavior received. These patterns should be independent and uncorrelated with each other. In order to ascertain these patterns, a factor analysis was performed on the matrix of 23 conflict variables over 73 nations which experienced conflict. This is the previously discussed conflict-received matrix. All nations that were the object of conflict in 1963 were employed in this analysis.[11]

While the unrotated factors define the most general factors in descending order of generality, the rotated factors delineate distinct clusters of interrelationships when they exist in the data. It is these Varimax rotated factors that are the basis of the following discussion.

Principal component analysis generally produces as many factors as there are variables in the original matrix. While this is generally true there seems to be a clear rationale for limiting our discussion to the first four factors. There are six factors with eigenvalues greater than 1.00, but factors 5 and 6 represented collections of variables already loading on factors 1 through 4. Since there were no loadings above .50 on factors 5 and 6, the addition in variance accounted for—about 10 percent—did not seem to warrant the lack of high loading variables which would have facilitated substantive naming.[12] Table 2 presents the Varimax loading matrix.

The first orthogonally rotated factor appears to be a combination of negative communications and unofficial acts of violence. Thus, nations receiving a good deal of negative communications—accusations, protests, etc.—are also likely to be experiencing unofficial violence from other nations. Unofficial violence refers to attacks by civilian populations of one nation against the embassy, flag, or representatives of another nation. To reiterate, these conflict acts need not be directed at the object nation by one specific nation but by a number of sources. Thus, the United States—a high scorer on this pattern—may have received negative communication mainly from the Soviet Union and China but received the unofficial acts of violence from Latin American nations. For the purpose of this study, neither the time sequencing of actions nor the sender of conflict acts is pertinent. This is a static look at the conflict environment.

The second factor indexes military violence. This pattern of conflict behavior seems to be statistically independent of other forms of conflict experience. The third pattern of conflict experience represents warning and defensive actions received by specific object nations. The fourth factor accounts for negative sanctions such as the severance of diplomatic relations and the expulsion of diplomats.

---

[11]The variables were intercorrelated using the product moment correlation. No transformations were performed on the data variables. The technique of factor analysis was principle component analysis. Initially a principle axis solution was obtained which was rotated to a simple structure employing a varimax criteria. For further information about these techniques, see Harry H. Harman, *Modern Factor Analysis*, 2nd ed., (Chicago: University of Chicago Press, 1967); R. J. Rummel, *Applied Factor Analysis* (Evanston, Ill.: Northwestern University Press, 1970).

[12]For a discussion of the choice of the number of factors, see Rummel, *Applied Factor Analyses*. I rotated four-, five-, and six-factor solutions before choosing four.

Table 2. Conflict Environment Patterns

Measures		h^2	Varimax Rotation[a]			
			$F1$	$F2$	$F3$	$F4$
1	WARNDF	90	11	05	93	14
2	ALRTMB	90	11	02	93	15
3	PLNVIL	94	19	94	11	−05
4	WARACT	96	14	96	11	−06
5	DISCMA	94	−01	97	−04	−04
6	DAYVIL	88	−03	93	−07	−04
7	NEGACT	93	37	−05	19	87
8	UNCNEG	56	53	−05	26	45
9	SEVDPR	41	−04	−03	23	60
10	EXPREC	50	51	04	−29	39
11	BCOTEM	49	−04	−06	−04	69
12	AIDREB	22	02	30	23	28
13	WRTCOM	96	96	07	−01	18
14	ORLCOM	84	86	04	−17	27
15	WRTORL	95	96	14	07	08
16	ACCUSN	97	97	08	−02	10
17	PROTST	76	74	−02	−16	43
18	MINTHM	72	81	08	19	16
19	UNOFVL	92	94	04	17	−10
20	ATKEMB	28	40	12	30	15
21	ATKPER	91	94	03	11	−12
22	ATKFLG	92	95	01	07	−12
23	NVIOLB	83	86	06	27	−07
Percent Total Variance			39.39	16.44	10.27	10.79

[a] Decimals omitted from loadings.

Substantively, the statistical independence of these four patterns means that there are four separate types of conflict experience. Foreign offices generally can be expected to experience four types of conflict in the international system, but the relationship between these patterns is unpredictable at the systemic level.[13]

PATTERNS OF NATIONAL OUTPUT

Oliva and Rummel[14] analyzed the bynation conflict of 107 nations for 1963. This was an analysis of the conflict behavior nations initiated. The result of their study along with those just reported comprise the conflict

---

[13]The fiindings do not apply to specific nations but to the system in general. Thus, a subsection of the system may experience jointly several of these patterns of conflict. For an attempt to compare parameters at both levels see Rummel, "Field Theory."

[14]Gary Oliva and R. J. Rummel, *Foreign Conflict Patterns and Types for 1963*, Research Report No. 22 (Honolulu: University of Hawaii, Dimensionality of Nations Project, April 1969).

Table 3.   Factor Analysis of Bynation Conflict Measures

Measures	h^2	Varimax Rotations[a]				
		$F1$	$F2$	$F3$	$F4$	$F5$
1 WARNDF	92	14	03	11	03	−94
2 ALRTMB	88	15	01	08	05	−92
3 PLNVIL	93	11	95	−01	−01	−12
4 WARACT	95	08	97	00	−03	−17
5 DISCMA	95	−04	97	−02	01	05
6 DAYVIL	87	02	93	−04	−03	07
7 NEGACT	97	21	−02	08	92	−27
8 UNCNEG	80	18	−01	−04	84	−25
9 SEVDPR	39	−11	−10	38	32	−35
10 EXPREC	41	11	−02	03	62	10
11 BCOTEM	50	04	−05	−16	68	−11
12 AIDREB	45	33	26	30	42	09
13 NEGCOM	98	96	04	−02	23	−08
14 WRTCOM	89	93	04	−03	11	05
15 ORLCOM	77	86	03	07	15	05
16 ACCUSN	91	95	05	−04	−10	00
17 PROTST	86	72	−01	−07	56	−13
18 MINTHM	74	76	04	−04	18	−34
19 UNCFVL	96	−01	−03	97	−01	−12
20 ATKEMB	35	05	02	52	11	−26
21 ATKPER	83	−06	−02	91	−02	04
22 ATKFLG	85	−02	−03	92	03	04
23 NVIOLB	49	−00	07	05	31	−62
Percent Total Variance		20.91	16.23	13.83	14.09	11.59

[a] Decimals omitted from loadings.

output and input of nations, respectively. In a factor analysis of the national output, Oliva and Rummel found five conflict patterns. A reanalysis of their data produced the same five factors,[15] which are presented in table 3. The patterns were termed negative communications, military violence, unofficial violence, negative sanctions, and warning and defensive acts, respectively. This five-factor solution points out an immediate difference between national input and output patterns of conflict. In the actions from the nation to the evironment, patterns of negative communications and unofficial acts of violence are differentiated while in the analysis of environmental input to nations, these behaviors are not differentiated.[16] Substan-

[15] I felt it was desirable to refactor the Oliva-Rummel analysis because three key communications variables (written, oral and written, or oral communications) were omitted from the earlier study and because the number of nations in their study was 107.

[16] This raises the question of the number of factors. When five factors were rotated, the same difference was found. Therefore, it can be assumed that the differences are not simply due to the four-factor solution for conflict received.

tively, the patterns of the conflict nations sent in 1963 were slightly more complex than the patterns of conflict received. While the patterns of conflict sent are slightly more complex than the conflict experienced from the international environment, it is the similarity that is much more striking.

COMPARISON OF CONFLICT AND RESPONSES

The conflict experiences of nations for 1963 can be analyzed by comparing conflict actions sent with actions received. The factor score matrices derived from the analysis of environmental conflict in section 3 will be compared with the factor-score matrix calculated in the reanalysis of bynation conflict reported earlier.[17] To compare them, I have chosen the canonical model in which linear combinations of conflict received by nations are related to linear combinations of national conflict actions.[18] Such combinations would take the form:

$$\alpha_{11}E_1 + \alpha_{12}E_2 + \ldots + \alpha_{1p}E_p =$$

$$\beta_{11}A_1 + \beta_{12}A_2 + \ldots + \beta_{1q}A_q + e_1 \quad (1)$$

where α = coefficients for conflict received, E = conflict received by nations from the environment, β = coefficients for national actions, A = conflict sent to the environment. This is the basic algebraic model of canonical analysis. Canonical analysis attempts to maximize the linear correlation between pairs of Variates.[19] Each Variate is independent of the other

---

[17]Factor scores are calculated by the formula

$$S_{nxp} = Z_{nxm}F_{mxp}(F'F)_{pxp}^{-1}$$

where S is the factor scores, Z is the standardized raw data, and F is the matrix of loading weights.

[18]The search for new models to express relationships between variables or concepts in political science and international relations has progressed to the stage of multiple regression where one variable is expressed as a linear combination of a series of other variables. A growing number of scholars have developed theories which attempt to relate a series of dependent variables to a series of independent variables. Just such a model—canonical regression—exists, but it has not been widely employed in international relations.

For the reader uneasy with mathematical discussion, canonical analysis can be compared to multiple regression procedures. The major difference is that there is more than one "dependent variable" in canonical analysis. This difference produces more than one solution—more than one possible combination of conflict sent and conflict received variables. There is, therefore, a "multiple correlation" or canonical correlation for each combination and an "overall correlation" or trace correlation for the generalized relationship of conflict sent to conflict received. Canonical coefficients (the $a + b$ of equation (1)) are similar in interpretation to regression coefficients. Similarly, variate scores are the "expected scores" of canonical relationships. In canonical analysis the "expected scores" are derived for both conflict sent and received sides of the equation, however. This explanation should allow the reader to skip to the interpretation beginning on page 134.

[19]I have capitalized "Variate" throughout this paper to help the reader distinguish between variable—a vector of observations—and Variate—a linear combination of variables weighted by canonical coefficients

Variates on its own side of the equation and all Variates on the other side of the equation with the exception of those on the same row, opposite itself.

By summing the standardized raw data—in this case the factor scores of both the original analyses—times the correct canonical weights, a Variate score for each nation on the linear combination of both input and output can be derived.

$$V_{nxq} = E_{nxq}A_{nxq}$$
$$W_{nxq} = A_{nxp}E_{pxq} \tag{2}$$

where $V_{n \times q}$ = the matrix of canonical Variates for the conflict received and $W_{n \times q}$ = the matrix of canonical Variates for the conflict sent. These canonical Variates are vectors of scores for each nation on the Variate. By subtracting the conflict-sent score of a nation from its conflict-received score, the degree of similarity between them is ascertained.

$$V_{i1} - W_{i1} = R_{i1} \tag{3}$$

where V_i is the first canonical Variate of conflict received, W_i is the first canonical Variate of conflict sent, and R_i is the residual vector for V_i - W_i. The standard deviation of R_i provides a benchmark for signaling when a difference between V_i and W_i is extreme. When such a residual is more than one standard deviation from the mean of the residual vector, the amount of conflict sent or received by that nation is abnormal, relative to other nations' input-output relationships.

This canonical model was applied to the matrices of factor scores of nations' conflict actions sent and received. The number of nations which received conflict was 73, the number that sent conflict was 82, and the number that received and sent conflict was 65. Two matrices, a conflict-sent matrix with 83 observations and a conflict-received matrix with 73 observations, were factored. In employing the canonical analysis all 73 nations which received conflict were employed. When a nation receiving conflict did not send conflict, scores for zero conflict were inserted for that observation.[20] The choice of sample is a function of this author's interest in nations' responses to conflict received from the environment. To have chosen the 65 nations which both sent and received would have biased the canonical results toward higher correlations since it would not allow for the possibility of no response.

The first matrix presented in this analysis is the canonical coefficient matrix, seen in table 4. The figures under headings 1–4 in table 4 are coefficients of the canonical equation and are interpretable in much the same way as regression coefficients. There is a separate set of canonical Variates

---

[20]These scores are not zero, but are the factor score equivalent of a zero raw score on each of the 23 variables.

Table 4. Canonical Variates for Comparison Between Conflict Sent and Conflict Received

Conflict Sent	h^2	Canonical Variates			
		1	2	3	4
1. Negative communications	.97	.03	.67	.72	.06
2. Military violence	1.00	1.00	−.04	.03	−.02
3. Unofficial acts of violence	.12	−.04	−.02	−.15	−.31
4. Negative sanctions	1.00	.06	.69	−.67	.27
5. Warning and defensive acts	.91	−.04	−.29	.09	.91
Canonical correlations		.98	.94	.74	.35
Conflict Received	h^2	1	2	3	4
1. Negative communications/ unofficial acts of violence	1.00	.07	.94	−.30	−.13
2. Military violence	1.00	1.00	−.05	.06	−.04
3. Warning and defensive acts	1.00	.07	.01	−.39	.92
4. Negative sanctions	1.00	−.00	.34	.87	.37

for each matrix. Thus, Variate 1 from the environmental conflict matrix is maximally related to Variate 1 of the conflict behavior matrix. Another statistic should be presented at this time, the canonical correlation. It is equivalent to the Pearson Product Moment correlation between V_i and W_j when $i = j$. It measures the degree of pattern similarity for nations on the corresponding Variates of conflict sent and received.[21] The correlations between V_i and W_j when i does not equal j, are all 0.[22] Turning to the communality estimates (h^2), they record the percent of variance from each variable that is accounted for by the Variates. In other words,

$$h_i^2 = \sum_{i=1}^{p} r_{ij}^2 \qquad (4)$$

where h_i^2 is the communality estimate of the variable, p is the number of Variates, and r is the correlation of the variable with the Variate.[23] All of

---

[21]The correlation is technically the square root of the eigenvalue.

[22]Care should be taken in interpreting V_i and W_j. The subscripts i and j refer to Variates and *not* nations. It means that only the *matched* linear combinations of variables from each of the two matrices will have correlations other than zero. Thus, for instance, all other W Variates are independent of V_i when the W Variate is not W_j, $i = j$.

[23]In calculating the canonical relationships, two sets of coefficients are derivable. The canonical coefficients are interpreted as regression coefficients. The second set of coefficients—usually labeled the canonical structure matrix—is interpreted as correlations of the initial variables with the newly formed Variates. The most important use of this second matrix is the calculation of the communality estimate which is simply the sum of these squared correlations. For parsimony in tables, I have added the communalities to the canonical coefficient matrix.

the variance in the matrix of factor scores for conflict received is accounted for in the analysis, thus all of communalities are 1.00. Since this is the smaller of the two matrices, all of its variance will be accounted for and there will be as many Variates as there are independent column vectors in this matrix.

As opposed to communalities of 1.00 for conflict received, the variance of the conflict sent variables can vary considerably. In this case, four of the five variables of conflict sent by nations are highly related to variables of conflict received by nations since their communalities show more than ninety percent of their variance is being accounted for in this analysis. In contrast, unofficial violence sent to the environment is not related to the relationships delineated here. Thus, it would appear that mass demonstrations, attacks on embassies, and other acts of unofficial protest are not related to experience with conflict received from the environment.

Turning from the communalities to the Variates themselves, only coefficients above .50 will be discussed. The first combination of Variates has a correlation of .98. Taking the high loading variables from table 4, and rearranging them to conform to the format as laid out in equation (1), we have the following equation:

$$\text{Military violence sent} \doteq \text{Military violence received}$$

The sign = is used in these equations to mean approximately equal, since only variables that strongly contribute to the Variates have been included. Some variables, such as clashes, are considered symmetric in character and automatically coded for both sides. While there is no conceptual difference between coding a clash on both sent and received and coding both a threat sent and a threat received, the reader should understand that it is in the nature of military conflict that sides fired upon tend to return that fire.

As a supplement to this interpretation of canonical coefficeints, the scores of each nation on the Variates can be computed. These scores represent a weighted combination of each nation's conflict sent and received. The weights are the canonical coefficients. By subtracting a nation's score on the Variate of conflict sent from its score on the conflict received Variate, the residuals are delineated. Table 5 presents those scores on the first pair of Variates which showed residuals of more than one standard deviation. With the exception of Saudi Arabia, the nations that display irregularities in excess of two standard deviations in conflict exchange with their environments on this pair of Variates were sending more violent conflict to the environment than they received.[24]

---

[24]The usual procedure here would be to interpret why these irregularities occur. In this case, however, deviations are explained in the next section.

Table 5.   Nations Not Well Predicted[a] by the Canonical Equations in the Military Violence Variate (Variate 1)

Nation	Conflict Received Score	Conflict Sent Score	Residual Score[b]
Albania	5.28	4.89	0.38*
Cambodia	0.10	−0.26	0.36*
China	0.31	−0.05	0.36*
Taiwan	0.17	−0.13	0.30*
Egypt	0.37	0.83	−0.46**
Haiti	−0.01	−0.34	0.33*
Indonesia	0.40	0.88	−0.48**
Iran	−0.15	−0.42	−0.27*
Iraq	−0.35	−0.14	−0.22*
Jordan	0.24	0.46	−0.22*
North Korea	−0.01	0.50	−0.51**
Malaysia	0.67	0.41	0.25*
Saudi Arabia	0.59	0.11	0.49**
Somalia	0.07	−0.18	0.24*
Syria	1.07	0.64	0.42*
Union of South Africa	−0.18	−0.42	0.24*
U.S.S.R.	−0.28	0.11	−0.39*
North Vietnam	−0.40	−0.18	−0.22*
South Vietnam	−0.40	0.11	−0.51**
Yugoslavia	4.89	5.31	−0.42*

* = one standard deviation
** = two standard deviations from the mean residual

[a] Nations at least a one-standard deviation away from the mean (X) residual are included in this table.

[b] Negative residuals indicate nations sending more behavior than expected.

Continuing with the second set of Variates, the following equation is applicable:

.67 Negative communications + .69 Negative sanctions sent
≐ .94 Negative communications/unofficial violence received.

The correlations between these Variate scores is .94. Thus, nations sending both negative communications and negative sanctions received negative communications or unofficial violence. Table 6 presents the nations with extreme residuals in this relationship. Those nations with extreme residuals are all sending much more to the environment than would be expected given that which they received.

In contrast to the nations sending both negative communications and negative sanctions delineated above, the third pairing of Variates highlights nations which send negative communications, but not negative sanctions.

Table 6.   Nations Not Well Predicted[a] by the Canonical Equations in the Mixed Diplomatic Variate (Variate 2)

Nation	Conflict Received Score	Conflict Sent Score	Residual Score[b]
Albania	−0.85	−0.39	−0.46*
Cambodia	−0.20	0.36	−0.56*
Egypt	0.06	0.49	−0.43*
Ethiopia	−0.18	0.23	−0.41*
France	0.77	0.22	0.54*
India	0.35	1.51	−1.16**
Iraq	−0.15	0.60	−0.75**
Malaysia	−0.22	0.53	−0.76**
Morocco	−0.20	0.16	−0.37*
Portugal	0.17	−0.45	0.62*
Senegal	−0.41	−0.03	−0.39*
Syria	0.17	−0.52	0.68*
United Kingdom	1.36	1.87	0.51*
Union of South Africa	0.43	−0.15	0.58*
U.S.A.	6.52	5.87	0.65*
South Vietnam	0.14	−0.45	0.60*
Yugoslavia	−0.55	−1.04	0.49*

* = one standard deviation
** = two standard deviations from the mean residual

[a]Nations at least a one-standard deviation away from the mean (X) residual are included in this table.
[b]Negative residuals indicate nations sending more behavior than expected.

.72 Negative communications − .67 Negative sanctions sent
$\doteq$ .87 Negative sanctions received

This relationship can be interpreted as those nations receiving negative sanctions from the environment respond with negative communications but not negative sanctions. These two sets of Variate pairs (sets 2 and 3) point out the diplomatic complexity of negative communications and negative sanctions. These two forms of behavior would appear to be the normal day-to-day processes of expressing diplomatic displeasure. There appear to be two patterns: one set of nations engages in both types of acts while another group usually chooses one but not the other.[25] The input-output relationships of conflict have been interpreted as though a nation sent and then received conflict. This sequencing is not necessarily correct. In fact, it may just as easily be that nations first receive negative sanctions, and then com-

[25]Whether or not a nation chooses to employ both types of acts in a single conflict relation with a specific opponent is not answerable in this analysis because the objects of conflict are not differentiated.

plain about it. Since there is no theoretical reason for placing first the nations' actions or the conflict received, canonical analysis is ideal because the relationships are symmetric and do not change with the direction of assumed sequencing.

Table 7 lists the nations with irregular exchanges with their environ-

Table 7. Nations Not Well Predicted[a] by the Canonical Equations in the Negative Communications Variate (Variate 3)

Nation	Conflict Received Score	Conflict Sent Score	Residual Score[b]
Brazil	−1.05	0.05	−1.10*
Cambodia	−0.00	−0.79	0.79*
China	1.51	4.30	−2.79**
Congo	0.03	−0.72	0.76*
Cuba	3.64	2.61	1.03*
Dominican Republic	1.71	0.92	0.79*
France	2.40	0.10	2.30**
Indonesia	−1.38	−0.62	−0.76*
Israel	−0.42	0.50	−0.93*
Lebanon	−0.29	0.42	−0.72*
Morocco	0.13	−1.15	1.28*
Netherlands	−0.05	−0.79	0.75*
Portugal	1.28	0.37	0.91*
Union of South Africa	2.41	0.87	1.54**
Venezuela	−0.56	−1.42	0.86*

* = one standard deviation
** = two standard deviations from the mean residual

[a] Nations at least a one-standard deviation away from the mean (X) residual are included in this table.
[b] Negative residuals indicate nations sending more behavior than expected.

ment. Now for the first time some of the nations with unexpected relations with their environment received more than they sent. The correlation between the Variate in this case was .74 or approximately 54 percent of the variance in Variate scores is held in common.

The final relationship only accounts for about 12 percent—or a correlation of .35—of the variation in exchanges with the environment.

− .31 Unofficial violence + .91 Warning and defensive acts sent
≐ .92 Warning and defensive acts + .37 Negative sanctions received

In other words, nations which send warning and defensive acts are quite likely to receive this in return as well as negative sanctions such as expulsions of diplomats. Since this relationship is not strong, it does not warrant extensive interpretation.

The preceding discussion has concentrated on specifying combinations of variables. There is yet a final set of relationships that should be discussed, however. It would be convenient to have a measure of the overall relationship of the two matrices and to know how much variance in each matrix is being accounted for by these relationships. The proportion of variance accounted for by respective sets of canonical Variates is shown in table 8. All of the variance in the conflict-received matrix is accounted for

Table 8.   Variance Accounted for by Canonical Equations

Variate	Canonical Correlation	Proportion of Conflict-Sent Variance	Proportion of Conflict-Received Variance
1	0.98	19.98	24.95
2	0.94	19.69	24.85
3	0.74	20.30	25.30
4	0.35	19.97	24.91
		79.94	100.00

in this analysis, since the conflict-received matrix is the smaller of the two matrices. Eighty percent of the variance in nations' conflict sent to the environment is reproduced by the Variates.

To ascertain an overall degree of the relationship between the matrices, Hooper derived a "trace correlation"[26] which is the average of all canonical correlations.

$$\text{Trace} = \bar{r} = \sqrt{1/p \sum_{j=i}^{p} r_j^2}$$

where p = the number of variables in the dependent matrix of conflict received and r_j is the jth canonical correlation between Variates V_j and W_j. It is an estimate of the average correlation between Variates for any set of basic vectors derivable in dimensionalizing the two spaces (matrices). The trace correlation in this analysis is .79 or better than 60 percent of the variance in nations' conflict actions is related to the conflict it receives from the environment. Conflict exchanges can be thought of as a tennis match in which the opponent's return is based upon the type of service he receives. This finding of a high relationship between conflict sent and received points to the high degree of influence that experiencing conflict received can play in making a nation conflictual toward others in the system. But how can the other 30+ percent of variation be explained? The next section is an attempt to explain that variance.

[26]J. W. Hooper, "Simultaneous Equations and Canonical Correlation Theory," *Econometrica* 27 (1959): 245–56.

Table 9. Marker Variables for the Patterns of National Attributes

Pattern Number	Marker Variables
1	GNP / population
2	Area
3	Defense expenditures
4	IFC and IBRD subscriptions / $(GNP)^2$ per capita
5	Domestic killed
6	Purges
7	Population / national land area (density)
8	Foreign college students / college students
9	Religious titles published / book titles
10	Unemployed / economically active population (percent unemployed)
11	Languages
12	Need affiliation scores
13	Export / GNP
14	Cost of living index
15	Military personnel / population
16	Balance of investments / gold stock
17	Arts and cultural NGO / NGO
18	Legality of government change
19	U.N. delinquencies / assessment
20	Constitutional status: 0 = totalitarian, 1 = authoritarian, 2 = constitutional
21	Factor scores on South African voting dimensions
22	Latitude measure of nation's capital

CHARACTERISTICS OF NATIONS DISPLAYING RESIDUALS IN THEIR CONFLICT SENT AND RECEIVED SCORES

Recall again that for each set of canonical Variates interpreted above, it was possible to calculate a nation score for conflict sent and conflict received, and by subtracting these estimates of conflict sent from that received, a residual score is calculated. The question to be answered now is: What are the characteristics of nations which account for the residuals? The DON project has factor analyzed 190 attribute variables for 107 nations in 1963. Twenty-two factors accounted for 78 percent of the variance. Table 9 lists a marker variable for each of the factors.[27] These twenty-two variables were then employed in an attempt to account for the residuals in conflict sent and received. The procedure employed was stepwise regression.[28] The theoretical approach here assumes that conflict begets conflict

[27]A marker variable is one which is highly correlated with the factor scores. It is used rather than factor scores for ease of interpretation.
[28]For a discussion of this technique see N. R. Draper and H. Smith, *Applied Regression Analysis* (New York: John Wiley and Sons, 1968).

and that deviation from the normal exchanges with a nation's environment can be explained by examining specific attribute characteristics of these nations.

It is particularly important to discuss the problem of random error when dealing with residuals of highly correlated variables. Most of the random error of the two variables is skimmed off in the residuals. Regression capitalizes on random error. Thus, for twenty-two independent variables, each variable will necessarily (practically speaking) increase the percent of variance explained, even if they were twenty-two error variables. The problem is then, when dealing with a dependent variable highly inflicted with random error (because it is a residual variable) and using a technique that capitalizes on random error, how much faith can we put in the results? To answer this question, the t-test for each variable and the F-ratio for the overall relationship is reported. Both tests are employed as answers to the random error problem and do not represent a sampling perspective in this paper.

The results of the first regression analysis of the deviations from the expected of military violence sent and received are presented in table 10.

Table 10.   Military Violence Received-Military Violence Sent: Regressed upon National Attributes

Variable	Multiple R	RSQ	Increase in RSQ	t = Test[a]	Sign
Domestic killed	29	8	8	9.86	−
Agriculture population/ population	40	16	8	9.84	
Legality of government change	47	22	6	6.04	
Cost of living index	51	26	4	4.68	−
Religious titles published/ book titles	55	30	4	5.18	
Latitude measure of nation's capital	57	33	3	2.88	−
Unemployed/economically active population (percent unemployed)	60	36	3	2.58	
Constant = .43					
F-ratio = 4.58					

[a] In this situation the t = test is used to estimate the probability that an observed regression coefficient might have been obtained by chance in random sampling from a population in which the true coefficient was zero.

Seven of the twenty-two attribute characteristics account for 36 percent of the variance in the residuals. The two most important variables are domestic killed and the percentage of population in agriculture. These two variables are inversely related to the deviation in scores for military exchanges. Positive deviations indicate the receipt of more official military conflict than expected, given the amount sent to the environment. Thus, attribute variables with positive coefficients vary directly with more conflict received than expected, given the conflict sent while attribute variables with negative coefficients vary directly with unexpected levels of conflict sent. *The conclusion here is that nations displaying domestic violence, having a low percentage of population in agriculture, who have tended to experience unlawful change of offices in the recent past, and have a high cost of living index, tend to send more military violence to the environment than would be expected, given normal exchange with the environment. In other words, modernized nations experiencing inflation and internal violence, possibly associated with the unlawful exchange of leadership, are likely to over respond militarily to their environment.* The finding supports much of the literature regarding the relationship between internal and external violence.[29] It is interesting in light of the general lack of relationship between internal and external violence uncovered in empirical studies.[30] It suggests that most military violence is directly related to the receipt of violence (the correlation above is .97) but that deviations or perhaps oversensitivity to military violence is found among those nations experiencing internal violence and rising costs of living.

The second variable of conflict residuals was taken from the relationship between negative communications and negative sanctions sent and received. It varied positively with more than expected amounts of negative communications and negative sanctions sent. Population is the marker variable for a factor which has a high loading for riots, indicating that nations with large, highly dense populations (as shown by another marker variable) tend to show population unrest in the form of riots but not domestic killed. This combination explains international conflict in the form of negative sanctions and negative communications. These nations are also active traders, as shown by results of their exports divided by gross national product, but not necessarily economically developed.

There are two substantive differences between this set of national characteristics and the characteristics accounting for deviations in military violence. First, the nations that were overreacting militarily are characterized as economically developed with a high cost of living index while those nations showing deviations in the second relationship are not necessarily economically developed but do have large, dense populations. The second and more important difference is that the first group exhibits domestic killed while the second relationship definitely is not accounted for by killing

[29]For example, see Rosecrance, *Action and Reaction in World Politics.*

[30]R. J. Rummel, "Dimensions of Conflict Behavior Within and Between Nations," chap 3, this volume; Tanter, "Dimensions of Conflict Behavior," pp. 41–64; Warren Phillips and Dennis R. Hall, "The Importance of Governmental Structure as a Taxonomic Scheme for Nations," *Comparative Political Studies* 3 (April 1970): 63–89.

**Table 11.   Negative Communications and Negative Sanctions Received–
Negative Communications and Negative Sanctions Sent:
Regressed upon National Attributes**

Variable	Multiple R	RSQ	Increase in RSQ	t-Test[a]	Sign
Export/GNP	35	12	12	3.91	–
Population	46	22	9	12.57	–
Unemployed/economically active population (percent unemployed)	56	31	10	9.62	
Factor scores on South African voting dimensions	61	37	6	5.58	–
Balance of investments/gold stock	64	41	4	9.19	
Foreign college students/college students	66	44	3	2.89	–
Population/national land area (density)	69	47	3	6.88	–
Domestic killed	70	49	2	3.44	
Legality of government change	72	52	2	4.13	
Arts and cultural NGO/NGO	74	55	3	3.47	

Constant = −.14
F-ratio = 6.52

[a] See note to table 10.

from internal violence. *Nations exhibiting deviations in the more diplomatic forms of conflict do, however, experience riots and internal unrest in levels less than domestic killing.*

Turning to the analysis of deviations from the third pair of Variates, the canonical coefficients accounted for negative communications or negative sanctions sent from nations to their environment, but not both. Ten attribute characteristics combine to predict almost 50 percent of the residual variance in this relationship. Since sending negative communications and receiving negative sanctions is the strongest relation, it will be the basis of this discussion. The variables most influential in explaining the release of more negative communications than expected were population, percent unemployed, military personnel as a percentage of population and voting on South African issues in the U.N. Countries with large residuals tend to have large populations, a relatively high level of unemployment, and are experiencing high cost of living problems. They also have a relatively large percentage of their population in the military, but do not spend a large portion of their budget on defense expenditures, the marker variable of a power factor. These characteristics vary positively with deviations in the amount of negative communications sent from nations to the environment. *Nations that are overactive on only one or the other of these more diplo-*

Table 12. Negative Communications or Negative Sanctions Received–Negative Communications or Negative Sanctions Sent: Regressed upon National Attributes

Variable	Multiple R	RSQ	Increase in RSQ	t-Test[a]	Sign
Population	38	14	14	20.26	–
Factor scores on South African voting dimensions	49	24	10	6.72	–
Unemployed/economically active population (percent unemployed)	52	28	4	8.95	–
Religious titles published/book titles	57	32	4	4.89	–
Military personnel/population	61	37	5	7.94	–
Cost of living index	63	39	3	1.34	–
Constitutional status: 0 = totalitarian, 1 = authoritarian, 2 = constitutional	65	42	3	1.02	
Languages	66	44	2	4.04	
Population/national land area (density)	68	46	3	3.77	
Defense expenditure	70	49	3	2.87	

Constant = .40
F-Ratio = 5.18

[a] See note to table 10.

matic forms of conflict are usually highly populated but with low density who are experiencing unemployment, high costs of living, and internal rioting.

The final canonical Variate accounted for warning and defensive acts

Table 13. Warning and Defensive Acts Received-Warning and Defensive Acts Sent: Regressed upon National Attributes

Variable	Multiple R	RSQ	Increase in RSQ	t-Test[a]	Sign
Arts and cultural NGO/NGO	31	10	10	10.83	
Religious titles published/book titles	45	20	10	9.28	
Balance of investments/gold stock	51	26	6	6.67	
Languages	55	31	4	3.63	

Constant = – 1.51
F-Ratio = 6.59

[a] See note to table 10.

sent and received. This saber-rattling was not highly correlated as shown by the correlation between input and output of .35. Thus, there was a good deal of variation in the residuals, but the ability for attributes to predict this deviation was not as large or as interpretable as the other regression analyses. While these four variables shown in table 13 account for 31 percent of the variance in deviations from input-output correlation, there does not seem to be a readily interpreted relationship.

CONCLUSIONS

Three levels of analyses have been employed in a first pass at the conflict input-output of nations. Factor analysis was used to find the independent patterns of conflict sent and received across nations for 1963. Then, canonical analysis ascertained the degree of relationship between input and output. And finally, stepwise regression techniques were employed to discover the attributes of nations which were related to deviations in input-output patterns of conflict. The individual results have been presented previously, but by bringing these results together we can make some statements about the nature of the conflict system. The five patterns of behavior found in analyzing conflict sent to the environment can be broken down into three subgroups. The patterns of official military violence and warning and defensive acts can be combined as the domain of the military. These are the behaviors that result from decisions of the executive and defense department. Of course, diplomatic experts and representatives from foreign offices are consulted, but the responsibility for the actions rests with the military. On the other hand, negative sanctions and negative communications usually originate in the diplomatic offices of the government. This classification of patterns of behavior leaves just the category unofficial acts of violence. These acts would originate in the mass public or among subgroups of that public.

The findings suggest a relationship between diplomatic and military acts of conflict: military initiative on the part of a specific nation is met with a military response from the environment. Thus, violence begets violence and warnings and defensive acts are the response to warning and defensive acts. The diplomatic initiatives are responsed to by diplomatic activities but in this case the actions are somewhat more complex. One strategy seems to be the use of both negative sanctions and negative communications while another appears to be the use of one or the other but not both.

Unofficial violence is not a separate pattern of environmental conflict, suggesting that across-nations in 1963 there was not a subset of nations which received this form of conflict as the sole pattern of conflict. In the canonical analysis, the low communality of the nation output factor for unofficial violence signaled that the type of behavior was not related to conflict exchanges.

The above findings specify a direct relationship between that which a nation sends to and receives from the international environment. Nations that send conflict to the environment can expect to receive conflict from it. The relationship of conflict behavior sent and received is quite high. It would also appear that at the macro level, diplomatic responses to diplomatic conflict are more probable than escalations from diplomatic to military conflict. The next step in this form of analysis would be to move to overtime analyses to ascertain the life cycle of conflicts.

The attempt at predicting deviations from expected in conflict sent and received highlighted the role of internal unrest in explaining these residuals. Residuals in each of the three largest relationships between input and output all pointed to the role of internal stress. Actual domestic violence resulting in domestic deaths was related to over expected initiatives of military violence. Other forms of domestic unrest and internal stress such as riots, high amounts of unemployment, or high cost of living indices were important in accounting for higher-than-estimated amounts of diplomatic conflict. These findings relate to a number of current theoretical statements. The linkage between domestic aspects of national units and international policies is viewed here as secondary to the actual give and take with the environment. The relationships of internal conflict to external conflict found in this work is close to the conceptualization of internal violence spilling over into international actions as suggested by Rosecrance and others.[31] Thus, the conflict environment of nations would be expected to have a dynamic of its own with deviations explainable by internal or domestic forces. These expectations require testing on data for a longer period of time, organized along time-series requirements.

[31]Rosecrance, *Action and Reaction in World Politics.*

.6. Externalizing Systemic Stresses: International Conflict as Adaptive Behavior

LEO A. HAZLEWOOD

TWO RESEARCH questions have been frequently discussed within the context of the linkage of national attributes to foreign conflict behavior. First, what are the relationships, if any, between domestic conflict and foreign conflict? Second, what configurations of national attributes, if any, predict to foreign conflict behavior? Theoretical statements by Rosecrance, Rostow, Wright, and others suggested the existence of a strong positive relationship between domestic and foreign conflict behavior.[1] A positive relationship between civil wars and international conflict was found in longitudinal analyses reported by Denton and by Denton and Phillips,[2] but cross-sectional studies by Rummel and Tanter indicated that no such significant domestic-foreign conflict relationships existed for the mid-1950s.[3] Subsequent research with the same data sets by Wilkenfeld and Stohl presented evidence that the relationships between domestic and foreign conflict behavior are mediated by the type of political system in which the conflict has occurred.[4]

[1] Richard N. Rosecrance, *Action and Reaction in World Politics* (Boston: Little, Brown and Co., 1963); Walt W. Rostow, *The Stages of Economic Growth* (London and New York: Cambridge University Press, 1960); Quincy Wright, *A Study of War* (Chicago: University of Chicago Press, 1965).

[2] Frank Denton, "Some Regularities in International Conflict, 1820–1949," *Background* 9 (1966): 182–95; idem and Warren Phillips, "Some Patterns in the History of Violence," *Journal of Conflict Resolution* 12 (1968): 182–95.

[3] R. J. Rummel, "Dimensions of Conflict Behavior Within and Between Nations," chap. 3, this volume; Raymond Tanter, "Dimensions of Conflict Behavior Within and Between Nations, 1958–1960," *Journal of Conflict Resolution* 10 (1966): 41–64.

[4] Jonathan Wilkenfeld, "Domestic and Foreign Conflict Behavior of Nations," *Journal of Peace Research*, no. 1 (1968): 56–69; idem, "Some Further Findings Regarding the Domestic and Foreign Conflict Behavior of Nations," *Journal of Peace Research*, no. 2 (1969): 147–56; Michael Stohl, "The Study of Conflict Behavior Within and Between Nations: Some New Evidence" (Paper delivered at the Midwest Political Science Association meetings, Chicago, April 1971).

The second research question involves the relationships between configurations of national attributes and foreign conflict. Rummel, on the basis of the correlations among 217 national attributes and 13 indicators of foreign conflict behavior, concluded that "the characteristics of a nation are not highly predictive of the intensity of its involvement in foreign conflict."[5] But Weede, reanalyzing subsets of the same data, discovered strong relationships between national power and verbal and violent foreign conflict.[6] An additional body of literature—dealing with the relationships between internal stresses induced by societal change and subsequent foreign conflict behavior—has produced similar results. Early studies of this linkage, including those by Sorokin, Rostow, Wright, and others, argued that internal stresses and external aggressiveness were positively related.[7] Burton, for example, asked "whether international strife results directly from communal conflict—that is, whether there can be international, in the absence of internal, conflict. Looking at states with a long history of peace, their internal integration is a conspicuous feature— Scandanavian states are examples. Looking at states that have been involved in war, internal strife is a conspicuous feature—African, Latin American, and Middle Eastern states are examples."[8] This external aggressiveness, according to Rostow, "can help maintain cohesion in a society where the concrete tasks of modernization raise difficult and schismatic domestic issues, which the leader of the coalition would seek to evade if possible. The gropings for a unifying national policy of, say, Nasser and Sukarno in the period 1955–58, represent a version of an old problem and a familiar response."[9] Such internal stresses were used, in part, to account for such diverse manifestations of foreign conflict as the European revolutions of 1848 and the colonial competition among European states in the 1890s.[10] Indeed, a classical explanation of the "barbarian" invasions of Western Europe at least implicitly drew on a supposed association between internal stress and foreign conflict.[11]

Haas explored one formulation of the bond between internal stress and foreign conflict and found that the supposed relationship between stress

[5]R. J. Rummel, "The Relationship Between National Attributes and Foreign Conflict Behavior," in *Quantitative International Politics*, ed. J. David Singer (New York: Free Press, 1968) pp. 213–14.

[6]Erich Weede, "Conflict Behavior of Nation-States," *Journal of Peace Research*, no. 3 (1970): 229–35.

[7]Pitirim A. Sorokin, *Social and Cultural Dynamics*, vol. 3 (New York: American Book Co., 1937); Rostow, *Stages of Economic Growth*; Wright, *Study of War*.

[8]John W. Burton, *Systems, States, Diplomacy and Rules* (Cambridge, Mass.: Cambridge University Press, 1968) p. 84.

[9]Rostow, *Stages of Economic Growth*, p. 114.

[10]Rosecrance, *Action and Reaction*, pp. 281–82.

[11]Crane Brinton et al. *The History of Civilization*, vol. 1 (Englewood Cliffs, N.J.: Prentice-Hall, 1967); Carroll Quigley, *The Evolution of Civilizations* (New York: Macmillan Co., 1961).

and "the military as a tool of statecraft" was positive but "not well supported," although "economic stress appeared to produce social strain" and strain and military behavior were positively "linked" over time for ten Western countries.[12] Both North and Choucri and Feierabend and Feierabend reported strong positive relationships between internal tensions or frustrations and external aggressiveness.[13]

This paper attempts to build upon these earlier findings to assess the strength and patterns of relationships between internal change, societal diversity, governmental response, domestic conflict, and foreign conflict behavior. It is my contention that (1) a configuration of measures of internal change, societal diversity and domestic conflict, together with governmental responses to such internal stresses, predict strongly to the levels of foreign conflict subsequently experienced, and (2) these relationships are interpretable and predictable within the context of general systems analysis, especially when the concepts of variety and adaptation are employed. Thus, the paper presents and tests a general systems-based model to account for some aspects of foreign conflict behavior in terms of adaptation to internal stresses. The model is presented and operationalized in the following section, while the basic relationships and specific patterns of dependency are tested with data from seventy-four states in the two subsequent parts. The last section presents a summary of the results and attempt to place them into a broad theoretical perspective.

THE MODEL

System-Environment Exchanges: Some General Principles

The model of society as a complex adaptive system presented here, relying heavily on general systems research, makes three assumptions about the nature of social behavior.

1. All social systems are open. Berrien defines open systems as "those which accept and respond to inputs (stimuli, information, and so on), and closed systems are those which are assumed to function 'within' themselves."[14] Implicit in the notion of system openness is "some interchange with its surroundings."[15] That is, open systems engage in environment-

---

[12]Michael Haas, "Social Change and National Aggressiveness, 1900–1960," in Singer, ed., *Quantitative International Politics*, p. 243.

[13]Nazli Choucri and Robert North, "Pressure, Competition, Tension, Threat: Toward a Theory of International Conflict" (Paper delivered at the annual meeting, American Political Science Association, New York, September 1969); Ivo Feierabend and R. L. Feierabend, "The Relationship of Systemic Frustration, Political Coercion, International Tension and Political Instability: A Cross-National Study" (Paper delivered at the American Psychological Association meetings, New York, 1966.

[14]Kenneth F. Berrien, *General and Social Systems* (New Brunswick, N.J.: Rutgers University Press, 1968), p. 15.

[15]Ibid., pp. 26–27.

system exchanges which are "an essential factor underlying the system's viability, its reproductive ability or continuity, and its ability to change."[16] Such environment-system exchanges introduce "variety" into the interaction patterns of the society. As defined by Buckley,[17] variety refers to the "distinguishable differences in an ensemble" or set, such as differing signs, signals, symbols or messages.[18]

2. Complex adaptive systems are "tension-oriented." They are oriented by the tensions of interaction which produce additional variety. Tension is assumed to be the basis of the society and its persistence. We must, however, distinguish between "ordinary" and "extraordinary" tensions. These complex adaptive systems do not manage expected tensions (for they are a normal part of interactions), but only stress and strain—that is, "greater mobilization of normal tensions under conditions of more than normal blockage."[19] Miller distinguishes stress as the behavior of variables forced "beyond the range of stability" by extraordinary tensions which in turn produces strains within the system."[20]

3. Complex adaptive systems are "inherently structure elaborating and changing."[21] Complex adaptive systems react to the stimulus of environmentally introduced variety by "elaboration or change of their structure to a higher or more complex level."[22] Such systems manage environmental variety by introducing "constraint," defined by Ashby as "a relation between two sets" which "occurs when the variety that exists under one condition is less than the variety that exists under another"[23] to utilize the tensions generated in the channels of existing and/or newly elaborated structures. To persist, a system must conform to what Ashby terms the law of requisite variety: "only variety in R can force down the variety due to D; only variety can destroy variety."[24] Buckley states this law for social systems as follows: "If a system or organization is to adapt to or control its environment, it must contain at least as much variety as there is in the environment to be controlled."[25] Social systems must develop sufficient constraint to respond to environmental variety while also employing the

[16]Walter Buckley, *Sociology and Modern Systems Theory* (Englewood Cliffs, N.J.: Prentice-Hall, 1967), p. 50.

[17]Ibid., p. 62.

[18]Ibid., p. 84.

[19]Walter Buckley, "Society as a Complex Adaptive System," in *Modern Systems Research for the Behavioral Scientist*, ed. Walter Buckley (Chicago: Aldine Publishing Co., 1968), p. 500.

[20]James G. Miller, "Living Systems: Basic Concepts; Structure and Process; Cross-Level Hypotheses," *Behavioral Science* 10 (1965): 224.

[21]Buckley, *Sociology*, p. 18.

[22]Ibid., p. 50.

[23]W. Ross Ashby, *An Introduction to Cybernetics*, science ed. (New York: John Wiley and Sons, 1963), p. 127.

[24]Ibid., p. 207.

[25]Buckley, *Sociology*, pp. 88–89.

tensions so generated. As Buckley states "The paradigm underlying the evolution of more and more complex adaptive systems begins with the fact of a potentially changing environment characterized by constrained variety and an adaptive system or organization whose persistence and elaboration to higher levels depends upon a successful mapping of some of the environmental variety and constraints into its own organization on at least a semipermanent basis.[26]

In effect, complex adaptive systems reduce the randomness of environmental variety by "harnessing" the tension generated through the development of new structures. Constraint is increased by mapping the environmental variety into employable form. Over time, "As open systems become more complex there developes within them more and more complex mediating processes that intervene between external forces and behavior." These processes (1) adjust the system to "external contingencies"; (2) direct systems "toward more congenial environments"; and (3) "permanently reorganize aspects of the system itself to deal perhaps more effectively with the environment."[27] In short, the structures of the complex adaptive system act as a regulator—a set of structures "block[ing] the flow of variety from disturbances to essential variables"[28]—which protects essential system variables by elaboration to map external variety more reliably into internally manageable form. Rather than equilibrium-seeking, such systems are constantly changing through the elaboration of structures for tension management.

Restating the Principles

The operation of these three principles has been summarized by Buckley. "This adaptive process thus involves a *source of variety* against which to draw, a number of *selective mechanisms* which sift and test this environmental variety against some *criteria* of viability, and processes which tend to *bind and perpetuate* the selected variety for some time."[29] As generally discussed in the general systems literature, the treatment of these environment-system exchanges is of limited utility to our present problem— the explanation of the foreign conflict behavior of nations through measures of societal stress and governmental response. The difficulty comes from emphasis rather than theoretical impoverishment. That is, there has been a predominant concern with accounting for adaptations such as morphogenesis (structural elaboration) as responses to the introduction of environmental variety. Exchanges from environment to system have been emphasized.

[26]Ibid., p. 63.
[27]Ibid., p. 58.
[28]Ashby, *Introduction to Cybernetics*, p. 201.
[29]Buckley, *Sociology*, p. 128.

Our concern is with the management of internal variety—generated through societal change and diversity—through system-environment exchanges originating within the system. Here, the internal variety is mapped against existing internal constraints and/or externalized through system-environment interaction. To cover this type of behavior, we can restate the law of requisite variety to deal with the problem of system adaptation to internal variety through constraint (mapping) and system-initiated variety externalization into the environment. In other words, if a system is to adapt to or control the variety of its internal components, it must contain or develop at least as much constraint as there is variety within those components to be regulated. Although, as noted, the exchanges from environment to system have been emphasized to date, a reorientation is at least implicit in the systems literature. Ashby's formulation of the law of requisite variety is devoid of directionality. Moreover, Buckley is concerned with the mapping by the system "of the variety of its external environment . . . and its internal milieu."[30]

When we attempt to apply these assumptions to the explanation of foreign conflict, a number of possibilities emerge within the law of requisite variety. The internal variety and constraints could be approximately equal, leading to relative system stability. Constraint could be more extensive than internal variety, a condition leading to systemic stagnation and disintegration. Finally, internal variety could be more extensive than existing systemic capacity to constrain, thereby predicting to widespread and perhaps violent change. It is this last configuration with which we are concerned.

As Ashby notes, we may postulate "two extreme forms" of response by the systemic structures (acting as a regulator) to a situation in which internal variety is more extensive than internal constraints. First, there is a simple blocking response in which the system "interposes something that acts as a single passive block to the disturbances." In this case, by such options as stringent regulation, quarantine, extensive societal segmentation and the like, the internal variety is countered while existing structures are elaborated. A second extreme response is what Ashby terms "counteraction," in which the disturbances of internal variety are met with counter-disturbances. The response involves the planned and systematic reaction to internal disturbances with counter-disturbances.[31] One illustration of this phenomenon might be a link between domestic and foreign conflict behavior where some internal problems are used to mobilize the populace for external aggressiveness in the hope of temporarily alleviating the internal problems. Such a linkage, then, is at least one pos-

[30]Ibid., pp. 128–29.
[31]Ashby, *Introduction to Cybernetics*, p. 201.

sible alternative system response when internal variety is more extensive than existing systemic constraints.

Tensions and Stresses

Clearly, the type and combination of responses by the system will be a function of a number of factors, including the magnitude and type of stress, the system orientation, and available resources. Accordingly, let us examine some sources of internal variety which might be producers of stresses. Variety, as noted, refers to the number and distribution of distinguishable elements within the system and its environment. Buckley notes that "A constant flow of potentially usable variety is provided by social differentiation, individual and subgroup differences, experience, exploration, turnover of components and cultural diffusion."[32] That is, societal heterogeneity or diversity—insofar as it designates cultural plurality, different (and perhaps mutually incompatible) life styles and orientations—may be examined as sources of internal variety in states. We must attempt to distinguish dimensions of societal diversity which can summarize internal variety for subsequent analysis. The literature on societal diversity distinguishes a number of different aspects of heterogeneity which may be relevant.[33] In operationalizing some of these indicators of societal heterogeneity, three distinct dimensions of societal variety emerged:[34]

1. *General societal diversity* accounted for 21.6 percent of the total variance and was marked by population size of the largest racial group as a percentage of the total population, the population of the largest ethnic group, group discrimination, potential separatism and percentage of the

[32]Buckley, *Sociology*, p. 129.

[33]S. M. Lipset and Stein Rokkan, eds., *Party Systems and Voter Alignments* (New York: Free Press, 1967); Douglas Rae and Michael Taylor, *The Analysis of Political Cleavages* (New Haven: Yale University Press, 1970); Tamotsu Shibutani and Kian M. Kwan, *Ethnic Stratification: Comparative Approaches* (New York: Macmillan Co., 1965).

[34]To facilitate concept formation and measurement, data on 13 indicators of societal diversity were gathered and factor analyzed using orthogonal rotation with varimax solution. The 13 indicators—population of the largest racial group as a percentage of the total population, population of the largest ethnic group, population of the largest language group, population of the largest racial group, percentage of the population which is Catholic, percentage of the population which is Buddhist, percentage of the population which is Mongolian, the number of ethnic groups larger than one percent of the population, the number of linguistic groups larger than one percent of the population, the number of religious holidays per year, group discrimination, potential separatism and the percentage of the population speaking the second largest language in the country—were drawn from three data sources: indicators 1–10 from the Dimensionality of Nations Project; indicators 11–12 from Ted R. Gurr, *New Error Compensated Measures for Comparing Nations: Some Correlates of Civil Violence*, Research Monograph No. 26, (Princeton, N.J.: Center for International Studies, 1966); and indicator 13 from Dankwart Rustow, *A World of Nations* (Washington, D.C.: Brookings Institution, 1967). The resulting three-factor solution is reported in the text of this paper.

population speaking the second largest language in the country. The pattern designated is one of differences and diversity within the society.

2. *Population diversity* (20.5 percent), denoting a pattern of societal heterogeneity, is marked by the population of the largest linguistic group, the population of the largest racial group, the percentage of the population which is Catholic, percentage Buddhist, percentage Mongolian, and the number of religious holidays per year.

3. *Ethnic diversity* (17.0 percent), marks a pattern of a multiethnic state with a number of nationality groups larger than one percent of the population and a number of language groups larger than one percent of the population loading highly on the factor.

These three major dimensions of societal diversity will be used in the model to assess societal variety. This internal variety is minimally likely in and of itself to have an impact on either system stability or change. We will expect it to be a part of the pool of variety available for structural elaboration to map both environmental variety and other societal variety. Moreover, we will expect it to be a partial producer of the normal tensions we have argued are ordinarily present in complex adaptive systems.

The key question is under what conditions these manifestations of internal variety are likely to be converted into systemic stresses, becoming manifestations of tension under severe blockage to normal interaction. Social change presents one set of conditions. Here, common interaction patterns among system components are disturbed, disrupted, and often permanently blocked. The properties of one aspect of social change, rapid economic growth, have already been examined as it relates to societal instability.[35] There is a reasonable expectation that rapid economic growth will be a short-run destabilizing force in the society. In the short run, such rapid economic growth will likely serve to disrupt the existing interaction patterns, uproot segments of the society, and give additional emphasis to tensions present in the society. That is, rapid economic growth can be disruptive insofar as it blocks ordinary interactions for tension reduction, thereby introducing stresses into the system. Over the long term, such rapid economic growth will be moderated and its impact—technological development, increased urbanization and industrialization, commercial agriculture—modified through structural differentiation and elaboration.[36] But such long-term development of constraints through structural change does not concern us. Rather, it is the short-term impact of such growth upon (1) the internal variety of the system and (2) the societal diversity which is part of this internal variety. In the short run, such rapid

[35]Mancur Olson, "Rapid growth as a Destabilizing Force," *Journal of Economic History* 27 (1963): 529–52.

[36]Neil J. Smelser, "Mechanisms of Change and Adjustment to Change," in *Industrialization and Society*, ed. B. F. Hoselitz and W. E. Moore (The Hague: UNESCO–Mouton, 1963), p. 35.

economic growth can serve to convert existing societal heterogeneity into societal divisions. This is not to suggest that the competition between and among the groups will take the form of economic rivalries, for as Horowitz has noted, there is evidence that such conflict is only of peripheral importance.[37] What is at issue, however, is the dislocation and disruption introduced with rapid economic growth inasmuch as it fosters conflict over the sharing in and distribution of the benefits of the short-term economic expansion. Social diversity is likely to be intensified over such "bread and butter" issues. Moreover, stresses created by the displacement and disruptions of rapid economic growth can also be manifested in what Horowitz terms "the components of racial conflict"—namely, career competition and political domination.[38]

Stress induced by short-term rapid economic growth which disrupts interaction patterns and intensifies divisions among social groups may begin to manifest itself within the system through a number of organized and anomic activities. Under severe stress, one can expect to see a mobilization of the populace and an incidence of minor social disruptions, especially by members of relatively disadvantaged groups. These disruptions may take the form of general strikes, demonstrations, riots, mass protests, or more individually oriented activities such as assassinations. As Rummel, Tanter, Bwy, and others have found, these activities tend to cluster together in a type of conflict behavior referred to as *turmoil*, a pattern of violence that is relatively unorganized, sporadic, of low intensity, short duration and of limited geographical scope.[39] It is our expectation, then, that the systemic stresses we have sketched above will tend to manifest themselves over time in turmoil. These expected relationships are outlined in figure 1.

Stress Management: Governmental Responses

From the assumptions outlined above, we would expect that the system will attempt to map increased internal variety generated through the stress of rapid economic growth and societal diversity on to existing constraints while trying to elaborate new structures (that is, increasing complexity) to cope with the problems. In short, complex adaptive systems, as open and inherently structure elaborating, will attempt to map the internal and en-

---

[37]Donald L. Horowitz, "Multi-Racial Politics in New States: Toward a Theory of Conflict," in *Issues in Comparative Politics*, ed. Robert L. Jackson and Michael B. Stein (New York: St. Martin's Press, 1971), p. 168.

[38]Ibid., pp. 172–77.

[39]Rummel, "Dimensions of Conflict Behavior"; idem, "A Field Theory of Social Action with Application to Conflict Within Nations," *General Systems Yearbook* 10 (1965): 183–211; Tanter, "Dimensions of Conflict Behavior": idem, "Dimensions of Conflict Behavior Within Nations, 1955–1960: Turmoil and Internal War," *Peace Research Society (International) Papers* 3 (1965): 159–83; Douglas Bwy, "Dimensions of Social Conflict in Latin America," *American Behavioral Scientist* 11 (1968): 39–50.

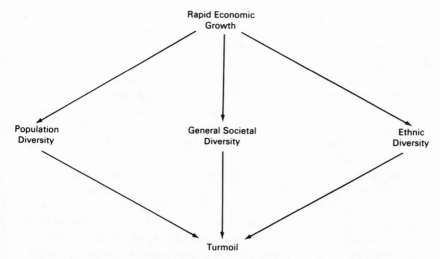

Figure 1.   Hypothesized Relationships Among Measures of Systemic Stress

vironmental variety on to existing structures or, utilizing the tensions generated by the newly created variety, develop new constraints and complexity. Our particular concern is with the internal variety generated through rapid economic growth induced stresses upon existing societal diversity which manifests itself in domestic turmoil. We must now delineate some of these system responses and specify their operation. Generally, we expect these structures to adsorb and neutralize all or part of the internal variety, thus reducing the disruptive impact of these internal stresses.

There are a number of alternative governmental responses, all oriented toward the reduction and management of the stresses and the appeals made on the governmental authorities and agencies. We shall distinguish two major classes of systemic structures involved in the governmental responses: (1) systemic capacity to reward, including the administration of social services; and (2) governmental capacity to coerce.

Governmental capacity to reward and provide social services will tend to aid the mapping of internal variety by facilitating the redress of demands on governmental authorities occurring from the stresses generated by social dislocations. Where this option of increased governmental activity in social welfare programs is emphasized, the implicit strategy is to reduce the stresses from rapid economic growth by alleviating the inequalities and societal discontinuities produced. Increased activity in social welfare can help reduce the inequalities in the distribution of collective goods resulting from the economic expansion through programs such as improved housing, health care, reduction of unemployment, and generally easing the adjustment of newly urbanized groups. Stresses on the society may be managed by supplementing the existing amounts of collective goods held by those disadvantaged groups and actively recruiting the more highly politicized members of these groups into the formal agencies of government. This type of governmental action may serve as a signal for the recipients that major benefits may be gained by remaining within the bounds of relatively orthodox behavior (defined by the norms of the particular system) rather than resorting to behavior considered "deviant." In this signaling process, a weak or ineffective governmental response could be interpreted as further evidence of the unsuitability of the existing social order, or have the effect of raising expectations without having the capacity to meet them.

The second strategy—the use of coercion against the mobilized populace—may be employed either independently or in coordination with increased governmental rewards. As Buckley notes, however, "Instruments of direct coercion, of course, often play a central role, at least until the slower processes of persuasion, socialization and member turnover become effective."[40] The objective in the effective and strategic use of force against such a group is to increase the costs of deviant behavior to a point where the benefits to be gained from these nonlegitimate activities are far less than the costs connected with their manifestation. In other words, governmental authorities will manipulate the coercive potential of the society to attempt to make the costs of deviance prohibitive.[41] In this instance, the behavior to be made costly is any action that will threaten the existing structures, institutions, and norms of the political system. When we refine the concept of capacity to constrain through coercion, we find that two major dimensions are involved.[42] The first, accounting for 37.8 percent of the total variance and termed *technological capacity*, is composed of indicators of the level of weapons development and firepower present within the armed forces of the country and measures of the level and size of the armed forces and military expenditures. The second dimension, *relative size and importance of the military* (25.8 percent), is a measure of the distribution of manpower and economic resources to the military by the society relative to the rest of the groups in the system. Thus,

---

[40]Buckley, *Sociology*, p. 129.

[41]Warren F. Ilchman and Norman T. Uphoff, *The Political Economy of Change* (Berkeley: University of California Press, 1969), pp. 70–72; Nathan Leites and Charles Wolfe, Jr., *Rebellion and Authority* (Chicago: Markham Publishing Co., 1970), passim.

[42]The ten indicators of systemic capacity to coerce were factor analyzed (orthogonal rotation, varimax solution) and the two-factor solution is discussed in the body of this paper. The source for three of these indicators—the military as a percentage of the population, the military as a percentage of the population aged 15–64, and defense expenditures as a percentage of the gross national product—was Bruce M. Russett et al., *The World Handbook of Political and Social Indicators* (New Haven: Yale University Press, 1964). The remaining seven indicators—size of the army, the technological advancement of the army, the navy, the air force and whether the military has advanced weapons systems, size of defense expenditures and defense expenditures as a percentage of governmental expenditures—came from the DON project.

it includes indicators such as the military as a percentage of the population, the military as a percentage of the population aged 15–64, defense expenditures as a percentage of governmental expenditures and as a percentage of the gross national product.

An additional note of caution is in order. Coercive measures are for the overt capacity of the system to buy compliance through coercion. No attempt has been made to measure either the actual utilization of this coercive potential by the state or fundamental inclinations of elites to resort to such coercive responses, although each one of these factors is clearly important. Rather, these measures merely assess *capacity* to coerce. Moreover, each indicator of the capacity to coerce, along with the final two factors of technological capacity and the relative size and importance of the military, have almost Janus-faced behavioral implications. That is, the capacity to coerce factors can easily be interpreted both as measures of external military preparedness and as measures of forces for internal control. Clearly, at an overt level—leaving aside all other systemic agencies of social control—those resources assessed by the technological capacity and relative size and importance factors will tend to be involved at least indirectly in attempts to buy compliance through the manipulation of coercion. Within this model, our concern is solely with their manipulation as vehicles for internal "deviance" control.

To the extent that variety-induced dislocations tend to be dissipated within the established reward and coercion process, they will be minimally manifested in foreign conflict behavior. Despite attempts to manage the stresses produced by rapid economic growth, some will go unresolved. It is possible that these stresses will be expressed in a structured and organized political violence aimed at bringing about a major change in the existing societal arrangements. However, another alternative open to the managing of the stresses is adaptation through externalization. In other words, the temporary excesses of internal variety can be reduced by mobilizing and directing the populace to support and/or engage in foreign conflict. Under conditions of high stress and insufficient or ineffectual systemic constraints (that is, minimal or inappropriate response) one strategy of adaptation is that of externalized aggressiveness. Wright suggests this position: the more intense the internal divisions between classes, parties or regions, the greater the necessity to intensify opposition to external scapegoats if state identity is to be preserved.[43] Elsewhere, Wright has noted that "to eliminate the [internal] dissentions, governments often resort to regimentation of opinion and the creation of scapegoats."[44] Finally, Wright argues that even extensive government response may not sufficiently reduce the stresses. "More intense political organization of a

[43]Wright, *Study of War*, p. 241.
[44]Ibid., p. 166.

nation, region, or other group will not therefore necessarily reduce the amount of conflict in which it is involved. Such organizations may merely divert opposition from its internal to its external relations."[45] More specifically, Rostow refers to the recent rise of some leaders ". . . who have chosen, in differing proportions and under differing influences, to build their domestic politics on 'anti-imperialism' and to channel a high proportion of the limited energies, talents, and resources available to them into external expansion. . . ."[46] Incorporating Wright and others, then, we expect that through scapegoating or some other such method, ineffectively managed systemic stresses are likely to result in foreign conflict behavior. The results of both Wilkenfeld and Stohl suggest that systems in which elites have broad decisional latitude tend to be characterized by moderately strong relationships between domestic and foreign conflict.[47]

Foreign Conflict Behavior

To this point we have referred to an undifferentiated dependent variable: foreign conflict behavior. We now turn to conceptualizing and specifying the empirical referents for this behavior. One useful way to consider foreign conflict behavior is along a continuum ranging from low to high of relative intensity and magnitude of the conflict exhibited. At the "high" end, we can place wars and large-scale military actions of varying degrees of severity and duration. At the low end fall smaller-scale disruptions or ordinary interstate interactions which are limited and marginal in impact. Between the two poles fall conflictual relations of increasing intensity and magnitude in which states take some actions toward physical conflict or more severe disruption of internation interactions but stop short of war.

Studies by Rummel, Tanter, and Phillips suggest some evidence for such a conceptualization.[48] For the 1955–57 and 1958–60 periods, Rummel and Tanter found three dimensions of foreign conflict behavior: belligerency, diplomatic conflict, and war.[49] Rummel and Phillips, using a more extensive set of indicators for 1955–57 and 1963, found five dimensions: negative communications, negative sanctions, warnings and defensive acts, anti-

[45]Ibid., p. 240.

[46]Walt Rostow, *Politics and the Stages of Growth* (London and New York: Cambridge University Press, 1971), p. 279.

[47]Wilkenfeld, "Domestic and Foreign Conflict Behavior"; idem, "Some Further Findings"; Stohl, "Study of Conflict Behavior."

[48]Rummel, "Dimension of Conflict Behavior"; Tanter, "Dimensions of Conflict Behavior"; Warren R. Phillips, "The Conflict Environment of Nations: A Study of Conflict Inputs to Nations in 1963," chap. 5, this volume; idem, "The Dynamics of Behavioral Action and Reaction in International Conflict" (Paper delivered at the Peace Research Society (International), Philadelphia Conference, 1970).

[49]Rummel, "Dimensions of Conflict Behavior"; Tanter, "Dimensions of Conflict Behavior."

foreign acts, and military violence.[50] Each one of these dimensions can be placed along a continuum of foreign conflict behavior to specify more clearly the meaning of the concept and the points along the continuum.

This study will use Tanter's factor analysis of thirteen indicators of foreign conflict behavior for 1958–60 to assess the dependent variable.[51] The first factor, *diplomatic conflict* (25.2 percent of the total variance), is marked by key loading items of negative sanctions, protests, expulsions of ambassadors and lesser officials, threats, and accusations. It denotes a pattern of conflict that is generally nonviolent and indicated by relatively commonplace disruptions of the interactions among contemporary states. Where such disruptions or disturbances do occur, they tend to be what Tanter refers to as of "a rational nature" compared to other kinds of conflict. That is, manifestations of diplomatic conflict tend to be relatively planned and controlled expressions of some incompatibilities of exhibited behavior with the norms of interstate interaction. Since such violations of the rules of the international game are relatively common, the responses tend to be of relatively low intensity. The second factor, *war* (21.8 percent), presents a pattern of activities involved in the preparation and waging of war. It is marked by such key loading items as troop mobilizations, military actions, wars, and the number killed in foreign conflict. Factor three, *belligerency* (10.1 percent), marked by severances of diplomatic relations and antiforeign demonstrations, presents a pattern of formal governmental and group response to some set of disturbing stimuli, either from within the nation or from the international system. In this case, the response is more severe than some minor disruptions of the common interaction patterns, yet less intense than the preparations for war included in the war factor.

The factor scores for these three dimensions, then, will give us an assessment of the level of each exhibited by the nations in the study for the 1958–60 time period. We must still confront a basic question of the relative importance of the bonds between systemic stresses, governmental responses, and the three dimensions of foreign conflict behavior. Will all three dimensions of foreign conflict behavior be equally (approximately) statistically accounted for by the other variables in the model, or is it reasonable to expect differences in the predictive power to the types of foreign conflict? Should we expect diplomatic conflict, war, or belligerency to

[50]R. J. Rummel, "International Patterns and National Profile Delineation," in *Computers and the Policy Making Community: Applications to International Relations*, ed. Davis Bobrow and Judah L. Schwartz (Englewood Cliffs, N.J.: Prentice-Hall, 1968); Phillips, "Conflict Environment"; idem, "Dynamics of Behavioral Action."

[51]While Tanter in "Dimensions of Conflict Behavior" included 83 countries in his study for 1958–60 and Rummel in "Dimensions of Conflict Behavior" included 77 for 1955–57, the countries common to both sets number 74. These 74 were utilized in the statistical analysis reported in this study.

be related to stresses and governmental responses in comparable or different ways? Earlier formulations of the systemic stresses → foreign conflict model tended to emphasize the explanation of war or warlikeness.[52] On the other hand, it seems reasonable to (1) expect differentials in explained variance, particularly (2) stronger relationships between stresses and responses and belligerency and diplomatic conflict. The relationships with war are expected to be weaker in magnitude on the grounds that war would be a more intense response than need be manifested to manage the stresses. In engaging in war, while one could easily mobilize the populace against some scapegoat, thereby distracting them from the dislocations induced by rapid economic growth and the intensification of societal divisions, the problems involved become apparent. In engaging in war the nation risks perhaps insufficient resources to buy time for structural elaboration to constrain the internal variety more effectively. With diplomatic conflict and belligerency, on the other hand, scapegoating to displace stresses can be undertaken with a much lower resource expenditure and risk. Thus, one nation could effectively manage the stresses of social change with the severing of diplomatic relations or antiforeign demonstrations (belligerency) to reduce internal variety or expel ambassadors or lesser officials, protest, sanctions, and so forth (diplomatic conflict) to achieve the same end. With diplomatic conflict, given its relatively minor long-range impact on the interactions of the international system, the internal advantages are quite significant while external costs are low. With belligerency, only slightly higher external costs are present, but the potential for the short-term management of internal variety is probably the highest of the three dimensions of foreign conflict behavior.

Summary

Thus far we have suggested that societies may be analyzed as open, tension-oriented, and structure-elaborating systems. We have argued that considerable amounts of foreign conflict behavior—especially belligerency and diplomatic conflict—can be accounted for as attempts at system adaptation through an externalization of internal variety into the international environment. Specifically, we have hypothesized that the intensification of societal diversity through rapid economic growth produces stresses on the system, manifested in domestic turmoil, which can be responded to through either increased social services and/or coercion to reduce and adsorb this internal variety. To the extent that internal variety is more extensive than internal constraint, the systemic stresses are likely to be manifested in foreign conflict behavior at a later time period. These relationships are summarized in figure 2.

[52]For example, see Haas, "Social Change"; Wright, *Study of War.*

Figure 2.   Summary of Hypothesized Relationships

TESTING THE MODEL: BASIC RELATIONSHIPS

Measurement Stability

Before proceeding to test the model, we must deal with a problem present in the analysis of data from large numbers of social systems. This problem is the establishment of the stability of the measurement and the results across subsets of the data matrix. As Alker and others have demonstrated, different factors and different statistical relationships can be obtained with alternative subsets of the data matrix.[53] Stated in the language

---

[53]Hayward Alker, "The Long Road to International Relations Theory: Problems of Statistical Non-Additivity," in *New Approaches to International Relations*, ed. Morton Kaplan (New York: St. Martin's Press, 1968).

of measurement, we must establish the stability and the equivalence of our measures across sets of countries. Przeworski and Teune have noted that "The criterion for inferring the equivalence of measurement instruments can be found in the structure of the indicators. Equivalence of measurement instruments must be demonstrated when there is some reason for believing that system interference is present, that is, when the same inference cannot be used in all systems."[54] Accordingly, we have attempted to test the stability of the foreign conflict factor structure across some divisions of the data matrix which might permit us to examine systemic interference in the otherwise generally observed relationships. In so doing we are asking whether our three dimensions of foreign conflict—belligerency, diplomatic, and war—can be found whenever we subdivide our data matrix into various categories of political systems. We shall employ a combination of discriminant function analysis[55] to cluster the countries and the Ahmavaara factor comparison algorithm[56] to compare the factors for each cluster to one another and to those obtained when all countries are jointly analyzed.

In our attempts to assess measurement stability, the initial research question is what single variable or configuration of variables might intervene upon the basic three-factor solution for foreign conflict behavior to produce the systemic interferences described by Przeworski and Teune. One such variable might be the national wealth level. Rostow hypothesized that different stages of economic growth strongly influence other areas of social behavior.[57] Adelman and Morris observed substantial

---

[54]Adam Przeworski and Henry Teune, *The Logic of Comparative Social Inquiry* (New York: John Wiley and Sons, 1970), p. 114.

[55]Representative literature on discriminant function analysis includes T. W. Anderson, *Introduction to Multivariate Statistical Analysis* (New York: John Wiley and Sons, 1958); Chester I. Bliss *Statistics in Biology, II* (New York: McGraw-Hill Book Co., 1970); William Cooley and Paul Lohnes, *Multivariate Procedures for the Behavioral Sciences* (New York: John Wiley and Sons, 1962); idem, *Multivariate Data Analysis* (New York: John Wiley and Sons, 1971); R. A. Fisher, "The Use of Multiple Measurement in Taxonomic Problems," *Annuals of Eugenics* 7 (1936): 179–88. The computations were performed with the University of Miami (Florida) discriminant function program for two groups with discrimination being made on the thirteen indicators of foreign conflict. Presented with the final clusters, listed in Appendix 1, is an *F*-test to evaluate the effectiveness of the discrimination.

[56]This procedure is presented in Yrjo Ahmavaara, "Transformation Analysis of Factorial Data," *Annales Academiae Scientiarum Fennicae* 88 (1954): 1–150. It is discussed in R. J. Rummel, *Applied Factor Analysis* (Evanston: Northwestern University Press, 1970). The procedure is utilized in Rummel, "Field Theory of Social Action." Rummel classes the Ahmavaara procedure as a transformation comparison in which factors of two different studies are compared in terms of jointly occupied vector space. The resulting coefficients are cosines of the angles between each factor in each study. Thus, they are interpretable as correlation coefficients. In other words, the results presented in table 1 are to be read as the correlation of factor 1 for all countries with factor 1 in the "Western" cluster and so forth. I wish to thank Willard Keim of the University of Pennsylvania for making the Ahmavaara procedure available to me.

[57]Rostow, *Stages of Economic Growth*.

differences in the behavior of a number of economic, political, and social variables once wealth level was controlled for.[58] Accordingly, our countries were divided into "high wealth" and "low wealth" groups using GNP/capita (1957) as the assignment criterion. These groups were then tested for homogeneity using discriminant function analysis, a generalized analysis of variance procedure. Working with a prespecified set of data—in this case, the thirteen indicators of foreign conflict—discriminant function analysis (1) isolates the key discriminating variables which distinguish the test groups, (2) gives a measure of differences between the test groups on each of the thirteen indicators as well as (3) an overall measure of the discrimination of the two sets of countries with the thirteen indicators, and (4) reclassifies the countries from one grouping to another in terms of most likeness on the discriminating variables. In our data, for example, reclassification meant that a formerly "high wealth" country had a pattern of foreign conflict closer to that of the "low wealth" countries than to that of the "high wealth" states. Thus, in reclassifying a state into the "high" or "low" wealth category we are stating that its pattern of foreign conflict for 1958–60 is closer to the other "high" or "low" wealth states than it is to countries in the opposite category. The final discriminated clusters of states, statistically significant at $p < 0.0001$, are listed in appendix 1. However intuitively troublesome some of the individual case classifications might be, they represent an empirically homogeneous categorization on foreign conflict for 1958–60. Table 1 presents thirteen indicators of for-

Table 1. Discriminating Variables for Wealth Clusters

Variable	"High Wealth" Mean	"Low Wealth" Mean	t
Antiforeign demonstrations	4.38	1.93	2.88[a]
Negative sanctions	0.86	1.37	0.90
Protests	6.21	2.22	2.67[a]
Severance of diplomatic relations	0.24	0.35	0.82
Expulsion of ambassadors	1.03	0.24	3.64[b]
Expulsion of lesser officials	2.38	0.31	5.91[b]
Threats	4.41	1.78	1.25
Military actions	0.48	0.65	0.79
Wars	0.10	0.28	1.01
Troop movements	1.34	0.31	1.92
Mobilizations	0.21	0.11	0.88
Accusations	13.62	7.09	1.60
Number killed in foreign conflict	5.79	14.93	1.87

[a] $p < .01$.
[b] $p < .001$.

[58]Irma Adelman and Cynthia Taft Morris, *Society, Politics and Economic Development* (Baltimore, Md.: Johns Hopkins University Press, 1967).

eign conflict and the final group means together with the difference of means tests for each. The *t* tests demonstrate that "high wealth" states experienced significantly higher levels of antiforeign demonstrations, protests, expulsions of ambassadors and lesser officials than did "low wealth" states. The pattern that appears to distinguish the "highs" from the "lows," then, is one of much more extensive belligerency in internation interactions on the part of the wealthier countries. Moreover, the strength of the overall discrimination (that is, all thirteen variables considered jointly) is statistically significant, $F(13, 69) = 13.862, p < 0.0001$.

A second possible source of systematic disturbances are those of the "cultural legacies" of "Western" and "non-Western" states.[59] After dividing the data matrix into "Western" and "non-Western" groups through a geographical criterion, we utilized discriminant function analysis to identify homogeneous groups based on the thirteen foreign conflict indicators (table 2). The final classification, also listed in appendix 1, shows that the mean value of the "non-Western" states is significantly higher than those of the "Western" states on severances of diplomatic relations (belligerency) dimension), number killed in foreign conflict (war dimension), number of antiforeign demonstrations, and number of negative sanctions (diplomatic dimension). The general pattern distinguishing the two clusters—statistically significant with $F(13, 69) = 18.763, p < 0.0001$—is one of "non-

Table 2.   Discriminating Variables for Cultural Clusters

Variable	"Western" Mean	"Non-Western" Mean	*t*
Antiforeign demonstrations	1.80	4.62	3.38[b]
Negative sanctions	0.72	2.07	2.46[a]
Protests	3.96	2.97	0.64
Severance of diplomatic relations	0.04	0.83	7.71[c]
Expulsion of ambassadors	0.54	0.48	0.23
Expulsion of lesser officials	0.96	1.17	0.50
Threats	2.89	2.34	0.26
Military actions	0.46	0.83	1.76
Wars	0.17	0.31	0.83
Troop movements	0.72	0.59	0.25
Mobilizations	0.07	0.28	1.89
Accusations	8.74	10.55	0.44
Number killed in foreign conflict	5.85	22.69	3.64[c]

[a]$p < .02$.
[b]$p < .01$.
[c]$p < .001$.

[59]Lucian W. Pye, "The Non-Western Political Process," *Journal of Politics* 20 (1958): 468–86; Alfred Diamant, "Is there a Non-Western Political Process?" *Journal of Politics* 21 (1959): 123–27.

Western" states engaging in substantially more of indicators from all three dimensions of foreign conflict.

After developing discriminated homogeneous clusters of countries and distinguishing their defining characteristics, we can now test whether the foreign conflict factor structure found for all countries is also found within each of these homogeneous subsets of the data matrix. Thus, we factor analyzed the thirteen indicators of foreign conflict in each one of the four clusters of countries ("high" and "low" wealth, "Western" and "non-Western") and compared the resulting factor structures with the Ahmavaara factor comparison procedure. This statistical technique permits one to compare any two sets of factor analyses utilizing the same variables on a factor by factor basis as well as by entire factor matrices. Presented in table 3 are the cosines between the factors (as vectors) in the all-country

Table 3. Comparison of Factor Analyses across Clusters of States

			All States		
		Diplomatic	War	Belligerency	
Non-Western	1	−0.52	−0.43	0.73	
states	2	−0.98	0.04	−0.17	$r = 0.88$
	3	0.85	0.49	−0.20	
Western	1	0.82	0.02	0.57	
states	2	−0.07	−1.00	−0.04	$r = 0.84$
	3	0.43	0.26	0.86	
High wealth	1	0.86	0.13	−0.48	
states	2	−0.15	0.98	−0.12	$r = 0.86$
	3	0.54	−0.56	−0.63	
Low wealth	1	0.69	0.72	−0.06	
states	2	0.74	−0.37	−0.57	$r = 0.87$
	3	0.52	0.73	−0.43	

analysis and those developed in each of the factor analyses within each of the four clusters of countries. These cosines describe the extent of similarity between the factors in the all-country analysis and those developed in each cluster. Since, as Jackson demonstrated, for standardized data the cosine between two variables as vectors equals their product moment correlation,[60] the figures given in table 3 may be interpreted as the correlation of each factor in the all-country analysis with each of those found in the within cluster analysis. We also obtain a product moment correlation between the two complete factor matrices. Thus, for example, on table 3 the *overall* relationship between the factor structure for all countries and for

[60]D. Jackson, "The Trigonometry of Correlation," *American Mathematical Monthly* 31 (1924): 275–80.

the "high wealth" countries is a robust $r = 0.86$, indicating that the two-factor structures share almost 74 percent in common variance.

In examining the results of the factor comparison, two issues are before us. First, is there present in each cluster of countries a factor structurally comparable to the one found when all of the countries are considered simultaneously? Second, is the nature of the relationships between and among the factors within each group of countries similar to the relationships found for all countries? The Ahmavaara factor comparisons generally demonstrate the existence of three factors—diplomatic conflict, war, and belligerency—in the various clusters of states. Overall relationships among the sets of data ranged from $r = 0.88$ for all states and "Western" countries to $r = 0.84$ for all and "non-Western" states. Only in the case of war in the "non-Western" states was a comparable factor pattern absent in the country clusters. While it is clear that there is presence in each cluster, the factors are obviously not orthogonal to one another. The overall relationships indicate measurement stability within the data matrix, however.

General Relationships

The first expected linkage in the model is between systemic stresses and foreign conflict. It was argued that stress would be positively and substantially related to foreign conflict. Rapid economic growth is measured by the change in gross national product per capita from 1950 to 1960, societal diversity by the three factors outlined above, and turmoil by Rummel's factor of domestic conflict behavior for 1955–57. These five variables, our measures of societal stress, will be examined for strength and direction of association with diplomatic conflict, war, and belligerency for 1958–60 with canonical correlation, a statistical procedure permitting the simultaneous assessments of the relationship of multiple "independent" and multiple "dependent" variables.[61] The results of the first canonical analysis present three empirical patterns between these two sets of variables. The first two canonical correlations are statistically significant,[62] account-

[61]Canonical analysis is formally discussed in Anderson, *Introduction to Multivariate Statistical Analysis;* Cooley and Lohnes, *Multivariate Procedures;* and idem, *Multivariate Data Analysis,* 1970. Recent applications of the technique in political science research include Roger W. Cobb and Charles Elder, *International Community: A Regional and Global Study* (New York: Holt, Rinehart and Winston, 1970); Warren R. Phillips and Dennis R. Hall, "The Importance of Governmental Structure as a Taxonomic Scheme for Nations," *Comparative Political Studies* 3 (1970): 63–89; Phillips, "Conflict Environment"; idem, "Dynamics of Behavioral Action." Calculations for the canonical correlations presented here were performed with BMD06M. In the canonical analysis, $N = 74$.

[62]Significance tests have been included not for the purpose of drawing inferences from a sample to a population (for we are dealing with a population), but rather to distinguish whether the observed population relationships could have been generated by underlying processes distinguishable from mere chance. Presentations of this position may be found in David Gold, "Some Problems in Generalizing Aggregate Associations, *"Ameri-*

ing for up to 45 percent of the common variance between stress and foreign conflict. They generally indicate that internal stresses do have a significant impact on foreign conflict behavior, at least for the latter 1950s.

The first canonical correlation (1.1) depicts a pattern in which popula-

0.23 GNP/capita − 0.11 general + 0.78 population + 0.44 ethnic + 0.54 turmoil →

0.35 diplomatic + 0.95 war − 0.09 belligerency (1.1)

$Rc_1 = 0.67$ $\chi^2 = 68.908$ $df = 15$ $p < 0.01$

tion diversity, ethnic diversity, and turmoil for 1955–57 are positively related to foreign conflict behavior, their association with war being particularly strong. In terms of the model, existing internal variety (societal diversity and turmoil), even without extreme economic expansion to activate it, is strongly associated with external conflict behavior. Economic stability, societal heterogeneity, and internal turmoil predict best to war. The second pattern (1.2) presents an inverse relationship of economic growth and ethnic diversity with foreign conflict while turmoil and foreign conflict are positively associated. That is, the greater the economic expansion and ethnic diversity, the lower the levels of foreign conflict, particularly diplomatic conflict and belligerency. Countries with high belligerency and diplomatic conflict also tend to be economically stagnant and homogeneous. On the other hand, those societies with high belligerency and diplomatic conflict will also tend to have high levels of internal turmoil. Thus, extensive economic expansion and high ethnic diversity, together with low levels of turmoil, predict to low levels of foreign conflict, especially belligerency and diplomatic, and vice versa. In this pattern, accounting for 26.6 percent of the common variance, the economic expansion and societal diversity do not result in any measured manifestations of stress. They are

0.53 GNP/capita − 0.06 general − 0.09 population + 0.41 ethnic − 0.68 turmoil →

−0.39 diplomatic − 0.04 war − 0.95 belligerency (1.2)

$Rc_2 = 0.53$ $\chi^2 = 28.358$ $df = 8$ $p < 0.001$

not positively associated with either domestic or foreign conflict. In terms of the model, one might speculate either that the tensions of interaction have not yet been sufficiently blocked to create stresses or that subsequent governmental responses have effectively defrayed these stresses before

---

can Behavior Scientist 8 (1964): 16–18; and Robert F. Winch and D. T. Campbell," Proof? No. Evidence? Yes. The Significance of Tests of Significance," *The American Sociologist* 4 (1969): 140–43. Alternative critical interpretations of the use of significance tests are presented in Denton Morrison and Ramon E. Henkel, eds., *The Significance Test Controversy: A Reader* (Chicago: Aldine Publishing Co., 1970).

either domestic or foreign conflict occurred. However, it is not a set of relationships expected in the model.[63]

To this point we have found that a combination of economic stagnation, population and ethnic diversity, and domestic turmoil is positively related to foreign conflict, especially war, and that high levels of economic expansion and ethnic diversity, when combined with low levels of turmoil, are associated with low levels of foreign conflict, especially belligerency and diplomatic conflict. Thus, the model has borne up well for the first pattern discovered and perhaps questionably for the second. Internal systemic diversity, although not economically induced, is positively associated with the level of foreign conflict for the latter 1950s. Nevertheless, the expected differences between systemic stresses and the three dimensions of foreign conflict behavior have not been observed. Rather than systemic stresses being more strongly related to belligerency and diplomatic conflict than to war, we find that the level of war for 1958–60 is better explained by systemic stresses than either of the other foreign conflict dimensions. In fact, economic expansion and relative ethnic heterogeneity, when combined with limited internal turmoil, tend to be more strongly and inversely associated with belligerency and diplomatic conflict than the stresses from rapid economic growth and societal diversity pattern which we had postulated. Nevertheless, the relationships between internal stresses and foreign conflict are clearly manifested in the canonical correlations. The relationships are strong and, for the first canonical, generally as predicted by the model. We conclude that foreign conflict is more likely under conditions of societal diversity and turmoil. Under economic expansion, some societal diversity and low levels of turmoil, foreign conflict is less likely. The apparently pivotal importance of domestic turmoil as a measure of internal stress to subsequent manifestations of foreign conflict will be explored later.

Second among the predictions of the model is the relationship of systemic stresses to governmental response. It was argued that governmental responses would map systemic stresses on to existing structures, thus constraining the internal variety and moving toward structural elaboration. In our analysis, we have assessed the relationship between the two sets, from which we shall draw inferences on mapping. The three internal responses are measured by change in the central governmental budget per capita from 1951 to 1961 and the two dimensions of the capacity to coerce.[64] The measures of systemic stress are the ones used previously. With this statistical analysis we are attempting to examine two questions raised in

---

[63]A third canonical correlation ($RC_3 = 0.28$) was also developed. Given its small size, however, it is not reported here.

[64]The data on central governmental budget growth per capita over time is from Gurr, *New Error Compensated Measures.*

the model: (1) what is the extent of the relationship (mapping) between systemic stresses and governmental responses? (2) what patterns of stress management are observed? That is, how do societies tend to manage the stresses of extensive internal variety with available system structures?

Three canonical correlations are developed between systemic stress and governmental responses, two of which are statistically significant. The first canonical correlation (2.1), accounting for over 38 percent of the common variance of the two sets of variables, summarizes the positive association of very rapid economic growth and population diversity with governmental responses, particularly the capacity to coerce. The weak weight of the budget growth measure—compared to the weights of the assessments of coercive capacity—indicate that this pattern might well be labeled the *coercive response*. Societies with very rapid economic growth

$$0.93 \, \text{GNP/capita} - 0.03 \, \text{general} + 0.36 \, \text{population} + 0.07 \, \text{ethnic} + 0.11 \, \text{turmoil} \rightarrow$$
$$-0.04 \, \text{budget} + 0.33 \, \text{technological} + 0.96 \, \text{relative size} \qquad (2.1)$$
$$Rc_1 = 0.62 \qquad \chi^2 = 50.051 \qquad df = 15 \qquad p < 0.001$$

and heterogeneous populations tend to be characterized by responses to systemic stresses based on force, thus attempting to make the costs of "deviance" too high. In this first canonical, it appears that the relationship of turmoil to governmental response is negligable. It may be the case that coercive responses tend to be exercised whenever rapid economic growth and population heterogeneity coincide with low levels of turmoil. Alternatively, the low levels of turmoil may be the product of governmental responses which raise the costs of deviance through coercion.

The second pattern uncovered (2.2) accounts for 21.1 percent of the variance between the two sets. Here, a combination of low levels of population diversity and turmoil is associated with a multiple-strategy governmental response involving low levels of budget growth and technological capacity to coerce. The more diverse the population and the more conflictual the society, the greater the likelihood that the governmental response to these systemic stresses will employ both noncoercive (budget growth) and coercive (technological capacity) actions. While our first canonical pattern (Rc_1) was one of purely coercive responses to these systemic stresses, in this canonical (Rc_2) we observe a "carrot and stick" pattern of governmental responses in which systemic stresses evoke a joint strategy of stress reduction through budget growth (social accommodation) and technological capacity to coerce (deviance penalization).[65]

[65]A third canonical correlation ($Rc_3 = 0.12$) produced between these sets of variables is not reported at this time.

$0.34\,\text{GNP}/\text{capita} + 0.24\,\text{general} - 0.88\,\text{population} + 0.11\,\text{ethnic} -$
$0.43\,\text{turmoil} \rightarrow$
$-0.74\,\text{budget} - 0.75\,\text{technological} + 0.32\,\text{relative size}$ (2.2)
$Rc_2 = 0.46 \qquad \chi^2 = 17.157 \qquad df = 8 \qquad p < 0.05$

Once again in these canonicals we note the apparently pivotal position of levels of domestic turmoil in predicting subsequent behavior—modes of governmental response, in this case. Societies in which rapid economic growth and population diversity are present along with minimal turmoil tend to generate a purely coercive response, while societies with stresses generated by population diversity and appreciable levels of turmoil generally tend to more complex coercive and noncoercive responses. The inclusion of noncoercive activities within the governmental responses to systemic stresses appears at least partially to depend upon the prior levels of domestic turmoil observed in the society.

Depending upon how well the internal variety is mapped on to system structures as constraints, certain levels of foreign conflict are predicted as the unmapped variety—the societal disorder—and externalized to aid adaptation while stress management capabilities are elaborated. With the canonical analysis presented below we shall examine two additional questions from the model: (1) how extensive is the relationship (mapping) between governmental responses and foreign conflict? (2) are there any dominant patterns in the externalization of societal variety? That is, do some governmental responses tend to be more important as externalizers of variety than others?

$0.20\,\text{budget} + 0.95\,\text{technological} + 0.33\,\text{relative size} \rightarrow$
$0.92\,\text{diplomatic} + 0.45\,\text{war} - 0.02\,\text{belligerency}$ (3.1)
$Rc_1 = 0.74 \qquad \chi^2 = 67.425 \qquad df = 9 \qquad p < 0.001$

The first canonical pattern (3.1) is one in which extensive governmental response (especially technological capacity) is positively associated with foreign conflict, particularly diplomatic conflict and wars. This pattern, which accounts for almost 54 percent of the common variance, is highlighted by the strong positive relationship between the capacity to coerce and extensive diplomatic conflict and warfare. In particular, the strength of the weights of technological capacity and diplomatic conflict seems to illustrate a general saber-rattling pattern in which states with well-equipped military attempt to utilize them through aggressive external behavior. On the other hand, a second significant canonical correlation between governmental response and foreign conflict (3.2) isolates an alternative pattern. A large and important capacity to coerce is positively associated with a foreign conflict pattern of warfare but low levels of belligerency and diplomatic conflict. Essentially, then, large size and importance of the military as a type of governmental response to systemic stresses tends to be associated with subsequent warlikeness along with minimal nonviolent (diplomatic) and semiviolent (belligerency) conflict.[66]

$$0.20 \text{ budget} - 0.35 \text{ technological} + 0.86 \text{ relative size} \rightarrow$$
$$-0.33 \text{ diplomatic} + 0.52 \text{ war} - 0.78 \text{ belligerency}$$
$$Rc_2 = 0.42 \qquad \chi^2 = 13.212 \qquad df = 4 \qquad p < 0.02 \qquad (3.2)$$

The two general patterns that emerge show coercive potential consistently dwarfing noncoercive governmental response as the method in which societies attempt to externalize system variety into international conflict to aid adaptation. What is still at issue, however, is the extent to which coercive versus noncoercive alternatives are utilized in response to internal conditions. Is it the case that extensive heterogeneity of the society together with domestic turmoil bring combined responses for adaptation through externalization? Or is externalization always likely through the coercive responses, regardless of the levels and orientation of the societal stresses?

These questions will be explored as we aggregate the components of the model and examine the networks of relationships among them. Thus far, however, we have seen that the relationships between stress and foreign conflict behavior, stress and governmental response, and governmental response and foreign conflict behavior are all of considerable magnitude. These linkages are summarized in figure 3. The first canonical correlation has been placed above the directional arrow and the percentage of the common variance placed below the line. How all of the components of the model will jointly relate to foreign conflict is the next question to which we shall turn.

Aggregating the Components of the Model

Having examined the general steps through the model, we turn now to a joint assessment of systemic stresses and governmental responses as they predict to foreign conflict. Three statistically significant canonical correlations are found in (4.1) to (4.3). The first of these (4.1), accounting for almost 66 percent of the common variance of the two sets, shows generally positive relationships between systemic stresses and responses and foreign conflict behavior. Particularly important in this association are turmoil and the capacity to coerce measures as they are related to diplomatic conflict and war. High turmoil and extensive capacity to coerce tend to be associated with both violent (war) and nonviolent (diplomatic conflict) foreign conflict behavior. At least for this first canonical, systemic stresses other than turmoil, and government responses other than the capacity to

[66]Although not discussed at this time, a third canonical correlation ($Rc_3 = 0.06$) was also developed between these sets of variables.

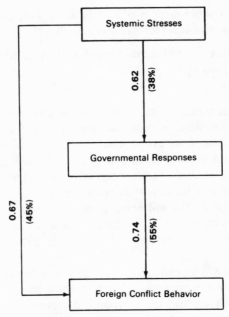

Figure 3.   Magnitude of Relationships Within the Model

coerce, appear to be unimportant predictors of belligerency, diplomatic conflict, and war.

0.07 GNP/capita + 0.05 general + 0.20 population + 0.17 ethnic +
0.42 turmoil + 0.11 budget + 0.74 technological + 0.33 relative size →
0.83 diplomatic + 0.62 war + 0.10 belligerency   (4.1)
$Rc_1 = 0.81$ $\chi^2 = 125.471$ $df = 24$ $p < 0.001$

While the magnitude of the relationship between the two sets is note-worthy, the resulting overall pattern is only partially consistent with the one specified in the model. Here, the measures of economic growth and societal diversity are not important individually, let alone in the hy-pothesized relationship of rapid economic growth accelerating societal divisions. Additionally, we find that war is predicted to much more strongly than anticipated within the model. On the other hand, diplomatic conflict, as expected, is strongly associated with the stress and governmen-tal response measures. Beyond these discrepancies, however, the findings are not inconsistent with our earlier theoretical specifications. That is, generally stressful societal conditions (producing additional internal variety), moderated by the governmental responses, tend to manifest them-selves in foreign conflict subsequently experienced. Turmoil and techno-logical capacity associated with diplomatic conflict and war are generally stronger aspects of this relationship.

In the second canonical correlation (4.2), sharing about 41 percent of the common variance, population and ethnic diversity are inversely related to a foreign conflict pattern combining high levels of diplomatic conflict and belligerency with infrequent wars. Technological capacity to coerce,

$$-0.17 \text{ GNP/capita} + 0.20 \text{ general} - 0.56 \text{ population} - 0.52 \text{ ethnic} +$$
$$0.05 \text{ turmoil} + 0.03 \text{ budget} + 0.48 \text{ technological} - 0.27 \text{ relative size} \rightarrow$$
$$0.46 \text{ diplomatic} - 0.65 \text{ war} + 0.58 \text{ belligerency} \tag{4.2}$$
$$Rc_2 = 0.64 \quad \chi^2 = 52.509 \quad df = 14 \quad p < 0.001$$

on the other hand, is strongly and positively associated with this same foreign conflict configuration. These results are interpretable as a variation on the saber-rattling pattern observed earlier in which generally nonviolent foreign conflict (diplomatic and belligerency) is engaged in by economically stagnating, homogeneous societies with a small but well-developed military. This second canonical demonstrates another aspect of the linkages specified in the model. In this case, we find societal diversity inversely associated with foreign conflict as long as the technological capacity to coerce is present. Whereas the first canonical presented turmoil and governmental response strongly related to foreign conflict, here we see the importance of societal diversity and the combination of the systemic stress and governmental response variables.

Another variation on the model is seen in the third canonical correlation (4.3) which accounts for 22 percent of the common variance. Here, there are minor differences from the results of Rc_2 in which one of the societal diversity and one of the governmental response variables is important as well as in which of the dimensions of foreign conflict behavior are more important. On the whole, however, the associations depicted in the two canonicals are really quite similar. In Rc_3 population diversity and turmoil

$$-0.01 \text{ GNP/capita} + 0.18 \text{ general} - 0.59 \text{ population} + 0.02 \text{ ethnic} -$$
$$0.58 \text{ turmoil} + 0.30 \text{ budget} + 0.46 \text{ technological} - 0.01 \text{ relative size} \rightarrow$$
$$0.33 \text{ diplomatic} - 0.45 \text{ war} - 0.81 \text{ belligerency} \tag{4.3}$$
$$Rc_3 = 0.47 \quad \chi^2 = 16.895 \quad df = 6 \quad p < 0.01$$

are inversely related to a foreign conflict pattern mixing diplomatic conflict with very little war and belligerency. This same foreign conflict configuration is positively associated with governmental responses, especially budget growth and technological capacity to coerce. Societies characterized by population homogeneity and low levels of domestic turmoil along with large per capita budget growth and technological capacity to coerce tend to engage in relatively limited foreign conflict, although that conflict which is observed positively associates with governmental response. Alternatively, societies with heterogeneous populations and high domestic turmoil levels, together with limited governmental responses (both coercive and noncoercive), tend to engage in foreign conflict more frequently, particularly war and belligerency. This third canonical, then, presents a pattern of societal diversity and domestic conflict being positively or negatively related to subsequent foreign conflict depending upon how effectively the governmental response variables function. Where governmental responses are positively related to foreign conflict behavior—in the language of the model, when they are effective in externalizing systemic stresses—societal diversity and turmoil are inversely associated with foreign conflict, and vice versa.

MODEL SPECIFICATION: SOME ADDITIONAL CONSIDERATIONS

To this point we have examined the associations over time among stress, governmental response, and foreign conflict behavior. Using canonical correlations, we have found strong relationships between stress and foreign conflict behavior, governmental response and foreign conflict behavior, and the combination of systemic stress and governmental response and foreign conflict behavior. At least the first canonical correlation in these findings has generally been interpreted as consistent with the predictions of the model. Nevertheless, a number of other canonical correlations indicated patterns within the data which were at least partially inconsistent with the model. That is, while the magnitudes of the overall relationships (for example, stress → foreign conflict) have been expected, the status of the linkages among the individual components of the systemic stress, governmental response and foreign conflict variable groups outlined in figure 2 is, at least, unclear. In this section we shall attempt to clarify further these internal interdependencies, utilizing path analysis.[67] The task now is to test the dependencies found among the variables in the model.

If we rely on figure 2 as an initial model for testing with path analysis, some changes must be made if the equations are to be identifiable—that is, if "the model is restrictive enough so that, given sufficiently large samples, the values of parameters can be determined."[68] By considering

[67]Representative literature on path analysis includes: Otis Dudley Duncan, "Path Analysis: Sociological Examples," *American Journal of Sociology* 72 (1966): 1-16; Kenneth C. Land, "Principles of Path Analysis," in *Sociological Methodology*, ed. Edgar F. Borgatta (San Francisco: Jossey-Bass, 1968); David Heise, "Problems in Path Analysis and Causal Inference," in ibid.; John Tukey "Causation, Regression and Path Analysis," in *Statistics and Mathematics in Biology*, ed. Oscar Kempthorne et al. (Ames: Iowa State Press, 1954); Sewell Wright, "The Interpretation of Multivariate Systems," in ibid.

[68]Carl Christ, *Econometric Models and Methods* (New York: John Wiley and Sons, 1966), p. 298. More extensive discussions of the identification problem can be found in Hubert M. Blalock, *Theory Construction: From Verbal to Mathematical Formulation* (Englewood Cliffs, N.J.: Prentice-Hall, 1969); Karl A. Fox, *Intermediate Economic Statistics* (New York: John Wiley and Sons, 1968); Arthur S. Goldberger, *Econometric Theory* (New York: John Wiley and Sons, 1964).

both foreign conflict behavior for 1955–57 and for 1958–60, the equations of the model can be made identifiable. Figure 4 presents this revised model. The variables which are "exogenous" or "predetermined" with respect to the model are denoted with Zs and letter subscripts from the start of the alphabet and those which are "endogenous" or "jointly dependent" with respect to the model are denoted with Ys and numeric subscripts. For simplicity sake, "disturbance" terms or unspecified residual factors—designated with Rs and letter subscripts from the end of the alphabet—have been excluded from the diagram, although they are, of course, included in the equations of the model. Straight lines on the figure connecting two variables designate hypothesized dependency relationships with the first subscript identifying the dependent variable and the second the variable whose direct impact is being assessed. Curved lines with double arrowheads, on the other hand, represent bidirectional correlations with either unspecified or nonexistent interdependence. The figures on the diagram are standardized; that is, they are path coefficients.[69] The relationships diagramed in figure 4 can be stated as a system of ten structural equations in which Y_0 = general societal diversity, Y_1 = population diversity, Y_2 = ethnic diversity, Y_3 = turmoil, 1955–57, Y_4 = relative size and importance of the capacity to coerce, Y_5 = technological capacity to coerce, Y_6 = central governmental budget growth per capita, 1951–61, Y_7 = diplomatic conflict, 1958–60, Y_8 = war, 1958–60, Y_9 = belligerency, 1958–60, Z_a = change in GNP per capita, 1950–60, Z_b = diplomatic conflict, 1955–57, Z_c = war, 1955–57, and Z_d = belligerency, 1955–57.

$$Y_0 = p_{0a}Z_a + p_{0q}R_q$$
$$Y_1 = p_{1a}Z_a + p_{1r}R_r$$
$$Y_2 = p_{2a}Z_a + p_{2s}R_s$$
$$Y_3 = p_{30}Y_0 + p_{31}Y_1 + p_{32}Y_2 + p_{3t}R_t$$
$$Y_4 = p_{43}Y_3 + p_{4u}R_u$$
$$Y_5 = p_{53}Y_3 + p_{5v}R_v$$
$$Y_6 = p_{63}Y_3 + p_{6w}R_w$$
$$Y_7 = p_{74}Y_4 + p_{75}Y_5 + p_{76}Y_6 + p_{7b}Z_b + p_{7x}R_x$$
$$Y_8 = p_{84}Y_4 + p_{85}Y_5 + p_{86}Y_6 + p_{8c}Z_c + p_{8y}R_y$$
$$Y_9 = p_{94}Y_4 + p_{95}Y_5 + p_{96}Y_6 + p_{9d}Z_d + p_{9z}R_z$$

The question of how to interpret the path coefficients is not a trivial one. Land suggests that one of two standards of evaluation might be used: (1) an absolute size of the coefficients, hopefully set with some theoretical criteria in mind; or (2) the standard t statistic used to evaluate

[69]Discussions of the relative merits of standardized vs. unstandardized coefficients may be found in Tukey, "Causation"; S. Wright, "Interpretation of Multivariate Systems"; and Hubert M. Blalock, "Theory Building and Causal Inferences," in *Methodology in Social Research*, ed. Hubert M. and Ann B. Blalock (New York: McGraw-Hill Book Co., 1968).

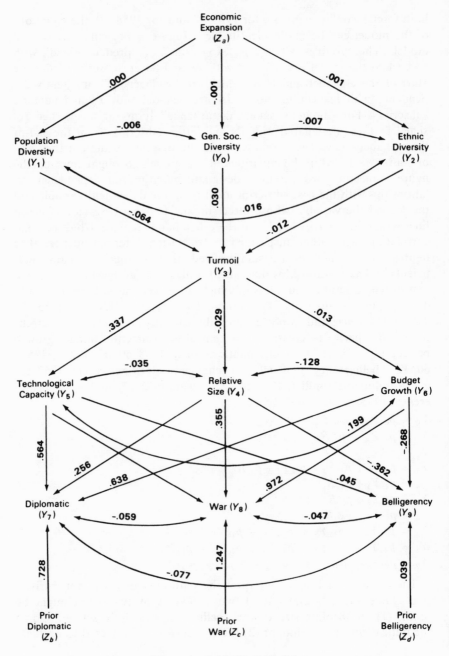

Figure 4.   Initial Path Model

regression coefficients.[70] This interpretation problem is further confounded by the fact that we are working with a population and not a sample. However, following Gold, we shall use the t as a test of significance
to signify difference from chance occurrence.[71] In so doing, we follow the
same line of reasoning used to interpret the canonical correlations
(see note 62).

Upon evaluation of the t statistics for the path coefficients for the
model in figure 4, the empirical inadequacies are clearly evident. Of the
twenty-one path coefficients, only nine are significantly distinguishable
from chance at $p < 0.10$ (one-tailed test)—p_{31}, p_{53}, p_{75}, p_{7b}, p_{74}, p_{84}, p_{86},
p_{8c} and p_{94}. Seven of these nine significant coefficients are present in the
relationships between governmental response, foreign conflict for 1955–57
and foreign conflict for 1958–60. The major inadequacies of the model
occur (1) in the ordering among the systemic stress measures and (2) in the
linkage of systemic stresses to governmental response. Only one such set
of dependencies is clearly traceable, that from population diversity to turmoil for 1955–57 to technological capacity to coerce as one type of governmental response. Within the governmental response–foreign conflict
paths, those involving diplomatic conflict and war are more strongly predicted to from the governmental response variables than those with
belligerency. Similarly, relative size and importance of the capacity to
coerce tends to be a stronger predictor to foreign conflict behavior, but
both technological capacity and per capita budget growth are also related
to one of the three dimensions.

While we have some reasonable evidence about the linkages of governmental responses and prior foreign conflict to foreign conflict behavior
for 1958–60, the model almost completely breaks down in expected internal relationships among the measures of systemic stress and the links
between these stresses and governmental responses. The task, then, is to
revise the model to specify these interdependencies accurately. One procedure is to examine all the measures of systemic stress as they relate to
all the governmental response variables and also relate governmental response and past foreign conflict to foreign conflict for 1958–60 in terms of
the earlier findings. Such a procedure was followed in developing the
revised model presented in figure 5. In this revision, Z_d (belligerency,
1955–57) has been dropped since it had minimal impact and was only included to help make the model identifiable. Wherever possible in the
revised model we have retained the original notation. However, since all
of the stress variables are now considered exogenous to this model, they
are designated with Zs and alphabetical subscripts. They do retain their

[70]Land, "Principles of Path Analysis," pp. 34–35.
[71]Gold, "Some Problems in Generalizing Aggregate Associations."

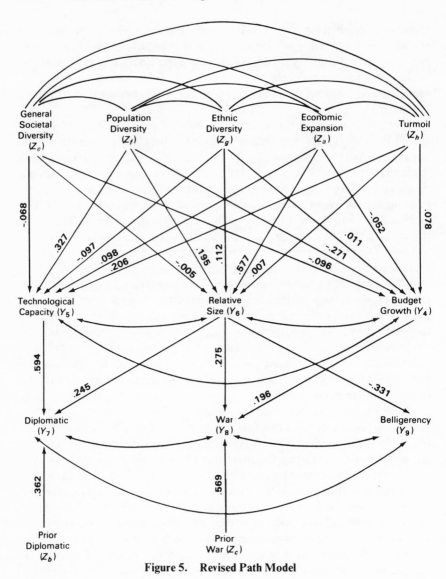

Figure 5.   Revised Path Model

former residual designations.   The new symbols and denotations are as follows:

Z_e = general societal diversity (formerly Y_0)
Z_f = population diversity (Y_1)
Z_g = ethnic diversity (Y_2)
Z_h = turmoil, 1955–57 (Y_3)

The structure of the model, composed of seven exogenous and six endogenous variables, is expressed with six identifiable equations. We now find much more encouraging results than with the earlier version of the model, having six of the fourteen path coefficients linking systemic stress and governmental response statistically significant at $p < 0.10$. The relationships between population diversity and all three governmental response variables, between rapid economic growth and the two dimensions of systemic capacity to coerce, and between turmoil and technological capacity can all be differentiated significantly from chance occurrence. Population diversity is inversely related to central governmental budget growth per capita ($p_{4f} = -0.271$), but positively related to technological capacity ($p_{5f} = 0.327$) and relative size and importance of the capacity to coerce ($p_{6f} = 0.195$). Change in the per capita gross national product is also positively associated with these same two variables ($p_{5a} = 0.098$; $p_{6a} = 0.577$). Finally, turmoil is directly related to technological capacity ($p_{5a} = 0.206$). All links between systemic stresses and governmental responses other than these cannot be significantly differentiated from chance occurrence.

$$Y_4 = p_{4a}Z_a + p_{4e}Z_e + p_{4f}Z_f + p_{4g}Z_g + p_{4h}Z_h + p_{4u}R_u$$
$$Y_5 = p_{5a}Z_a + p_{5e}Z_e + p_{5f}Z_f + p_{5g}Z_g + p_{5h}Z_h + p_{5v}R_v$$
$$Y_6 = p_{6a}Z_a + p_{6e}Z_e + p_{6f}Z_f + p_{6g}Z_g + p_{6h}Z_h + p_{6w}R_w$$
$$Y_7 = p_{7a}Z_a + p_{7e}Z_e + p_{7f}Z_f + p_{7g}Z_g + p_{7h}Z_h + p_{7x}R_x$$
$$Y_8 = p_{84}Y_4 + p_{86}Y_6 + p_{8c}Z_c + p_{8y}R_y$$
$$Y_9 = p_{94}Y_4 + p_{9z}Z_z$$

In the management of systemic stresses and the subsequent links to foreign conflict, we find that the relative size and importance of the capacity to coerce is significantly related to all foreign conflict, while per capita budget growth and technological capacity are positively related to war and diplomatic conflict, respectively. Past war (Z_c) is related to war for 1958–60 ($p_{8c} = 0.569$) as is past diplomatic conflict to diplomatic conflict for 1958–60 ($p_{7b} = 0.362$), but belligerency over the two time periods under study is not significantly related.

Now we must reduce the insignificant paths, further specify the relationships among measures within the same conceptual categories and recompute the path coefficients. The end product, located in figure 6, is a seven-equation overidentified recursive model of the relationships between systemic stress, governmental response, and foreign conflict behavior. All path coefficients included in the figure are significant at least at $p < 0.10$. Correlation coefficients have been placed on the curved arrows of the diagram while the residual terms have been deleted from the diagram but included in the equations. In figure 6, the four exogenous and seven endogenous variables are designated as follows: Z_a = change in GNP/

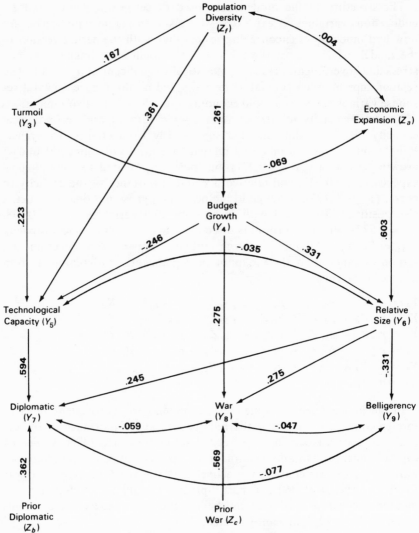

Figure 6.   Final Path Model

capita; Z_b = diplomatic conflict, 1955–57; Z_c = war, 1955–57; Z_f = population diversity; Y_3 = turmoil, 1955–57; Y_4 = governmental budget growth/capita; Y_5 = technological capacity to coerce; Y_6 = relative size and importance of the capacity to coerce; Y_7 = diplomatic conflict, 1958–60; Y_8 = war, 1958–60; Y_9 = belligerency, 1958–60. In turn, the expected relationships among these variables may be expressed in the following equations:

$$Y_3 = p_{3f}Z_f + p_{3t}R_t$$
$$Y_4 = p_{4f}Z_f + p_{4u}R_u$$

$$Y_5 = p_{53}Y_3 + p_{54}Y_4 + p_{5f}Z_f + p_{5v}R_v$$
$$Y_6 = p_{64}Y_4 + p_{6a}Y_a + p_{6w}R_w$$
$$Y_7 = p_{75}Y_5 + p_{76}Y_6 + p_{7b}Z_b + p_{7x}R_x$$
$$Y_8 = p_{84}Y_4 + p_{86}Y_6 + p_{8c}Z_c + p_{8y}R_y$$
$$Y_9 = p_{96}Y_6 + p_{9z}R_z$$

This final model permits us to examine a number of direct and indirect effects among the variables, including the impact of the measures of systemic stress on foreign conflict. It is argued in the model that systemic stress increases system variety which, depending on the type and effectiveness of the governmental response, may be externalized and manifested in subsequent foreign conflict behavior. By expanding the basic equations, as is suggested in the literature on path analysis, we can assess the direct and indirect impact of systemic stresses on foreign conflict. In other words, we can examine the relative importance of the various paths from systemic stresses through governmental responses to foreign conflict behavior.

When we expand the equations diplomatic conflict (Y_7), war (Y_8) and belligerency (Y_9) for Y_3 we obtain the direct and indirect impact of turmoil for 1955–57 on foreign conflict for 1958–60. The expanded equation for diplomatic conflict (Y_7) and results[72] clearly indicate that the path between turmoil, technological capacity, and diplomatic conflict is far more powerful than any other tested. The second most important effect of turmoil on diplomatic conflict is by way of past diplomatic conflict (for 1955–57) through path $p_{7b}r_{3b}$, but this path is much less important than the one through technological capacity. On the other hand, turmoil operating through rapid economic growth and the relative size and importance of the capacity to coerce tends to be weakly and inversely related to diplomatic conflict. It appears that the management of systemic turmoil through technological capacity is strongly related to subsequent diplomatic conflict, while the governmental response through budget growth per capita or relative size and importance is either weakly or inversely related to subsequent diplomatic conflict. The method of governmental response makes a major difference for the subsequent manifestation of systemic stress as externalized variety in diplomatic conflict. Indeed, the strongest path (turmoil–technological capacity–diplomatic conflict) is one of saber-rattling with a well-armed military to externalize internal stresses.

The impact of turmoil on war (Y_8) is much weaker, however, where the strongest path in the model relates turmoil to war for 1958–60 through prior warfare. This finding—that the best single predictor of at least some foreign conflict may be prior foreign conflict behavior—is not unique to

---

[72]The expansions of those equations in the model linking the stress variables to the conflict variables are presented in appendix 2.

this study.[73] The smallness of the other paths is more interesting, how-ever, insofar as this may indicate the stress management capabilities of noncoercive (budget growth per capita) and coercive (relative size and importance of the capacity to coerce) governmental response. With bud-get growth, the compound path $p_{4f}p_{3f}$ is substantially smaller than the path p_{84} from budget growth to war. This appears to indicate that budget expansion has the impact of multiplying rather than decreasing the sys-temic stress. Such behavior by systemic structures has been discovered elsewhere.[74] Somewhat similar behavior is obtained with the path from turmoil to war through the relative size and importance variable and economic growth over time ($p_{86}p_{6a}r_{3a}$). Here, the weak tie between economic growth and turmoil does more to defray systemic stresses than does the governmental response variable. Rapid economic growth to relative size and importance to war is a strong path, although relative size and importance—acting as a stress manager—does substantially re-duce the magnitude of the relationship from economic growth. When-ever turmoil is included as the starting point of the path, however, it is negligible in effect and negative in direction, the whole path equaling -0.011. With the turmoil-belligerency relationship, the most important path is through rapid economic growth and relative size and importance of the capacity to coerce. While turmoil and rapid economic growth are inversely related—as are relative size and importance and belligerency—the relationship between rapid economic growth and relative size and importance is strongly positive and contributes most of the final product. It is interesting to note how relative size and importance appears to man-age the stresses of economic expansion. The size of the path coefficients is substantially reduced, thus continuing a pattern observed regarding rela-tive size and importance and war.

The effects of population diversity (Z_f) on foreign conflict behavior present essentially the same pattern. Upon expansion, we see that the impact of population diversity on diplomatic conflict is greatest through technological capacity to coerce as a governmental response. All other paths are much weaker and those through budget growth or past diplo-matic conflict are either small or inversely related. Technological capacity (as a governmental response) appears to multiply rather than reduce systemic stresses. With budget growth, on the other hand, we find a pat-tern of stress management in which significant positive associations with technological capacity to coerce is made negative when task expansion rather than the use of force is the governmental response. All paths

[73]See Dina A. Zinnes and Jonathan Wilkenfeld, "An Analysis of Foreign Conflict Be-havior of Nations," in *Comparative Foreign Policy: Theoretical Essays*, ed. Wolfram F. Hanrieder (New York: David McKay Co., 1971).

[74]Maruyama, "The Second Cybernetics."

between population diversity and war are weak, with the expansion of this relationship introducing a variation on the pattern observed in the turmoil-belligerency link. Here, the strongest path to war is not through prior warfare but rather through budget growth per capita. In the population diversity-budget growth-war sequence, budget growth seems to reduce the impact of population diversity on war. When both budget growth and relative size and importance are considered as governmental responses, however, the performance of budget growth as a stress-managing response is less efficient than that found in $p_{84}p_{4f}$. In other words, when the stresses of population diversity are responded to by governmental budget growth—indicating task expansion and increased social services—the effectiveness of the response is greater than when both budget growth and relative size and importance of the coercive capacity are employed. Budget growth alone appears to reduce stress adequately. The introduction of coercion—to yield a carrot-and-stick response—serves to multiply rather than reduce the stresses, resulting in a greater externalization of internal variety. Similarly, the best path (albeit very weak) from population diversity to belligerency is through per capita budget growth and the relative size and importance of the capacity to coerce ($p_{96}p_{64}p_{4f}$), but the relationship is negative. We can again note the importance of relative size and importance in managing stresses generated by societal diversity as well as the changing behavior of budget growth, depending upon whether it is considered alone or with other responses.

Finally, when we expand the equations of diplomatic conflict (Y_7), war (Y_8), and belligerency (Y_9) to assess the direct and indirect effects of economic growth (that is, change in the GNP/capita, 1950–60) on foreign conflict, the results consistently show the importance of the relative size and importance of the capacity to coerce as a type of governmental response. The other two types of governmental response we have considered in this model—technological capacity and budget growth—tend to be parts of weak paths from economic growth (Z_a) to foreign conflict. With relative size and importance, on the other hand, there is a very strong reduction in the association between systemic stresses and governmental response as the stresses are passed on to foreign conflict. In the economic growth–diplomatic conflict association the only path to make any appreciable impact is economic growth to diplomatic conflict through the relative size and importance of the capacity to coerce ($p_{76}p_{6a}$). All other paths are unimportant. The correlation between economic growth and diplomatic conflict is substantially reduced whenever governmental response is controlled for. Moreover, the path coefficients illustrate the operation of relative size and importance as a stress-managing governmental response which substantially reduces the magnitude of the stress generated by economic growth.

When we assess the direct and indirect impact of economic growth on war or belligerency we observe a repitition of the pattern encountered previously. The paths from economic growth to war and belligerency are almost identical to those encountered with the economic growth-diplomatic conflict relationship. In each case, the path from rapid economic growth to war or belligerency through relative size and importance is the strongest. Only the path from economic growth to prior war to war for 1958–60 contributes additionally to the impact of economic growth on warfare. For economic growth–belligerency, only the path through relative size and importance ($p_{96}p_{6a}$) contributes at all. That is, we encounter in the economic growth–belligerency association an example of extremely effective stress management in which the systemic stresses of economic expansion are controlled and made inversely related to belligerency (Y_9) by the relative size and importance of the capacity to coerce.

SUMMARY AND CONCLUSIONS

In this paper we have conceptualized society as an open, tension-oriented, and structure-elaborating system in which stresses generated by blockages to ordinary interactions, brought on by social change and diversity, are responded to in a number of ways. Since our principal concern has been system responses to these stresses in terms of subsequent foreign conflict, we have examined the relationships among systemic stresses, governmental responses to these stresses, and foreign conflict. Very strong relationships among these three sets of variables were observed whenever canonical analysis was employed. While some patterns of the relationships in the canonical correlations were not readily identifiable, the results generally were consistent with the notion of governmental response as stress management being strongly related to subsequent foreign conflict behavior. However, our expectations concerning the relative importance of the three dimensions of foreign conflict behavior were not accurate. Contrary to predictions, war rather than diplomatic conflict or belligerency tended to be more strongly accounted for with the first canonical correlation. Moreover, a test of the systemic stresses–governmental responses–foreign conflict model with path analysis indicated that the orderings of the variables within each of the conceptual categories (stresses and responses) differed from those initially hypothesized. Instead, we found that population diversity predicted to societal turmoil and that three measures of systemic stresses—population diversity, turmoil, and change in the gross national product per capita—predicted to the dimensions of coercive capacity (technological capacity and relative size and importance of the military) and budget growth per capita over time. These governmental response variables, especially the relative size and importance of the military, then predicted to the three dimensions of foreign conflict behavior.

In addition to clarifying the ordering of the dependencies among the variables in the model, the path analysis demonstrated some relationships among the governmental response variables that had not been included in the earlier formulations of the model. One expectation of the model was that these response variables would mediate the systemic stresses, perhaps by defraying them—that is, channelling them into use for structural elaboration—or by externalizing them into foreign conflict. In fact, the behavior of the governmental response variables differed depending upon the type of systemic stresses and the governmental resources committed in these responses. Initially, technological capacity and the relative size and importance of the military were dependent upon budget growth per capita. Second, the relative size and importance variable was the single best stress-managing structure assessed in the model. Finally, combined responses— for example, budget growth and one of the capacity to coerce variables— often served to increase rather than decrease the impact of systemic stresses on foreign conflict. In other words, they become deviation-amplifying responses[75] rather than stress-managing responses.

One question for additional research is the operation of these governmental responses. Are there distinguishable types of variety which can more effectively be responded to by alternative systemic structures? Under what conditions might these varying forms of variety be produced and under what conditions have they tended to be more or less effectively managed—either by externalization, absorption, or some other procedure? The canonical correlations between systemic stresses and governmental responses may lend themselves to the handling of this kind of question. These relationships indicate two general patterns in the data. The first (2.1) is one in which economic expansion and some societal diversity is principally responded to by the relative size and importance of the capacity to coerce. The second pattern (2.2) indicates societal diversity (either population or ethnic) together with some social conflict evoking a combined response of budget growth and coercion. If one assumes the representativeness of these results, to what extent are the patterns observed indicative of more coercive responses being used to counter economic expansion in the presence of societal diversity as opposed to societal diversity and some social turmoil leading to a more complex response strategy of increased governmental activity along with the use of coercive capacity?

Further research must be undertaken before any concrete conclusions can be drawn in this area. However, the statistical analysis does clearly indicate that systemic stresses—in this study, social change, societal diversity, and internal conflict—are significantly related to subsequent foreign conflict behavior, at least for the 1950s. Equally important as generators of

[75]Ibid.

these stresses are population diversity, turmoil, and the rate of economic growth. Moreover, prior conflict—particularly warfare—and governmental responses tend to be important predictors to foreign conflict. As previously noted, the relative size and importance of the military tends to be a major explanatory variable in the model. Nevertheless, these findings must be considered tentative. To what extent they are representative of similar behavior in other time periods and accurately predictive of dynamic relationships over time are questions which must be placed on the agenda for subsequent research.

APPENDIX 1.1.   Final Clusters Developed with Discriminant Function Analysis

"Western" States		"Non-Western" States
Afghanistan	Korea (North)	Argentina
Albania	Laos	Cambodia
Australia	Liberia	China (P.R.C.)
Austria	Libya	China (Taiwan)
Belgium	Mongolia	Colombia
Bolivia	Nepal	Costa Rica
Brazil	Netherlands	Cuba
Bulgaria	New Zealand	Ecuador
Burma	Norway	Guatemala
Canada	Pakistan	Haiti
Ceylon	Panama	India
Chile	Philippines	Indonesia
Czechoslovakia	Poland	Iraq
Denmark	Portugal	Ireland
Dominican Republic	Romania	Jordan
El Salvador	Saudi Arabia	Korea (South)
Ethiopia	Spain	Lebanon
Finland	Sudan	Mexico
France	Sweden	Morocco
Germany (D.D.R.)	Switzerland	Nicaragua
Germany (F.D.R.)	Thailand	Paraguay
Greece	U.S.S.R.	Peru
Honduras	United Kingdom	Tunisia
Hungary	U.S.A.	Turkey
Iran	Vietnam (North)	Union of South Africa
Israel	Vietnam (South)	Uruguay
Italy	Yugoslavia	Venezuela
Japan		

$$F(13, 69) = 18.7627$$
$$p < 0.0001$$

APPENDIX 1.2. Final Clusters Developed with Discriminant Function Analysis

"Low Wealth" States		"High Wealth" States
Afghanistan	Korea (South)	Argentina
Albania	Laos	Austria
Australia	Liberia	Belgium
Brazil	Libya	Bolivia
Bulgaria	Mongolia	Chile
Burma	Morocco	Cuba
Cambodia	Nepal	Czechoslovakia
Canada	New Zealand	Dominican Republic
Ceylon	Nicaragua	El Salvador
China (P.R.C.)	Pakistan	France
China (Taiwan)	Panama	Germany (F.D.R.)
Colombia	Paraguay	Haiti
Costa Rica	Peru	Hungary
Denmark	Philippines	Iran
Ecuador	Portugal	Ireland
Ethiopia	Saudi Arabia	Italy
Finland	Spain	Japan
Germany (D.D.R.)	Sudan	Lebanon
Greece	Sweden	Mexico
Guatemala	Thailand	Netherlands
Honduras	Tunisia	Norway
India	Turkey	Poland
Indonesia	Union of South Africa	Romania
Iraq	Uruguay	Switzerland
Israel	Venezuela	U.S.S.R.
Jordan	Vietnam (North)	United Kingdom
Korea (North)	Vietnam (South)	U.S.A.
		Yugoslavia

$$F(13, 69) = 13.9562$$
$$p < 0.0001$$

APPENDIX 2.   Expanded Path Coefficient Equations

$r_{37} = p_{75}p_{53} + p_{75}p_{54}p_{4f}p_{3f} + p_{75}p_{5f}p_{3f} + p_{76}p_{64}p_{47}p_{3f} + p_{76}p_{6a}r_{3a} + p_{7b}r_{3b}$

   (0.132)   (−0.006)   (0.036)   (0.004)   (−0.010)   (0.090)

   (A.1)

$r_{38} = p_{84}p_{4f}p_{3f} + p_{86}p_{64}p_{4f}p_{3f} + p_{86}p_{6a}r_{3a} + p_{8c}r_{3c}$ (A.2)

   (0.009)   (0.004)   (−0.011)   (0.141)

$r_{39} = p_{96}p_{64}p_{4f}r_{3f} + p_{96}p_{6a}r_{3a}$ (A.3)

   (−0.005)   (0.014)

$r_{f7} = p_{75}p_{53}p_{3f} + p_{75}p_{54}p_{4f} + p_{75}p_{5f} + p_{76}p_{64}p_{4f} + p_{76}p_{6a}p_{fa} + p_{7b}r_{fb}$

   (0.022)   (−0.038)   (0.214)   (0.021)   (0.001)   (−0.058)

   (A.4)

$r_{f8} = p_{84}p_{4f} + p_{86}p_{64}p_{4f} + p_{86}p_{6a}p_{fa} + p_{8c}r_{fc}$ (A.5)

   (0.051)   (0.024)   (0.001)   (0.039)

$r_{f9} = p_{96}p_{64}p_{4f} + p_{96}p_{6a}r_{fa}$ (A.6)

   (−0.029)   (−0.001)

$r_{a7} = p_{75}p_{53}p_{3f}r_{af} + p_{76}p_{64}p_{4f}r_{af} + p_{76}p_{6a} + p_{7b}r_{ab}$ (A.7)

   (0.000)   (0.000)   (0.148)   (0.001)

$r_{a8} = p_{84}p_{4f}r_{af} + p_{86}p_{64}p_{4f}r_{af} + p_{86}p_{6a} + p_{8c}r_{ac}$ (A.8)

   (0.000)   (0.000)   (0.166)   (−0.017)

$r_{a9} = p_{96}p_{64}p_{4f}r_{af} + p_{96}p_{6a}$ (A.9)

   (−0.000)   (−0.200)

.7. Societal Development and International Conflict*

MICHAEL HAAS

THEORIES OF DEVELOPMENT

Political and economic development for centuries were regarded as disruptive of the social fabric of mankind and as precursors to war. Plato recommended that states develop very modestly, since the production of too much wealth would bring the downfall of regimes through civil strife and foreign war. Aristotle, too, rejected the advance of technology, and the later Stoics and Christians equated development processes with barbarous and sinful forms of behavior. When Adam Smith's *The Wealth of Nations* appeared in 1776 an entirely new thesis arose. Development was regarded as a precondition to a democratic and peaceful world. Just how this transformation in human thought occurred over the centuries is beyond the scope of this essay, but what is important is that Smith's thesis was accepted not only by David Ricardo and other nineteenth-century economic thinkers but also by Karl Marx himself.[1] Nevertheless, most wars in the mid-twentieth century have involved the developing countries of Asia and Africa.[2] Meanwhile, a serious questioning of the utility of man's continuing exploitation of nature in the name of economic and technological progress has come from experts in problems of environmental pollution in the advanced countries. Are Plato and Aristotle correct in cautioning against societal development? The purpose of this essay is to explore this question in greater depth, in relation to the problem of war and peace.

*This is a condensed version of Part III of the author's forthcoming *International Conflict* to be published by Bobbs-Merrill Publishing Company, with the permission of the author and publisher.

[1] Edmund Silberner, *The Problem of War in Nineteenth Century Economic Thought*, trans. Alexander H. Krappe (Princeton, N.J.: Princeton University Press, 1946).

[2] Bruce M. Russett, *International Regions and the International System* (Chicago: Rand McNally Co., 1967), p. 197.

Development has six major dimensions.[3] One of the most basic societal dimensions is *time*—that is, whether characteristics of developing societies change over time. The *spatial* dimension is concerned with how evenly development is spread across the geographic terrain of a country. The ratio between actual attainment of development and potentialities in a country is a third dimension, which may be called *kinetic. Entropy*, a fourth dimension, refers to the state of disorganization in a system; negentropy characterizes a developed society, in which forces for change are not at loggersheads but instead coordinated together. The *allocational* dimension refers to whether benefits from development are distributed equitably across various strata of the population. The *transactional* dimension, finally, tells us the extent to which inputs into a system are at an equilibrium with outputs.

Keeping in mind these six basic aspects of development, we may next review alternative strategies, or theories of how best to achieve societal development. For each strategy there is a unique definition of development, and this accounts for confusion on the meaning attached to the term development as well as the diversity in emphases across development theorists. There are six ideal-typical development theories.

According to the *technological* theory of development, the basic problem for a developing country is to increase resources and achieve economic wealth; a common synonym for the technological approach is the term *modernization.*[4] Modernizationists are content when societies are increasing resources over time, extending into the hinterlands in pursuit of economic gain, have mobilized resources from an actual to a potential state, have provided sufficient goods for societal needs, have distributed wealth to strata that will accelerate the pace of further modernization, and when a country has a favorable balance of trade. A second theory focuses on *human development* as the key not only to modernization but also to development in general. Advocates of this theory use the term *nation-building*[5] to refer to their desire to cosmopolitanize a people over time, break down pockets of residential segregation, increase social mobility, bring about more compatible life styles among the population, distribute social values

[3]Cf. Michael Haas, "Types of Asymmetry in Social and Political Systems," *General Systems Yearbook* 12 (1967): 69–79; idem, "Regional Cooperation for What?" (Paper presented to the Southeast Asia Development Advisory Group Regional Development Seminar, Conference on Industrialization, Trade, and Regional Cooperation in Southeast Asia, Honolulu, July 1970).

[4]Cf. David E. Apter, *The Politics of Modernization* (Chicago: University of Chicago Press, 1965); C. E. Black, *The Dynamics of Modernization* (New York: Harper & Row, 1966); W. M. Rostow, *The Stages of Economic Growth* (London and New York: Cambridge University Press, 1960).

[5]Karl W. Deutsch and William J. Foltz, eds., *Nation-Building* (New York: Atherton Press, 1963); Reinhard Bendix, *Nation-Building and Citizenship* (New York: John Wiley and Sons, 1964).

broadly to all strata, and eliminate barriers to the migration of labor, travelers, and students.

Although advances in economic and human resources are primary *goals* for proponents of development, we may ask instead which *means* are most appropriate. The *populist* approach emphasizes the need to capture the hearts and minds of mass publics and, therefore, studies national attitudes.[6] The salience of development processes should increase over time and be embraced by all regions of the country; moreover, there should be so much public interaction that the populace will become more attitudinally homogeneous, subcultures acquiring more empathy for one another, and friendly foreign policies should be developed as well. *Elitists* assert that political leaders, rather than the masses, provide the knowhow to bring about development.[7] The elites should grow in size, become scattered about the countryside, be cohesive in times of stress, avoid internal rivalry between cliques in and out of power, tackle festering or dormant conflict situations through direct intervention, and take the initiative in bringing about a foreign policy that bolsters the national interest. The populist and elitist approaches, in short, stress the role of leadership.

The two final theories are of *political* development. One is concerned with executing and the other with the making of decisions. *Structuralists* identify development with the attainment of greater bureaucratic capabilities.[8] For this theory what is essential is a continued structural differentiation of the administrative operations of a government, deconcentration in their situs if necessary to improve services, reorganization to provide streamlining rather than bottlenecking, a breakdown of localized resistance to the penetration of government operations, an increase in tasks for each structure so that further structural differentiation will seem necessary, and a high degree of reciprocated interchange within intergovernmental institutions. *Functionalists* are concerned with the effectiveness of a polity in making decisions.[9] Specificially this means that the performance of political functions should accelerate in pace, with wide participation from all regions of a country; dynamism rather than immobilism

[6]Cf. David C. McClelland, *The Achieving Society* (Princeton, N.J.: D. Van Nostrand Co.; 1961); S. N. Eisenstadt, *Essays on Comparative Institutions* (New York: John Wiley and Sons, 1965).

[7]J. P. Nettl, *Political Mobilization* (New York: Basic Books, 1967); Samuel P. Huntington, *Political Order in Changing Societies* (New Haven: Yale University Press, 1968); Amitai Etzioni, *The Active Society* (New York: Free Press, 1968).

[8]Fred W. Riggs, *Administration in Developing Countries* (Boston: Houghton Mifflin Co., 1964); Joseph LaPalombara, ed., *Bureaucracy and Political Development* (Princeton: N. J.: Princeton University Press, 1963).

[9]Robert T. Holt and John E. Turner, *The Political Basis of Economic Development* (Princeton, N.J.: D. Van Nostrand Co., 1966); Joseph LaPalombara and Myron Weiner, eds., *Political Parties and Political Development* (Princeton, N.J.: Princeton University Press, 1966); Gabriel A. Almond and G. Bingham Powell, Jr., *Comparative Politics* (Boston: Little, Brown and Co. 1966).

should describe decision-making processes; a variety of political channels should be available for action; there should be a democratic allocation of values to the population; and mutual responsiveness should be promoted with a wide set of foreign allies.

EMPIRICAL ASPECTS OF DEVELOPMENT

Each of the six development strategies singles out a societal attribute for emphasis—resources, demographic characteristics, mass attitudes, elite behavior, and government structures and functions. Elsewhere I have assembled data appropriate for each dimension, attribute, and theoretical approach, 183 variables in all for 85 countries in the 1955–60 period.[10] A list of the countries in this analysis appears in the appendix. The purpose of collecting so many variables is to obtain as balanced a view as possible. What theoretical approach, dimension, or attribute is most crucial in accounting for foreign conflict behavior? A single-factor study would yield only a partial answer, so a broad sample of all types of data was preferred. (A classification of the variables into each of the six dimensions and six attributes is provided in table 1.) A disadvantage of having so many vari-

Table 1.   Conceptual Map of Societal Variables

Dimension	Attribute					
	Resources	Demotypes	Attitudes	Behavior	Functions	Structures
Temporal	1–12	13–15	16	17–23	24–30	31–33
Spatial	34	35–38	39–40	41	42–44	45–47
Kinetic	48–54	55–59	60–66	67–73	74–81	82–91
Entropic	92–96	97–101	102–7	108–13	114–15	116–26
Allocational	127–33	134–42	143–46	147–54	155–61	162–63
Transactional	164–67	168	169–70	171, 180–83[a]	172–75	176–79

[a]The gap between 171 and 180 is due to the fact that 180–83 are dependent variables, which for convenience are flagged at the end of the enumeration.

ables is that the underlying structure of many variables will not be obvious if we merely compute bivariate correlations between those indexing foreign conflict and those indicating developmental processes or strategies. We therefore need to employ multivariate analysis of the data so that we can weed out spurious relationships between variables and thereby provide a basis for validating models which depict the direction and pattern of causation between variables related to foreign conflict. *Factor analysis* is

[10]Michael Haas, *International Conflict* (Indianapolis: Bobbs-Merrill Co., forthcoming), chap. 8; idem, "Dimensional Analysis in Cross-National Research," *Comparative Political Studies* 3 (April 1970): 3–35.

particularly useful in determining the underlying empirical structure within a group of variables; one ascertains the smallest number of independent, that is, *noncorrelated*, sets of variables. *Cluster analysis*, rather than finding which types of variables are unrelated to each other, provides a treelike configuration of variables that are most *similar* to each other; one can look at the results of a cluster analysis as clumps of highly related variables which merge with all other clumps, starting with clumps that are most similar and concluding with the convergence of large, loosely related super-clusters. The two techniques are profitably used in tandem when we desire to move beyond conclusions based solely on measures of correlation in order to construct models that postulate and test cause-and-effect relationships.

In undertaking both factor analysis and cluster analysis, I found that the structure of the 183 variables was extraordinarily complex. A total of 43 factors emerged in a factor analysis, so higher-order factors were extracted as summarized in figure 1. In the cluster analysis there were 28 clusters (figure 2). From the factor analysis we discover that the most basic distinction between developmental processes is between those in which tensions are involved vs. those where tasks are being accomplished. The cluster analysis presents a contrast between countries with liberal democratic polities and sustained industrial economies as opposed to directive polities and faltering economies.

The path of mergers in the liberal-democratic sustained modernization cluster (figure 2) permits some speculation on priorities to assign to various problems in undertaking political development within the newer states of Africa and Asia. Indeed, Lucian Pye has suggested that developmental change is achieved when states are able to solve six basic societal tasks,[11] all of which are depicted in figure 2. An *identity crisis* is solved when societies are homogenized by means of an interpenetration of social life with political and universalistic structures; the unified society cluster pulls together these elements. A *legitimacy crisis* is overcome when legal and formal mechanisms are accepted as authoritative and utilized adaptively, and this is a theme of our formalism cluster. But we can also observe that solution of identity and legitimacy crises goes hand in hand with technological development. The next two of Pye's so-called crises are solved without any necessary connection between each other (and are unrelated to the bureaucratized productivity cluster). Democracy represents solution of a *participation crisis*, at which time political parties are viable and enable infrastructural groups to have a high degree of access to decision making by political elites. A *penetration crisis* is solved when conditions in the secularization cluster are present: most inhabitants are urbanized and politi-

[11]Lucien Pye, *Aspects of Political Development* (Boston: Little, Brown and Co. 1966), chap. 3.

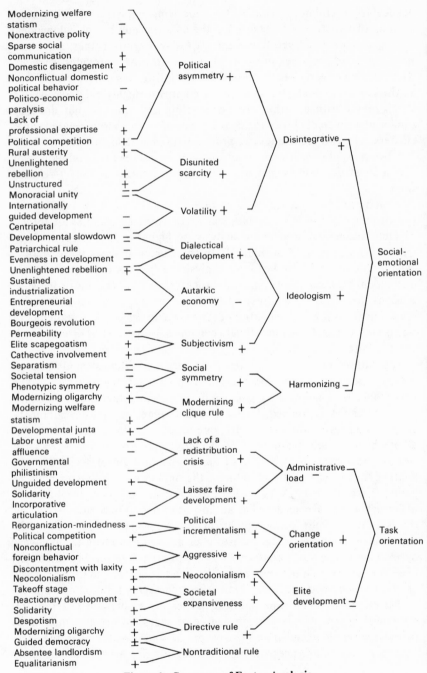

Figure 1. Summary of Factor Analysis

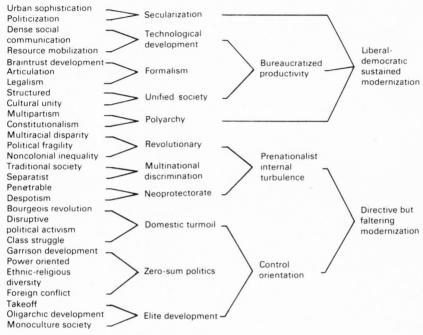

Figure 2. Summary of Cluster Analysis

cized in outlook. (Variables pertaining to a *distribution crisis* are closely related to secularization as well.)

Within this framework of findings from the cluster analysis, we may argue that an *integration crisis* is passed when all of the above crises have been solved and thus a country is a liberal-democratic polity with an economic system that can maintain a steady rate of growth. What Fred Riggs refers to as a dialectical path of development, in which demands of right- and left-wing interests produce alternations in officeholders or changing emphases in developmental goals over time,[12] is thus seen as a problem which Pye labels as the *integration crisis*. Figure 2 demonstrates the process. At earlier levels of development the need to achieve legal-rational authority to service the economy sets in motion tasks that are empirically separable from a need to respond to demands for democratic decision making and popular consultation, on the one hand, and desires for income redistribution and welfare statism, on the other. Political decay, a concept developed by Samuel Huntington, thus means the erosion in any resolutions of these crises.[13]

[12]Fred W. Riggs, "The Dialectics of Developmental Conflict," *Comparative Political Studies* 1 (July 1968): 197–226.
[13]Huntington, *Political Order*, chap. 1.

If we look at factors and clusters related to indicators of foreign conflict, we discover that an aggressiveness factor is related to a discontentment with laxity factor (figure 1), and a foreign conflict subcluster is adjacent to clusters labeled garrison development, power-oriented and ethnic-religious diversity (figure 2). If our analysis of the role of development in encouraging foreign conflict were to stop here, we would say (looking at the cluster analysis) that countries going to war are likely to be garrison states, power oriented, extremely diverse in demographic composition, and (based on the factor analysis) suffering from a decline in developmental efficiency. A closer look at the composition of variables with each of these factors and clusters is provided in table 2 and figure 3, respectively.

Table 2.   Factor Analysis of Societal Variables

Variables	Foreign Conflict Factor[a]	Discontentment with Laxity Factor
Deaths due to foreign conflict	90	06
Wars	83	−07
Foreign military clashes	79	05
Per capita foreign killed	72	00
Military mobilizations	51	−01
Bloc prominence	49	19
Military-administrative expenditures/ GNP	47	05
Foreign aid sent or received	43	16
Central government expenditures/GNP	36	02
Electricity generation/consumption	−10	77
Government revenue/expenditures	10	−39
Change in government expenditures	−07	−33
Percent total variance	2.5	1.6

[a]Signs are reversed, so the label is changed from nonconflictual foreign conflict behavior to foreign conflict to be consistent.

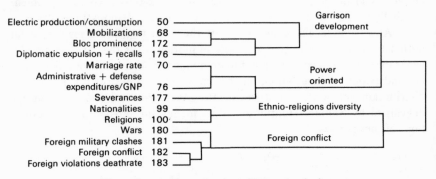

Figure 3.   A Closer Look at Cluster Analysis

But what is the causal ordering between these variables? In order to construct a causal model we cannot use all of the variables listed in table 2 or figure 3. We must choose one variable from each of the key clusters and factors on the basis of explicit criteria.

Our dependent variable, indexing *international violence*, is the most prominent variable on a factor composed mainly of indicators of war propensity. In table 1 we find that deaths due to foreign conflict has the highest loading. Other variables are chosen on at least two of three grounds. Some variables have high loadings on the foreign conflict factor but are not types or foreign conflict per se; if we use these variables, we end up with *bloc prominence* and an index of the size of a country's *military-industrial complex*, namely, the variable military and public administration expenditures as a percentage of total gross national product. Second, variables adjacent to the foreign conflict cluster (figure 3) are combed for possible inclusion; this criterion justifies all variables picked so far and nets three additional variables for casual models. The cluster labeled garrison development is best summed up by measuring changes in governmental budgets as percentages of total gross national product; we thereby obtain an indicator of *governmental expansion* for our roster of critical variables. The ethnic-religious diversity cluster is composed of two variables; we choose *ethnic diversity* because it loads higher on the phenotypic symmetry factor (which is listed in the middle of figure 1) than the variable religious diversity. The power-oriented cluster contains several equally plausible candidates for inclusion in a causal model, so we must invoke a third criterion: a variable with the highest loading on a factor merging with foreign conflict in a higher-order factor analysis is deemed acceptable. Accordingly, we will select a measure of *electricity inefficiency*, namely, the disparity between electric generation and consumption figures; this variable tops the discontentment with laxity factor (table 2).[14] A second-order factor containing both discontentment with laxity (with a positive loading) and nonconflictual foreign behavior (with a negative loading) is named aggressiveness; in the third-order factor analysis, aggressiveness merges with two other factors—political incrementalism and neocolonialism. Taking the highest loading factor of the two, political incrementalism, and decomposing it to its principal factor, reorganization (figure 1), we can isolate the variable loading highest on the reorganization factor—lack of

[14]A disparity between electricity generation and consumption is due either to transmission loss or faulty statistical records. The label "discontentment with laxity" is selected to describe this factor because it appears that electric inefficiency is associated with an inability to collect taxes to pay for government spending and thus a freeze in government budget figures. Meanwhile, there is a short tenure of chief executives despite the reliance on a traditional bureaucracy (the latter two variables load .26 and .21, respectively, on the discontentment with laxity factor and are among the upper ten variables in magnitudes of factor loadings).

change in the number of government ministries between the years 1955 and 1960; this latter variable is used to index *administrative stagnation.*

In all, our search comes up with seven variables for a causal model of societal factors disposing countries to become involved in war (figure 4). Each of the six basic attributes is represented with the exception of the attitudinal, for which data is the most difficult to locate. Four of the six postulated societal dimensions are included in the seven variables to be fit into the causal model; only spatial and allocational dimensions are left out of the search for causation. Thus, an emphasis on only one of the six dimensions or theories of development is inadequate in representing all the sources of independent variation that may account for the incidence of international conflict.

Our first model tests Plato's theory of war, and it may be designated a *polis model* (Model I).[15] We encounter four causal paths leading to a high incidence in war deaths (figure 5). Plato suggests that middle powers are least likely to engage in war, so one path starts with bloc prominence and

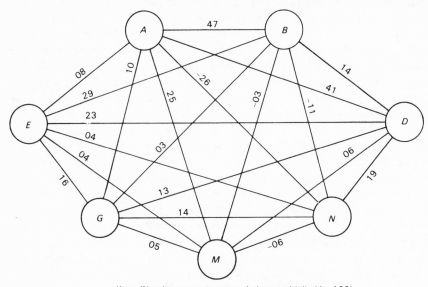

Key: (Numbers represent correlations multiplied by 100).

A = military-administrative budget/GNP
B = bloc prominence
D = deaths due to foreign conflict
E = electricity production ≠ consumption
G = change in government budget per capita
M = unchanged number of government ministries
N = number of nationalities

Figure 4.   Variables Selected for Models of War Propensity

[15]Plato, *The Republic*, trans. Benjamin Jowett (Garden City, N.Y.: Doubleday and Co., n.d.), pp. 64–67.

Figure 5.   Polis Model of War Propensity[a]

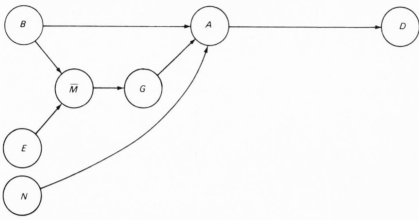

[a]The symbol M̄ indicates that the sign of the variable is reversed.

is mediated only by the level of expenditures on armed forces and public administration ($B \rightarrow A \rightarrow D$). A poor country with an inefficient conversion of electricity from production to consumption ends up in war, according to the theory, if it is also administratively active and undergoes a rapid increase in government expenditures ($E \rightarrow \bar{M} \rightarrow G \rightarrow A \rightarrow D$). Bloc leaders, similarly, might become administratively overactive yet, when overall government budgets soar, the outcome is a higher military-administrative budget and thence war ($B \rightarrow \bar{M} \rightarrow G \rightarrow A \rightarrow D$). Plato's preference for cohesive states, finally, is represented by a fourth major path. Countries with a large number of national groups are prone to enter war if, and only if, they devote a large proportion of their gross national product to military-administrative purposes ($N \rightarrow A \rightarrow D$). Despite some plausibility for this argument, however, many of the predictions generated by the polis model depart from actual observations with the data from 85 countries in the late 1950s (table 3). Of 14 predictions, only 5 are less than ±.10 and thus roughly within the range of our predicted .00 correlation.

A second alternative is a *bourgeois capitalist model* (Model II) that accords with the image supplied by both Marx and Lenin (figure 6).[16] Economic inefficiency, as indexed by the measuring disparity between electricity production variable and consumption is seen as coming from two main sources. First of all capitalist states do not take wishes of workers into serious consideration; the number of government ministries remains frozen, since government structures are not encouraged to accommodate

[16]Karl Marx and Friedrich Engels, *Manifesto of the Communist Party* (New York: International Publishers, 1948); Vladimir I. Lenin, *Imperialism* (New York: International Publishers, 1939).

Table 3.   Predictions and Degrees of Fit for Societal Models

Model	Prediction	Observation
I	1. $r_{bn} = 0$	$-.11$
	2. $r_{en} = 0$	.04
	3. $r_{\bar{m}n} = 0$	.06
	4. $r_{be} = 0$	.29
	5. $r_{gn} = 0$	.14
	6. $r_{dn \cdot a} = 0$	.34
	7. $r_{dg \cdot ab} = 0$	.10
	8. $r_{eg \cdot \bar{m}} = 0$	.16
	9. $r_{ae \cdot g} = 0$	.80
	10. $r_{am \cdot bg} = 0$	.30
	11. $r_{bg \cdot m} = 0$	.03
	12. $r_{bd \cdot a} = 0$	$-.06$
	13. $r_{de \cdot a} = 0$	$-.18$
	14. $r_{d\bar{m} \cdot a} = 0$	.05
II	1. $r_{bm} = 0$	$-.03$
	2. $r_{mn} = 0$	$-.06$
	3. $r_{en \cdot b} = 0$	.08
	4. $r_{gn \cdot b} = 0$	.14
	5. $r_{gm \cdot e} = 0$	.04
	6. $r_{am \cdot eg} = 0$	.37
	7. $r_{dm \cdot a} = 0$	$-.05$
	8. $r_{bg \cdot e} = 0$	$-.02$
	9. $r_{ab \cdot egn} = 0$	.41
	10. $r_{bd \cdot a} = 0$	$-.07$
	11. $r_{de \cdot a} =$	$-.18$
	12. $r_{dn \cdot a} = 0$	.34
	13. $r_{dg \cdot a} = 0$	.10
III	1. $r_{bd \cdot ae} = 0$	$-.10$
	2. $r_{dm \cdot a} = 0$	$-.05$
	3. $r_{dg \cdot an} = 0$	.04
	4. $r_{bm} = 0$	$-.03$
	5. $r_{bg} = 0$	.03
	6. $r_{bn} = 0$	$-.11$
	7. $r_{em} = 0$	.04
	8. $r_{gm} = 0$	.05
	9. $r_{mn} = 0$	$-.06$
	10. $r_{eg} = 0$	.16
	11. $r_{en} = 0$	.04
IV	1. $r_{bd \cdot aen} = 0$	$-.10$
	2. $r_{dm \cdot a} = 0$	$-.05$
	3. $r_{dg \cdot aen} = 0$	.13
	4. $r_{bm} = 0$	$-.03$
	5. $r_{bg} = 0$	.03
	6. $r_{gm} = 0$	.05
	7. $r_{en \cdot bg} = 0$	.05

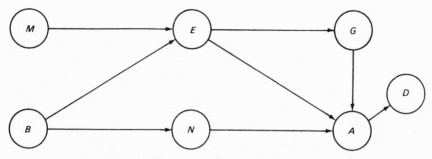

Figure 6.   Bourgeois Capitalist Model of War Propensity

desires of the working class ($M \rightarrow E$). Second, once a capitalist state assumes bloc leadership, the internal contradictions within capitalism are most severely manifest ($B \rightarrow E$). Economic inefficiency, in turn, means that capitalists will try to use government to bail them out of financial disaster ($E \rightarrow G$). More money will be spent on administrative and military programs designed to conquer peoples of foreign lands ($E \rightarrow G \rightarrow A \rightarrow D$ and $E \rightarrow A \rightarrow D$). Yet another consequence of being top-dog in the international system is that a country will eventually grow larger and more diverse in ethnic composition ($B \rightarrow N$), posing problems for internal maintenence, and a larger army will be needed to quell possible internal revolt; but a country with a large army will be tempted to employ it in foreign arenas to build national patriotism and to divert attention from pressing domestic problems ($N \rightarrow A \rightarrow D$). This second model has a somewhat better fit than the polis model but is still off the mark: 5 of the 13 observations exceed $\pm.10$ (table 3).

An alternative to an emphasis on capitalist overdevelopment as a prime source of tension in societies is to trifurcate our sample of countries into three groups—least developed and traditionalist states, developing countries which are using either capitalist or socialist methods of achieving new economic levels, and highly developed countries (figure 7). These three categories resemble an ideal-type analysis based on a comparative analysis of longitudinal trends in ten countries between 1900 and 1960, in which three distinct causal paths are suggested.[17] In all countries an arms buildup is seen as preparatory to warfare. Advanced countries that serve as bloc leaders may find it necessary to play the role of an international policeman in behalf of their own interests ($B \rightarrow A \rightarrow D$); if not, however, bloc leaders can slip into war as well if they happen to be inefficient for a time ($B \rightarrow E$), whence they might go to war immediately or after some military preparations ($E \rightarrow A \rightarrow D$ or $E \rightarrow D$). The least developed coun-

---

[17]Michael Haas, "Social Change and National Aggressiveness, 1900–1960," in *Quantitative International Politics*, ed. J. David Singer (New York: Free Press, 1968), pp. 238–42.

tries, if stagnant administratively, go to war so long as they devote a high proportion of their national wealth to military expenditures ($M \rightarrow A \rightarrow D$). Developing countries, third, may be dragged into war if they contain populations that are diverse in ethnic composition ($G \rightarrow N \rightarrow D$ or $G \rightarrow N \rightarrow A \rightarrow D$). But a country with much ethnic similarity may still be unable to develop without spending a large portion of its rising government budget on military preparations ($G \rightarrow A \rightarrow D$). The 11 predictions generated by this moderately overidentified[18] *developmental model* (Model III) are very close to actual observations, with 8 of the predictions at the ±.06 level or lower and the 3 higher predictions topped only by a .16 correlation (table 3).

Because of the relative success of the third model, a more *eclectic model* seems possible (Model IV). The aim in this final model is simply to patch up incorrect predictions of the third model by adding more causal linkages, thus controlling for more variables (figure 8). Every exogenous variable is filtered through the level of military-administrative expenditures, although ethnic diversity and economic inefficiency may make war attractive among developing and developed countries. The increase in causal arrows entails an overidentified structure of equations, though the number of predictions is simplified and in only 2 of the 7 cases do we encounter results higher

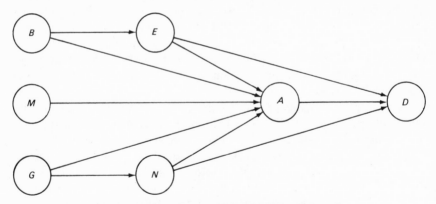

Figure 7.   Developmental Model of War Propensity

[18]When the model was constructed originally, the $B \rightarrow A$ and $G \rightarrow A$ links were left out so as to avoid an overidentified model. The predictions $r_{ab \cdot e} = 0$ and $r_{ag \cdot n} = 0$ were so far from actual observations, however, that it was necessary to add these two arrows in order to improve the fit. It is utopian to expect a perfect fit between theory and data, but there is some justification for an overidentified model in social, as opposed to statistical, theory: human behavior is itself overdetermined, with many possible causes and conditions present at any one time. Social behavior, thus, takes place amid many sufficient conditions, no unique combination of which is indispensable for a new sequence of behavior, according to Karl W. Deutsch and Dieter Senghaas, "Towards a Theory of War and Peace: Propositions, Simulations, and Reality" (Paper presented to the annual convention of the American Political Science Association, New York, September 1969).

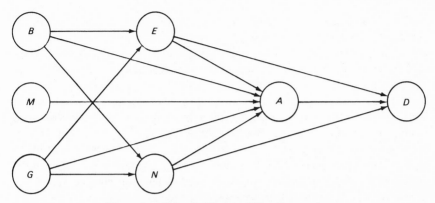

Figure 8.   Eclectic Model of War Propensity

than the ±.05 level (table 2). The average difference between predictions
and observations, derived by summing absolute partial correlations for
each prediction and dividing by the total number of prediction equations,
is nearly identical for Models III and IV, so parsimony will be invoked to
decide in favor of the developmental model.

IMPLICATIONS FOR A PEACEFUL DEVELOPMENTAL STRATEGY

Among the six competing theories of development, there is some support for each at various levels of development. Among countries newly
emerging from colonial or traditional rule, there is a tendency for some
to have changed political forms by a smooth transition while others re-
sorted to military coups or even wars of independence. Structuralism is
an especially apt strategy in either situation; increased civilian bureaucratic capabilities provide the most effective check on a tendency for military rule to emerge. Even for advanced countries with a large military establishment, civilian control of the military remains a problem. Countries
that stagnate in bureaucratic development, however, are likely to enter
war if the military budget is high, for there is little political infrastructure
to control the impact of a large army in a society.

The functionalist strategy, indexed by rapid increases in governmental
expenditures as would be encountered in transitional societies, can avoid
war so long as military spending does not account for most of the rise in
overall governmental budgets. In addition, problems of human development are most difficult among transitional countries. Too much internal
diversity may pose problems of civil unrest or alienation from the developmental process, so it is exigent to counterbalance intercultural communication problems by providing widespread public education wherein chil-
dren can learn values appropriate for development while beginning to understand and appreciate the cultural pluralism within their own country.

Advanced countries, notably those that have become bloc leaders, may tend to feel themselves qualified or trapped into assuming the role of international policemen. If so, a garrison state or a military-industrial complex may become so entrenched in the social fabric of the country that continuous wars will be seen as needed to keep weapons development going. George Orwell's *1984* is a description of the type of society where military goals are seen as crucial for maintaining high levels of development. Modernization theorists are usually thought to speak with more relevance to underdeveloped countries, but the fact that a lag in technological growth can trigger highly industrialized countries to go to war suggests that problems of resource development will never reach a stage of peacefully self-sustained growth, as Rostow has suggested.[19] The complex technological era of modern times has been described as the result of so many decisions that ours is an "accidental century" of "unprepared societies."[20] Planning is needed in advance for business firms to survive in the contemporary capitalist world, and the same need for anticipation of the future exists within government if leaders are ever to keep ahead of events that might otherwise outrun their past experience. The past is not a model for the future postindustrial society, as traditional societies were transformed into modern ones at lower levels of development. The new science of futuristics, thus, is an integral part of peace research.[21] Without knowledge about the present and planning for the future, industrial states are destined to engage in war when large military contracts for weapons development constitute a subsidy for inefficient businesses, thus causing the economy to malfunction. Thus it is business itself which has much to fear from the rising power of a military-industrial complex in which contracts for the manufacture of nonproductive weapons are the payoff, war the byproduct, and funds for investment and futuristic analysis are decreasingly available.[22]

Since indicators for the populist and elitist development strategies are difficult to obtain for cross-national comparisons, it is impossible to sketch the role of mass opinion and of political elites directly, but such variables probably intervene between each link in the causal chains described above. It is clear that all six strategies of development provide wise counsel for statesmen wishing to prevent internal problems from spilling over into costly and wasteful wars. Whatever reduces an exaggerated role for the

[19]Rostow, *Stages of Economic Growth.*
[20]Michael Harrington, *The Accidental Century* (New York: Macmillan Co., 1965); Donald N. Michael, *The Unprepared Society* (New York: Basic Books, 1968).
[21]Cf. John McHale, *The Future of the Future* (New York: George Braziller, 1969). For the link with peace research, Robert Jungk's "Mankind 2000" project is the most notable. Jungk and a collaborator, Hans Josef Mundt, are editing a fifteen-volume series, *Designs for a New World,* of which the first three volumes have appeared thus far in German.
[22]The decreasing availability of funds for investment during eras with an upswing in military expenditures is documented in Bruce M. Russett, *What Price Vigilance?* (New Haven: Yale University Press, 1970), chap. 5.

military in any country will assist in avoiding wars as well as promoting development. The argument that foreign enemies necessitate a large defense establishment is a sound one; but when causation works the other way around, as we have arranged our models, it is because of developmental stagnation, problems of human development within developing countries, and an inability to think futuristically in the wealthiest and most powerful countries among the family of nations. In answer to Plato and Aristotle, it is not development per se that causes violence between nations but rather the role accorded to the military that is crucial in accounting for wars. As a country develops, new societal problems may—if mishandled—lead to wars between nations.

APPENDIX
List of Countries Investigated

1. Afghanistan	30. West Germany	59. Paraguay
2. Albania	31. Greece	60. Peru
3. Argentina	32. Guatemala	61. Philippines
4. Australia	33. Haiti	62. Poland
5. Austria	34. Honduras	63. Portugal
6. Belgium	35. Hungary	64. Rumania
7. Bolivia	36. India	65. Saudi Arabia
8. Brazil	37. Indonesia	66. Spain
9. Bulgaria	38. Iran	67. Sweden
10. Burma	39. Iraq	68. Switzerland
11. Cambodia	40. Ireland	69. Syria
12. Canada	41. Israel	70. Thailand
13. Ceylon	42. Italy	71. Turkey
14. Chile	43. Japan	72. South Africa
15. China	44. Jordan	73. U.S.S.R.
16. Taiwan	45. North Korea	74. U.K.
17. Colombia	46. South Korea	75. U.S.A.
18. Costa Rica	47. Lebanon	76. Uruguay
19. Cuba	48. Liberia	77. Venezuela
20. Czechoslovakia	49. Libya	78. Yemen
21. Denmark	50. Mexico	79. Yugoslavia
22. Dominican Republic	51. Nepal	80. Laos
23. Ecuador	52. Netherlands	81. North Vietnam
24. Egypt	53. New Zealand	82. South Vietnam
25. El Salvador	54. Nicaragua	83. Morocco
26. Ethiopia	55. Norway	84. Sudan
27. Finland	56. Mongolia	85. Tunisia
28. France	57. Pakistan	
29. East Germnay	58. Panama	

.8. Field Theory and National-International Linkages

RICHARD H. VAN ATTA[1]

VARYING PERSPECTIVES on the question of the linkage between internal aspects of nation-states and the behavior of states toward each other have been formulated. Field theory as developed by R. J. Rummel can be considered an attempt to create a theory of such linkages at the most general level. This chapter explicates field theory as a general theory of linkage. The field theory perspective is compared to the linkage framework formulated by James N. Rosenau. The body of the chapter consists of an assessment of the basic linkage proposition of field theory that the dyadic behavior of nation-states results from the differences between nations on their attribute characteristics. Following this assessment are some general conclusions regarding the possible theoretical evolvement of field theory.

In this study the general concern with the linkage of the internal properties of nations and the behavior between nations is assessed from the perspective of field theory. Some consideration is given here to substantively interesting behavior linkages in the presentation of the research results. To give the discussion some perspective, it should be noted that in field theory any particular behavior, such as the conflict behavior between nations, is treated as part of a behavior space which includes the entire realm of dyadic interaction between nations. The concept of social distance is introduced as the basic linkage between the set of nation characteristics and the behavior of the nation. Field theory provides a general framework

[1]The author acknowledges a great indebtedness to R. J. Rummel in the preparation of this article. An earlier draft coauthored by the author and Rummel appeared as, "Testing Field Theory on the 1963 Behavior Space of Nations," Research Report No. 43 (Honolulu: University of Hawaii, Dimensionality of Nations Project, August 1970). The present paper remains very much a joint endeavor drawing upon Rummel's continuing development of field theory. The author also wishes to thank Warren Phillips for his comments on the earlier draft and Jonathan Wilkenfeld for his editorial assistance.

into which each behavior is incorporated, relative to other behavior and in relation to the attribute properties of nations.

Field theory will be summarized here, having been presented in detail elsewhere.[2] A field of social reality is posited, analytically distinguishing between the attributes of social units and their interactions. Attribute and behavior spaces are defined, such that attributes and interactions are projected into these spaces as vectors. The distance vectors between the values for social units on the dimensions of attribute space are conceived of as social forces determining the location of nation-pairs (dyads) on the dimensions of behavior space. Thus, field theory focuses on the relative distances of nations on attribute dimensions in explaining the behavior of nations. The theory postulates the existence of finite sets of attribute and behavior dimensions, and specifies the linkage between distances on attribute dimensions and the projection on the dimensions of behavior space. The substantive characteristics of the dimensions are not specified, nor are the relative weightings of the attribute distances predicting specific dyadic behavior. In these respects, one might say that field theory is rather abstract in comparison to most theoretical formulations of international relations.

Figure 1 gives a hypothetical representation of attribute space in which two dimensions are shown. The relationship between attributes, and the relative location of nations in attribute space, is defined by the dimensions. In the figure six nations are located with respect to the dimensions called economic development and power base. These two dimensions and that of political orientation are rather basic to the delineation of attribute space. In empirical studies using factor analysis these dimensions have consistently emerged, explaining over 40 percent of the variation in attribute variables.[3]

Behavior space can similarly be diagramed. The units located in the space are nation-pairs, or dyads, rather than single nations. The position of a dyad, e.g., U.S. → Thailand, is determined by the value of the interaction from the actor (U.S.) to object (Thailand) as measured on the dimensions of behavior space. Figure 2 presents a hypothetical behavior space for

[2]Field theory was first elucidated by Rummel in the article "A Field Theory of Social Action with Application to Conflict Within Nations," *General Systems: Yearbook of the Society for General Systems Research* 10 (1965): 183–211. A revised version of the theory was presented in "Field Theory and Indicators of International Behavior" (Paper presented before the Sixty-fifth Annual Meeting of the American Political Science Association, New York, September 1969). Also available as Research Report No. 29, Dimensionality of Nations Project.

[3]For the pictoral representation only two dimensions of attribute space are illustrated. Empirical studies have shown there are at least ten dimensions. These studies will be specifically treated when the attribute data is presented.

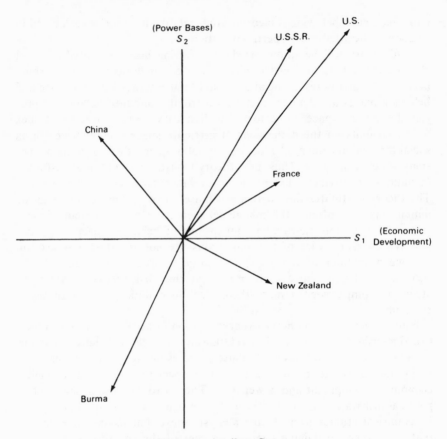

Figure 1. Attribute Space

two dimensions (exports and official conflict) showing the location of five dyads.

The purpose of this spatial representation is to present a theoretical conceptualization that organizes a whole domain of interrelated phenomena. Such a theoretical system should encompass a large number of diverse variables, and to do so must be more abstract in its formulation than the specific variables that are of substantive concern. Field theory's spatial format offers an organizing framework for the vast array of aggregate level variables of concern for international relations. Within this structure middle-range theories, such as status theory[4] can be connected to sub-

[4]Status theory in international relations predicts the behavior of nations in terms of the social structure existing between them. The basic presentation of such a theory is in Johan Galtung, "A Structural Theory of Aggression," *Journal of Peace Research*, no. 2 (1964): 15–38. Rummel has specifically incorporated the status concept into field theory in his monograph "Status, Field Theory and International Relations," Research Report No. 50 (Honolulu: University of Hawaii, Dimensionality of Nations Project, 1971).

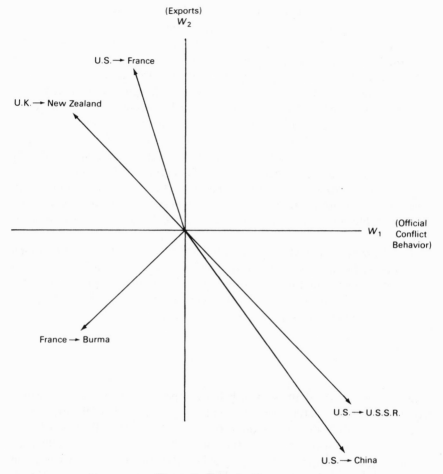

Figure 2. Behavior Space

stantive concerns. In this fashion, while field theory is abstract in relation to those hypotheses treating specific variable relationships, its ability to subsume such hypotheses provides a general framework within which such relationships can be developed and structured.[5]

In field theory the entities of analysis are the social units—nation-states. The theoretical statements of field theory deal with the relative position of nations within the abstractly defined attribute space and the position of dyads, consisting of ordered pairs of nation-states, in behavior space. These

[5]In R. J. Rummel, "U.S. Foreign Relations: Conflict, Cooperation, and Attribute Distances," in *Peace, War, and Numbers*, ed. Bruce M. Russett (Beverly Hills; Sage Publications, 1972), an effort is made to analyze within the context of field theory several specific propositions drawn from various theoretical works.

spaces are defined analytically in terms of linear algebra and are operationally delineated through factor analysis, through which the dimensions of attribute and behavior space are ascertained. The dimensions which define the location of nations and dyads in the two spaces are the variables of theoretical importance in field theory. The use of dimensions as variables in international relations theory is unusual although not without precedence. Even though analyses usually treat such concepts as power, development, conflict, stratification, penetration, etc. in terms of single variables or as composite indicators, it was recognized by Wright that these concepts, taken together, can be depicted within a multidimensional space. Wright located nations in this space in reference to several dimensions he proposed.[6] The existence of a multidimensional space has subsequently been verified in a number of cross-national analyses, which have established rather stable descriptions of the dimensions delineating international relations.[7]

Field theory specifically asserts a linkage between attributes of nations and the dyadic behavior of nations. This linkage is contained in the statement that the location of a dyad on a dimension of behavior space is determined by the distance vectors that connect nations in attribute space. Mathematically this linkage may be expressed as

$$w_{i \to j, k} = \sum_{l=1}^{p} \alpha_l d_{l, i-j}, \tag{1}$$

where w_k is the kth dimension of behavior space and $i \to j$ is a particular dyad, with nation i acting toward j. On the right hand side of the expression the symbol $d_{l,i-j}$ is defined as the distance vector on the lth dimension of attribute space for the actor and the object. The vector gives the difference between the two nations on the particular attribute. The behavior position on each behavior dimension is predicted by a weighted sum of the differences on the attribute space dimensions.

International behavior is the consequence of relative differences between nations on their attributes. This particular expression of the linkage between attribute and behavior spaces has been subsequently called Model I of field theory. An alternative, Model II, has also been proposed. Instead of proposing a general equation over all nation pairs, in Model II the linkage is specific to the particular actor nation i. The mathematical expression of this model, where the parameter α is specific to actor nation i, is

    [6]Quincy Wright, *The Study of International Relations* (New York: Appleton-Century-Crofts, 1955).
    [7]See, for example, Bruce M. Russett, *International Regions and the International System* (Chicago: Rand McNally, 1967), and R. J. Rummel, "Indicators of Cross-National and International Patterns," *American Political Science Review* 63 (1969): 127–47.

$$w_{i \to j,k} = \sum_{l=1}^{\rho} \alpha_{li} d_{l,i-k} \tag{2}$$

That is, the particular predictive relation for each actor is a separate theoretical structure. While the dimensions of attribute space are the same for each actor, the relative weighting of these dimensions in predicting behavior differs from actor to actor in Model II. This difference is designated by the additional subscript on the coefficient. Although the substantive interpretations of these two models are quite different,[8] they view similarly the nature of the linkage relationship between attribute and behavior space.

This theoretical focus of field theory on the attribute difference of nations as the predictor of internation behavior invites comparison between it and the general notion of "linkage politics" which has been presented most cogently by James Rosenau.[9] The fundamental similarity is the emphasis in both formulations upon internal properties of nations as explanation of the external behavior of nations. Yet, this similarity is almost too basic, since it takes very little penetration below it to reveal some marked differences in the orientations of these approaches. A brief comparative discussion of these two approaches may offer some insight into the strategy, as well as the state, of theory-building in the study of international relations. At the outset it should be noted that Rosenau's linkage formulation is a much looser and much broader body of thought than is field theory. Field theory is consciously developed as a strict analytical structure specifically delimiting its range by initial assumptions. The presentation by Rosenau of the idea of "linkage politics" is the specification of an area of theory, a need for theory of a particular kind, with some preliminary ideas as to what might be included in such a theory. The appropriate question, then, is to what extent and in what way is field theory a theory of linkage politics as described by Rosenau.

Let us return to the basic similarity noted between field theory and linkage politics: behavior is explained by internal properties. Field theory proposes a specific version of this assertion in the form of equations (1) or (2). The theory does not contain an explanation of this linkage, however. Neither does it provide an explanation of the variety of empirically ascertainable patterns this linkage might take. Field theory is, then, a framework for analyzing linkages. It says very little about their substantive characteristics.

---

[8] See Rummel, "Field Theory and Indicators of International Behavior," pp. 31–32.

[9] The reader is referred to the article by James N. Rosenau, chap. 2, this volume, as well as to James N. Rosenau, ed., *Linkage Politics* (New York; Free Press, 1969). This discussion of linkage politics also relies upon Rosenau's article, "Pre-Theories and Theories of Foreign Policy," in *Approaches to Comparative and International Politics*, ed. R. B. Farrell (Evanston: Northwestern University Press, 1966), pp. 27–96.

In its original statement (Model I) the linkage between attribute differences and behavior was proposed to be uniform across all actors. To weight the differences on a dimension the same over all actors is to imply that unique cultural, social, and political forces of each nation are irrelevant in forecasting its behavior toward other nations. The parameters of the linkage between attributes and behavior are posited in this model to be constant, regardless of variation in internal structure. Such a general model of the linkage between attribute and behavior can be classified, following Bobrow's scheme, as a "system" model, since the relationships it specifies cut across the universe of actors in the system.[10] Such a general, systemic interpretation of linkage, is not precluded in the Rosenau formulation. The emphasis it places on the importance of varying structure and process within nations, however, is indicative of much less generality (a greater role for unique factors) than is allowed in Model I of field theory.

While the "linkage politics" formulation of Rosenau deals with the relationship between nation characteristics and foreign behavior, the emphasis is rather different from field theory. Nation characteristics are used as the basis of a societal typology according to which five sets of "process" variables (idiosyncratic, role, governmental, societal, and systemic) are scaled in terms of relative potency. The typology is based upon characteristics of size, development, and political orientation. A specific ordering of the process variables is presented according to this typology. Presumably this ordering of process variables, together with proper description of the "issue areas," should allow one to predict foreign policy behavior. Rosenau's characteristics of nations provides a classification scheme. Characteristics of nations are not themselves explanatory of behavior; they provide a key for ascertaining or zeroing-in on the explanatory process variables.

In contrast, field theory utilizes attributes themselves as the explanatory variables, and does not specifically treat the process whereby attributes through a mediatory social decision structure generate the behavior. In field theory relative distance on attribute dimensions is developed as a social force that produces the interaction between nations. The theory does not address itself to that which Rosenau feels is an important source of variation in foreign policy—the internal political process.

Process variables enter into field theory somewhat through the back door when Model II is compared with Model I. Model II, in allowing weights for similarities and differences on attribute dimensions to vary by actor, implies there are two kinds of forces in the international system. One kind is the general force affecting all nations. The second kind consists

---

[10]Bobrow differentiates a "system approach" and an "actor approach" in which the linkages are developed for an actor separately, rather than in the context of the entire system. See Davis Bobrow, "Ecology of International Games: Requirement for a Model of the International System," *Peace Research Society Papers* 11 (1969): 67–87.

of forces unique to the internal structure of each nation. These specific influences acting in conjunction with general forces could then cause each nation to react differently in response to the same attribute difference.[11] While Model II does not state what these unique influences might be, Rosenau's categorization of process variables certainly enumerates the more important possibilities.

The comparison of field theory and the linkage politics "pre-theory" exemplifies the growing tendency to merge the systemic concerns of international relations theory with the consideration of internal national properties which has been the purview of comparative politics. These formulations are neither the first nor the only attempts to join together internal properties of nation-states with the behavior between them. Kaplan in *System and Process in International Politics*[12] delves into subsystem processes including decision making and national interest. The work of Fred Riggs and Charles McClelland represents early concerns with the linkage between the larger system, particularly as manifest in the behavior between units, and the properties of the units themselves.[13] Recently more empirically oriented theoretical works have attempted to bring to bear the assessment of linkages through the analysis of quantitative data. The Bobrow paper cited earlier is one study of the linkage between attributes and behavior that seeks a middle ground between system-level generalization and individual actor uniqueness. The work of Choucri and North and that of Cobb and Elder are other examples of formulations that combine in research studies the "building blocks" of nation characteristics, internal process, and international behavior.[14] These studies and others constitute preliminary efforts at developing theory through an inductive procedure.

Field theory offers a systematic analytical framework, which deals with the linkage question at an initially more abstract level, but, as it continues to evolve, treats more concretely the specific patterns of linkages.[15] Its orientation has been to treat first the most general systemic relationship

[11]Rummel, "Field Theory and Indicators of International Behavior," p. 5.

[12]Morton A. Kaplan, *System and Process in International Politics* (New York: John Wiley and Sons, 1957).

[13]See Fred W. Riggs, "International Relations as a Prismatic System," and Charles A. McClelland, "The Acute International Crisis," both in *The International System*, ed. Klaus Knorr and Sidney Verba (Princeton, N.J.: Princeton University Press, 1961).

[14]Reports of North and Choucri's work are available in Nazli Choucri and Robert C. North, "The Determinants of International Violence," *Peace Research Society Papers* 12 (1969): 33–63; and idem, "Pressure, Competition, Tension, and Threat: Toward a Theory of International Conflict" (Paper prepared for delivery at the sixty-fifth Annual Meeting of the American Political Science Association, New York, September 1969). For the work of Cobb and Elder, see Roger Cobb and Charles Elder, *International Community: A Regional and Global Study* (New York: Holt, Rinehart and Winston, 1970).

[15]Examples of more specific treatments of the linkage relationships in field theory are Rummel, "U.S. Foreign Relations," and S. Rhee, "Communist China's Foreign Behavior: An Application of Field Theory Model II" (Ph.D. diss., University of Hawaii, 1971). Also available as Research Report No. 57, Dimensionality of Nations Project.

in the most parsimonious fashion, with subsequent developments giving more specific treatment of the relationships accepting loss of generality and increasing theoretical complexity in trade for greater explanatory capacity.

ASSESSMENT OF FIELD THEORY

This section presents the results of some exploratory research regarding the linkage between attribute distances and the dyadic behavior of nations. This basic proposition of field theory has already been subjected to some empirical analysis. With the original presentation of field theory only some partial analyses were possible because of the need for extensive data collection and preliminary subanalyses.[16] As part of the Dimensionality of Nations Project, however, data collection and analysis have proceeded to the point where attributes and behavior spaces for two time periods, 1955 and 1963, have been defined, enabling the more complete assessment of the field theory linkage proposition. Canonical regression analysis was applied to the attribute and behavior data to assess the predicted fit between attribute distance vectors and behavior dimensions. While a more thorough consideration of this method of analysis is given in an earlier paper,[17] a brief explanation of the technique appears below.

Separate analyses were conducted for the 1955 and 1963 data. For each of these data points both Model I and Model II were analyzed. To afford maximum comparability the same selected sample of nation dyads were used for the 1955 and 1963 analyses. In addition 1963 data on a random sample of dyads was also compiled for analysis. The selected sample provides a basis for assessing the stability of the research findings across the same sample at different time periods and the random sample serves as a benchmark against which the generalizability of the selected sample results can be assessed. The findings of the data analyses will be presented after considering the methods involved. The tests of Model I will be discussed first.

FIELD THEORY TESTS: MODEL I

The steps in the analysis of Model I for both the 1955 and 1963 data followed the research design displayed in figure 3. A full explanation of the research methodology is presented in the report on the 1955 data analysis.[18] A brief outline of the research procedure is given below. Data on attributes of nations and dyadic behavior of nations were separately factor

[16]R. J. Rummel, "A Social Field Theory of Foreign Conflict Behavior," *Peace Research Society Papers* 4 (1965).
[17]Rummel, "Field Theory and Indicators of International Behavior."
[18]Ibid.

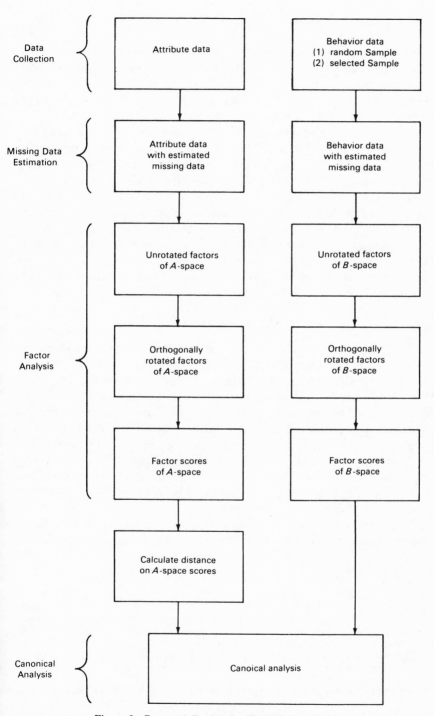

Figure 3. Research Design for Field Theory Tests

analyzed to delineate the dimensions of attribute and behavior spaces respectively. For attribute space, data on the entire set of nations could be used in determining the dimensions of the space. However, the data collection task made it prohibitive to include all possible dyads (11,342 for the 1963 data) in the calculation of behavior space dimensions.

For the behavior space analysis, two samples were analyzed. One sample is that composed of 182 dyads, which were all of the pairings of 14 selected nations. The other sample contained 166 dyads randomly selected from all possible nation pairs. (For a list of the dyads included in the random sample, see appendix 1.)[19] The factor scores of the individual nations on the attribute space dimensions and of the dyads on the behavior space dimensions were computed for the orthogonally rotated factors. For the selected and random sample dyads, the factor score differences on each attribute dimension were then computed. Canonical regression was then used to determine the fit between these differences (distance vectors) and dyadic scores on the behavior dimension.

Data: Attribute Distance

For the analyses of field theory using 1955 data, attribute distances were calculated on indicator variables of the dimensions of attribute space. The use of these indicators, rather than the factor scores for the dimensions, was due to the lack of a missing data estimation program which would have enabled the calculation of factor scores. The delineation of attribute space for 1955 has been reported in earlier studies.[20] A component factor analysis of 236 attributes for 82 nations was conducted.[21] The dimensionality of the space was found to be fifteen. These dimensions were rotated according to the Varimax criteria to orthogonal dimensions best measuring the clusters of attribute vectors in *A*- space. The indicators for thirteen dimensions are listed in table 1.[22]

The data for the 1963 attribute space was collected for 107 nations on 94 variables. The procedures for selecting the 94 variables were as follows.

[19]The tests of Models I and II were applied to only the selected sample for the 1955 data.

[20]Jack Sawyer, "Dimensions of Nations: Size, Wealth, and Politics," *American Journal of Sociology* 73 (September 1967): 145–72; R. J. Rummel, "Some Attributes and Behavioral Patterns of Nations," *Journal of Peace Research* 2 (1967): 196–206; idem, "International Pattern and Nation Profile Delineation", in *Computers and the Policy-Making Community*, ed. Davis B. Bobrow and Judah L. Schwartz (Englewood Cliffs, N.J.: Prentice-Hall, 1968) pp. 154–202.

[21]The nations used in both analyses comprised all nations having a foreign ministry, exchanging ambassadors with other nations, containing a population over 750,000, and having been independent for two years.

[22]The fifteen dimensions account for 75 percent of the variance in the attribute data. In the analysis indicators for thirteen of the fifteen orthogonally rotated dimensions were used. The two dimensions were excluded for different reasons. For one dimension there was no attribute sufficiently correlated with it to select as an indicator. For the other dimension the best indicator proved to be linearly dependent on the other thirteen indicators.

Table 1.   Indicators of Attribute Space Dimensions for 1955 Data

Dimension	Indicator
1. Economic development	energy consumption per capita
2. Power capability	national income
3. Political orientation	freedom of group opposition
4. Catholic culture	Roman Catholic/population
5. Foreign conflict	number of threats
6. Density	population/national land area
7. Oriental culture	number of religious groups
8. Domestic conflict	domestic killed
9. (Unlabeled)	foreign college students/college students
10. Traders	exports/gross national product (GNP)
11. Diversity	number of language groups
12. Equality	educational expenditures by government/ government expenditures
13. Sufficiency	proteins/calories

1. Five of the highest loading and substantively distinctive variables were taken from each oblique factor found in 1955 data for 236 variables.
2. Ten of the variables with the lowest communalities and not otherwise selected by (1) above were included. Any change in the common and unique components of attribute space from 1955 to 1963 can thus be observed.
3. Eight political variables rescaled from Banks and Textor, *Cross Polity Survey*, and three United Nations voting variables were included to give a better definition to the political dimensions found in 1955 data.

Missing data for the attribute variables was estimated using a multiple regression technique.[23] A component factor analysis was performed on the complete matrix and twenty-two dimensions were orthogonally rotated using the varimax technique.[24] Table 2 summarizes these dimensions, most of which are similar to those found for 1955. For these 1963 dimensions factor scores were computed and differences (distance vectors) were calculated for those nations in the random and selected samples.

One difference between the 1955 and 1963 attribute spaces should be mentioned. The 1955 attribute space did not include geographic location. Accordingly, in the tests of field theory a geographic distance variable was added to the set of distances on the indicators of the 1955 attribute dimen-

[23]The technique is discussed in Charles Wall and R. J. Rummel, "Estimating Missing Data," Research Report No. 20 (Honolulu: University of Hawaii, Dimensionality of Nations Project, 1969).
[24]All dimensions for which the eigenvalue exceeded 1.00 were rotated. A factor analysis of the initial data matrix with missing data delineated twenty-two factors for which the eigenvalue exceeded this value. Although the reanalysis of the data with missing data estimated produced twenty-four factors with eigenvalues exceeding 1.00, it was decided to rotate the same number as appeared in the missing data analysis.

**Table 2. 1963 Attribute Space:
Orthogonally Rotated (Varimax) Dimensions for 94 Variables**

Variable Name	Loading
Factor 1: Economic development[a]	
percent total variance = 10.3	
1. agricultural population/population	.85
2. Gross National Product/population	.85
3. bureaucratic[b]	.82
4. telephones/population	.80
5. dwellings with running water/dwellings	.80
Factor 2: Political orientation	
percent total variance = 9.8	
1. constitutional status[b]	−.86
2. bloc membership (0 = Western, 1 = neutral,	−.79
2 = Eastern)	
3. system style[b]	.79
4. Communist party membership/population	.75
5. Russian titles translated/titles translated	.75
Factor 3: Power	
percent total variance = 7.8	
1. defense expenditure	.95
2. national income	.94
3. investment balance	.93
4. demonstrations	.93
5. U.N. assessment/total U.N. assessment	.92
Factor 4: Catholic culture	
percent total variance = 5.5	
1. latitudinal measure of nation's capital	.87
2. Catholic population/population	−.80
3. air distance from U.S.	.69
4. factor scores on Cold War issue dimension of	.52
U.N. voting[c]	
5. membership in neutral bloc (yes = 1, no = 0)	.52
Factor 5: Domestic conflict[a]	
percent total variance = 4.4	
1. population	.90
2. number of riots	.84
3. number of accusations	.78
4. population × energy production	.66
5. number of foreign killed	.63
Factor 6: Linguistic-ethnic diversity[a]	
percent total variance = 3.7	
1. number of languages	.75
2. population of largest language group/population	−.75
3. number of religions	.59
4. number of ethnic groups	.51
5. age of nation	.47
Factor 7: Density	
percent total variance = 4.1	
1. density	.80
2. railroad length/national area	.68

Table 2. (Continued)

Variable Name	Loading
3. arable land/total land area	.67
4. foreign mail sent/foreign mail	.58
5. road length/national area	.56
Factor 8: Trade	
percent total variance = 2.6	
1. exports/gross national product	.83
2. seaborne goods/gross national product	.59
3. imports/trade	.51
Factor 9: Unlabeled	
percent total variance = 2.9	
1. cost of living index	.91
2. balance of payments/gold stock	−.84
3. percent increase in national income/percent increase in population	.64
Factor 10: Unlabeled	
percent total variance = 2.2	
1. arts and culture NGO/total NGO[d]	−.71
2. average rainfall	.69
Factor 11: Military	
percent total variance = 2.3	
1. military personnel/population	.71
2. number of military actions	.61
Factor 12: Unlabeled	
percent total variance = 3.1	
1. foreign college students/college students	.78
2. radial measure of geographic location of nation's capital	.64
Factor 13: Unlabeled	
percent total variance = 2.1	
1. factor scores on South African issue dimension of U.N. voting[c]	.86
2. number of purges	.74
Factor 14: Unlabeled[a]	
percent total variance = 2.2	
1. number of purges	.74
2. desire for achievement	.51
Factor 15: Unlabeled	
percent total variance = 2.2	
1. legality of government change	.84
2. participation of military in government[b]	−.55
Factor 16: Unlabeled[a]	
percent total variance = 1.8	
1. IFC and IBRD subscription/GNP^2 per capita	.63
Factor 17: Unlabeled	
percent total variance = 2.1	
1. desire for affiliation	.69
2. proteins/calories	.64

Table 2. (Continued)

Variable Name	Loading
Factor 18: Unlabeled[a]	
percent total variance = 2.0	
1. unemployed/economically active population	.72
2. military treaties/treaties	.58
Factor 19: Unlabeled	
percent total variance = 1.7	
1. number killed in domestic violence	.77
Factor 20: Unlabelled[a]	
percent total variance = 1.8	
1. balance of investment/gold stock	.80
Factor 21: Unlabeled[a]	
percent total variance = 1.6	
1. religious titles published/book titles	.63
Factor 22: Unlabeled[a]	
percent total variance = 2.2	
1. U.N. delinquencies/assessments	.76
2. national area	.59

[a]Signs reversed.

[b]From A. Banks and R. Textor, *A Cross Polity Survey* (Cambridge, Mass.: MIT Press, 1963).

[c]From R. Pratt and R. J. Rummel, "Issue Dimensions in the 1963 United Nations General Assembly," *Multivariate Behavioral Research* (July 1971): 251–86.

[d]NGO = nonintergovernmental organizations.

sions. For 1963, however, geographic variables locating a nation's capital were included among the 94-attribute variables factor analyzed. The dimensions of the 1963 attribute space subsume geographic location and the distances between nations on these dimensions capture geographic distance.

Data: Behavior Scores

As mentioned above, the data on the behavior of dyads was collected on two dyadic samples. One of these was a selected sample of 182 dyads comprising all possible couplings of 14 selected nations (excluding, of course, the nation with itself). The fourteen nations were selected to represent high, middle, and low values on the major dimensions found to define the 1955 attribute space and to reflect the major cultural and regional groupings of nations.[25]

[25]Several sources were utilized in making the selection. In particular, R. B. Cattell, "The Principle Cultural Patterns Discoverable in the Syntal Dimensions of Existing Nations," *Journal of Social Psychology* 32 (1950): 215–53; and Russett, *International Regions*, were useful guides.

The selected list of dyads ensured that the full scope of differences and similarities *among* nations would be analyzed as they relate to interaction *between* nations. The nations included in the selected sample dyads were: Brazil, Burma, China, Cuba, Egypt, India, Indonesia, Israel, Jordan, Netherlands, Poland, U.S.S.R., U.K., and U.S.A.

To determine the 1963 dyadic random sample, all 107 sovereign nations that had been independent prior to January 1962 were numbered. Eighty dyads of nations then were selected using a random number table. Due to substantive interest, three dyads, U.S. → U.S.S.R., U.S.S.R. → China, and U.S. → France, were added to the sample. Since two directions of relationship, $i \rightarrow j$ and $j \rightarrow i$ are considered for each pair $i \rightarrow j$, the sample included 166 dyadic relations out of a population of 11,342 such relationships for 1963. The random sample dyads are listed in appendix 1.

Forty behavior variables were included in the analysis of behavior space for 1955.[26] The number of variables for the 1963 analysis was enlarged to fifty-six, adding some variables, such as economic aid, official visits, and co-participation in international conferences, for which 1963 data had become available.[27]

The data for 1955 nation behavior was factor analyzed (principle component model) after missing data had been estimated. To better delineate clusters of behavior the Varimax orthogonal rotation is presented in table 3. Twelve dimensions were delineated for which the eigenvalue was greater than 1.0. However, the twelfth dimension was eliminated since the variables it included were considered to be of little importance to international behavior. The remaining eleven factors account for approximately 74 percent of the variance in the behavior variables. The factor analysis of the 1963 behavior data for the selected sample of dyads delineated sixteen factors; for the random sample, thirteen dimensions were defined. Factor scores were then calculated for both data sets on the orthogonally rotated dimensions. Table 4 presents the behavioral dimensions for the selected sample. Since those for the random sample are similar,[28] they are not presented here.

[26]These variables were selected to index the diversity of interaction between nations, including mail exports, tourists, students, U.N. voting, conflict, etc. For a report on the 1955 component factor analysis results, see Rummel, "Indicators of Cross-National and International Pattern."

[27]For the variable definitions and the 1963 data sources, see R. J. Rummel, "Field Theory and the 1963 Behavior Space of Nations," Research Report No. 44 (Honolulu: University of Hawaii, Dimensionality of Nations Project, 1970), appendix I. Missing data were estimated for the 1963 behavioral data, as were the data for 1955.

[28]The trace correlation (using canonical analysis) between the random and selected samples is .77. The least squares estimates of the selected sample 1963 behavior dimensions from the 1955 dimensions have a correlation of .84 with the 1963 dimensions; the corresponding correlation for the factor scores is .60. These results indicate that while the dimensions were fairly stable between 1955 and 1963, the behavior dyads (as measured by the factor scores) shifted considerably. It is of interest to see, then, whether the field theory tests come out the

Table 3.   1955 Behavior Space:
Orthogonally Rotated (Varimax) Dimensions[*][a]

Variable Name[c]	Loadings
Factor 1: Salience	
percent total variance = 11.2	
1. relative translations	.87
2. translations	.86
3. relative tourists	.75
4. tourists	.65
5. treaties	.58
Factor 2: Communications	
percent total variance = 6.6	
1. relative mail	.90
2. mail/domestic mail[d]	.81
3. emigrants	.64
Factor 3: Exports	
percent total variance = 8.1	
1. exports/GNP	.95
2. tourists/population	.87
3. relative exports	.78
4. relative treaties	.67
Factor 4: Students	
percent total variance = 6.5	
1. students	.91
2. relative students	.83
Factor 5: Migrants	
percent total variance = 7.8	
1. relative emigrants	− .89
2. emigrants/population	− .80
3. mail	− .71
4. treaties	− .62
Factor 6: Diplomatic	
percent total variance = 4.9	
1. relative embassy or legation	.88
2. embassy or legation	.83
Factor 7: International organizations	
percent total variance = 6.9	
1. relative IGO[f]	− .86
2. relative NGO[d]	− .79
3. IGO	− .65
4. NGO	− .51
Factor 8: U.N. voting	
percent total variance = 9.8	
1. weighted U.N. voting distance[g]	.89
2. U.N. voting distance 1[g]	.80

same given that the behavior of dyads has changed so. A detailed comparison of 1955 and 1963 behavior space analyses is presented in Rummel, "Field Theory and the 1963 Behavior Space of Nations."

Table 3. (Continued)

Variable Name[c]	Loadings
3. common bloc membership[h]	−.78
4. common bloc position[i]	.78
5. U.N. voting distance 2[g]	.67
Factor 9: Self-determination vote	
percent total variance = 4.0	
1. U.N. voting distance 3[g]	.80
2. unweighted U.N. voting distance[g]	.68
Factor 10: Negative sanctions	
percent total variance = 3.6	
1. negative sanctions[j]	−.73
2. previous enemies[k]	−.62
Factor 11: Deterrence	
percent total variance = 4.4	
1. military violence[j]	.86
2. negative communications[j]	.81

*Footnotes for tables 3 and 4 follow table 4.

It is of interest for our subsequent discussion to note briefly the substantive composition of the behavior space dimensions. Unlike a previous analysis of the international activity of nations, no predominant factor emerged in the analysis of dyadic behavior space.[29] A major difference between that study and the one reported here is that in the former the total behavior of individual nations, rather than the directed behavior of dyads, was analyzed. The predominant factor in the earlier study, labeled "Participation," indicated that a general interrelationship exists in the basic transactions in which a nation engages. In the dyadic behavior studies this general interrelationship was much less pronounced, with the transactional variables being dispersed over several separate factors. Another prominent factor in the individual nation study, that labeled "Conflict," becomes a more dispersed phenomenon when the data is treated dyadically. When total behavior is disaggregated into its dyadic components, conflict behavior forms at least two separate factors. In the 1963 dyadic analysis three separate factors of conflict behavior were delineated: "Conflict acts," in which negative communications is the most salient individual variable; "Defensive acts," isolating the variable designated "Warning and defensive acts"; and a factor encompassing the less severe conflict variables of negative sanctions and antiforeign violence. The military violence variable appears jointly on the first two conflict dimensions. This multidimensional

[29]R. J. Rummel, "Some Dimensions in the Foreign Behavior of Nations," *Journal of Peace Research* 3 (1966): 201–24.

Table 4.   1963 Behavior Space:
Selected Sample Orthogonally Rotated (Varimax) Dimensions

Variable Name	Loading
Factor 1: Salience	
percent total variance = 11.1	
1. export of books and magazines	.87
2. tourists	.87
3. exports	.83
4. military treaties	.73
5. coparticipations in internation conferences	.71
Factor 2: Cold War[b]	
percent total variance = 6.3	
1. common bloc membership[i]	.87
2. bloc position index	− .86
3. similarity in U.N. voting on procedural issue dimension	.81
4. weighted similarity in U.N. voting on major issue dimensions[l]	.80
Factor 3: Diplomatic	
percent total variance = 4.1	
1. relative diplomatic representation	.91
2. embassy or legation $i \rightarrow j$	.78
3. relative diplomats sent	.63
Factor 4: Conflict acts	
percent total variance = 6.9	
1. conflict incidents	.89
2. total conflict	.87
3. negative communications	.86
4. time since on opposite side in war	.66
5. military violence	.56
Factor 5: International organization	
percent total variance = 8.1	
1. weighted relative IGO[f]	.88
2. relative IGO	.86
3. weighted relative NGO[d]	.83
4. relative NGO	.82
5. IGO	.64
Factor 6: Migrants[b]	
percent total variance = 5.6	
1. emigrants/population	.91
2. relative books exported	.81
3. emigrants	.78
4. relative emigrants	.63
Factor 7: Unlabeled	
percent total variance = 3.7	
1. independence of i and j predates 1946	.84
2. time since on same side in war	.78

Table 4. (Continued)

Variable Name	Loading
Factor 8: Aid[b]	
percent total variance = 3.6	
1. economic aid	.93
2. relative economic aid	.92
Factor 9: Exports[b]	
percent total variance = 6.0	
1. relative exports	.86
2. largest commodity export/exports $A \rightarrow B$	.85
3. export/GNP	.80
Factor 10: Unlabeled[b]	
percent total variance = 2.9	
1. territory of i lost to j and not regained	.85
2. book translations	.53
Factor 11: Defensive acts	
percent total variance = 3.6	
1. warning and defensive acts	.80
2. military violence	.59
Factor 12: Unlabeled[b]	
percent total variance = 2.9	
1. i once a colony or part of j	.84
2. relative students $i \rightarrow j$	.53
Factor 13: Military treaties[b]	
percent total variance = 3.3	
1. relative military treaties	.79
2. book translations	.50
Factor 14: Students	
percent total variance = 5.8	
1. students $i \rightarrow j$	.86
2. official visits	.73
3. relative treaties	.63
4. treaties	.60
Factor 15: U.N. voting	
percent total variance = 4.8	
1. similarity in U.N. voting on major issue dimensions[1]	.78
2. similarity in U.N. voting on South African issue dimension	.73
3. relative NGO	−.51
Factor 16: Negative sanctions	
percent total variance = 2.8	
1. negative sanctions	.63
2. antiforeign violence	.61

Footnotes for Tables 3 and 4.

[a]Orthogonally rotated to a Varimax solution. The unrotated solution was from a principal axes factoring of a product moment correlation matrix. This is the component factor model. All dimensions with eigenvalues greater than 1.0 were rotated. The labels given each dimension are meant to describe the behaviors highly correlated with the dimensions.

[b]Signs reversed.

[c]All behaviors are for nation i to nation j. A "relative" behavior is defined as (behavior of nation i to j)/nation i's total behavior. For example, relative exports is (exports $i \rightarrow j$/i's total exports). The data matrix was complete for all variables. Missing data had been estimated using a regression estimation technique.

[d]NGO = Nonintergovernmental international organizations.

[e]The denominator refers to the actor.

[f]IGO = Intergovernmental international organizations.

[g]The voting variables are the Euclidean distance between nations on the orthogonal dimensions of U.N. voting in the 10th (1955) Session of the General Assembly. To determine these distances, Assembly Committee and Plenary sessions roll-call votes first were separately component factor analyzed to define the issue dimensions. Then, roll calls on those issues central to the committee and Plenary dimensions were combined and refactored. The resulting dimensions describe the most general clustering of issues in the U.N. The voting variables used here were computed from factor scores on these dimensions:

Weighted U.N. voting distance: Euclidean distance between nations i and j on the seven major dimensions of U.N. voting, with each dimension weighted by the variance in roll calls for which it accounted.

Unweighted U.N. voting distance: Euclidean distance between nations i and j on the seven major dimensions of U.N. voting.

U.N. voting distance 1: Euclidean distance between nations i and j on a "Cold War" dimension of U.N. voting.

U.N. voting distance 2: Euclidean distance between nations i and j on a "admission of new states" dimension of U.N. voting.

U.N. voting distance 3: Euclidean distance between nations i and j on a "self-determination" dimension of U.N. voting.

[h]Common bloc membership of nations i and j = 2; different = 1; opposite = 0. Blocs considered are Communist, neutral, and Western. Neutral bloc membership is defined as not having a mutual defense treaty with either the U.S. or U.S.S.R.

[i]Bloc position between nations i and j measured as the absolute difference on the following scale:

1	2	4	6	7
U.S.A.	non-U.S.A. Western bloc member	neutral bloc member	non-U.S.S.R. Communist bloc member	U.S.S.R.

[j]These variables are (orthogonally rotated) factor scores resulting from a previous component factor analysis of all nation dyads (340) manifesting foreign conflict behavior on any one of 16 variables: violent acts, planned violent acts, incidences of violence, discrete military acts or clashes, days of violence, negative acts, diplomatic rebuffs, negative communications, written negative communications, oral negative communications, written or oral negative communications, unclassified negative communications, accusations, representations or protests, warnings, and antiforeign demonstrations. See R. J. Rummel, "Some Attributes and Behaviorial Patterns of Nations" *Journal of Peace Research* 2 (1967).

[k]This is rated as the time since nations i and j were on opposite sides of a war: 0 = pre-1900 or never; 1 = 1901–10; 2 = 1911–20; 4 = 1921–30; 8 = 1931–40; 16 = 1941–50; 32 = 1951–60; 64 = 1961–present.

[l]Similarity in roll-call voting on six dimensions of U.N. voting, 18th session.

breakdown of conflict is similar to that found in the specific analyses of foreign conflict reported by Rummel and Tanter.[30] Conflict behavior when considered dyadically shows the same characteristic of general independence from other behavior variables as noted in the nondyadic foreign behavior studies.[31]

ANALYSIS: THE CANONICAL REGRESSION MODEL

The objective of our empirical research is to obtain an assessment of the linkage between distances on attribute dimensions and the behavior between nations. This linkage for Model I is defined as

$$w_{i \to j,k} = \sum_{l=1}^{p} \alpha_l d_{l,i-j},$$

which can be given the matrix representation

$$W_{mxq} = D_{mxp} P_{pxq}, \tag{3}$$

where W is a matrix of m dyads by q behavioral dimensions (an element w of the matrix is the score for a dyad $i \to j$ on behavior dimension k), D is a matrix of distance vectors (a typical element of which d_{i-j}, the distance between nations i and j on the lth attribute dimension), P is a matrix of parameters.[32]

Equation (3) states that international behavior is a linear transformation of the attribute distances between two nations. One criterion on which the statement can be assessed is the degree to which it represents our observations. An estimate of the behavior, W, can be obtained using regression equation:

$$\begin{aligned} W &= DP + U, \\ W^* &= DP \end{aligned} \tag{4}$$

and $U = W - W^*$ is the matrix of linear deviations between the estimated behavior W^*, obtained from observations S and parameters P, and the actual behavior W. Assuming the deviations U are uncorrelated by column with D, then

$$\begin{aligned} D'W &= D'DP + D'U \quad (D'U = 0) \\ (D'D)^{-1} D'W &= P \end{aligned} \tag{5}$$

---

[30] R. J. Rummel, "Dimensions of Conflict Behavior Within and Between Nations," chap. 3, this volume; R. Tanter, "Dimensions of Conflict Behavior Within and Between Nations, 1958–1960," *Journal of Conflict Resolution* 10 (1966): 41–64.

[31] Rummel, "Some Dimensions in the Foreign Behavior of Nations," p. 207.

[32] This presentation of the regression model to assess field theory is adapted from Rummel, "Field Theory and Indicators of International Behavior," pp. 18–26.

The parameters P will be regression coefficients and W^* will be the least squares estimate of W.

The square of the *trace correlation*, $\bar{r}$, is the appropriate statistic to assess the empirical fit between the actual behavior space, W, and that predicted from the attribute distance, W^*. The equation for the trace correlation squared for this data is

$$\bar{r}^2 = \frac{1}{q} \sum_{k=1}^{q} \left(\frac{1}{m} W_k' W_k^* \right)^2 = \frac{1}{q} \sum_{k=1}^{q} R_k^2, \qquad (6)$$

where W_k is assumed standardized and R_k is the multiple correlation coefficient for the regression of W_k onto D and the W_k dimensions are mutually orthogonal. The coefficient $\bar{r}^2$ measures the proportion of variance in behavior space accounted for by attribute distances.

The trace correlation can be calculated using any rotation of the dimensions of behavior space, since the variation within the space is not altered by rotating its coordinates. It is possible than to perform a linear transformation of W that will yield orthogonal behavioral dimensions ordered such that the first will have the maximum correlation with D, the second dimension will have the maximum residual correlation, etc. This can be done by applying canonical analysis to solve for the least squares fit between W and D. Let T be the appropriate transformation for W. Then, the canonical model is

$$\begin{aligned} WT &= DP + G, \\ Y &= V + G, \end{aligned} \qquad (7)$$

where $WT = Y$, $DP = V$, and G is the least squares error. The restrictions on Y and V are:

$$\begin{aligned} Y_k' V_g &= r_{kg} \text{ (canonical correlation)}, k = g; \\ Y_k' V_g &= 0, k \neq g; \\ Y_k' Y_k &= V_g' V_g = 1; \\ Y_k' Y_g &= V_k' V_g = 0. \end{aligned} \qquad (8)$$

The canonical analysis, then, will yield the least squares fit between attribute distances and behavior dimensions, such that the rotated dimensions Y of behavior successively have the maximum correlations with attribute differences. The trace correlation is unaltered by using the canonical model and can be calculated from the canonical results by replacing R_k^2 by r_k^2, the canonical correlation, in equation (6).

ANALYSIS: RESULTS OF CANONICAL REGRESSION

Canonical regression analysis results for Model I are reported below for the 1955 data on the selected sample and the 1963 data for both the selected and random sample. The results of these canonical regressions are summarized in table 5 for the 1955 study, table 6 for the 1963 analysis using the selected sample, and table 7 for the 1963 analysis using the random sample. The trace correlation obtained for the 1955 data was .36 for the selected sample. The square of this coefficient shows that only 13 percent of the variation of behavior within behavior space is dependent upon attribute distances. For the 1963 selected sample data, the trace correlation again is .36 and for the random sample the trace is .34. The results of the test of Model I using 1955 data and data for 1963 indicate a lack of fit with empirical data.

Table 5. Canonical Analysis Results[a] for Model I, 1955 Selected Sample

Behavior Dimension Y_k[b]	Canonical Correlation with $V_g(k = g)$[c]	Chi-square[d]	Degrees of Freedom (D.F.)[e]	Z-transformation for D.R. $\geq$ 30[f]
Y_1	.79 (.63)	355.3	180	7.71
Y_2	.63 (.40)	190.4	154	2.00
Y_3	.50 (.25)	105.6	130	−1.56
Y_4	.38 (.15)	58.0	108	−3.89
Y_5	.30 (.09)	31.7	88	−5.27
Y_6	.20 (.04)	15.5	70	−6.22
Y_7	.15 (.02)	8.5	54	−6.22
Y_8	.12 (.01)	4.7	40	−5.81
Y_9	.08 (.01)	2.3	28	
Y_{10}	.07 (.01)	1.1	18	
Y_{11}	.03 (.001)	.2	10	
Y_{12}[g]	.01 (.000)	.03	4	
Trace correlation[h] = .36 (.13)				

[a] Minimization of U in equation (5) under restrictions (6) given in text.

[b] Y_k is a column vector from Y, $Y = WT$, where W is the matrix of scores on behavior dimensions of B-space and T is a transformation matrix.

[c] V_g is a column vector from V, $V = DP$, where D is composed of distance vectors on thirteen indicators of attribute dimensions and two measures of geographic distance (capitol distance and territorial distance). Canonical correlations squared given in parentheses.

[d] The chi-square equals $- [n - 0.5(p + q + 1)] \log_e \wedge$, where n = number of dyads, q = the number of behavioral dimensions of W, p = the number of columns of D, and

$$\wedge = \prod_{k=1}^{q} (1 - r_k^2).$$

where r_k^2 is the kth squared canonical correlation.

[e] The degrees of freedom = $[p - (k - 1)][q - (k - 1)]$.

[f] The Z-transformation is for reference to corresponding areas under the normal curve.

[g] A twelfth dimension of W was included in the canonical analysis. Since this dimension involved four variables which are not behavioral (in the sense of action), it is not discussed in the text.

[h] Trace correlation is $\left(\sum_{k=1}^{q} r_k^2 / g \right)^{1/2}$, where r_k^2 is the kth squared canonical correlation and g the number of behavioral dimensions of W.

Table 6.   Canonical Analysis Results for Model I, 1963 Selected Sample[a]

Behavior Dimension Y_k	Canonical Correlation with $V_g(k = g)$	Chi-square	Degrees of Freedom (D.F.)	Z-transformation for D.F. $\geq$ 30
Y_1	.70 (.49)	393.37	352	1.53
Y_2	.64 (.41)	282.14	315	−1.33
Y_3	.49 (.24)	198.07	280	−3.74
Y_4	.43 (.18)	153.25	247	−4.70
Y_5	.89 (.15)	119.58	216	−5.30
Y_6	.33 (.11)	92.30	187	−5.73
Y_7	.30 (.09)	73.18	160	−5.76
Y_8	.27 (.07)	57.62	135	−5.67
Y_9	.26 (.07)	45.13	112	−5.43
Y_{10}	.25 (.06)	33.97	91	−5.21
Y_{11}	.20 (.04)	23.59	72	−5.09
Y_{12}	.20 (.04)	16.73	55	−4.66
Y_{13}	.18 (.03)	9.90	40	−4.44
Y_{14}	.14 (.02)	4.85	27	
Y_{15}	.08 (.01)	1.74	16	
Y_{16}	.07 (.00)	0.79	7	
Trace correlation = .36 (.13)				

[a] See footnotes to table 5.

Table 7.   Canonical Analysis Results for Model I, 1963 Random Sample[a]

Behavior Dimension Y_k	Canonical Correlation with $V_g(k = g)$	Chi-square	Degrees of Freedom (D.F.)	Z-transformation for D.F. $\geq$ 30
Y_1	.75 (.56)	274.87	286	−0.45
Y_2	.59 (.34)	152.18	252	−4.98
Y_3	.46 (.21)	89.07	220	−7.61
Y_4	.38 (.14)	53.79	190	−9.10
Y_5	.33 (.11)	31.35	162	−10.05
Y_6	.19 (.04)	14.63	136	−11.05
Y_7	.17 (.03)	9.25	112	−10.63
Y_8	.12 (.01)	4.82	90	−10.27
Y_9	.09 (.01)	2.59	70	−9.51
Y_{10}	.07 (.00)	1.41	52	−8.47
Y_{11}	.06 (.00)	.69	36	−7.25
Y_{12}	.03 (.00)	.21	22	
Y_{13}	.02 (.00)	.07	10	
Trace correlation = .34 (.12)				

[a] See footnotes to table 5.

It is important to note that in the 1955 selected sample there were twelve dimensions and sixteen in the 1963 tests. Thus, for 1963 there were many more bits of information for canonical analysis to fit together to achieve a maximum correlation. Taking the different sizes of the two spaces into account, then, how do we compare them?

The Z-transformation column in the tables measures the significance of the canonical correlations in terms of the dimensionality of the spaces. For 1955, we can see that the first canonical correlation is highly significant ($p < .0000003$) and the second is significant at $p \leq .02$ (one-tailed.)[33] Because of this significance, the first canonical *variates* can be given an interpretation and discussed. Inspection of the transformation matrix T (not shown) indicates that Y_1 is largely a transformation of the salience and international organization behavioral dimensions shown in table 3. That is,

$$Y_1 \doteq -.56 \, (\text{salience}) - .60 \, (\text{international organizations}), \qquad (9)$$

where $\doteq$ means approximately equal since the minor contribution of the other dimensions is not included. This particular linear combination of two behavioral dimensions yields the transformed behavior dimension, Y_1, having the highest dependence on the 1955 attribute space. Further inspective of the parameters solved for in matrix P (also not shown) indicates that Y_1 is maximally dependent upon V_1, where

$$V_1 \doteq \quad 2.70 \begin{pmatrix} \text{distance between nations on} \\ \text{energy consumption per capita} \end{pmatrix}$$
$$- 2.54 \begin{pmatrix} \text{distance between nations} \\ \text{on national income} \end{pmatrix}. \qquad (10)$$

Putting (9) and (10) together and taking into account the loadings of table 3 for salience and international organization, the analysis shows that differences between nations on energy consumption per capita (an indicator of the development dimension) and national income (an indicator of the power dimension) account for 63 percent of the variation in the behavior of a nation toward another in terms of translations, tourists, treaties, and cojoining international organizations.

For the 1963 Model I selected sample results, however, the significance of the *first* canonical correlation is only $p \leq .07$, while for the random sample the corresponding Z-transformation indicates pure chance results.[34] Therefore, we must conclude that although the trace correlation

[33]The one tailed test is appropriate, since field theory predicts that the Z-transformation be positive.

[34]For several of the canonical results, the negative Z-transformations are highly significant in tables 5–7. This indicates that there is some systematic (nonchance) reason for these low canonical correlations. Our guess is that the cause of these low correlations is the nature of Model I, which assumes that the $i \rightarrow j$ behavior on the kth dimension will be of equal magnitude but opposite in sign to $j \rightarrow i$ behavior. That is, behavior is antisymmetrical.

is as high for 1963 as for the 1955 test, this is due to the greater variance included in the 1963 analysis: the 1963 test suggests that Model I does not fit the data at all and that little confidence could be placed in any interpretation of the canonical variates.

FIELD THEORY TESTS: MODEL II

In Model II of field theory the linkage between attribute distances and behavior is expressed by the equation

$$w_{i \rightarrow j,k} = \sum_{l=1}^{p} \alpha_{li} d_{l,i-k}.$$

Replacing the coefficient α_i of Model I with α_{li} of Model II relieves the field theory linkage of a severe constraint. In Model II, as opposed to Model I, it is not assumed that the forces linking attribute differences to behavior act uniformly across all actors. Model II does imply, however, that the forces operating for *a particular actor* are consistent across all of its dyadic linkages. Furthermore, Model II allows for symmetric, asymmetric and antisymmetric behavior, whereas for Model I the behavior of nation i to nation j is constrained to be the exact opposite of the behavior of j to i.[35]

The analysis of Model II follows the design presented previously for Model I. The data on attribute distances and behavior dimensions for the selected sample of dyads were separated into fourteen subsamples such that the actor is the same nation for all of the dyads in the subsample. The attribute difference values and the behavior dimension scores are the same values for the dyads as used in the Model I tests. However, because of the small sample size for each Model II subsample (13 dyads) it was necessary to reduce the number of variables (dimensions) for both attribute and behavior space. Since each subsample is composed of only thirteen dyads, the degrees of freedom for the canonical regression equation, $WT = DP + U$, is a problem. Consider a regression analysis of international behavior involving thirteen cases and thirteen predictors (independent variables). The multiple correlation will necessarily equal 1.00. Regardless of the predictors used, we would get a perfect fit. Since our interpretation of the value of Model II depends in part on the variance in behavior accounted for, the degrees of freedom problem has to be carefully considered. The problem is to reduce the number of variables in the regression equation and still include the substantive content of the data used in the analysis of Model I. The data manipulations reported below are an attempt to overcome this problem.

[35]Ibid., p. 32.

Data: Attribute Distances

Attribute distance variables for the 1955 tests of Model II are selected to represent the three dimensions accounting for the greatest amount of variance in attribute space: economic development, size or power capability, and political orientation. Together these dimensions accounted for about 41 percent of the total variation in the 236 attributes.[36] The indicators employed for these dimensions were, respectively: energy consumption per capita, national income, and freedom of group opposition. The differences on these indicators were used for the Model II test along with an indicator of geographic distance (the closest geographic distance between the political territories of nations *i* and *j*). For the 1963 Model II tests, the variables on which attribute differences were calculated are the factor scores for the four factors of attribute space: economic development, power capability, political orientation, and Catholic culture. The first three dimensions are very similar to the dimensions for which indicators were developed in the study of 1955 data. The fourth dimension, besides accounting for the next greatest amount of variance, also includes geographic location measures as high loading variables. These four dimensions account for about 33 percent of the variation in attribute space.

Data: Behavior Scores

To reduce the number of behavior variables to be analyzed the orthogonal dimensions of behavior space are summed to form a smaller number of orthogonal dimensions. A substantive interpretation of the dimensions delineated in the factor analyses of behavior variables classifies these dimensions into three categories: private international relations, administrative behavior, and conflict behavior. Table 8 shows the dimensions making up each of these three categories of international behavior for the 1963 data. The signs above the dimensions indicate whether they were summed or subtracted[37] to form the composite three dimensions. Scores on these three orthogonal dimensions for each of the fourteen subsamples of thirteen dyads each constitute the behavior data for the Model II field theory tests.

Analysis: Results of Canonical Regression

The canonical regression for each of the subsamples of dyads fits a four-dimensional subspace of the original attribute space to a three-dimensional subspace of the original behavior space. The results of these canon-

---

[36]Sawyer, "Dimensions of Nations."
[37]Whether the dimension was summed or subtracted depended on the sign of the loadings on the dimension.

Table 8.   Behavior Dimensions for Model II Analysis with 1963 Data

	I. Private International Relations			
	+	−	+	−
Behavior	Salience	Exports	Students	Migrants
Export of books	.88			
Tourists	.87			
Exports	.83			
Military treaties	.73			
Co-participation	.71			
Relative exports		−.86		
Largest commodity		−.85		
Export/GNP		−.80		
Students			.86	
Official visits			.73	
Relative treaties			.63	
Treaties			.60	
Emigrant/population				−.91
Relative books				−.81
Emigrants				−.78
Relative emigrants				−.63

	II. Administrative Behavior			
	+	− Inter- national Organi-	−	− Military
Behavior	Diplo- matic	zation	Aid	Treaties
Relative embassy or legation	.91			
Embassy or legation	.78			
Relative diplomats sent	.63			
N-IGOS		−.88		
Relative IGO		−.86		
N-NGOs		−.83		
Relative NGOs		−.82		
IGOs		−.64		
Economic aid			−93	
Relative economic aid			−.92	
Relative military treaties				−.79
Book translations				−.50

	III. Conflict Behavior				
	−	+	+	+	+
	U.N.	Cold	Deter-	Deter-	Negative
Behavior	Voting	War	rence I	rence II	Sanctions
U.N. voting similarity	.78				
South African issue dimension	.73				
NGOs	−.51				

Table 8.   (Continued)

Behavior	− U.N. Voting	+ Cold War	+ Deter- rence I	+ Deter- rence II	+ Negative Sanctions
Common bloc member		−.87			
Common bloc position		.86			
Procedural issue dimension		−.81			
Weighted U.N. vote similarity		−.80			
Conflict incidence			.89		
Total conflict			.87		
Negative communication			.86		
Time opposite war			.66		
Military violence			.56	.59	
Warning and defense				.80	
Negative sanction					.63
Antiforeign violence					.61

ical analyses, summarized in table 9 for the analyses of 1955 data, may be compared with the results from the study using 1963 data, reported in table 10. The tables are arranged with the substudies arrayed as columns across the page. For each of the substudies the trace correlation giving the overall fit between the attribute distance and the behavior dimensions is presented in the first row below the actor label. For example, the Brazil substudy for 1955 data shows a trace correlation of .74. Below the trace correlation is a row containing two values for each substudy. These values are the canonical correlations for the first two canonical variates for the substudy. The first two canonical correlations are highly significant in all of the substudies. In very few cases are the correlations substantial for the subsequent variates. Therefore, only the first two variates are presented in the tables. In the 1955 Brazil substudy the canonical correlations are .98 for the first canonical variate and .78 for the second variate. From the column of figures directly below each of these correlations the structure of the relationship producing these correlations can be ascertained. The values in these columns are the coefficients for the first two canonical equations. These coefficients give the composition of the first two canonical variates in terms of the relative contribution of the original attribute distances and behavior dimensions. Only those coefficients exceeding .50 are included in the tables (with a few exceptions marked by parentheses). For the Brazil example, the first canonical variate chiefly comprises the relationship between national income difference and the private international relations behavior dimension. This relationship can be expressed in

Table 9.   Canonical Analysis Results for Model II, 1955 Data

Actor	Brazil		Burma		China		Cuba		Egypt		India		Indonesia	
Trace Correlation	.74		.67		.77		.76		.77		.73		.65	
Canonical Correlation	.98	.78	.92	.66	.97	.85	1.00	.80	.95	.78	.93	.82	.84	.73
D — Energy consumption per capita	−1.08							1.00	−1.08	.71	.54	−1.39		(−.30)
D — National income	−.77		−.73	−.51	−.75		.96		.67			.64		
D — Freedom of group opposition						.78								
D — Territorial distance	.81		1.18			−.56		−1.40	.81	.60	−.62		.83	(−.30) (−.35)
W — Conflict	.73		.84		1.00			−.80			−.57		.88	
W — Administrative behavior	−.64			.89		.59		.60	.83		−.52			
W — Private international relations	.99					.76	−1.00			−.97	.63	.97	.70	.71

Actor	Israel		Jordan		Netherlands		Poland		U.S.S.R.		U.K.		U.S.	
Trace Correlation	.80		.71		.63		.69		.77		.75		.75	
Canonical Correlation	1.00	.80	.93	.72	.93	.49	.88	.74	.95	.80	.96	.82	.95	.83
D Energy consumption per capita	.57	-1.22		-.65	.87	.56		-.56				.76		
National income	(.49)	1.45	-1.31	.56		-1.25	-1.92	1.13	-.81		-.75	-.94	-.65	-.85
Freedom of group opposition					.62	.51								-.65
Territorial distance				-.78		-.66		.83		.78		1.08		.57
W Conflict			.53				.70		.99			.82		
Administrative behavior		.87	.62	.84	-.69	-.70		.71						.87
Private international relations	-.97		.58		-.72	.71		.92		.89	.97	-.50		.99

Note: Each sample consists of thirteen dyads comprising the same actor. The actor for each sample is shown heading the canonical results for that sample. Only the first two canonical correlations are shown and only the canonical coefficients greater or equal to an absolute value of .50 (with the exception of Indonesia's second canonical variate) are given.

equation form as

-1.08 national income $\doteq .99$ private international relations.

The second variate has the structure

$-.77$ national income $+ .81$ territorial distance $\doteq$
.73 conflict $- .64$ administrative behavior.

The results of the analyses will be summarized below, followed by a discussion of the more interesting relationships which were ascertained.

As mentioned in the Model I analyses, the trace correlation is a measure of the overall fit between the two variable spaces. In the Model II studies the *square* of the trace correlations across all of the subsamples for the 1963 data averages .53 and .57 for the 1955 data. The trace correlations range from .61 to .80 for the 1963 studies, compared to a range of .63 to .80 for 1955. While for the 1963 data the average of the first canonical correlation is .93, the average for the 1955 data was .96. Thus, both analyses of Model II, using data on attributes and behavior data for 1955 and 1963 show a substantial fit of the two spaces. On the average over 50 percent of the variance in behavior space can be accounted for by attribute distances when Model II is employed.

Given the small sample it is somewhat hazardous to generalize the empirical relationships found in the analyses. A substantial relationship between attribute differences and behavior is ascertained for all subsamples, as shown by the trace correlations. However, a comparison of the composition of the canonical variates shows that not only do they vary greatly from 1955 to 1963 for the same subsample of dyads, but also that there is a lack of uniformity of structure across the subsamples. The fact that these relationships are quite strong and yet so disparate establishes as the next stage of theoretical concern the development of an explanatory synthesis of these findings. Before discussing some possible directions for this theoretical development, some comments on the specific relationships are in order.

An extremely prevalent relationship was that linking differences on internal characteristics with conflict behavior. Yet the structure of this relationship reflects both the temporal inconsistency and the actor-to-actor incongruity mentioned above. A good example of the temporal change is the shift in the relationship for Chinese conflict. The findings for the two time periods were most striking. For the 1955 analysis a nearly perfect relationship was ascertained between the difference in power (as indexed by national income) between China and another state and the conflict behavior China directed toward that state. The equation expressing this relationship is $-.75$ power $\doteq 1.00$ conflict. However, for 1963 another dimension shows a predominant relation with Chinese conflict behavior although the difference on the power dimension still plays a considerable role. From the equation expressing the relationship for 1963,

$$.84 \text{ political orientation} - .53 \text{ Power} \doteq .99 \text{ conflict,}$$

it can be seen that the relative difference on the political orientation dimension is an important factor separate from similarity in power in predicting Chinese conflict behavior. This more complicated relationship for the later time period can be attributed primarily to the marked increase in Chinese conflict directed toward the Soviet Union. The shifting of political orientation was not very substantial over the period, but those shifts that did occur were accompanied by commensurate change in conflict behavior.[38]

Other examples of shifts, perhaps even more striking that that illustrated by Chinese conflict, are manifested in the Cuban and Indonesian subsamples. Most other subsamples show a definite change in the structure of their relationships, but none as dramatic as those just singled out. The most consistent, but still by no means constant, relation between the two time periods is that found for the Soviet Union. Here the similarity in power best predicts Soviet conflict behavior—a manifestation of the continuing predominance of the United States as the recipient of Soviet conflict.

In comparing the results of each subsample analysis, there is a lack of a general relationship between conflict behavior and any particular attribute dimension or combination of dimensions. To a large extent the sampling of nations itself militated against such findings. Since the nations included in the studies were selected so as to capture the wide variation in national characteristics, it is not surprising that there should be a good deal of variety in the patterns of behavior of these actors.

The attribute dimension that is most prevalent in the relationships between conflict behavior and attribute distance is power. In examining the relations delineated for behavior variates which include this conflict dimension, thirteen of the subsamples show power difference being negatively related to the behavior variate. Table 11 lists the combination of internal attributes which predict to behavior variates which include the conflict dimension. This summary shows the prevalence of power difference in predicting to conflict. Yet the divergence in the results is still the main feature. The simple relationship of power similarity predicting conflict is found for only six of the subsamples, and for one of these power similarity conjointly predicts conflictful and cooperative behavior. For other subsamples the relationship is more complex with power similarity additively

---

[38] A much more detailed assessment of this relationship utilizing data on China's relations to 82 dyads (as opposed to the 13 dyads used in this analysis) gives very similar findings to those reported here. See Rhee, "Communist China's Foreign Behavior," esp. pp. 140–50.

Table 10.   Canonical Analysis Results for Model II, 1963 Data

Actor	Brazil		Burma		China		Cuba		Egypt		India		Indonesia	
Trace Correlation	.80		.73		.61		.69		.77		.72		.70	
Canonical Correlation	.99	.84	.90	.81	.91	.45	.95	.58	.90	.84	.95	.71	.93	.68
D — Difference on economic development	-1.04		.64						.96					(.43)
D — Difference on power capability					-.53		-.74	-.71		-.85		-.95	-.87	
D — Difference on political orientation		-.52		.52	.84			-.94						
D — Difference on Catholic culture				-.54		-.53						.64		
W — Conflict	.76		.77		.99		.96		.89		.68		.71	
W — Administrative behavior				.92		.66						.61		-.70
W — Private international relations	.94	-.51	-.64		.63		.94		.88		.99		.92	

Actor	Israel		Jordan		Netherlands		Poland		U.S.S.R.		U.K.		U.S.	
Trace Correlation	.73		.78		.74		.79		.65		.67		.79	
Canonical Correlation	.99	.76	.95	.73	.94	.84	.93	.75	.84	.73	.98	.59	.92	.82
D — Economic development		.93												
Power capability	-.76	.81	-.87		-.64	(.39)		-.67	-.58	-.79		-.99		-.78
Political orientation					.81	(.39)		1.09				.71		1.25
Catholic culture			(-.46)											
W — Conflict			.67		-.87		.78		.78			-.84		.71
Administrative behavior		.98	.99			.52						.76		
Private international relations	.95		.70		-.76	-.76	.62	-.84	.53	.92	1.00	-.60		.67

Note: Each sample consists of thirteen dyads comprising the same actor. The actor for each sample is shown heading the canonical results for that sample. Only the first two canonical correlations are shown and only canonical coefficients greater than or equal to an absolute value of .50 are presented (with a few exceptions noted in parentheses.)

combined with another attribute difference in the prediction. These results suggest subsequent analyses being done with samples of actors and objects constructed such that the question of particular relational properties among the actor and object (particularly power difference) predicting their conflict interaction can be more systematically explored.

**Table 11.   Relations Between Attribute Differences and
Behavior Variates including the Conflict Dimension**

Relationship Between Attribute Differences and Behavior Variate Containing Conflict	Subsamples Showing the Relationship
– Power	$U.S.S.R._{.55}$, $China_{55}$, $Cuba_{63}$, $Poland_{63}$, $U.S.S.R._{.63}$, $U.S._{.63}$[a]
– Power + Political	$U.S._{.55}$, $China_{63}$, $Netherlands_{63}$
– Power + Distance	$Brazil_{55}$, $India_{55}$
– Power – Distance	$Jordan_{55}$
– Power + Political + Development	$U.K._{.55}$
– Political	$Brazil_{63}$, $Jordan_{63}$, $U.S._{.63}$[a]
Distance	$Indonesia_{55}$, $India_{63}$[b]
Distance – Development	$Burma_{55}$, $Cuba_{55}$
Distance – Development + Power	$Poland_{55}$
No relationships	$Netherlands_{55}$, $Egypt_{55}$, $Israel_{55}$, $Israel_{63}$, $U.K._{.63}$

[a] Two separate relationships delineated for U.S. in 1963.
[b] Attribute dimension in 1963 was Catholic culture.

The discussion of the structure of the relationships determined by this study has dwelled upon the linkage between attribute differences and the conflict behavior dimension. The analyses also show that cooperative interaction is related to attribute differences. Here again no simple pattern of relationship emerges across the subsample. The most prevalent finding is the prediction of private international relations from the negative difference on the power capability dimension. For the 1963 data such a relationship is found for the actors Brazil, Egypt, India, Indonesia, Israel, U.S.S.R., U.K., and U.S. For the less powerful of these nations, this relationship shows they tended to engage in private international relations with nations more powerful than they. The more powerful actors also directed their private relations to the higher power nations or to those more close to parity with themselves, rather than toward the less powerful. These findings were anticipated by such theorists as Galtung who have focused on the role of status in international relations.[39] The relationship was almost

[39] The work of Johan Galtung has most consistently dealt with the relationship between status dimensions of nations and their resultant behavior. This theoretical perspective, while

specific to the 1963 time period, as only the U.K., Cuba, and Brazil sub-samples elicited the same pattern for the 1955 data. It is interesting to note that the only nation for which power difference predicted both its conflictual and cooperative relations was the most powerful nation in the system—the United States. Rummel's study of U.S. behavior has substantiated these findings.[40] The two studies by Rummel and Rhee using the field theory framework both show the status relationship as a predictor of private relations.[41] Yet, this finding appears to be by no means universal, inviting more explicit exploration of the role of international status relationships.

CONCLUSION

The results of these studies have some strong implications for the development of field theory as an approach to linking the attributes of nations to international relations. First, it is readily apparent that the most general model of such a linkage, Model I, is inadequate. The assumptions of the model are much too constraining for this model to have empirical viability. Revision of this model so as to maintain the level of generality it expresses across actors has been suggested by Park.[42] While this revision does lead to some improvement in the model's explanatory capacity, it is still rather marginal in relation to the results of Model II. It would seem that the notion of a completely general linkage theory equally applicable across all actors will have to be abandoned, at least temporarily. The question of whether it is necessary to retreat to the individual actor perspective, as some might argue is the implication of Model II, has not been demonstrated. Certainly actor uniqueness will plague, as it always has, the general theorist in international relations. Rummel's original theoretic argument rather boldly attempted to avoid the effect of uniqueness. This perspective proved to be unsuccessful.

a separate development from field theory, clearly augments field theory by providing specific *substantive* deductions of linkage between differences (and similarities) on national characteristics and the behavior of the nations. Galtung's more theoretically oriented articles include, "A Strucutral Theory of Aggression," *Journal of Peace Research* 2 (1964); "A Structural Theory of Integration," *Journal of Peace Research* 4 (1968); and "A Structural Theory of Imperialism," *Journal of Peace Research* (1971). Rummel has specifically incorporated substantively defined status dimensions in an elaboration of field theory, "Status, Field Theory, and International Relations."

[40]Rummel, "U.S. Foreign Relations."

[41]Ibid.; and Rhee, "Communist China's Foreign Behavior."

[42]Tong-Whan Park, "The Role of Distance in International Relations: A New Look at the Social Field Theory" (Paper presented at International Studies Association, South-Southwest Regional Meetings, New Orleans, October 1970). The paper suggests including both distance vectors and distance magnitudes in the linkage equation. Distance vectors in Model I cannot, as Park demonstrates, accommodate symmetric behavior. His suggestion is to add distance magnitudes (the absolute value of distance) as a component of the model.

The relative success of Model II in contrast to the results of Model I opens up the question of what level of generality is appropriate for field theory. Is there some regularity in the structure of the relationship below that inclusive of all actors? This is at least initially an empirical question inviting a replication of the analyses reported here with additional sub-samples. Yet, perhaps more importantly, this is a theoretical question. The proliferation of empirical results without theoretical guidance may not readily clarify the situation. Specifically, in terms of the theory itself there will have to be created additional axioms from which may be deduced particular types or clusters of actors which should manifest similar attribute-behavior linkages. The work with the social status concept previously cited is a step in this direction. In rebuilding in this manner the generality of the theory may be enhanced, but the cost, of course, is loss of parsimony—the theory will have to be made more complex.

Another perspective for elaborating the structure of field theory is to analytically differentiate between types of behavior. This tack has already been explicitly taken by Park.[43] It may be useful in making the differentiation of behavior to consider such conceptualizations such as Rosenau's "Issue Area"[44] or Bobrow's "Ecology of Games."[45] Drawing particularly upon Bobrow, it may be that linkage, in the field theoretic sense, may be best discerned not across actor subsamples or groupings of actor subsamples, but across actor-object couplings defined in terms of the behavioral situation. Does it not make sense to think of the Soviet Union ⇆ United States dyads, as contextually different from other Soviet Union or United States dyadic relationships? Are there not dyadic interdependences, perhaps China ⇆ India, China ⇆ U.S.S.R., which might not theoretically correspond to those for the U.S. and U.S.S.R.? There has been much said of such patterns of interrelationship as penetration and integration.[46] These would also seem to represent situational concepts which could provide a theoretical basis for inferring particular actor-object linkage patterns within the field theory context. The status concept here again seems particularly promising.

In this paper we have looked at field theory as a framework which provides an integrative structure to research linkages. The initial structure, Model I, has been shown to be empirically inadequate. The analysis of Model II, however, yields more encouraging results. The research findings presented here, while demonstrating some difficulties in the field theoretic

[43]Ibid. Park distinguishes four types of dyadic behavior—symmetric-homogeneity, symmetric-complementarity, asymmetric transaction from "topdog to underdog," and asymmetric transaction from "underdog to topdog."

[44]Rosenau, "Pre-Theories and Theories of Foreign Policy," esp. p. 53.

[45]Bobrow, "Ecology of International Games."

[46]J. N. Rosenau, "Theorizing Across Systems: Linkage Politics Revisited," chap. 2, this volume.

statement of linkages, have also given some insight as to possible paths for future theoretical developments.

APPENDIX 1.
1963 Dyadic Relations Random Sample

All 107 sovereign nations that had been independent prior to January 1962 were numbered. Eighty pairs (dyads) of nations then were selected by consecutive numbers in a random table (page of random numbers and first number used were selected randomly as well).

As with the 1955 random sample study, three dyads, U.S.-U.S.S.R., U.S.-France, and U.S.S.R.-China were added to the sample. Their theoretical value is believed to outweigh the consequent slight loss of randomness.

Since two directions of relationship $A \rightarrow B$ and $B \rightarrow A$ are considered for each dyad $A-B$, the sample of 83 dyads becomes a sample of 166 dyadic relations out of a population of 11,342 such relationships for 1963.

Table A1. DYADIC STUDY: 1963 Dyadic Relations Sample (N = 166)

Number	Dyad	Code
1.	Afghanistan → Bolivia	AFG → BOL
2.	Albania → China	ALB → CHN
3.	Australia → Denmark	AUL → DEN
4.	Australia → Germany (D.D.R.)	AUL → GME
5.	Austria → Belgium	AUS → BEL
6.	Austria → Bulgaria	AUS → BUL
7.	Belgium → Austria	BEL → AUS
8.	Bolivia → Afghanistan	BOL → AFG
9.	Bolivia → Rumania	BOL → RUM
10.	Bolivia → Togo	BOL → TOG
11.	Brazil → France	BRA → FRN
12.	Brazil → Guinea	BRA → GUN
13.	Brazil → Israel	BRA → ISR
14.	Brazil → Portugal	BRA → POR
15.	Brazil → Senegal	BRA → SEN
16.	Brazil → Togo	BRA → TOG
17.	Bulgaria → Austria	BUL → AUS
18.	Burma → Japan	BUR → JAP
19.	Cambodia → Italy	CAM → ITA
20.	Cambodia → Portugal	CAM → POR
21.	Cambodia → U.S.A.	CAM → USA
22.	Cameroon → Congo (Brazzaville)	CAO → CON
23.	Cameroon → Hungary	CAO → HUN

Table A1. (Continued)

Number	Dyad	Code
24.	Cameroon → Korea (Rep. of)	CAO → KOS
25.	Cameroon → Peru	CAO → PER
26.	Canada → Ethiopia	CAN → ETH
27.	Central African Rep. → Costa Rica	CEN → COS
28.	Central African Rep. → Rumania	CEN → RUM
29.	Chad → Columbia	CHA → COL
30.	Chad → Switzerland	CHA → SWZ
31.	Chile → Senegal	CHL → SEN
32.	China → Albania	CHN → ALB
33.	China → U.S.S.R.	CHN → USR
34.	Rep. of China → Turkey	CHT → TUR
35.	Columbia → Chad	COL → CHA
36.	Congo (Brazzaville) → Cameroon	CON → CAM
37.	Congo (Brazzaville) → Norway	CON → NOR
38.	Congo (Brazzaville) → Sudan	CON → SUD
39.	Congo (Brazzaville) → Upper Volta	CON → UPP
40.	Congo (Leopoldville) → Guinea	COP → GUN
41.	Congo (Leopoldville) → Israel	COP → ISR
42.	Congo (Leopoldville) → Jordan	COP → JOR
43.	Congo (Leopoldville) → Vietnam (South)	COP → VTS
44.	Costa Rica → Central African Rep.	COS → CEN
45.	Czechoslovakia → Korea (Dem. Rep.)	CZE → KON
46.	Czechoslovakia → Yemen	CZE → YEM
47.	Dahomey → Union of South Africa	DAH → UNS
48.	Denmark → Australia	DEN → AUL
49.	Dominican Rep. → Guinea	DOM → GUN
50.	Ecuador → Korea (Rep. of)	ECU → KOS
51.	Egypt → Germany (Fed. Rep.)	EGP → GMW
52.	Egypt → Malaysia	EGP → MAL
53.	Ethiopia → Canada	ETH → CAN
54.	Ethiopia → Mali	ETH → MLI
55.	Ethiopia → Yemen	ETH → YEM
56.	Finland → Spain	FIN → SPN
57.	France → Brazil	FRN → BRA
58.	France → U.S.A.	FRN → USA
59.	Ghana → Upper Volta	GHA → UPP
60.	Germany (D.D.R.) → Australia	GME → AUL
61.	Germany (D.D.R.) → Niger	GME → NIR
62.	Germany (Fed. Rep.) → Egypt	GMW → EGP
63.	Germany (Fed. Rep.) → Upper Volta	GMW → UPP
64.	Greece → Iran	GRC → IRN
65.	Greece → Nigeria	GRG → NIG
66.	Guatamala → Vietnam (North)	GUA → VTN
67.	Guinea → Brazil	GUN → BRA
68.	Guinea → Congo (Leopoldville)	GUN → COP
69.	Guinea → Dominican Republic	GUN → DOM
70.	Hungary → Cameroon	HUN → CAO
71.	Indonesia → Korea (Dem. Rep.)	INS → KON
72.	Iran → Greece	IRN → GRC

Table A1. (Continued)

Number	Dyad	Code
73.	Iran → Jordan	IRN → JOR
74.	Iraq → Lebanon	IRQ → LEB
75.	Iraq → Liberia	IRQ → LBR
76.	Ireland → Lebanon	IRE → LEB
77.	Ireland → Sweden	IRE → SWD
78.	Ireland → Turkey	IRE → TUR
79.	Israel → Brazil	ISR → BRA
80.	Israel → Congo (Leopoldville)	ISR → COP
81.	Israel → Mauritania	ISR → MAT
82.	Italy → Cambodia	ITA → CAM
83.	Ivory Coast → Syria	IVO → SYR
84.	Japan → Burma	JAP → BUR
85.	Jordan → Congo (Leopoldville)	JOR → COP
86.	Jordan → Iran	JOR → IRN
87.	Korea (Dem. Rep.) → Czechoslovakia	KON → CZE
88.	Korea (Dem. Rep.) → Indonesia	KON → INS
89.	Korea (Rep. of) → Cameroon	KOS → CAO
90.	Korea (Rep. of) → Ecuador	KOS → ECU
91.	Korea (Rep. of) → Thailand	KOS → TAI
92.	Lebanon → Iraq	LEB → IRQ
93.	Lebanon → Ireland	LEB → IRE
94.	Liberia → Iraq	LBR → IRQ
95.	Madagascar → Togo	MAD → TOG
96.	Malaysia → Egypt	MAL → EGP
97.	Mali → Ethiopia	MLI → ETH
98.	Mauritania → Israel	MAT → ISR
99.	Mexico → Nigeria	MEX → NIG
100.	Morocco → Netherlands	MOR → NTH
101.	Nepal → Saudi Arabia	NEP → SAU
102.	Nepal → Switzerland	NEP → SWZ
103.	Nepal → Yugoslavia	NEP → YUG
104.	Netherlands → Morocco	NTH → MOR
105.	Nicaragua → U.S.A.	NIC → USA
106.	Niger → Germany (D.D.R.)	NIR → GME
107.	Nigeria → Greece	NIG → GRC
108.	Nigeria → Mexico	NIG → MEX
109.	Norway → Congo (Brazzaville)	NOR → CON
110.	Panama → Tanganyika	PAN → TAN
111.	Paraguay → United Kingdom	PAR → UNK
112.	Peru → Cameroon	PER → CAO
113.	Philippines → Portugal	PHL → POR
114.	Philippines → Union of S. Africa	PHL → UNS
115.	Portugal → Brazil	POR → BRA
116.	Portugal → Cambodia	POR → CAM
117.	Portugal → Philippines	POR → PHL
118.	Rumania → Bolivia	RUM → BOL
119.	Rumania → Central African Rep.	RUM → CEN
120.	Rumania → U.S.A.	RUM → USA
121.	Saudi Arabia → Nepal	SAU → NEP

Table A1. (Continued)

Number	Dyad	Code
122.	Senegal → Brazil	SEN → BRA
123.	Senegal → Chile	SEN → CHL
124.	Sierra Leone → Tanganyika	SIE → TAN
125.	Spain → Finland	SPN → FIN
126.	Sudan → Congo (Brazzaville)	SUD → CON
127.	Sweden → Ireland	SWD → IRE
128.	Switzerland → Chad	SWZ → CHA
129.	Switzerland → Nepal	SWZ → NEP
130.	Switzerland → Vietnam (South)	SWZ → VTS
131.	Syria → Ivory Coast	SYR → IVO
132.	Tanganyika → Panama	TAN → PAN
133.	Tanganyika → Sierra Leone	TAN → SIE
134.	Thailand → Korea (Rep. of)	TAI → KOS
135.	Togo → Bolivia	TOG → BOL
136.	Togo → Brazil	TOG → BRA
137.	Togo → Madagascar	TOG → MAD
138.	Togo → Vietnam (North)	TOG → VTN
139.	Turkey → China (Rep. of)	TUR → CHT
140.	Turkey → Ireland	TUR → IRE
141.	Turkey → Union of S. Africa	TUR → UNS
142.	Union of S. Africa → Dahomey	UNS → DAH
143.	Union of S. Africa → Philippines	UNS → PHL
144.	Union of S. Africa → Turkey	UNS → TUR
145.	U.S.S.R. → China	USR → CHN
146.	U.S.S.R. → U.S.A.	USR → USA
147.	United Kingdom → Paraguay	UNK → PAR
148.	U.S.A. → Cambodia	USA → CAM
149.	U.S.A. → France	USA → FRN
150.	U.S.A. → Nicaragua	USA → NIC
151.	U.S.A. → Rumania	USA → RUM
152.	U.S.A. → U.S.S.R.	USA → USR
153.	Upper Volta → Congo (Brazzaville)	UPP → CON
154.	Upper Volta → Germany (Fed. Rep.)	UPP → GMW
155.	Upper Volta → Ghana	UPP → GHA
156.	Upper Volta → Vietnam (North)	UPP → VTN
157.	Vietnam (North) → Guatamala	VTN → GUA
158.	Vietnam (North) → Togo	VTN → TOG
159.	Vietnam (North) → Upper Volta	VTN → UPP
160.	Vietnam (South) → Congo (Leopoldville)	VTS → COP
161.	Vietnam (South) → Switzerland	VTS → SWZ
162.	Yemen → Czechoslovakia	YEM → CZE
163.	Yemen → Ethiopia	YEM → ETH
164.	Yugoslavia → Nepal	YUG → NEP
165.	Honduras → Malaysia	HON → MAL
166.	Malaysia → Honduras	MAL → HON

Note: The arrow between the members of the dyad indicates the direction of the relationship that is considered. For example, ARG → CUB symbolizes the behavior of Argentina toward Cuba in such asymmetrical variables as exports, threats, and mail sent.

.9. Foreign Conflict Behavior and Domestic Disorder in Africa*

JOHN N. COLLINS

A PARTIAL THEORY OF AFRICAN FOREIGN CONFLICT BEHAVIOR

Foreign conflict behavior by nation-states is undoubtedly a result of a complex mixture of causes. These causes may reside in features of the international system, in features of the political and social systems of the individual countries so behaving, in features of the interactions between countries, and possibly also in the personal predispositions of the leaders responsible for making policy in the individual countries.[1] It is the intent of this research to examine one widely hypothesized *sufficient* condition of foreign conflict behavior—the condition of domestic disorder as it applies in the African International System.

The Hypothesis in International Relations Theory

The idea that there is a causal relationship between internal disorder and foreign conflict behavior of states is a very old and venerable one in international relations literature.[2] The full causal sequence consists of three stages, thus making it more difficult to test rigorously than if there was not a reciprocal cause and effect. This sequence is as follows: (1) domestic dis-

*This is a revised version of a paper delivered at the Sixty-fifth Annual Meeting of the American Political Science Association, New York, 1969.

[1]See especially, Kenneth Waltz, *Man, the State, and War* (New York: Columbia University Press, 1959).

[2]Richard N. Rosecrance, *Action and Reaction in World Politics: International Systems in Perspective* (Boston: Little, Brown and Co., 1963), pp. 281–83; Quincy Wright, *The Study of International Relations* (New York: Appleton-Century-Crofts, 1955), p. 562; Steven Withey and Daniel Katz, "The Social Psychology of Human Conflict," in *The Nature of Human Conflict,* ed. Elton McNeil (Englewood Cliffs, N.J.: Prentice-Hall, 1965), p. 81; Hans Morgenthau, *Politics Among Nations* (New York: Alfred A. Knopf, 1954), p. 98; Ithiel de Sola Pool, *Symbols of Internationalism,* Hoover Institute Studies, Series C, no. 3 (Stanford, Calif.: Stanford University Press, 1951), p. 21.

order in country A causes country A to (2) exhibit foreign conflict behavior, and a subsequent result of real or imagined foreign conflict between country A and other countries is to (3) increase the internal solidarity in country A and thus reduce the domestic disorder. There is thus a hypothesized reciprocal causal relationship between domestic disorder and foreign conflict behavior.

Haas and Whiting's statement of the relationship is quite explicit in noting that nonviolent, rather than violent conflict behavior is the more likely outcome of internal disorder.

In time of extreme domestic tension among elites, a policy of uniting a badly divided nation against some real or alleged outside threat frequently seems useful to a ruling group. Elites, fearful of losing their position in the nation as a result of sharp ideological and group conflict, . . . attempt to displace the attention of the disaffected portion of the nation away from its grievance and toward some outside target. . . . This form of the search for self-preservation rarely results in war, though the "hate America" or "hate the Jews" campaigns may give rise to such propaganda barrages as to make war appear imminent.[3]

This relationship is considered by theorists to be especially applicable in underdeveloped areas. The reputed xenophobic behavior of militant nationalist leaders is attributed to a search for external scapegoats to direct domestic attention away from the domestic disorder and instability which particularly plague new states. The scanty literature on foreign policy or international relations of developing states frequently asserts that leaders intentionally externalize hostility as a response to internal solidarity problems. For example, Robert Good states that:

The cohesive functions of the "common enemy" must be perpetuated even when the foreign "enemy" is no longer a real threat, for the invocation of the putative threat is useful in maintaining unity at home.[4]

Speaking more specifically about Africa, Doudou Thiam finds that,

It often happens, particularly with new states, that inflexibility abroad coincides with a period of internal difficulties, and that peace abroad goes hand in hand with quiet and well being at home. The extremism of Guinea or Mali is often connected with internal problems.[5]

Zartman, citing numerous instances in Africa where this relationship applies, posits that, ". . . the magnitude of the problem [of internal security

---

[3]Ernst B. Haas and Allen S. Whiting, *Dynamics of International Relations* (New York: McGraw-Hill Book Co., 1956), p. 62.

[4]Robert C. Good, "State Building as a Determinant of Foreign Policy in the New States," in *Neutralism and Nonalignment*, ed. Lawrence W. Martin (New York: Frederick A. Praeger, 1962), p. 5.

[5]Doudou Thiam, *The Foreign Policy of African States* (New York: Frederick A. Praeger, 1965), p. XI.

and of development] and the elusiveness of their sources constitute a temptation to view the insecurity in external terms."[6]

Citing authorities, however, does not prove or explain why this relationship should have special relevance for new or developing states. Is this because new nations are subject to generally *more* internal instability or domestic disorder, or is it because new nations are more *sensitive* to the disorder which does occur within their borders? This question can be approached by examining in more detail some key aspects of the development or nation-building process itself. Good in particular has emphasized that the foreign policy for new states must be understood as an integral part of the more general nation-building process.[7] By distinguishing between two key aspects of the development or nation-building process we can more clearly see why the relationship between domestic disorder and foreign conflict behavior is especially relevant for understanding African foreign behavior.

The Twin Developmental Tasks

Zartman has made an insightful and, for our purpose, useful distinction between what he calls the "problem solving" task and the "solidarity building" task of development.[8] The problem-solving task is directed toward solving the economic and technical development problems and meeting the inflamed aspirations of the newly independent peoples for the better material way of life promised with independence. This task requires rational and technical decision making primarily in the economic sphere, relying upon an efficient bureaucracy and upon expert, technical knowledge. In terms of foreign policy, this problem-solving task can be translated into a call for greater reliance on outside help in the form of technical assistance, reliance on expatriate personnel and foreign aid, and a search for economically profitable foreign trade. Treaties and other special cooperative arrangements, and alignments with countries that can most effectively contribute to the economic development, would also contribute to this problem-solving task.

The solidarity-building task, on the other hand, involves the job of creating a sense of attachment and unity toward the new national unit. The people that comprise the nation-state must have a feeling of community. They must be aware that they belong to the same political unit and must be willing to give their loyalty to that unit. Success for the developmental goals and the maintenance of law and order both depend on a sense of at-

---

[6]William Zartman, "National Interest and Ideology," in *African Diplomacy: Studies in the Determinants of Foreign Policy*, ed. Vernon McKay (New York: Frederick A. Praeger, 1966), p. 28.

[7]Good, "State Building."

[8]Zartman, "National Interest."

tachment and involvement by the people towards the central political system. The leadership must legitimize itself and its new government. The leadership must, in short, develop a sense of solidarity among the population that will allow the national authority to prevail, and that will provide the motivation for the hard work of development to proceed. This is the aspect of nation building that is often more suspect to Western observers, in part because it is often seen as just an exercise in self-aggrandizing politics by the nationalist leaders. The use of inflammatory slogans and highly ideological appeals are the stock in trade of the nationalist leader as he seeks to foster this sense of solidarity.

Domestic disorder is both a sign of the incompleteness of this solidarity building, and a threat to the unity which is sought. Because of the tenuousness of the existence of the state, such disorder has a special threatening effect. Zartman gives special emphasis to the seriousness of domestic disorder in the new African states.

Yet, in a general sense, the very existence and instability of the new states is far more tenuous than the small number of incidents . . . would indicate. Insecurity is endemic, even if not always specific. The threats are not external as much as internal.[9]

The distinction between two types of tasks in the developmental process can also be seen in the ideas of Lucian Pye.[10] His "developmental syndrome" is comprised of three aspects. The first aspect is a "general spirit or attitude toward *equality*," meaning "mass participation and popular involvement in political activities."[11] This is directly comparable to the solidarity-building task described above. Pye's second and third syndrome characteristics, the *capacity* of the political system, and *differentiation* and *specialization* of the social system, are both concerned with the ability of the political system to effectively and efficiently execute public policy of a technical developmental nature. These characteristics are thus similar to the problem solving task as explained above.

The task of African leaders is therefore to convert the geographically defined nation-state, inherited from the colonial era, into a social and political unit that is internally unified. Its citizens must either extend or convert their traditional, parochial loyalties to a national loyalty. There must be a sense of legitimacy about a set of rules of the game for operating the political unit. In addition, the leader must foster rapid economic and social development of his country, tasks that require unified action, high support, hard and dedicated work, and perhaps some personal sacrifices. The nationalist leader contends that the tasks ahead are so urgent and overwhelm-

[9]Ibid., p. 28.
[10]Lucian Pye, *Aspects of Political Development* (Boston: Little, Brown and Co., 1963).
[11]Ibid., p. 45.

ing that only a unified national interest should be considered, rather than the diverse regional, tribal, ethnic, socioeconomic, or other special interests that seek a hearing if not a veto position in the political arena.

Insofar as nationalist leaders, just as political leaders elsewhere, attempt to enhance their own political power as well as their tenure in office, so they will be concerned with solidarity-building and the correlative symbol manipulation and dependence upon an ideology. The maintenance of internal security and of obedience to central government laws are tenuous achievements at this stage of development for most African states and the potential for violence that rests just under the thin surface of domestic order is an understandable justification for pursuing with all possible vigor the solidarity needs of the new political unit.[12] But the analyst does not need to pass judgment on the propriety of solidarity-building to recognize that this is indeed a major preoccupation of these new nation leaders. And insofar as the two different developmental tasks, problem solving and solidarity-building, call for different types of foreign behavior, we can reasonably expect the solidarity-building-determined foreign behavior to be especially prevalent, if not dominant.

Domestic Links with Foreign Behavior

A second perspective on the possible relationship between domestic disorder and foreign behavior can be gained by considering not just the nature of the dominant domestic needs, as done above, but by also considering the nature of the links between domestic and foreign policies in general. A common theme in studies of foreign policy making in developed countries is that internal groups make specific policy demands upon the government which must be met in part by particular, specified foreign policies.[13] Foreign relations are thus conceived to be in part an extension of internal policy making because the foreign policy decision-making process is responsive to the demands of internal interest groups.

Is this a relevant model for understanding the formation of African foreign policy? Probably not, for several reasons. Internal articulation processes are not very developed in most new African nations. There is little development of diverse social or socioeconomic interest groups that feel sufficiently involved or concerned with the foreign policies of their country to make demands for specific foreign policies. The size of the politically relevant public, that is, the public which is aware of, and concerned with,

---

[12]See Aristide Zolberg, "The Structure of Political Conflict in the New States in Tropical Africa," *American Political Science Review* 62, no. 1 (March 1968).

[13]Haas and Whiting, *Dynamics of International Relations*, pp. 21–55; James N. Rosenau, ed., *International Aspects of Civil Strife* (Princeton, N.J.: Princeton University Press, 1964); George Modelski, *A Theory of Foreign Policy* (New York: Frederick A. Praeger, 1962).

most governmental policy making is quite small under normal circumstances. According to Zartman, "Public opinion and pressure groups have little weight in the decision-making process and foreign policy leaders frequently have little access to them."[14] The net result is that policy making, especially in the foreign sphere, is predominantly left up to a relatively small group of elites in each country. This certainly allows a greater flexibility and perhaps capriciousness in policy making, and lessens the chances that specific domestic policies and demands will be related to foreign policy.

In addition to separate domestic group interests and pressures, theories of foreign policy making commonly assert that there is some conception of the "national interest" which guides the foreign policy makers. This national interest seeks to take account of the economic, military, and general physical needs of the country in specific terms. Such a conception of the national interest or national interests can then serve as a direct policy guide in the country's international dealings.

This notion of a national interest is, however, of questionable relevance in the African setting. Zartman has emphasized the gross underdevelopment in African countries of the wide range of information generating and gathering processes so essential for any state to come to a realistic appraisal of its national interest. Thus, information about resource capabilities, development potential and priorities, population characteristics and needs, etc., are generally sadly lacking. These countries also lack adequate information about other countries, African as well as non-African, because of their inexperience and inadequate diplomatic establishments. In addition, these new states characteristically have an incomplete set of tools for conducting foreign relations. Both the diplomatic skills and manpower and the elements of national power that can be exerted externally in pursuit of particular national goals are underdeveloped.[15] All of these factors certainly mitigate against the possibilities of conducting an enlightened foreign policy that is guided by a firm conception of the national interest.[16]

What conclusion can be drawn from these perspectives on foreign policy in the new African states? They suggest that the substantive policy content will be minimally related to domestic policy, and that consequently the domestic political need of solidarity-building will predominate over the problem-solving concerns in the conduct of foreign relations. We might thus expect a much closer relationship between domestic and foreign *politics* rather than between domestic and foreign *policies*. In particular, the *politics* of overcoming domestic disorder and elite insecurity can be ex-

[14]William Zartman, *International Relations in the New Africa* (Englewood Cliffs: Prentice-Hall, 1966), p. 35.
[15]Zartman, "National Interest and Ideology," pp. 120–22.
[16]Zartman, *International Relations*, pp. 30–35.

pected to be a major determinant of foreign policy, especially a policy of external conflict behavior.

General Conflict Theory

The theory of foreign conflict behavior by African states suggested above posits that the major determinant of such behavior resides *within* rather than *between* the nation states involved. In this sense, *foreign conflict behavior* is essentially the same as *hostility*. The alternate conception would be to treat foreign conflict behavior as a response to conflict situations which exist between nations.

What is involved here is a basic distinction made by students of social conflict between two *types* of conflict. The utility of the distinction is both for obtaining greater conceptual clarity in understanding the general phenomenon that we label as conflict and for studying more rigorously the ways that conflict in its destructive aspects can be resolved or eliminated.[17]

The distinction between types of conflict is often clouded in various terminology or definitional attempts. Wright, for example, places conflict in a more general category as a species of opposition, defined as a "process by which social entities function in the disservice of one another."[18] Competition and conflict are then distinguished as different species of opposition, by restricting the term conflict to "opposition among social entities directed against one another," whereas "competition" is an independent "striving for something of which the supply is inadequate to satisfy all parties." Conflict thus requires action directed *against* other parties, whereas competition is action directed *for* some object in a fixed-sum game without awareness necessarily of the other parties. Thus competition may lead to conflict, but can exist without conflict. Likewise, conflict can take place without competition, that is, without mutually incompatible or exclusive goals.

Other theorists enlarge their usage of the term conflict and make their distinction between competitive and noncompetitive conflict. Bernard refers to noncompetitive conflict as the social-psychological conception of conflict, emphasizing its expressive, nonrational, and tension characteristics. She contrasts this conception, considered more applicable on the individual, psychic level, with the sociological conception. Sociological or competitive conflict involves the notion of cost, as from mutually incom-

---

[17]Lewis Coser, *The Function of Social Conflict* (Glencoe, Ill.: Free Press, 1957), makes the strong argument that not all conflict is bad, but rather it has some socially useful "functions." I do not mean to suggest that all conflict should be eliminated, but that the easily identifiable destructive conflicts between nation-states are an appropriate focus for scholarly attempts at understanding means of conflict resolution.

[18]Quincy Wright, "The Nature of Conflict," *Western Political Quarterly* 4 (1951): 197.

patible or exclusive goal-values, and is considered more appropriate for studying relations between larger systems, as in war.[19]

The same distinction is made by Coser, but under different labels. Social-psychological or noncompetitive conflict is considered to be non-realistic conflict. As he states it, "non-realistic conflict is conflict which is the end in itself, that is, arises exclusively from aggressive impulses which seek expression no matter what the object." Realistic conflict, on the other hand, is more instrumental or a means to an end, and is thus more akin to competitive or sociological conflict. It is in response to some "objective" external threat or competitive object, such as a hostile move by another country or a dispute over trade outlets or external assistance. Expressive or nonrealistic conflict is thus a mainifestation of hostility, whereas realistic conflict as a social relationship can exist without hostility or emotional feelings involved.[20]

The important thing to note is the conceptual distinction made by these cited theorists between *real-object-based conflict* and conflict rooted more in *psychological processes*. Certainly any real-world conflict situation might contain both types of conflict, thereby confusing the real bases of the conflict. Coleman finds in his study of community conflicts that realistic conflicts, if left unresolved, can lead to an accompanying unrealistic conflict which then can outlive the original real-object bases of the dispute.[21]

In terms of the distinction made earlier between foreign policy making in developed states and the characteristic foreign policy process in new African states, the conceptual distinction between the two types of conflict would seem to fit. That is, insofar as African foreign policy is guided not by internal or external substantive policy goals or differences, but rather by internal political needs of the new state (especially the solidarity-building need), the social-psychological or nonrealistic conception of conflict would seem more appropriate.

If, therefore, the hypothesis that domestic disorder is a sufficient condition of foreign conflict behavior is upheld in the present research, then some weight could be given to the proposition that for the new African states the social-psychological conception of internation conflict, rather than the realistic or real-object-based conception, is especially relevant. As mentioned earlier, this finding would then have relevance for better understanding the means of conflict resolution. And by so identifying the conceptual type of conflict characteristic of African foreign behavior, the analyst could, in future research, tie these findings into the more general

---

[19]Jessie Bernard, "The Sociological Study of Conflict," in *The Nature of Conflict*, ed. International Sociological Association (Paris: UNESCO, 1957), p. 34.

[20]Coser, *Function of Social Conflict*, p. 48.

[21]James S. Coleman, *Community Conflict* (Glencoe, Ill.: Free Press, 1957).

body of conflict theory dealing with this type of conflict as found in other social conflict contexts, for both inductive and deductive purposes.

Our next step in understanding the hypothesized relationship between domestic disorder and foreign conflict behavior is to seek a deeper explanation of this theoretical linkage. For this we will turn to research in social psychology and in particular to research on ethnocentrism.

FURTHER EXPLICATION OF THE HYPOTHESIS

By far the richest body of literature which has attempted to go beyond the descriptive theory stage in hypothesizing a relationship between in-group disorder and externalized conflict behavior is that by sociologists and social psychologists.[22] These studies focus primarily on personality factors and small groups, but deal with the common theoretical relationship between in-group characteristics and processes, and relations between groups. Campbell and LeVine have admirably surveyed and summarized this literature, focusing on the organizing concept of "ethnocentrism."[23] The following discussion draws heavily on this work as well as the work of Rosenblatt[24] which surveys propositions on ethnocentrism and nationalism.

Ethnocentrism Conceptualization

The term ethnocentrism is attributed to William Sumner. The central proposition made by Sumner, and the one relevant for the present research, is stated thus:

The relation of comradeship and peace in the we-group and that of hostility and war towards others-groups are correlative to each other. The *exigencies of war with outsiders are what make peace inside*, lest internal discord should weaken the we-group for war. Loyalty to the group, sacrifice for it, hatred, and contempt for outsiders, brotherhood within, warlikeness without—all grow together, common products of the same situation.... (italics added).[25]

[22]John W. Thibaut and Harold Kelly, *The Social Psychology of Groups* (New York: John Wiley and Sons, 1959); George E. Simpson and J. Milton Yinger, *Racial and Cultural Minorities*, 3rd ed., (New York: Harper & Row, 1965); Leonard Berkowitz, *Aggression: A Social Psychological Analysis* (New York: McGraw-Hill Book Co., 1962); Otto Klineberg, *Tensions Affecting International Understanding: A Survey of Research* (New York: Social Science Research Council, 1950); Georg Simmel, *Conflict: The Web of Group Affiliations* (Glencoe, Ill.: Free Press, 1955); R. M. Williams, Jr., *The Reduction of Intergroup Tensions* (New York: Social Science Research Council, No. 57, 1947); T. W. Adorno et al., *The Authoritarian Personality* (New York: Harper & Bros., 1950); Gordon W. Allport, *The Nature of Prejudice* (Cambridge, Mass.: Addison-Wesley Publishing Co., 1954).
[23]Donald T. Campbell and Robert LeVine, "Propositions about Ethnocentrism from Social Science Theories" (ms., Northwestern University, 1965).
[24]P. C. Rosenblatt, "Origins and Effects of Group Ethnocentrism and Nationalism," *Journal of Conflict Resolution* (June 1964).
[25]William A. Sumner, *Folkways* (Boston: Ginn & Co., 1906), p. 12.

Stated more simply, this descriptive hypothesis asserts that external conflict or threat situations for a group are correlated with and cause in-group solidarity. The causal direction is implied by the italicized phrase of Sumner's quote, but elsewhere he posits just association between the two phenomena.

Realistic Conflict Theory

What is lacking in the above formulation of this basic linkage is any deeper explanatory theory. To answer this question, Campbell and LeVine suggest a number of alternative theories, two of which are relevant here. The first is called the "realistic conflict theory." This argument states that a group faced with real external threats can more effectively confront and surmount this threat if it draws together internally, if all its members cease internal conflicts and contribute to a united group effort to repel the threatening situation. Greater production of war materials, greater spirit among its armed forces, fewer demands directed to the government for goods or services which detract from a war effort—all of these are seen to follow from increased in-group solidarity generated in time of war, which thus serves to increase the ability of the group to survive the external threat.

Campbell applies his selective survival model of sociocultural evolution to explain why such a reactive mechanism should be set in motion. The evolutionary model, which is elaborated by Campbell,[26] is based on random variation of social forms and processes, and selection and retention of those forms and processes which work well for the group, including contribution toward group survival. This, therefore, seems a more satisfactory way than the strict functionalism argument of explaining how men have learned to respond to threat situations by increasing their in-group solidarity.

How, though, does this discussion of realistic conflict situations fit into our present study, which is not measuring the objective conflicts or threats facing African states, but rather is measuring foreign conflict or hostile behavior? The linkage is provided by realizing that it is *not* the objective existence of threat situations that is sufficient to trigger a response by the reacting state, but rather the *perception* of a threat. We can assume a *possible*, although not *necessary*, correspondence between real and perceived threat. And since the external threat is relevant to national response only insofar as it is perceived as such, the way is opened for opportunistic manipulation of threat situation perceptions by national leaders.

---

[26]Donald T. Campbell, "Evolutionary Theory in Social Science: A Reappraisal" (Paper delivered at the conference on Social Science and the Underdeveloped Areas: A Revival of Evolutionary Theory, Northwestern University, June 1961).

The situation whereby national leaders "perceive" fictitious external threats or enemies, in order to increase internal solidarity, can thus be explained by the same functional argument that Campbell and LeVine use to explain national reactions to real conflicts or threats. As Campbell and LeVine phrase it,

This is certainly one of the most ubiquitous observations on the exploitative opportunism of nationalist politics. . . . While this principle does not involve real threat, it does involve an opportunistic exploitation of the major principle of Realistic Group Conflict Theory. . . . Thus the major proposition of Realistic Group Conflict, extended to its "artificial" exploitation in the solution of internal problems, brings us around to a position in which intergroup conflict becomes a "projective" product of internal problems—at the social level if not the psychic.[27]

Therefore, although African foreign conflict behavior was depicted in the previous section as nonrealistic or social-psychological conflict, a theoretical explanation can be applied from realistic conflict reasoning.

Frustration-Aggression-Displacement Theory

A second and alternate line of theorizing which can be used to explain the co-occurrence of external conflict and in-group solidarity is the frustration-aggression-displacement theory. This theory has been given wide currency especially by Dollard et al. and MacCrone.[28] The F-A-D theory simply states that frustrations will lead to aggressions. Central to this theory is the concept of scapegoating. As stated by MacCrone:

. . . privations of everyday life . . . may readily enough find expression in hostility directed against an "out-group"—hostility that would otherwise vent itself at the expense of the "in-group." . . . The greater the discipline of group life, its repressions, privations, and exactions . . . , the greater we can expect its aggressiveness to become at the expense of some other group or groups.

As a form of insurance, the existence of the "out-group" covers the "in-group" against the risks of internal conflict and aggressiveness. If we could imagine a state of affairs in which such a group did not exist, it would become necessary to invent one, if only to enable members of the "in-group" to deal with conflicts, internal and external, without wrecking their own group.[29]

The premises of the theory that are important for our purposes are: (1) the expression of aggression is gratifying in itself, and thus results in a lowering of aggressive tendencies (catharsis); (2) the true source of frustration for an individual is most difficult to determine, so the selection by the

---

[27]Campbell and LeVine, "Propositions About Ethnocentrism," pp. 50–51.

[28]J. Dollard et al., *Frustration and Aggression* (New Haven: Yale University Press, 1939); Ian Douglas MacCrone, *Race Attitudes in South Africa: Historical, Experimental and Psychological Studies* (Johannesberg: Witwatersrand University Press, 1937 (1957)).

[29]MacCrone, *Race Attitudes*, pp. 250–51.

subject of the appropriate target for aggression is not uniquely or specifically determined; and (3) aggression can thus be displaced toward objects other than the frustration-creating object or situation. With the inhibitions against internal aggressiveness found, albeit in varying degrees, in organized societies, it is reasonable to expect in-group members to perceive out-groups as a cause of their frustrations. Campbell and LeVine[30] refer to this propensity of groups to perceive out-groups as the cause of frustration as "the socially institutionalized target mechanism."

Although this theory is appealing in its simplicity, it does have a drawback in that it implies a reification of the social group or nation-state. A mechanism has been lifted from the individual psychic level of analysis and applied to a large group, implying that nation-states are organic "things" that also can experience frustration and aggressive impulses. This interpretation can be avoided, however, by viewing the frustrations within the new African states to be individually held and to be "displaced" to other nation-states when their own country acts in an externally hostile manner toward other countries. In applying this mechanism to the nation-state, we can posit that the national leadership behaves hostilely toward other countries in order to provide an available target for individual catharsis by the population. From the point of view of the national leadership, this external displacement is preferable to having its population act out their frustrations in an internally disruptive way.

Conclusion

Accordingly we have two theories, the "realistic" conflict theory and the frustration-aggression-displacement theory, each predicting that domestic disorder will lead to foreign conflict behavior. Each theory, however, explains this causal relationship in different ways. The two theories do not differ in their prediction so either both or neither theory will be subject to rejection. No handle can be obtained in this research as to which of the competing theories better "explains" the phenomenon. At this tentative state of research about the international behavior of African states, however, both theories can aid in understanding the data.

RESEARCH DESIGN

Data Collection

The sample used in this study is comprised of thirty-three independent African countries.[31] Data were collected for the three year period 1963 through 1965. The data were obtained from a frequency content analysis of

[30]Campbell and LeVine, "Propositions About Ethnocentrism," p. 106.

[31]The sample includes all countries on the African continent which had attained independence by January 1, 1964, with the exception of the Republic of South Africa which has been excluded. South Africa has been excluded because it does not share the lower levels

several African news summaries, supplemented by *Deadline Data* and various encyclopedia yearbooks.[32] The coding procedure is based largely on Rummel's foreign and domestic conflict study[33] and Rummel's later and more elaborate foreign conflict code sheet.[34] Although the present study is a replication of the earlier Rummel and Tanter studies, it was found desirable to vary somewhat the construction of variables used in those studies. These variations, however, should not jeopardize the comparability between the present research and those which are being replicated. The variable definitions and coding rules used in this data collection are shown in the appendix.

Data Preparation

The data which were collected by a simple frequency count of events were grouped initially into seventeen variables of foreign conflict behavior and twenty-two variables of domestic disorder.

All reported events were recorded which intuitively (1) had a domestic disruptive effect or which indicated domestic disruptions or disorder, or (2) involved conflictful or hostile behavior by one nation directed towards other nations either individually or in general. Coding categories sought to capture clear empirical differentiation between such events, that is, mutually exclusive ones. Each of these variables had occurrences for at least 10 percent of the countries in the sample in order to reduce the statistical distortions that would have resulted from using uniquely occurring categories.

In the earlier Rummel and Tanter studies,[35] nine domestic disorder variables and thirteen foreign conflict behavior variables were recorded. The larger number of variables in the present study is a product of a wider, more extensive search for events, and a desire to make as many distinctions as was feasible in the initial collection of data to maximize the utility of the data for possible future analyses.

---

of economic and political development which so characterize the rest of Africa. The theory used in this research is premised on lower levels of development. North African countries are included despite the common tendency to exclude these from studies of Africa. The five North African countries are important participants in African international relations both in terms of the international politics and the international organizations and alliances of the continent. There is a corresponding degree of identification by these five countries with the idea of "Africa." These countries also have many characteristics similar to sub-Saharan African countries, thus permitting their inclusion in such a regional analysis.

[32]The African news summaries used were the *African Research Bulletin* (1964–65) and *Africa Diary* (1963). Both publications are periodic summaries of what was reported in major African newspapers and radio broadcasts as well as in other major world news media.

[33]R. J. Rummel, "Dimensions of Conflict Behavior Within and Between Nations," chap. 3, this volume.

[34]R. J. Rummel, "A Foreign Conflict Behavior Code Sheet," *World Politics* (1966): 283–96.

[35]Rummel, "Dimensions of Conflict Behavior"; Raymond Tanter, "Dimensions of Conflict Behavior Within and Between Nations, 1958–1960," *Journal of Conflict Resolution* 10 (1966): 41–64.

The two earlier studies of Rummel and Tanter applied factor analysis to the data to identify major empirical clusters or dimensions which were then used as the composite variables for their analyses. In the foreign domain, both Rummel and Tanter obtained three dimensions, and in the domestic domain Rummel obtained three dimensions and Tanter, two. This approach requires the researcher to give a conceptually meaningful label to the empirically derived dimensions so they can be used as variables which have a specific meaning or interpretation. This is done by analyzing those variables which load most heavily on the given dimension to determine what underlying similarity they share.

Factor analyses of the data in the present research were compared with the factor analysis results of the earlier studies. Two general conclusions emerged from these comparisons. First, the African data showed a greater empirical complexity, requiring in the domestic domain six factors to pattern the data whereas the earlier data drawn from non-African countries required only two or three factors. Seventy-one percent of the total variance was accounted for by three factors in Rummel's analysis, whereas five factors in the African data were required to account for 69.4 percent of the total variance. The 64.4 percent of total variance accounted for by Tanter's two-factor solution of the domestic data required four factors in the African data.

In the foreign conflict domain, Rummel's three factors accounted for 66.3 percent of the total variance as compared with the 62.6 percent of the total variance accounted for by the six African factors. Similarly, Tanter's three factors accounted for 57.0 percent of the total variance, compared with the 56.7 percent of the total variance accounted for by the first five African factors. This greater number of factors in the African data may, of course, be due to the larger number of variables used in the African analysis, but if the dimensions delimited by the Rummel and Tanter studies were, in fact, stable underlying dimensions of domestic disorder and foreign conflict behavior, then that result should have been replicated in the present African study.

The second conclusion to be drawn from the comparison of the factor analyses of Rummel and Tanter with that of the African data is simply that the empirically derived factors resulting from the African data do not appear to be conceptually meaningful dimensions according to the labels used in the previous studies nor even by any other labels that could be deduced. Variables loading heavily on one factor do not have any readily apparent underlying similarity nor conceptual distinctiveness from those variables used to compose other factors. Thus the researcher is unable to use these empirical factors as new, meaningful composite variables. In the foreign conflict domain, this lack of a meaningful and parsimonious structuring of foreign conflict behavior could be accounted for in part by the argument advanced in the first section. That is, African countries conduct their foreign relations in a somewhat less structured way, without the ordering effect of specified national goals or past experience, as found among older and more developed states. One could also speculate that the lack of structuring of the domestic disorder domain in the African countries is a reflection of their greater domestic disorder. Quantitatively, the African states had a mean of 2.72 domestic events per country (1963–65), as compared with the mean for the Rummel study of .64 events per country. This does not, of course, demonstrate that the African domestic domain is less *structured*, but simply more populated with disorder events.

THE VARIABLES

Domestic Disorder Data

Although the theoretical discussion in the previous sections referred to the hypothesized cause of foreign conflict behavior by several different terms—domestic instability, domestic frustrations, domestic tensions, domestic malintegration, domestic cohesion, etc.—this research does not seek to distinguish or operationalize these terms separately. The literature often uses these terms interchangeably, indicating the difficulty of rigorous conceptual and operational separation.

Working on the level of the nation-state, all of these concepts are very hard to operationalize and measure directly. Especially for most African countries, the quality and quantity of data, such as attitudinal measures, or precise measures of governmental legitimacy or political system stability, is not available for a comparative study of thirty-three countries. This research is, therefore, using one type of data that is available and comparable for African states, namely, specific observable events which are manifestations of, or indicative of, disruptions in the political system. We are not attempting to say by what our observed disorder events—assassinations, coup attempts, terroristic acts, antigovernment demonstrations, etc.—are produced, but simply that these events are likely manifestations of social tensions or lack of cohesion or lack of solidarity, etc., *and* that the events themselves are signals to the government that elite tenure and political system maintainance and effectiveness are endangered.

Domestic Disorder Composite Variables

The twenty-two initial domestic disorder variables are formed into seven consolidated variables as defined in table 1.[36]

[36]The composite variables in both the domestic and foreign domains were formed by summing the raw values for the component indices. This more parsimonious approach was chosen over the complex approaches, such as factor analysis or z-score summing, because of the unjustifiable weighting of events which these more complex approaches introduce.

Table 1. **Construction of Domestic Disorder Consolidated Variables**

Composite Variables	Code	Components
1. Anomic outbreaks	ANOMIC	riots strikes political clashes intertribal conflict antigovernment demonstrations mutiny
2. Subversive activities	SUBVER	guerrilla warfare terroristic acts assassinations plots
3. Revolutionary activities	REVOLU	revolutions civil war antigovernment riots political boycotts
4. Elite instability	ELIINS	major governmental crises elite deletions
5. Number killed/domestic violence	DOMKIL	
6. Domestic suppression	DOMSUP	ban on demonstrations ban on political groups proclamation of emergency freedom/press curtailment
7. Number of political arrests	ARREST	

1. The first composite variable is labeled *anomic outbreaks* and groups together riots, antigovernment demonstrations, strikes, political clashes, intertribal warfare, and mutinies. All these events are unchanneled dissent among the population, not primarily directed toward challenging the government, and involving a very low level of violence. They are not exclusively the activities of counterelites in the societies, but involve to a large extent the participation of nonelites. A certain degree of spontaneity is also characteristic of these events. This composite variable is most similar to Rummel's and Tanter's "turmoil" dimension. Anomic outbreaks quite clearly are a type of domestic disorder that detracts from national solidarity or is indicative of low domestic solidarity, which is then hypothesized to contribute to a government's foreign conflict behavior.

2. The second composite variable is labeled *subversive activities* and is comprised of guerrilla warfare, terroristic acts, assassinations, and plots. Subversive activities are conceived to be covert acts of violence that are

For a discussion of this methodological point, see John N. Collins, "Factor Analysis and the Grouping of Events Data: Problems and Possible Solutions" (Paper delivered at the First Annual Events Data Conference, Michigan State University, 1969).

aimed at the toppling of the current government or its incumbents. They are perpetrated from outside the government and aimed at the current regime, and thus pose direct threats to the tenure of the incumbent elites. They involve the actions of counterelites who are seeking not only to make their dissent known, but also to substitute themselves for the incumbent elites. This variable is conceptually similar to the "subversive" dimension found by Rummel and the "conspiracy" dimension used by Gurr.[37]

3. The third composite variable, *revolutionary activities*, incorporates political boycotts, antigovernment riots, revolutions, and civil war. This variable, similar conceptually to Rummel's "revolutionary" dimension, differs from the subversive activities variable only in that the constituent events are defined as overt activities, mostly violent ones. Otherwise, the conceptual meaning is the same as the subversive activities variable.

4. The fourth composite variable, identified as *elite instability*, groups the two events of major governmental crises and elite deletions. The distinguishing characteristic of these two events is that they represent sharp differences among the governmental elites which threaten the stability of the current regime. They thus indicate instability directly within the governmental elite structure. Support for pulling out a specifically elite instability variable from other measures of political instability is found in Russett et al., where it is noted that:

Perhaps one of the most important things to note about violence [domestic violent deaths] and executive instability is their low linear correlation with each other—only .30 . . . supporting our original contention that these two indices are measuring quite different aspects of political stability and are complementary to each other.[38]

This distinction would have been lost if the factor analysis dimensions from the African data had been utilized.

5. The fifth variable to be used in the analysis, *number killed in domestic violence*, is a single rather than composite variable. To correct the badly skewed distribution of this variable in its raw data form, it has been transformed into common log form. The number killed is an alternate way of measuring the *severity* or *extent* of violence which has already been measured by the particular event that resulted in the deaths, such as guerrilla warfare, riots, etc. Since the violent events which these deaths are a result of are spread among several of the composite variables discussed above, it was thought best to keep number killed as a separate summary variable of domestic violence in general. The use of this "body count" in-

[37]Ted Gurr, "A Causal Model of Civil Strife: A Comparative Analysis Using New Indices," *American Political Science Review* 62, no. 4. (1968): 1104–24.

[38]Bruce M. Russett et al., *World Handbook of Political and Social Indicators* (New Haven: Yale University Press, 1964), pp. 289–90.

dex as a single best indicator of domestic violence is suggested by Russett.[39]

6. The sixth composite variable is labeled *domestic suppression*. This variable groups together four events—bans on demonstrations, bans on political groups, proclamation of emergencies or martial law, and freedom of the press curtailments. These events are internal governmental responses to political disorder which are designed to suppress such disorder. The domestic suppression variable can be conceived to be either an indication of the degree of internal disorder, or the degree of insecurity as perceived and responded to by the governmental elites arising from domestic disorders. Our theory hypothesizes that political elites may utilize foreign conflict behavior to reduce the threat to their regime that is posed by internal disorder. An alternate governmental response to domestic disorder, however, may be to suppress the sources of the disorder, rather than turning to the corrective linkage via foreign conflict behavior, as explained in earlier sections. Therefore, in using the domestic suppression variable in the analyses, both interpretations of this variable must be considered—domestic suppression as an indicator of domestic instability *or* as an alternate governmental response (alternate to foreign conflict behavior) to such domestic instability.

7. The seventh variable is again a single variable, the *number of political arrests*. As with the previous "body count" variable (domestic violent deaths), it was found necessary to transform the number of political arrests into common log form. This variable is conceptually the same as the "domestic suppression" composite variable (above), in that it is a governmental response to political disorder and dissent.

Foreign Conflict Behavior Data

The data on foreign conflict behavior are actions taken by one national government against other countries. Mack and Synder define conflictful behaviors as "those designed to destroy, injure, threaten, or otherwise control another party or other parties."[40] We are, therefore, not necessarily measuring *foreign conflict* between nations, but rather conflictful responses by one nation against others. This research is not attempting to measure the extent to which countries respond conflictfully to *external* conflict situations. It is asking the more limited question whether domestic disorder is a *sufficient*, rather than *necessary*, condition of foreign conflict behavior.

Foreign Conflict Behavior Composite Variables

The seventeen initial foreign conflict behavior variables were formed into eight composite variables as defined below: (see table 2)

---

[39] Ibid., p. 98.

[40] Raymond W. Mack and Richard Snyder, "The Analysis of Social Conflict—Toward an Overview and Synthesis," *Journal of Conflict Resolution* 1 (June 1957): 212–48.

Table 2.   Construction of Foreign Conflict Behavior Consolidated Variables

Composite Variables	Code	Components
1. Diplomatic hostility	DIPHOS	disruption of diplomatic relations diplomatic rebuffs boycott or walkout of international conference or organization
2. Negative behavior	NEGBEH	closing of border expulsion of foreigners disruption of economic relations severance of pacts and treaties miscellaneous hostility assistance to another's enemies
3. Military violence	MILVIO	troop mobilizations official military violence
4. Number killed/foreign violence	FORKIL	
5. Antiforeign unofficial activity	ANTUNO	antiforeign anomic activity unofficial foreign violence
6. Negative communications, "internal interference"	INTINF	
7. Negative communications, "hostile policies"	HOSPOL	
8. Negative communications, "general criticism"	GENCRI	

1. The first foreign composite variable is labeled *diplomatic hostility.* This groups together severance of diplomatic relations, expulsion and re-call of diplomatic personnel, walkout or boycott of an international conference or organization, and diplomatic rebuffs. These actions are conceptually related in that they are nonviolent acts taken against another country which convey primarily a formal diplomatic meaning of hostility. This variable is conceptually similar to Rummel's and Tanter's "diplomatic" dimensions.

2. The second foreign composite variable is *negative behavior.* This includes any official nonviolent action taken against another country, and which is not included under the formal diplomatic variable above. These hostile actions include closing of borders, expulsion of foreigners, severance of economic relations, severance of pacts and treaties, assistance to another country's enemies—internal and external—and a residual category of miscellaneous hostile activities such as proclamation of a hostile policy, banning another country's publications within the acting country, etc.

This composite variable is very similar in definition to the *negative sanction* variable used by Rummel and Tanter. Their factor analyses revealed, however, an indeterminacy as to which major dimension it should be grouped with. Rummel's factor analysis placed it in the belligerency dimension while Tanter's analysis placed it in the diplomatic dimension.

3. The third foreign composite variable is *official military violence*. These are actions that are either preparation for, or the execution of, military violence by one state directed against other states. This is the definition given by Rummel and Tanter to their "war" dimensions, and brings together in all three studies such actions as troop mobilizations, military clashes, military actions, and war. In the Rummel and Tanter studies, the war dimension included number killed in foreign conflict. In the present study, this "body count" variable has been kept as a separate summary measure of the extent or severity of foreign violence just as was done with the "body count" variables in the domestic domain.

4. The fourth variable is the *number killed in foreign violence*. This includes deaths from both official military violence and unofficial cross-border violence. The common log transformation form of this variable is used in the analysis.

5. The fifth foreign composite variable is *antiforeign unofficial activity*. This is unstructured, mostly nonviolent activity taken by citizens. rather than the government, of one country against another country to demonstrate hostility toward that country. This includes antiforeign riots and demonstrations, citizen boycotts, and cross-border banditry and tribal violence. This is similar to the *foreign demonstrations* variable used by Rummel and Tanter, where it was grouped with severance of diplomatic relations on their "belligerency" dimension. The distinguishing characteristic of their belligerency dimension was the emotional, actively hostile mood it conveyed. In the present research, however, no clear conceptual distinction can be made between severance of diplomatic relations, as one type of formal diplomatic activity, and other formal diplomatic moves such as expulsion or recall of diplomatic personnel. Thus all formal diplomatic hostile activities are kept separate to form the first composite variable, *diplomatic hostility*. Rummel's belligerency dimension also grouped foreign demonstrations with negative sanctions. In the present research, *antiforeign anomic activity* is distinguished by its nongovernmental or nonofficial nature from the official governmental actions included in the *negative behavior* composite variable. This same nongovernmental versus governmental distinction also separates the *antiforeign anomic activities* from the *negative sanctions* variable used by Rummel and Tanter.

In addition to the above-listed five foreign conflict behavior composite variables, the domain of "negative communications" yielded three more composite variables. In contrast with the Rummel and Tanter researches, which coded "negative communications" according to the *form* of the message, the present research coded messages according to the *theme* or *substance*. Thus the earlier studies used threats, accusations, and protests as the coding categories for "negative communications."

> Threats: any official diplomatic communication or governmental statement asserting that if a particular country does or does not do a particular thing it will incur negative sanctions.
>
> Accusations: any official diplomatic or governmental statement involving charges and allegations of a derogatory nature against another country.
>
> Protests: any official diplomatic communication or governmental statement, the purpose of which is to complain about or object to the policies of another country.[41]

In rejecting this approach in the present research, three considerations were applied:

Protest notes, as a well-defined tool of diplomacy, were found too infrequently in the African data to warrant treatment as a separate coding category. This tends to support the earlier speculation that African diplomacy is more personal and less bounded by the established rules of diplomacy.

All three *form* categories (threats, accusations, protests) showed fairly high empirical relationships in both Rummel's and Tanter's data and accordingly were grouped together in their factor analyses. This indicates a relatively low discriminating power between the various negative communications when coded into these *form* categories.

In the two earlier studies, threats, accusations, and protests were grouped into different dimensions. Rummel's factor analysis grouped all three of these negative communication *forms* with the war dimension, whereas Tanter's factor analysis grouped them with his diplomatic dimension. This suggests that the *content* and *substance* of negative communications varied between the two studies in a way that was not identified by the *form* categories which they used to record their data.

Through preliminary analysis of the data sources, three *substantive* and *theme* differences were discernible in the negative communications issued by African governments. The criteria used in selecting these three theme categories were simply those of (a) conceptual clarity and distinctiveness; (b) empirical delimitation, that is, that each message could be fairly unambiguously categorized into just one category; and (c) theoretical import for the theory being tested. The three "negative communications" variables used in this research as the last three foreign conflict behavior variables

[41]Rummel, "Dimensions of Conflict Behavior."

are as follows:

6. *Internal interference* includes all complaints about subversive activity or internal interference activities alleged to have been directed against the country making the complaint. Such messages are typically of a more emotional nature both because of the difficulty of objectively verifying the charge, and because of the seriousness of the alleged activity, i.e., challenging and threatening the internal sovereignty of the complaining country.

7. *Hostile policies* includes all complaints about hostile foreign policies and violent or threatening activities alleged to be perpetrated by a country against the complaining country, and not included under *internal interference*. Included are complaints about threatening military moves, violations of national air space or territorial waters, hostile trade or diplomatic policies, etc. Not only are these actions more susceptible to objective verification by the international community, but they usually do not generate the same degree of emotional heat as do allegations of subsersive intent.

8. *General criticism* includes all complaints about illegal action, un-African behavior or ideology (siding with imperialism or international communism, etc.), and general criticism of another country's internal or external policies. The target country of these complaints is not alleged to be acting directly against the complaining country, but rather the complaint is against the activities or policies of the target country in general.

ANALYSIS

In order to determine what the relationship is between our eight measures of foreign conflict behavior and seven measures of domestic disorder, several techniques are employed. First, working with the combined data for a three-year period, we can evaluate the cross-sectional concomitant variation by studying both the zero-order correlations and the multiple correlations. Second, in order to determine the causal direction, time-series analysis with one-year lags are used. If domestic disorder is a sufficient condition of foreign conflict behavior, then the domestic disorder should not follow after (in time) the incidents of foreign conflict behavior. By using one-year lags we are attempting to find out if domestic disorder in one year can predict foreign conflict behavior in the next year. There is, of course, nothing in the theory that says that it takes on the average one year for the full impact of hypothesized foreign conflict behavior to result from domestic disorder. The one-year lag is admittedly an arbitrary time period, selected because sufficient data did not occur for shorter periods. If one-year time-series associations do not show up, we are, therefore, faced with the alternate plausible hypothesis that a different time period is the cycle that connects domestic disorder as a sufficient condition of foreign conflict behavior. Both zero-order correlations and multiple correlations are also used for the time-series analysis.

Cross-Sectional Analysis

In table 3 are displayed the zero-order correlations among all fifteen variables for the full three-year period.[42] The following preliminary observations, based on table 3, merit attention.

1. Among the foreign conflict behavior variables, *diplomatic hostility* does not correlate above .35 with any other foreign conflict variables, thus indicating that this one type of foreign behavior, as practiced by African states, is empirically a somewhat independent dimension of foreign conflict behavior. African states participating in diplomatic conflict do not necessarily participate in other types of foreign conflict behavior.

2. Among the domestic disorder variables, *elite instability* is correlated (n = .49) with only one other type of domestic disorder, *subversive activities.* This indicates that within African states, instability within the governmental elite structure can exist somewhat independent of other types of domestic disorder, except for subversive activities.

3. Continuing with the same threshold criteria of r = .35, we can note that the correlations between the domestic disorder domain and the foreign conflict behavior domain contain 15 out of 56 correlations which are positive and above the .35 level. There are, further, only 8 negative correlations, and these are uniformly very small. This suggests a basis of positive concomitant variation between these two domains, as predicted by our theory and in the direction predicted by our theory.

4. One final observation that can be made from table 3 is that the intercorrelations *among* the foreign conflict variables contain 10 out of 28 correlations above the .35 threshold, and the intercorrelations *among* the domestic disorder variables contain 12 out of 21 correlations above the threshold. From this we can conclude that within each of the two domains —foreign and especially domestic—there is a fairly high degree of empirical covariance of these types of events. Countries characterized by more domestic disorder of one type seem also to have more domestic disorder of other types, and likewise in the foreign domain. There are exceptions, however, to this interrelationship within each domain, as noted in (1) and (2) above. This indicates that within African states instability within the governmental elite structure can exist somewhat independent of other types of domestic disorder except for subversive activities, activities which are covert threats to the elites themselves.

---

[42]Even though we are not dealing with a random sample, but indeed with the universe of African states, we can use the statistical significance level of r = .35 (significant at the .05 probability level for a sample of this size) as a rough guide in sorting out more interesting correlations.

Table 3.   Correlations Among 15 Variables of Domestic Disorder and Foreign Conflict Behavior for 1963–65, African Countries[a]

| | | | | Foreign Conflict | | | | | | | | Domestic Disorder | | |
	1	2	3	4	5	6	7	8	9	10	11	12	13	14	15
Variables															
1. DIPHOS	1.00														
2. NEGBEH	32	1.00													
3. MILVIO	12	06	1.00												
4. FORKIL	-01	12	(59)	1.00											
5. ANTUNO	13	32	(39)	(54)	1.00										
6. INTINF	29	(57)	-10	05	02	1.00									
7. HOSPOL	25	24	(68)	(55)	(44)	13	1.00								
8. GENCRI	13	(50)	31	23	(48)	17	(56)	1.00							
9. ANOMIC	32	(35)	12	21	(58)	26	07	10	1.00						
10. SUBVER	22	(53)	-04	09	-01	(74)	13	05	28	1.00					
11. REVOLU	16	26	(39)	31	(55)	-03	20	01	(42)	27	1.00				
12. ELIINS	05	17	-02	02	-10	18	-13	-13	12	(49)	17	1.00			
13. DOMKIL	19	(63)	31	33	(47)	(44)	27	15	(67)	(48)	(51)	20	1.00		
14. DOMSUP	(39)	(59)	11	(36)	(47)	(48)	17	05	(70)	(49)	(41)	24	(73)	1.00	
15. ARREST	(53)	32	-19	-09	12	28	03	04	(51)	(38)	30	32	25	(40)	1.00

[a] Decimals are omitted. Correlations ≥ .35 are in parentheses.

Multiple regression for the total three-year period can tell us somewhat more specifically than can the zero-order correlations how well each foreign conflict behavior variable, taken individually, can be predicted by the full set of domestic disorder variables. The multiple regression results are shown in table 4. In general it can be noted that the multiple correla-

Table 4.   Regression of 7 Domestic Disorder Variables onto Foreign Conflict Behavior Variables, 1963–65, for 33 African Countries.

Criterion	Standard Deviation of Criterion	Standard Error of Estimate	Multiple R	R²
1. DIPHOS	3.391	3.055	.60	.37
2. NEGBEH	7.314	5.575	.74	.55
3. MILVIO	2.547	2.386	.56	.31
4. FORKIL	1.034	1.015	.50	.25
5. ANTUNO	2.251	1.664	.76	.57
6. INTINF	5.103	3.101	.85	.71
7. HOSPOL	6.226	6.492	.40	.16
8. GENCRI	3.775	4.118	.27	.07

tions (*R*) are quite strong. The first six values are greater than or equal to *R* = .50. This reflects the generally high zero-order correlations between the domestic domain variables and the foreign domain variables which were displayed earlier. Since *R* can vary only between 0 and +1, we must refer to table 3 to verify that the strong multiple correlations are reflecting positive associations rather than negative associations.

The predictive power of the domestic disorder variables for the first six criterion variables is also indicated by the difference in value between the standard deviations and the standard errors of estimate. The smaller values for the standard errors of the estimate tell us that there is less unexplained variance in the criterion variables when the domestic disorder variables are used as predictors than when simply the mean of the criterion variable is used as a predictor.

Analysis of the multiple regression results yields the following conclusions:

1. The most strongly predicted type of foreign conflict behavior is the negative communications variable, *internal interference* (*R* = .85). All the significant zero-order correlations composing this multiple *R* are positive, indicating that the multiple correlation is in the predicted direction. As we noted in discussing the internal interference variable earlier, these com-

plaints are about events or behaviors that are very hard to verify, and thus are susceptible to fabrication and manipulation by the complaining government. These messages also directly specify that the target foreign government is responsible for the domestic unrest, rather than simply complaining in general about the activities of the target government as the other message variables are measuring. Referring back to the zero-order correlations in table 3, we can see that there is a particularly strong correlation between internal interference messages and subversive activities ($r = .74$), suggesting that domestic subversive attempts are quite readily attributed by African states to foreign involvement and assistance, accurately or not. This correlation is illustrated by the high level of subversive activities in the Congo (K), which that country blamed on neighboring African countries, and by the subversion attempts in Niger, Togo, and Dahomey, which those countries blamed on Ghana. Thus, there is both face validity and empirical support for the hypothesis that domestic disorder can be a sufficient condition for "internal interference" messages.

2. Two negative communications variables—*hostile policy* and *general criticism*—are not well predicted by the domestic variables ($Rs = .40$ and .27, respectively). If foreign scapegoating is a common reaction of governments to domestic disorder, as our theory hypothesizes, then this suggests that negative communications which simply complain about other countries' foreign policies in general are not among the ways used to scapegoat. As we saw above, however, negative communications that accuse the target country of internal interference are the most likely verbal outcome of domestic disorder.

3. The second most strongly predicted type of foreign conflict behavior is *antiforeign unofficial behavior* ($R = .76$). Once again the zero-order correlations are positive, thus confirming that the multiple correlation is in the predicted direction. The domestic disorder variables most strongly associated with *antiforeign unofficial behavior* are *anomic disorder, domestic suppression, revolutionary activities*, and *domestic killed*. The last two domestic disorder variables are measures of overt domestic violence. We can, therefore, conclude that violent domestic disorder is characteristic of those African states which also exhibit unofficial foreign conflict behavior. However, it is difficult to ascertain whether this is due to our hypothesized linkage between domestic disorder and foreign conflict behavior, or more simply to a general spilling over of domestic violence across national boundaries. The latter speculation finds support from the situation in the Congo (K), the Sudan, Somali, and Kenya. In all of these states the high levels of domestic violence or overt unrest did spill over inadvertently into neighboring countries (Congo, Sudan) or else were an integral part of the internal unofficial foreign conflict (Somali, Kenya).

The *unofficial antiforeign conflict behavior* variable is also tapping antiforeign demonstrations and riots that do not extend across borders, but are directed at foreign embassies, business establishments, and other foreign presences within the acting country. In these instances the hypothesized relationship may still hold, which suggests another observation. Since *antiforeign unofficial behavior* is the most direct form in which nonelites can express external conflict behavior (in contrast with the monopoly elites have over the other forms of foreign conflict behavior), this association suggests that the theorized linkage between internal and external conflict can operate at the mass, nonelite level as well as at the level of nation-state official actors, as found elsewhere in this article. This distinction between an elite and a nonelite level of linkage is further substantiated by noting that the one type of domestic disorder which is specifically elite in nature, *elite instability*, is not part of the multiple association with *antiforeign unofficial behavior*.

4. The next most strongly predicted type of foreign conflict behavior is *negative behavior* ($R = .74$), also based on only positive zero-order correlations. There are four zero-order correlations above or at the .35 threshold level contained in this multiple correlation, thus indicating that *negative behavior* is broadly related to domestic disorder.

5. A relatively more modest multiple correlation is found between the domestic disorder domain and *diplomatic hostility* ($R = .60$). Two zero-order correlations contained within this multiple correlation exceed the .35 threshold, and all zero-order correlations are in the predicted, positive, direction. This multiple correlation lends support to the hypothesized linkage between internal and external conflict. However, it also appears that African countries rely more on nonformalized, nondiplomatic types of conflict behavior such as is captured by the *negative behavior* variable, as suggested in the first section of this paper.

6. A relatively modest multiple correlation is also found between the domestic disorder domain and *military violence* ($R = .56$). This multiple correlation is based on a set of zero-order correlations which contain only one correlation above the .35 threshold. *Military violence* appears to be strongly related only to *revolutionary activies*, which can be explained by the frequent association of border clashes in the wake of internal revolutionary warfare. This co-occurrence, however, is not necessarily a product of our hypothesized linkage between internal and external conflict, but can be adequately explained as either (a) part of a common military context, or (b) the product of aggression by outside forces.

7. The multiple correlation between the domestic domain and the *foreign killed* variable ($R = .50$) is even more modest. Although the zero-order correlations are in the predicted direction, again only one zero-order

is above the .35 threshold (*domestic suppression*). However, since *domestic suppression* can represent either domestic disorder *or* governmental suppression, this finding alone can not lend great support to the hypothesized linkage.

Comparing the regression results from the African data with those from the Rummel and Tanter studies (tables 5 and 6), we can see that the findings of the present study differ markedly from those earlier studies. The highest multiple correlation in the Rummel study is $R = .31$, for his "belligerency" dimension. The most directly comparable foreign conflict variable in the present study is *negative behavior*, which has a much higher multiple correlation ($R = .74$) with domestic disorder in African states.

Similarly with the diplomatic foreign conflict variable, Rummel and Tanter both obtained multiple correlations of $R = .26$ which is markedly lower than the $R = .60$ obtained with the African data. This strongly suggests that governmental hostility—both formal diplomatic and other types of foreign conflict policies—by African states is, in contrast with countries elsewhere, directly associated with conditions of domestic disorder.

The multiple correlations with the variables *official military violence* and *foreign violence deaths* are modest in the African sample, but are still con-

Table 5.   Regression of 3 Domestic Conflict Dimensions onto Foreign Conflict Behavior Variables, 1955–57, Rummel Analysis.[a]

Criterion	Standard Deviation of Criterion	Standard Error of Estimate	Multiple R	R^2
1. War	2.40	2.36	.26	.07
2. Diplomacy	1.49	1.46	.26	.07
3. Belligerency	1.00	.97	.31	.10

[a]Taken from Rummel, "Dimensions of Conflict Behavior."

Table 6.   Regression of 3 Domestic Conflict Variables onto Foreign Conflict Behavior Variables, 1958–60, Tanter Analysis.[a]

Criterion	Standard Deviation of Criterion	Standard Error of Estimate	Multiple R	R^2
1. Wars	.75	.76	.03	.00
2. Severance of diplomatic relations	.15	.15	.26	.07
3. Protests	.35	.35	.24	.06

[a]Taken from Tanter, "Dimensions of Conflict Behavior."

siderably higher than the comparable values for the "war" dimension (Rummel) and the "war" variable (Tanter). This suggests that foreign violence is related to conditions of domestic disorder more so in African states than elsewhere, although certainly the size of these correlations indicates that foreign violence is a product of other factors as well.

The relatively high multiple correlation ($R = .76$) between *antiforeign unofficial activity* and the domestic variables in the African sample is not comparable with any of the figures in the Rummel and Tanter studies, since this type of foreign conflict behavior was not included in those studies directly.

To summarize the results of the cross-sectional regression analysis, we have seen that for African states there is a fairly strong association between domestic disorder and foreign conflict behavior other than overt foreign violence or general critical messages. This has added to our understanding of the strong overall zero-order associations, and has also allowed direct comparison of the African data with the findings of Rummel's and Tanter's studies of non-African states. This comparison revealed a consistent reversal of those earlier findings, suggesting that for African states domestic disorder is a much more relevant factor for foreign conflict behavior than is the case in non-African countries.

Time Lagging

Throughout our analysis so far we have been holding in abeyance any firm statements about causality, even though we have been making some causal speculations from the concomitant variation we have observed. Although we must admit at the outset that the social sciences are generally unable to prove causality directly, we can accept Blalock's advice to "*think causally and to develop causal models that have implications that are indirectly testable.*"[43]

Our causal model, which hypothesizes that domestic disorder is a sufficient condition of foreign conflict behavior, can be tested in part by determining if domestic conflict in one time period can "predict" to foreign conflict in the next period. This method can not be used to determine causality in the rigorous sense that we may desire, but it can add or detract from the plausability of the hypothesized relationships underlying the cross-sectional associations. A cross-sectional relationship which is *not* maintained in time lagged analysis is certainly more difficult to explain with the hypothesized linkage set forth in this article.

The following conclusions can be drawn from the time-lagged analysis:

1. In table 7 are displayed the comparative correlations of the various

---

[43]Hubert M. Blalock, Jr., *Causal Inferences in Nonexperimental Research* (Chapel Hill: University of North Carolina Press, 1964), p. 6.

Table 7.   One-Year Time-Lagged Correlations, Domestic Disorder and Foreign Conflict Behavior

		Multiple R^a	ANOMIC	SUBVER	REVOLU	ELIINS	DOMKIL	DOMSUP	ARREST
						Domestic Disorder			
1964 foreign– 1963 domestic	NEGBEH	(.67)	.47	.35	.13	-.09	.42	.16	.11
	DIPHOS	(.69)	.55	.17	.34	.03	.38	.24	.36
	MILVIO	.35	.03	-.16	.07	-.26	.08	.01	-.24
	FORKIL	(.54)	.28	.06	.07	-.12	.22	-.03	-.09
	ANTUNO	.37	.15	.01	.16	-.09	.06	-.07	-.13
1965 foreign– 1964 domestic	NEGBEH	(.79)	.37	.49	.31	-.03	.52	.71	.44
	DIPHOS	(.55)	.34	.12	.30	-.09	-.02	.22	.22
	MILVIO	.36	.01	-.12	.24	.01	-.01	.14	-.12
	FORKIL	.39	.06	-.02	.19	-.13	.21	.28	.03
	ANTUNO	.50	.28	-.20	.19	-.13	.18	.32	.18
Total 1963–65 cross-sectional	NEGBEH	(.74)	.35	.53	.26	.17	.63	.59	.32
	DIPHOS	(.61)	.32	.22	.17	.05	.19	.39	.53
	MILVIO	(.56)	.12	-.04	.39	-.02	.31	.11	-.19
	FORKIL	.47	.21	.09	.31	.03	.33	.36	-.09
	ANTUNO	(.76)	.58	-.01	.55	-.10	.47	.47	.12

[a] The multiple Rs in parentheses meet the criteria that the standard deviation of the foreign conflict variable (criterion) is larger than the standard error of the estimate.

domestic disorder variables with a foreign conflict variable, *negative behavior*. First, we can note that the rather large multiple correlation from the cross-sectional analysis, $R = .74$, is sustained with the one-year lagging for both 1963–64 and 1964–65. Since there are no significant negative zero-order correlations we can conclude that *negative behaviors are fairly well predicted by high levels of general domestic disorder in the preceding one year period.*

2. Looking at the zero-order correlations we can see one other pattern. *Anomic outbreaks* and *subversive activities* predict well to *negative behaviors* in the next year across both time-lag periods, although both of the subversive activities correlations are somewhat less than the cross-sectional correlation. The conclusion still remains, however, that based on these two cross-lag periods we *cannot reject* the hypothesis that *displays of general, nonviolent negative behaviors toward other nations* (such as expelling foreigners, assisting another nation's enemy, closing borders, severing economic relations, breaking pacts, etc.) *can be explained in part as a response to domestic conditions, in the preceding year, of general anomic disorder and subversive threats to the government.* This lends some credence to the partial theory of African foreign policy posited earlier.

3. In a similar fashion we can analyze the comparative values of the various domestic disorder variables with the foreign conflict variable of *diplomatic hostility*, displayed in table 7. First, we can note that the multiple correlation from the cross-sectional analysis, $R = .61$, is sustained by the two time-lag periods, again with predominately positive zero-order correlations. As in the analysis above, we can conclude that *diplomatic hostility is fairly well predicted by high levels of general domestic disorder in the preceding one-year period.*

4. Focusing on the zero-order correlations we can note that only one domestic disorder variable, *anomic outbreaks*, is consistently comparable or larger (1963–64: $r = .55$; 1964–65: $r = .34$) in size than the cross-sectional correlation ($r = .32$). It would appear, therefore, that *displays of diplomatic hostility can be explained in part as a response to general anomic disorder in the preceding year.*

5. Referring again to table 7 we can examine the relationships between the three foreign violence measures and the various domestic disorder measures. The $R = .56$ for *military violence* from the cross-sectional analysis is not supported by the two time-lag regression correlations ($R = .35$ and $R = .36$), which are not only small but also smaller than the cross-sectional figure. We therefore *cannot support the hypothesis that official military hostility and violence is a product of domestic disorder in the preceding year.* The moderate cross-sectional association ($R = .56$) is perhaps explained best by the relationship posited earlier. That is, that much

of the foreign violence, both official and unofficial, is in part a concomitant spillover of domestic violence and disorder. Much of the border area in Africa is weakly controlled by any government, and it is thus fairly easy for internal dissident groups, such as in the Congo (K) and the Sudan, to range across the border and encounter almost accidently the military forces of a neighboring state. Rwanda and Burundi represent another pattern where dissident elements of one country (Burundi) launch raids or regroup forces in the weakly controlled border area of a neighboring country (Rwanda) and, in the ensuing cross-border unofficial violence and internal violence, involve the armed forces of one or both countries. It may be also that military activities against other states in Africa are either a response to real conflict situations or else accidental border violations which provoke a limited military response.

6. Continuing our analysis of table 7 it can be noted that although there is no significant cross-sectional association (R = .47) between the number of people killed in foreign violence and general domestic disorder, in the 1963–64 time lag there is a moderate (R = .54) association. *Support is therefore very weak for any causal or concomitant association between the severity of foreign conflict, both official and unofficial, as measured by the total killed in the conflict, and any pattern of domestic disorder.* Probably what this is indicating is that it takes at least two countries to have foreign violence deaths, and the involvement in such violence is as much a reaction to external threats and attacks as it is to internal conditions. Another factor may be operating here, as illustrated by the brief Algerian-Moroccan border war which occurred in this time period. This action involved near full-scale mobilization of both countries and direct confrontations between the two armies, but the news sources reported only "about" ten deaths in the entire one-month war. This one example indicates that perhaps either (a) death counts are not a good indicator of the degree of foreign conflict intent, and/or (b) the notoriously inaccurate reporting on battle deaths counts is even more serious in the African setting. These two speculations cast doubt on the validity of this "killed" measure as an indicator of the overall severity of foreign conflict.

7. One final observation can be made from table 7. The foreign conflict variable, *antiforeign unofficial activity*, shows a strong cross-sectional relationship (R = .76) with the full set of domestic disorder variables, but the two time lags do not reproduce this degree of association (1963–64: R = .37; 1964–65: R = .50). *Antiforeign unofficial activity cannot, therefore, be seen as a product of domestic disorder in the preceding year.* It can, however, be viewed as a direct corollary of concomitant general domestic disorder. The fairly strong zero-order correlation with *anomic outbreaks* (r = .58) in the cross-sectional analysis suggests that demonstrations against and attacks on foreign objects occur frequently as spillover

from general anomic disorder in the country, without requiring any cause-and-effect relationship as hypothesized in this paper. If there is a causal relationship of anomic outbreaks *producing* antiforeign anomic activities it could occur in the immediate context of internal general anomic disorder without involving the lengthy societal reaction time that our one-year time lag is capturing.

8. *Antiforeign unofficial activities* are also, in the cross-sectional analysis, correlated fairly strongly ($r = .55$) with the domestic disorder variable of revolutionary activity. The direct spillover explanation posited above in the analysis of foreign violence deaths would seem to apply here also. That is, such unofficial antiforeign activity can be viewed as an immediate integral part of revolutionary activities, rather than as a causal product of such domestic violence as hypothesized in the causal model.

9. In table 8 are displayed the comparative correlations of the various domestic disorder variables with the three foreign conflict message variables—"internal interference," "hostile policy," and "general criticism" theme messages. Messages about internal interference have a strong ($R = .84$) cross-sectional relationship with the full array of domestic disorder variables, and this relationship is sustained in one time period (1963–64: $R = .82$). *This suggests that for this one-time period the level of internal interference messages can be viewed as a product, in part, of general domestic disorder in the previous year.* The lack of any sizable relation, however, in the 1964–65 time lag makes it difficult to assert this as a general relationship, and indicates the need for further time analysis with more time periods.

10. The relatively strong zero-order relationships between domestic disorder of a subversive type and internal interference conflict messages (1963–64: $r = .64$; cross-sectional $r = .74$) suggests that *African states with internal subversive troubles often seek to identify foreign scapegoats as the alleged direct cause of the subversive activities.* The cross-sectional association may be better explained by shorter time lagging as the allegations of foreign interference in internal subversive activities would likely be a more direct and immediate reaction than is captured by the one-year time lagging used herein.

11. One further observation from table 8 can be made about foreign conflict messages which contain only general criticism of another country. There is a consistent lack of relationship between this type of foreign conflict message and domestic disorder. *This strongly suggests that general criticism of other nations by African states need not at all be a function of domestic disorder*, and that at least this one aspect of their foreign policy may be more guided by *policy* considerations rather than just domestic *politics* considerations. This is of course contrary to the general view of African foreign policy put forth in the first two sections.

Table 8.   One-Year Time-Lagged Correlations, Domestic Disorder and Foreign Conflict Messages

		Multiple R^a	ANOMIC	SUBVER	REVOLU	ELIINS	DOMKIL	DOMSUP	ARREST
1964 foreign–	INTINF	(.82)	.65	.64	.13	.14	.38	.14	.33
1963 domestic	HOSPOL	(.65)	.24	-.04	.22	-.28	.25	-.00	-.15
	GENCRI	.36	.00	-.13	.00	-.17	-.04	-.16	-.21
1965 foreign–	INTINF	.28	-.04	.20	-.03	.02	.03	.06	.09
1964 domestic	HOSPOL	.44	.03	.01	.09	-.15	.29	.30	-.02
	GENCRI	.44	.13	.24	-.16	-.11	.26	.14	.25
Total 1963–65	INTINF	(.84)	.26	.74	-.03	.19	.44	.48	.28
cross-sectional	HOSPOL	.40	.07	.13	.20	-.13	.27	.17	.03
	GENCRI	.27	.10	.05	.01	-.13	.15	.05	.04

^{a}Multiple *R*s in parentheses meet the criteria that the standard deviation of the foreign conflict variable (criterion) is larger than the standard error of the estimate.

Comparison of Results with Earlier Studies

Comparing now our findings with the three-year time-lag regression analysis introduced by Tanter[44] to the data collected by him (1958–60) and Rummel (1955–57), we can see a convergence of results. Tanter's analysis, regressing the domestic disorder (or domestic conflict, as Rummel and Tanter refer to the domestic phenomena) for 1955–57 onto the foreign conflict behavior for 1958–60, is shown in table 9. Using "protests" in 1958–

Table 9. Multiple Regression of Rummel 1955–57 Domestic Conflict Variables (antigovernment demonstrations, revolutions, and guerrilla warfare) onto 1958–60 Foreign Conflict Behavior Variables.[a]

1958–60 Criterion	Standard Deviation of Criterion	Standard Error of Estimate	Multiple R
1. Protests	35	32	42
2. War	68	69	12
3. Severance of diplomatic relations	16	14	40

[a] Taken from Tanter, "Dimensions of Conflict Behavior."

60 Tanter obtained a multiple correlation with domestic disorder in 1955–57 of $R = .42$. This is lower than the 1963–64 regression Rs for the African data (for the comparable foreign conflict behavior variables of internal interference and hostile policy messages, Rs $= .82$ and $.65$, respectively). *It does, however, indicate a consistency of the causal relationship between domestic disorder and these types of foreign conflict behaviors.*

Tanter also obtained a multiple correlation of $R = .40$ between 1958–60 severance of diplomatic relations and 1955–57 domestic conflict. The comparable foreign conflict behavior variable in the present study is *diplomatic hostility*, which we found was predicted by domestic disorder in both of the one-year time lags (Rs $= .69$ and $.55$). *This consistency of findings between the two studies adds support to the causal relationship between domestic disorder and foreign diplomatic hostility.*

The third foreign conflict variable reported by Tanter ("war") is shown not to be predicted by domestic conflict in the earlier three-year period ($R = .12$). The corresponding foreign conflict variable in the African study, military violence, was also shown not to be associated with domestic disorder in either time lag (Rs $= .35$ and $.36$). This shows additional consistency between the two studies on the time analysis.

Two possible reasons why the Tanter three-year time lagging produced

[44] Tanter, "Dimensions of Conflict Behavior."

multiple correlations lower than those obtained with the African data can be speculated. First, the one-year time lag used with the African data may be a more sensitive time period to capture the causal sequence than the three-year period. This question can only be determined through further research. Second, it may be that the causal relationship between domestic disorder and foreign conflict behavior is more relevant in African states than for the non-African states which were studied by Rummel and Tanter. In our theoretical discussion in the first two sections we hypothesized that the characteristics of new, developing African states would make such a linkage particularly relevant. Since, however, the Rummel and Tanter samples included other, non-African developing states as well as highly developed states, their analysis would not allow a strict sorting out of this proposition. This question could be answered more fully by breaking the Rummel and Tanter data down by regions, to see if other developing areas are particularly prone to foreign conflict manifestations of domestic disorder, and to see if there is still a difference between other developing states and the new African states with respect to this causal relationship between domestic disorder and foreign conflict behavior.

CONCLUSION

The hypothesis that domestic disorder is a sufficient but not a necessary condition for foreign conflict behavior by African states has been formulated and explained by several theoretical perspectives. Viewing the nature and the difficulty of internal nation building in new states and the less structured policy-making process, especially for foreign policy, we have posited that African states are much more subject to foreign conflict behavior motivated by domestic disorder than are older, more developed states. Theoretical explanations of the internal-external conflict relationship are posited from both the realistic conflict perspective and the frustration-aggression perspective.

Using seven measures of domestic and eight measures of foreign conflict behavior, cross-sectional analysis for the time period 1963–65 for thirty-three African countries demonstrated a strong basis of concomitant variation between the domestic and foreign domains. Multiple regression of all seven domestic disorder measures into each foreign conflict behavior variable individually showed that: (1) negative communications messages which complain about "internal interference" are strongly "predicted" by domestic disorder, but other types of negative communications are not associated with domestic disorder; (2) antiforeign unofficial behavior is well predicted by domestic disorder; (3) negative behavior and diplomatic hostility, as the two more commonly occuring types of foreign conflict behavior, are strongly "predicted" by domestic disorder; (4) foreign military violence and number of foreign killed are only weakly related to domestic disorder.

These cross-sectional results are shown to be markedly different from the findings of Rummel and Tanter in their analysis of non-African countries. Their multiple regression analysis showed no relationship between each of the three dimensions of foreign conflict and all measures of domestic conflict.

In the time-lag analysis, using one-year periods, the following results were obtained: (1) multiple regression of domestic disorders onto both negative behavior and diplomatic hostility, for the time lags 1963–64 and 1964–65, were strong and positive, thus supporting the posited causal relationship; (2) multiple correlation of domestic disorder with foreign military violence and foreign killed across the two time lags do not support the hypothesized relationship; (3) time lagging of domestic disorder with antiforeign unofficial activity does not support the strong association found between these variables in the cross-sectional analysis (thus, the causal inference relating the form of foreign conflict behavior with domestic disorder is not supported); (4) Negative communication complaining of internal interference, shown to be strongly associated with domestic disorder in the cross-sectional analysis, is sustained in only one of the two time lags, 1963–64, so the causal inference is only partially supported; (5) the lack of cross-sectional association between domestic disorder and the other types of negative communication is supported by the lack of time-lag relationships, thus failing to support the causal inference for these variables.

Comparison of these one-year time lags with a three-year lag done by Tanter shows (1) time-lag relationships between domestic disorder and general, nonviolent, nondiplomatic conflict are present in both analyses, indicating a consistency of the causal relationship in the African and non-African system, although the one-year African time lag is much stronger of the two; (2) consistency of findings in the two time lags is also found between domestic disorder and foreign diplomatic hostility, supporting the causal inference; and (3) the lack of relationship between foreign violence and domestic disorder in the African time lag is sustained by Tanter's time lag.

APPENDIX
Variable Definitions and Coding Rules

The initial seventeen foreign conflict behavior variables used to construct the final composite variables are operationally defined below.

General notes on coding of foreign conflict behavior variables:
(a) "actor" and "object" refer respectively to the country doing the for-

eign conflict behavior, and the target of such behavior. The object can be individual states as well as recognized groups of states or international bodies of some sort.

(b) all events are to be coded under only one variable except where noted otherwise.

(c) the unit of analysis is the relationship between the actor country and a recognizeable object. Thus, if diplomatic relations are severed with five countries all at once, five occurrences are recorded rather than just one.

(d) variables 1, 4, and 9 (DIPREL, CLOBOR, AND ASSENM) are events that can be conceived to have a continuing bad effect on relations between countries even after their initiation, and generally are amenable to specific revocation of the action in order to signify removal of the continuing state of hostile relations. Reinstating diplomatic relations and opening of borders are examples. Such events are coded once initially and again once for each one-half-year period during which they are still operating. Thus severance of diplomatic relations in February 1964 which are not reestablished until August 1964 will register twice—once for the period January–June, and once for the period July–December.

The seventeen foreign conflict behavior variables and their coding procedures are as follows:

1. (DIPREL). Disruption of diplomatic relations: any action which acts to disrupt or to indicate the disruption of the formal diplomatic relations with another state, including expulsion or recall of diplomatic personnel and severance or suspension of formal diplomatic relations. Each such event is coded rather then the number of personnel involved.

2. (DIPREB). Diplomatic rebuff: according to Rummel, "a diplomatic rebuff may be a clear diplomatic snub or insult, such as having a minor official meet a chief of state, or having an ambassador fail to attend a diplomatic reception when invited. A rebuff is evidenced by an intentional violation of diplomatic protocol." Also included would be the cancellation of an official visit by self or other elites because of bad relations between the two countries.

3. (IOBOYC). International organization or conference boycott or walkout: the purpose of such actions must be to register a diplomatic offense against some other country or group of countries or the international organization.

4. (CLOBOR). Closing of border: sealing a border either partially or completely. Both countries involved are coded if the action seems mutual. Otherwise, in the absence of data to confirm mutual acceptance or mutual intent, only one country, so identified by the news account, is coded for it. An event may be coded here as well as under item 1 above.

5. (EXPFOR). Expulsion or jailing of foreigners: this is for nondiplomatic foreign personnel, whether private citizens or employees of the object country. Each *event* is coded rather than the number of persons involved. An event may be coded here as well as under item 1 above.
6. (ECOREL). Disruption of economic relations: behavior which acts primarily to impair the economic relations between actor and object, or action taken by actor against the economic relations between the object country and some third country. This includes boycotts, blockades, embargoes, severance of economic relations, discontinuance of giving or receipt of economic assistance, severance of trade or agreement, freezing of assets of object, nationalization of object's assets, etc. These actions can be either partial or categorical. An event may be coded here as well as under item 1 above.
7. (PACTOFF). Breaking of pacts, treaties, and agreements: abrogation of a treaty, agreement, or pact, or discontinuance of negotiations for such by a discrete event, even though negotiations were not actively in progress at the time. These actions can be unilateral or by mutual action, but must have hostile intent. Economic treaties and agreements are not coded here but are included under ECOREL above.
8. (MSCHOS). Miscellaneous hostile behaviors: actions other than those included above that are taken by the actor against the object, which are nonviolent, and which reflect hostile or unfriendly intent or relations between the countries. This includes such things as banning the distribution of a publication which is produced by the object, or proclaiming a policy which will operate adversely for the object and which has hostile intent.
9. (ASTENM). Assistance to another country's enemy: material, rather than just moral or verbal, aid and support to a subversive or rebellious group which is acting against the object government, or giving military aid to object's violent enemy, or allowing an exile rebel headquarters to be established in the actor country. Since these activities are usually of a continuing nature, the presence or absence of such assistance during each one-half-year period is recorded.
10. (TROOPS). Official nonviolent military moves: this includes troop alerts and mobilizations, and military movements intended to communicate a warning or defensive message and which are related to a developing conflict situation.
11. (OFVIOL). Official military violence: this is defined by Rummel as "any military clash of a particular country with another and involving gunfire." Rummel has a separate category for military clashes involving at least .02 percent of the population as soldiers, but this "size of force" distinction is not used herein. Conflicts within each six-month period of 1–10 days duration are scored 1, 11–30 days are scored 2,

between 1 and 2 months are scored 3, and greater than 2 months are scored 4.

12. (FORKIL). Number killed in foreign violence: these figures have been transformed to common log form. This is of course a summary measure of events which have already been coded elsewhere. This is total killed by all countries in the foreign violence that country has been involved in.

13. (ANOFOR). Antiforeign anomic activity: antiforeign demonstrations and riots, which, according to Rummel, "includes attacking an embassy, legation, or information office of another country, or attacking for political reasons either foreign nationals on the street or their property" as well as "strikes against the goods of another nation, either by dock workers or consumers."

14. (UNOFVI). Unofficial antiforeign violence: this includes attacks on border posts by unofficial irregular groups, cross-border banditry, cross-border tribal warfare, and acts of terrorism by unofficial groups against foreigners. Violence incident to ANOFOR (above) is not included here. Events which are continuous for more than three days are recorded once for each one-month period they continue.

The last three foreign conflict behavior variables are different types of negative communications, and are the same variables as used in the final analysis. These can be a statement by any major governmental elite, including government-controlled press and radio, providing such statements are not at obvious variance with governmental policy in the matter. The unit of measure here is the message from actor to object, rather than just the verbal or written utterance itself. Thus, if in one speech, negative communications are directed to three specific countries, then three messages are recorded.

15. (INTINF). Negative communications concerning complaints about internal interference by the object in the affairs of the actor. These include charges that the object is engaging in subversive activities against the actor, or is assisting such subversive activities either materially or by moral support.

16. (HOSPOL). Negative communications concerning complaints about general hostile policies of the object toward the actor. These include charges of provocations by the object, of intimidation or blackmail, of responsibility or complicity for violence, aid or comfort to the actor's enemies (including granting diplomatic recognition to actor's enemies), of territorial violations of actor's territorial space by the object, of threats to the peace of the actor, and of general aggressive policies.

17. (GENCRI). Negative communications concerning complaints in general of the object country. The object of these complaints is not alleged to be acting directly against the actor. This includes complaints about

an internal policy of the object (such as complaints about the South African racial policy), general criticism of the object's foreign policy, charges of illegal actions, of violation of treaties or agreements, and charges of ideological deviance by the object (such as not following a true pan-African or pan-Arab policy, or of being undemocratic, imperialistic, or neocolonialistic.)

The initial twenty-two domestic disorder variables used to construct the final composite variables are operationally defined as follows:

1. (RIOTNP). Nonpolitical riots: any violent demonstration or clash of people, the primary purpose of which is *not* to protest governmental actions or policy, and which has at least 25 people.

2. (ANTDEM). Antigovernment demonstration: "Any peaceful public gathering of at least [25] people for the primary purpose of displaying or voicing their opposition to government policies or authority, excluding those demonstrations of a distinctly anti-foreign nature" (taken from Rummel, but with a change in the minimum number of people required from 100 to 25).

3. (STRIKE). Strikes: any strike by employees involving at least 25 workers. In contrast with the Rummel definition, these strikes do not need to have an explicit political protest intention. If an antigovernment demonstration or riot also occurs, this is coded in addition. These strikes do not have to be general strikes involving more than one employer as the Rummel definition specifies.

4. (POLCLA). Political clash: any violent clash between two or more political groups, factions, or parties within the country, and which are not intended as actions against the government.

5. (INTRIB). Intertribal conflict: any event between tribal groups which is simply showing hostility between the two groups and does not involve governmental opposition, and which is sporadic and discrete in nature.

6. (MUTINY). Revolt against authority by the armed forces of a country, but not necessarily with any intention of overthrowing the government.

7. (GUERWA). Guerrilla warfare: presence or absence, within each three-month time period, of any *covert* armed activity carried on by independent bands of citizens or irregular forces and aimed at the overthrow of the present regime.

8. (TERRSA). Acts of terrorism or sabotage: any violent, discrete, covert action with antigovernment intent.

9. (ASSASS). Assassinations: any politically motivated murder or attempted murder of a high government official or politician. Such deaths which accompany coups will not be counted separately as an assassination event.

10. (PLOTAC). Plots for coups: any attempt, successful or not, by one or more parts of the power elite to take over the government by extralegal means.
11. (POLBOY). Political boycott: any boycott of an election or other governmental activity by internal groups.
12. (ANTRIO). Antigovernment riot: any violent demonstration against the government, its leaders, or policy, which thereby threaten in a violent, physical way the maintenance of law and order.
13. (REVOLU). Revolution: presence or absence, within each three-month period, of any *overt*, organized armed attempt to overthrow the existing government.
14. (CIVWAR). Civil war: presence or absence, within each three-month period, of any *overt*, organized armed attempt to secede from the national government by some group within the country. The breakaway attempt by the Katanga in the Congo (Leopoldville) would be an example.
15. (MAJCRI). Major governmental crisis: According to Rummel, "any rapidly developing situation that threatens to bring the down-fall of the present regime—excluding situations of revolt aimed at such an overthrow." A very narrow vote of confidence in a parliamentary form of government, or an actual downfall of the government, would be included here.
16. (ELTDEL). Elite deletions: the number of individuals dismissed from or resigning from the top elite structure and which indicates disunity among the elite structure.
17. (DOMKIL). Number killed in domestic violence, transformed to common log form. The events which resulted in these deaths have probably been coded elsewhere in addition.
18. (BANDEM). Presence or absence of ban, either partial or categorical, on demonstrations or public gatherings for political purposes. If such a ban extended over the entire country, then it would probably show up as a proclamation of emergency (below) rather than here.
19. (BANGRP). Banning of politically relevant group: any ban on a politically relevant group which severely restricts the political relevance or activities of that group or groups. The unit of measurement is the governmental action, regardless of how many groups are so affected by each such ban.
20. (PROEMR). Proclamation of emergency or martial law: presence or absence, for each six-month period, of a declaration of a state of emergency or martial law in any significant part of the country and which is a response to political conditions and not simply due to a natural disaster such as an earthquake.
21. (FRPRCU). Freedom of the press curtailment: any governmental re-

striction on the freedom of the press as discrete events, such as censoring a particular publication, or closing down a newspaper. Long-term governmental policies which restrict the freedom of the press by their deterence effect will show up in this variable only when the government has to remind the press of such curtailments in the form of specific actions. The event of the governmental action is the unit of measurement, and not the number of newspapers so affected.

22. (ARREST). Political arrests: the number of people arrested for political reasons, transformed into common log form. This includes arrests resulting from events coded elsewhere, such as coups, elite deletions, etc.

.10. The Strength and Direction of Relationships Between Domestic and External Conflict and Cooperation: Syria, 1961-67*

ROBERT BURROWES
and
BERTRAM SPECTOR

> *"Diverting popular attention from domestic troubles by starting foreign wars is one of the most venerable dodges of statecraft."* —Harry Eckstein
> (1965)

> *"It seems that Syria wished to achieve some easy external victories in order to cover up her domestic difficulties."* —Levi Eshkol
> (January 1967)

THE DISCIPLINE of international politics currently reveals a striking discrepancy between the conclusions of a number of highly regarded nonquantitative studies of international politics and recent statistical inquiries into the relationships between the domestic and external conflict behavior of nations. The former tend to assume a strong relationship between domestic and external conflict. On the one hand, much of the traditional literature

*This study is part of the Middle East Conflict and Cooperation Analysis (MECCA) Project, and is currently supported by the National Science Foundation under Grant #GS-2775. Earlier versions of this paper were prepared for presentation at the annual meeting of the Middle East Studies Association, Austin, Texas, November 15–17, 1968, and the annual meeting of the American Political Science Association, Commodore Hotel, New York City, September 2–6, 1969. We wish to thank the Center for International Studies at New York University for assistance in the preparation of these earlier versions. We also wish to thank Harriet Zagor and Ellen Hochman for help in collecting the data, and Douglas Muzzio and Jose Garriga for suggestions and criticisms of this effort. Finally, we wish to thank Elena Arena for typing and proofreading this and earlier versions of the manuscript.

regards between-nation conflict as largely determined by within-nation conflict. It has been suggested that: (1) international instability tends to fluctuate with the domestic insecurity of elites;[1] (2) elites fearing the loss of position during periods of rapid industrialization and widespread social change may be driven to a foreign policy of conflict in order to displace attentions of a disaffected population onto some outside target;[2] and (3) politicians seeking internal solidarity, stability, and order use war and preparation for war to maintain or expand the power of government, class, or party.[3] On the other hand, the traditional literature also contains suggestions that the presence of external conflict may lead to internal instability and civil violence, particularly for the nation that loses or pays a high price for victory in external conflict.[4] Whatever its direction, the assumption of a strong relationship between domestic and external politics can fairly be described as part of the conventional wisdom of the discipline.

In sharp contrast to this assumption are the findings in the separate multivariate statistical studies of R. J. Rummel and Raymond Tanter. Rummel collected a single cross-section of data on twenty-two domestic and external conflict indicators over seventy-seven nations for the years 1955–57.[5] These data were intercorrelated and factor-analyzed; the dimensions of domestic and external conflict which emerged were then subjected to multiple regression analysis. The factor analysis suggested that there was no significant relationship between domestic and external conflict dimensions; similarly, multiple regression of each external conflict dimension on the set of domestic conflict dimensions, and each domestic conflict dimension on the set of external conflict dimensions, led to the conclusion that the two domains of politics "generally cannot be predictors of each other."[6] Tanter subsequently replicated Rummel's study using data on the same twenty-two indicators collected across eighty-three nations for the years 1958–60.[7] Derived by similar techniques, his findings tended to confirm Rummel's conclusions. Furthermore, when Tanter regressed his

---

[1]Richard Rosecrance, *Action and Reaction in World Politics* (Boston: Little, Brown and Co., 1963), p. 304.

[2]Ernst Haas and Allen Whiting, *Dynamics of International Politics* (New York: McGraw-Hill Book Co., 1956), pp. 61–62.

[3]Quincy Wright, *A Study of War* (Chicago: University of Chicago Press, 1942), vol. 1, pp. 140, 254; vol. 2, pp. 225, 727, 1016.

[4]Harry Eckstein, "On the Etiology of Internal Wars," *History and Theory* 4, no. 2 (1965): 155; and F. H. Denton, "Some Regularities in International Conflict, 1820–1949" (Rand Corporation, 1965), p. 20.

[5]R. J. Rummel, "Dimensions of Conflict Behavior Within and Between Nations," chap. 3, this volume.

[6]Ibid.

[7]Raymond Tanter, "Dimensions of Conflict Behavior Within and Between Nations, 1958–60," *Journal of Conflict Resolution* 10 (March 1966): 41–64.

1958–60 data on Rummel's 1955–57 data, he found that the relationship between internal and external conflict became only slightly stronger.

DESIGN OF THIS STUDY

This study had its origins in this discrepancy between traditional theory and these recent empirical findings. The attempt to determine where truth lay between these two positions did not begin without prejudice. The weight of international relations theory, a reading of the history of international politics, and "common sense" all conspired to cast doubt upon the results reported by Rummel and Tanter. Their data and features of their research designs nurtured these doubts.[8] First, it seemed questionable whether nonspecialists relying solely on such sources as the *New York Times Index* and *Deadline Data* could gather a reasonably reliable and valid cross-section of data on both the domestic and external conflict of seventy-seven or more nations. Second, the sheer paucity of data on many of the indicators for most nations suggested that the failure of Rummel and Tanter to find a stronger relationship between domestic and external conflict was partly an artifact of distributional irregularities in those data. Third, the fact that the data on domestic and external conflict were collected for the same time period suggested the possibility that the results were caused by their failure to allow for an appropriate time lag between an external or foreign dependent variable and the set of domestic or internal independent variables. Fourth, and related to the previous point, it was thought that the search for unlagged or lagged relationships between domestic and external conflict may have been confounded by the use of time units of so long a duration as three years. Finally, it was believed that the decision not to analyze cooperation separately or in combination with conflict might account for the failure to find a stronger relationship between domestic and external politics.

For these reasons, this study was begun with the assumption that the actual relationship between domestic and external politics was more in accord with traditional theory than with the findings of Rummel and Tanter. It was believed that a multiple time-series analysis of carefully collected data on the conflict and cooperation of a single nation would yield evidence of such a relationship. It was assumed that the systematic lagging of domestic and external politics on one another would reveal a temporal pattern in which the two political domains are strongly related, and that the sequential pattern that emerged would indicate the direction of the relationship between the two domains. The general and contradictory hypotheses which guided the design of this study were:

[8]Many of these data and design questions are raised by Rummel in the excellent concluding section of his study.

(1) that increases (decreases) in domestic conflict and/or cooperation tend to precede increases (decreases) in external conflict and/or cooperation; and,

(2) that increases (decreases) in external conflict and/or cooperation tend to precede increases (decreases) in domestic conflict and/or cooperation.

Syria was chosen as the subject of this study for four reasons. First, Syria has evidenced a remarkably high degree of variation on precisely those dimensions to which propositions regarding the conflict behavior of nations are usually addressed; the levels of both domestic[9] and external[10] conflict in Syria have been subject to wide and repeated fluctuations during her three decades of independence. Second, most narrative histories of Syria's modern politics assume and are even organized around the close interdependence of Syria's domestic and external politics.[11] Third, a number of factors—among them the Arab-Israeli dispute and Great Power competition in the Eastern Mediterranean—have worked to sustain high journalistic and scholarly interest in Syria over the past two decades. This promised relatively easy access to an unusually rich body of political data. Fourth, one of the authors has spent considerable time in the Middle East and has had some training in Middle East area studies. This was deemed crucial to the collection of valid and reliable data.

This case study of Syrian politics covers the period between the breakup of the United Arab Republic and the outbreak of the Six-Day War—September 29, 1961 through June 4, 1967.[12] This was a period of unstable multiparty rule and only slightly more stable Baath party and/or military rule. The brief period of harmony after the breakup of the U.A.R. gave way in 1962 to increasingly intense domestic conflict between the conservative Syrian nationalists and the Baathist and pro-Nasser revolutionary Arab nationalists. Resolved in favor of the revolutionaries by a coup in early 1963, this conflict was quickly superseded by a much more bitter and bloody struggle between the two revolutionary groupings. The level of conflict declined sharply by the spring of 1964, when the already weakened pro-

[9]We have counted 43 new cabinets between October 1945 and June 1967. Daniel Lerner has referred to Syria as "statistically the most unstable country, in terms of regime turnovers, anywhere in the world." Daniel Lerner, "Some Comments on Center-Periphery Relations," in *Comparing Nations*, ed. Richard Merritt and Stein Rokkan (New Haven: Yale University Press, 1966).

[10]See, for example, Malcolm Kerr, *The Arab Cold War 1958-1967* (New York: Oxford University Press, 1967); and Patrick Seale, *The Struggle for Syria* (London: Oxford University Press, 1965).

[11]Kerr, *Arab Cold War*, and Seale, *Struggle for Syria*, are good examples of this thesis.

[12]This period has not yet received adequate treatment in the scholarly literature. Some of the events of this period are presented in Kerr, *Arab Cold War*. See also Walter Laqueur, *The Road to Jerusalem* (New York: Macmillan Co., 1968), and Nadav Safran, *From War to War: The Arab-Israeli Confrontation*, 1948-1967 (New York: Pegasus Press, 1969).

Nasser elements were finally smashed in an aborted coup; however, the period of relative domestic tranquillity between mid-1964 and mid-1967 was broken by a coup of major consequences in early 1966, an attempted coup in late 1966, and a severe outbreak of domestic unrest in early 1967.

Syria's external politics during the same six-year period was marked by an active and progressively more militant pattern of international relations. Cautious cooperation with the United Arab Republic in 1966 and 1967, after four years of mostly bitter conflict, stands in marked contrast to the extremely high and increasing level of conflict toward Jordan, Israel, and the West. Syria worked hard in 1965 and 1966 to destroy the "spirit of the Arab summits," and to redraw the battlelines between the conservative monarchies and the progressive forces in the Arab world. At the same time, she led the way to a renewal of military conflict with Israel. Her almost exclusive patronage and control of the Palestine guerrilla movement between the beginning of 1965 and mid-1967 was a major component in her new policy of confrontation toward Israel. Initiatives by Syria during 1966 and early 1967, more than those of either the U.A.R. or Israel, set the stage for the coming of the Six Day War.

Data Making

The analysis in this study is performed on political event data. Different categories of events were used to operationalize the domestic and external politics of Syria; changes in the frequency of occurrence of these events were used to measure changes in the two political domains. This record of overt behavior—a record of who did what to (and/or with) whom in Syrian politics—was drawn from nine published sources: (1) the *Cahiers de l'Orient contemporain*, (2) the *Middle East Journal*, (3) the *New York Times Index*, (4) the *New York Times*, (5) the *Times* (London), (6) *Deadline Data*, (7) *Facts on File*, (8) *Keesing's Contemporary Archives*, and (9) the *Asian Recorder*. The *Cahiers* was decidedly the most productive source of event data on Syria. The *Middle East Journal, New York Times*, and *Times* (London) also yielded a considerable amount of data. The other sources were of a far more marginal nature.

The abstraction of events from these nine sources was guided by a large set of specific event categories. These categories were designed to be as mutually exclusive and exhaustive as possible. The category scheme used to abstract events, as well as the modified one used in the subsequent analysis, differed considerably from that used by Rummel and Tanter. The differences were dictated by practical and, to a lesser extent, theoretical considerations. The set of categories reflects a desire to measure cooperative as well as conflictual behavior in both the domestic and external political domains. In particular, external cooperation indicators were included in the belief that politicians may use external cooperation as often as conflict to cope with or manage domestic political difficulties. The choice of domestic indicators was also guided by a desire to distinguish between conflict and cooperation *by* the ruling elite and conflict and cooperation *toward* the ruling elite. A further distinction was desired in the domestic domain between acts by or toward counterelites and those by or toward nonelites. Finally, an attempt was made in both the domestic and external domains to maintain verbal/nonverbal and violent/nonviolent distinctions.

Practical considerations forced a partial retreat from the category scheme which was regarded as ideal conceptually and theoretically. Many categories had to be collapsed into more general categories or deleted altogether. In some instances, the recording of events by sources was not detailed or unambiguous enough to support the desired distinction. As often, the decision to delete or collapse categories was guided by low frequencies or severe distributional irregularities. An inspection of the scatterplots of pairs of indicators suggested that, even when log transformed, many of the series of data produced correlations which were highly unstable and the artifacts of many "zero-entries" and a few high values. In such cases, the choice lay between conceptual refinement and reliable results. In most instances, we chose to delete or collapse categories in order to increase our confidence in the results of the analysis. This process of compromise between prior concepts and the available data led to a final set of twenty-four domestic and external conflict and cooperation indicators, listed below.[13]

EXTERNAL DOMAIN

Conflict

1. Informal protests or accusations
2. Informal threats or warnings
3. Formal protests or warnings
4. Negative sanctions or other minor unfriendly acts
5. Isolated border skirmishes
6. Sustained military actions
7. Guerrilla acts

Cooperation

8. Low-level visits or meetings
9. High-level visits or meetings
10. Unilateral statements of friendship or common cause
11. Joint statements of friendship or common cause

[13]See appendix for both a brief discussion of some of the category decisions and the definitions of the final set of categories.

12. Acts of support or other minor friendly acts
13. Cultural, social, or minor economic agreements
14. Major economic, political, or military agreements

DOMESTIC DOMAIN

Conflict

15. Demonstrations or strikes against the government
16. Riots against the government
17. Verbal and nonverbal acts by counterelites against the government
18. Verbal conflict by the government
19. Government imposition of restrictions
20. Government punitive acts against nonelites
21. Government punitive acts against counterelites

Cooperation

22. Verbal and nonverbal support for the government
23. Government requests for support
24. Government acts designed to win support

The process of abstraction and coding yielded 4,710 domestic and external conflict and cooperation events. Nearly three times as many external as domestic events were identified (3,478 and 1,232 respectively). Whereas the external events were distributed rather evenly over the six years covered by this study, the domestic events were concentrated in the period before mid-1964.

The frequency of occurrence of each of the 24 indicators was summed for each of the 74 four-week periods from September 29, 1961 through June 4, 1967. Each of the 24 series of 74 observations was log transformed in order to minimize the effects of extreme values.[14] The resultant 24 × 74 matrix of transformed data provided the basis of the subsequent analysis.

Data Analysis

The search for relationships between Syria's domestic and external politics was preceded by a search for relationships within each of these two political domains. Pearson's product moment correlation was chosen to measure the strength of the intradomain bivariate relationships. The ten domestic and fourteen external indicators were then factor-analyzed[15]

[14]While the log $(x + 1)$ base 10 transformation did bring in the extreme values, it by no means created data that closely approximated a normal distribution. A large number of zero entries usually defeats all attempts to normalize the distributions on event indicators. This problem is especially prevalent when one is working with highly discriminating event categories and/or short time intervals.

[15]For a good discussion of factor analytic techniques, see R. J. Rummel, "Understanding Factor Analysis" *Journal of Conflict Resolution* 11 (December 1967): 444–80. See also the applications of these techniques by Rummel and Tanter, cited in notes 5 and 7.

separately to determine whether the two political domains could be described in terms of a smaller number of theoretically interpretable dimensions.

The search for relationships between the two domains of Syrian politics began with the correlation of each of the domestic indicators with each of the external indicators. The entire set of twenty-four domestic and external indicators was then factor-analyzed together. The purpose of this stage of the analysis was to determine whether certain dimensions of Syrian politics cut across the domestic and external domains. The relationships between the two domains were explored further by means of multiple stepwise regression. Factor scores for each four-week interval were computed for each dimension that had emerged in the separate factor analyses of the domestic and external domains. These scores were then used to determine the degree to which each of the external dimensions of Syrian politics could be predicted from the set of domestic dimensions, and vice versa.

Up to this point, the analyses were undertaken without the use of time lags. The search for relationships between Syria's domestic and external politics proceeded under the assumption that whatever relationships existed were simultaneous (i.e., relationships operated within rather than across four-week intervals). In the final stage of analysis, the factor scores on each domestic and external dimension were lagged one and two intervals on every other dimension, and then correlated. The lagged and unlagged correlation matrices were then compared to determine the effect of lagging upon the strength of the relationship between the members of each pair of dimensions. The temporal structure that provided the highest correlations among the several domestic and external dimensions was then utilized to create a set of nonsimultaneous regression models. The results of the multiple regression analysis based on lagged dimensions were then compared to those based on unlagged dimensions to determine the effect of time upon the ability of the entire set of domestic dimensions to predict each of the external dimensions, and vice versa. Finally, these results were used to draw some tentative conclusions about the direction of the relationship between domestic and external politics in Syria.

RESULTS

The following results and analyses apply only to Syria during the six years covered by this study. No claim can be made for their validity for other nations or even for Syria during any other period of time. Since the seventy-four four-week intervals are treated as a universe, rather than a sample drawn from a larger universe, tests of significance are not reported with the results.

Intradomain Correlations. The intercorrelation of the measures of each domain revealed striking differences in the domestic and external

Table 1.   Correlations Between Domestic Conflict and Cooperation Indicators[a]

	1	2	3	4	5	6	7	8	9
1. Demonstrations and strikes									
2. Conflict by counterelites	41								
3. Riots against government	65	58							
4. Verbal conflict by government	49	50	67						
5. Imposition of restrictions	56	42	74	63					
6. Punitive acts against counterelites	29	39	37	39	41				
7. Punitive acts against nonelites	58	51	81	67	65	43			
8. Acts of support for government	42	42	46	36	49	38	42		
9. Government requests for support	28	35	31	40	52	19	29	42	
10. Government acts to win support	45	21	44	36	50	29	44	32	44

[a]Correlations were rounded off and multiplied by 100. $N = 74$. Correlations $\geq .40$ are underlined for the purpose of visual clarity only.

politics of Syria. Table 1 shows a pattern of high correlations within the domestic domain, and suggests a strong tendency for many of the measures of domestic politics to vary with one another simultaneously over the period of this study. All of the domestic domain correlations were positive. Many of the domestic conflict measures correlated at .40 or higher with most of the other forms of domestic conflict. For example, riots, government imposition of restrictions and government punitive acts against nonelites were highly correlated[16] with each other, and were moderately or highly correlated with nearly every other form of domestic conflict or cooperation. Relationships were only slightly less strong in the case of demonstrations and strikes, verbal conflict by the government, and conflict by counterelites. The one domestic conflict measure that had no high domestic correlates was punitive acts against counterelites. The three domestic cooperation indicators were only moderately correlated with each other, and tended to have low or only moderate correlations with the measures of domestic conflict. Of the three, government requests for support varied most independently from the conflict indicators.

In marked contrast, the measures of Syria's external conflict and cooperation were far less highly intercorrelated. The 14 × 14 matrix shown in table 2 contains only eight correlations of .40 or higher. Moreover, six of the eight occurred between pairs of external conflict measures. The several forms of external cooperation were not strongly related to one another or to the several forms of external conflict. Informal protests,

[16]For the purposes of this paper, a "strong" or "high" correlation is .50 or higher, and "moderately" high or strong correlation is .40 or higher.

Table 2. Correlations Between External Conflict and Cooperation Indicators[a]

	1	2	3	4	5	6	7	8	9	10	11	12	13
1. Informal protests													
2. Informal threats	58												
3. Formal protests and warnings	31	35											
4. Minor unfriendly acts	47	53	30										
5. Insolated border skirmishes	27	23	25	13									
6. Military actions	06	14	46	13	24								
7. Guerrilla acts	55	59	19	33	10	12							
8. Low-level visits	29	41	28	35	19	21	14						
9. High-level visits	15	09	-11	28	-01	00	02	00					
10. Unilateral statements of friendship	18	24	-03	-11	13	-06	15	08	-07				
11. Joint statements of friendship	26	24	-05	22	-10	01	26	29	47	-04			
12. Minor friendly acts	-11	-13	-15	-05	-10	-20	-17	06	02	09	-06		
13. Minor agreements	20	22	03	15	07	07	24	22	00	-08	27	-13	
14. Major agreements	-05	05	-14	-03	00	-07	-03	03	25	11	20	-06	21

[a]Correlations ≥ .40 were underlined for the purpose of visual clarity only. Correlations were rounded off and multiplied by 100. $N = 74$.

informal threats, and guerrilla acts were strongly related to one another and were somewhat less strongly related to minor unfriendly acts. Formal protests or warnings was the only moderately high correlate of military actions, and neither of these two forms of conflict was a moderately high correlate of informal protests, informal threats, minor unfriendly acts, or guerrilla acts. The only moderately strong relationship between an external conflict indicator and an external cooperation indicator was that of informal threats and low-level visits, and the only moderately strong relationship between two external cooperation indicators was that of high-level visits and joint statements of friendship. Isolated border skirmishes, quite surprisingly, was the one external conflict measure that failed to have a moderately high correlation with any of the other indicators of external conflict or cooperation. The same was the case for four of the external cooperation measures: unilateral statements of friendship, minor friendly acts, minor agreements, and major agreements.

Intradomain Factor Analyses.   The separate factor analyses of the domestic and external domains revealed a fundamental structural difference in the domestic and external politics of Syria. Intimations of this difference had appeared in the correlational analyses of the separate domains. The attempt to extract factors according to Kaiser's criterion[17] indicated the unidimensional nature of domestic conflict and cooperation in Syria. Unfortunately, the single domestic factor that emerged using this criterion explained only 51.7 percent of the variance among the ten domestic political measures. For this reason, and for reasons of interpretation, this solution was discarded in favor of a three-factor solution. (A two-factor solution was discarded for the same reasons.) The three factors extracted in the principal components solution were then subjected to orthogonal (varimax) and oblique (oblimin) rotations to achieve simple structure and a more invariant solution. The low correlations among the obliquely rotated factors led us to choose the orthogonal solution. Table 3 presents the orthogonally rotated three-factor solution. Certain characteristics of this solution recommended it for use in the subsequent analysis. First, the three factors collectively explained a considerable portion of the total variance among the indicators (70.1 percent). Second, every indicator had a high loading on one and only one factor, and had a considerable portion of its variance (h^2) explained. Third, the distribution of high loadings on the three factors was susceptible to a meaningful and fairly straightforward interpretation.

The first factor extracted explains nearly half (47.6 percent) of the com-

----

[17]According to Kaiser's criterion, factors are extracted only so long as the eigenvalue or characteristic root of the factor is 1.00 or more. In other words, every factor extracted must explain one "unit" of variance, there being as many units of variance as variables in the factor analysis.

Table 3. Factor Analysis of Domestic Domain Indicators

Measures	Factors and Factor Loadings [a]			h^2 (Percent)
	I	II	III	
1. Demonstrations and strikes	75	−13	23	63
2. Riots against government	85	−32	16	86
3. Government verbal conflicts	69	−36	20	65
4. Imposition of restrictions	66	−28	47	74
5. Punitive acts against nonelites	83	−33	12	80
6. Conflict by counterelites	39	−69	07	64
7. Punitive acts against counterelites	21	−74	08	60
8. Support for government	19	−61	47	63
9. Government requests for support	10	−25	85	80
10. Government acts to win support	46	06	68	67
Percent Common Variance	47.6	27.2	25.2	100.0
Percent Total Variance	33.4	19.1	17.6	70.1

[a]Factor loadings are rounded off and multiplied by 100. Orthogonally rotated factor solution. $N = 74$. Unities were placed in the main diagonal.

mon variance, and is clearly the most important factor in the Syrian domestic domain. This factor apparently is tapping an underlying dimension of conflict in Syria's domestic politics. Two of the five measures that load highly on this factor are measures of conflict by the government toward unspecified targets—verbal conflict by the government and government imposition of restrictions. However, the three indicators with the highest loadings on this factor—demonstrations and strikes, riots, and punitive acts against nonelites—all involve large numbers of nonelites. For this reason, we have chosen to interpret this as a "mass conflict" dimension in Syrian domestic politics.

The two remaining factors share rather equally the common variance not explained by the "mass conflict" dimension. As in the case of mass conflict, the second factor contains both conflict by and conflict toward the government. In this case, however, the targets of government conflict or agents of conflict against the government are counterelites. The reason for the relatively high loading of acts of support for the government is not self-evident. In reexamining the data comprising this indicator, we found that most of the events in this category were acts of support for the government by nonruling elites during periods of high level political conflict. Therefore, despite the tenuousness of this explanation, we have chosen to interpret this factor as an "elite conflict" dimension. The third factor lends itself more easily to interpretation. The two indicators with high loadings on this factor are government requests for support and government acts designed to win support. We have chosen to interpret this factor as a "government cooperation" dimension.

The factor analysis of the Syrian external indicators revealed a tendency directly opposite to the tendency toward unidimensionality in the domestic domain. The application of Kaiser's criterion for the number of factors extracted yielded a six-factor solution which explains 71.0 percent of the variance among the fourteen measures of external conflict and cooperation. The fact that twice as many factors were required to explain the same amount of variance suggests that the external politics of Syria was less highly structured than her domestic politics during the period of this study. The absence of a large number of high correlations between external indicators, as shown in table 2, anticipated the greater fragmentation in the external domain than in the domestic domain.

The orthogonally rotated factor solution was selected for analysis after oblique rotation established that the six factors were negligibly correlated. Table 4 presents the orthogonal solution for the seven external conflict

Table 4.   Factor Analysis of External Domain Indicators

Measures	\multicolumn{6}{c}{Factors and Factor Loadings[a]}	h^2 (Percent)
	I	II	III	IV	V	VI	
1. Informal protests	81	13	10	02	12	−02	70
2. Informal threats	79	22	07	16	18	−07	74
3. Minor unfriendly acts	62	25	31	−02	−27	−21	66
4. Guerrilla acts	81	−04	−04	15	06	22	73
5. Formal protest/threats	31	72	−15	−05	−13	−02	65
6. Border skirmishes	11	60	−01	−03	40	01	54
7. Military actions	00	78	02	06	−12	12	65
8. High-level visits	08	−02	91	−15	−04	00	86
9. Joint friendly statements	30	−13	63	35	−13	07	65
10. Major agreements	−21	−03	50	45	44	14	70
11. Minor agreements	19	00	−01	85	−08	06	77
12. Unilateral friendly statements	21	−08	−10	−09	84	−11	78
13. Low-level visits	28	39	07	42	02	−58	74
14. Minor friendly acts	−14	−25	−02	−16	08	−81	76
Percent Common Variance	27.6	18.7	16.3	13.5	12.4	11.5	100.0
Percent Total Variance	19.6	13.3	11.6	9.6	8.8	8.1	71.0

[a] Factor loadings are rounded off and multiplied by 100. Orthogonally rotated factor solution. $N = 74$. Unities were placed in the main diagonal.

and seven external cooperation measures. As in the case of the solution chosen for the domestic domain, this solution has much to recommend it. First, with the exception of major agreements, each indicator loads quite highly on one and only one factor. Second, with the exception of isolated border skirmishes, at least 65 percent of the variance (h^2) of each indicator is explained by the six factors. Finally, the loadings permit a fairly straightforward interpretation of the factors.

Distinctly different patterns are apparent among the measures of

Syria's external conflict and external cooperation. Conflict and cooperation indicators do not load highly together on any of the factors, suggesting that the two subdomains vary quite independently of one another. As important, the external conflict subdomain is far more highly structured than the cooperation subdomain. Two factors explain approximately two-thirds of the variation in the seven external conflict indicators, whereas four factors are required to explain only slightly more variance in the same number of external cooperation indicators.

The two external conflict factors together explain more than 45 percent of the common variance. The distribution of high conflict loadings on these two factors suggests an "indirect conflict" dimension and a "direct conflict" dimension. The former is defined by informal protests, informal threats, minor unfriendly acts, and guerrilla acts; the latter is defined by formal protests, isolated border skirmishes, and military actions. The "direct conflict" factor can be distinguished from the "indirect conflict" factor in terms of the formal and official nature of the indicators which load highly on it.

The external cooperation factor which contributes most to the common variance consists of high-level visits, joint statements of friendship, and major agreements. This factor clearly seems to be tapping a "high-level cooperation" dimension, and has been interpreted as such. Each of the three remaining cooperation factors explains approximately one-eighth of the common variance. Two indicators, minor friendly acts and low-level visits, load highly on one of these factors, leading us to interpret it as a "low-level cooperation" dimension. Each of the two remaining factors has only one very high loading: minor agreements in the one case and unilateral statements of friendship in the other. Major agreements has moderately high secondary loadings on both of these factors. These two rather questionable factors have been interpreted as a "minor agreements" dimension and a "unilateral verbal friendship" dimension.

Interdomain Correlations. The search for relationships between the domestic and external domains of Syrian politics began with the simple correlation of each of the original domestic indicators with each of the original external indicators. The results presented in table 5 suggest that the bivariate relationships between the two domains are considerably weaker than even those found within the external domain. Only 11 of the 144 interdomain correlations are .30 or higher, and only 1 of the 11 is higher than .40. Nevertheless, if treated with caution, these results do yield information which goes beyond the fact of general independence between Syria's domestic and external politics. To the degree that the two domains are not completely independent, they seem to covary in an inverse relationship. In other words, as the frequency of many of the types of events in the one domain increases, the frequency of many of the types of

Table 5. Correlations Between Domestic and External Conflict and Cooperation Indicators[a]

Domestic \ External	Informal protests	Informal threats	Formal protests and warnings	Minor unfriendly acts	Isolated border skirmishes	Military actions	Guerrilla acts	Low-level visits	High-level visits	Unilateral statements of friendship	Joint statements of friendship	Minor friendly acts	Minor agreements	Major agreements
Demonstrations and strikes	02	−06	−01	01	11	(−20)	−16	−07	−10	16	−10	04	−15	−19
Conflict by counterelites	17	00	−18	−05	06	(−33)	−01	03	(−26)	18	03	04	09	−03
Riots against the government	(−22)	−14	(−20)	−06	04	(−26)	(−22)	04	(−22)	16	−03	05	−11	−04
Verbal conflict by the government	14	07	−08	−06	00	−17	−12	09	−07	(30)	−04	11	(−20)	−07
Imposition of restrictions	08	−18	−14	−09	05	(−21)	(−21)	−05	−11	(20)	02	16	(−24)	−06
Punitive acts against counterelites	(30)	10	−05	−03	06	(−20)	−04	−02	04	09	12	05	−11	−01
Punitive acts against nonelites	00	−06	−06	−04	04	(−39)	(−30)	−07	−12	18	−03	12	−18	−12
Acts of support for the government	(37)	16	04	−07	16	(−27)	12	01	−17	(26)	−03	07	−08	06
Government requests for support	−07	(−33)	−03	−19	−06	(−20)	(−26)	−09	−16	15	−19	00	(−31)	−12
Government acts to win support	−13	(−33)	−16	−14	00	(−20)	(−41)	01	01	(20)	−12	(26)	(−39)	−12

[a] Correlations were rounded off and multiplied by 100. N = 74. Correlations ≥ .20 were put in parentheses for the purpose of visual clarity only.

events in the other domain decreases. Eight of the eleven correlations of .30 or higher are negative in form; furthermore, disregarding for a moment the negligible degree of relationship in most cases, nearly two-thirds of the total set of interdomain correlations are negative.

In addition, the small number of even modestly strong positive or negative relationships between domestic and external measures are not randomly distributed over the matrix of interdomain correlations. A disproportionately large number of these modest interdomain correlations involve the external conflict subdomain or the domestic cooperation subdomain. Eight of the eleven correlations of .30 or higher involve an external conflict indicator; only three involve an external cooperation indicator. At the same time, six of these eleven correlations of .30 or higher involve a domestic cooperation indicator, even though only three of the ten domestic indicators measure cooperation.

Turning to the individual indicators, it appears that certain external conflict or cooperation indicators are more strongly related to the domestic domain than are others. Military actions and guerrilla acts, which are very weakly related to each other, are the two external conflict indicators most strongly related to measures of Syria's domestic conflict and cooperation. Each has two interdomain correlations of .30 or higher, and each has a number of other interdomain correlations of .20 or higher. (Only one interdomain correlation for military actions fell below .20.) Neither the isolated border skirmishes nor the minor unfriendly acts indicator is even modestly related to measures of domestic conflict or cooperation. Of the external cooperation measures, minor agreements and unilateral statements of friendship both have a number of interdomain correlations of .20 or higher, whereas major agreements, joint statements of friendship, and low-level visits do not.

In contrast to the external domain, the domestic domain exhibits a pattern in which the individual domestic measures share more equally in the modestly strong interdomain relations. Nevertheless, some differences are apparent. Government acts designed to win support is the domestic measure which is most strongly related to the external domain. (Of its fourteen interdomain correlations, three are .30 or higher and another three are .20 or higher.) Government punitive acts against nonelites is unique in that all of its interdomain relationships are extremely weak except for correlations of .30 or higher with military actions and guerrilla acts. Finally, demonstrations and strikes seem unusually unrelated to any of the measures of Syria's external conflict or cooperation.

Interdomain Factor Analysis. The factor analysis of the total set of twenty-four original indicators served to confirm further the general independence of the domestic and external domains in Syria between 1961 and 1967. The application of Kaiser's criterion resulted in the extraction

Table 6. Factor Analysis of Domestic and External Domain Indicators

Measures	Factors and Factor Loadings[a]							h^2 (Percent)
	I	II	III	IV	V	VI	VII	
1. Demonstrations and strikes	73	-04	06	-08	12	09	01	58
2. Conflict by counterelites	69	13	-22	-21	-24	-11	-08	67
3. Riots	90	-15	-05	-08	-11	-01	-03	85
4. Government verbal conflict	77	06	01	00	09	-04	-16	64
5. Imposition of restrictions	81	-09	-02	04	22	-10	-01	72
6. Punitive acts against counterelites	55	23	-13	19	18	-05	15	47
7. Punitive acts against nonelites	86	-10	-05	-02	-01	06	-15	78
8. Support for government	58	34	-05	-13	20	-37	13	67
9. Government acts to win support	52	-30	02	09	47	-11	13	58
10. Government requests for support	47	-14	-03	-15	46	-15	-27	63
11. Low-level visits	10	21	47	16	-39	-01	-47	68
12. Informal protests	15	82	18	17	00	-06	07	77
13. Informal threats	-04	78	26	10	-23	-07	-13	76
14. Minor unfriendly acts	02	51	29	35	-13	37	-20	65
15. Guerrilla acts	-21	81	-02	-03	-14	-05	11	74
16. Formal protests/threats	-09	31	70	-13	09	18	05	65
17. Border skirmishes	11	13	61	-06	-04	-26	09	48
18. Military acts	-31	-03	73	01	-01	09	10	65
19. High-level visits	-15	05	-04	87	15	-01	-02	81
20. Joint friendly statements	03	23	-09	70	-30	02	01	65
21. Minor agreements	-11	15	01	-04	-79	06	12	67
22. Unilateral friendly statements	18	24	05	-15	14	-68	-28	68
23. Major agreements	-10	-16	-03	41	-31	-63	14	72
24. Minor friendly acts	04	-08	-25	-03	16	-06	-78	70
Percent Common Variance	32.2	17.8	12.2	11.1	11.0	8.2	7.5	100.0
Percent Total Variance	21.7	12.0	8.2	7.5	7.4	5.6	5.0	67.4

[a] Factor loadings are rounded off and multiplied by 100. Orthogonally rotated factor solution. $N = 74$. Unities were placed in the main diagonal.

of seven factors which collectively explained 67.4 percent of the variance. As in the previous factor analyses, the obliquely rotated solution revealed very low correlations among the factors. Table 6 presents the orthogonally rotated solution chosen for analysis. Factor I reveals the tendency toward undimensionality in the domestic politics of Syria; Factors II–VII for the most part faithfully reproduce the previously revealed structure of the external politics of Syria. What is of greatest interest to this study is the absence of any instances in which indicators from the two domains have loadings of .50 or higher on the same factor. The extremely low loadings of the external indicators on the single domestic conflict and cooperation dimension is particularly striking; except for the military actions indicator, which has a loading of .31, no measure of Syria's external politics has a loading higher than .21 on this dimension. Similarly, no domestic indicator had a moderately high loading on either the external "direct conflict" dimension or the external "indirect conflict" dimension. The same situation prevailed with three of the four external cooperation dimensions. The "minor external agreements" dimension is the one exception. Two domestic indicators—government acts designed to win support and government requests for support—had loadings of .46 and .47, respectively on this essentially external dimension. The former domestic indicator also had a loading of .52 on the domestic conflict and cooperation dimension, whereas the latter had a loading of .47 on this same dimension. Weakly related to the other measures in their own domain, these were the only measures of domestic politics that came close to forming a dimension which cut across the domestic and external politics of Syria between 1961 and 1967.

Interdomain Regression Analysis. The results of the factor analysis of the combined set of measures, which showed the domestic and external measures separated into different dimensions, suggest virtually no relationship between the two domains during this recent and turbulent period of Syria's political history. This apparent lack of relationship can be further investigated by means of multiple regression analysis. Whereas simple correlation can measure the strength of bivariate relationships, and factor analysis can detect underlying patterns of interrelationships among a large set of indicators, multiple regression analysis is particularly well suited to determine the form and strength of the relationship between a dependent variable and a small set of independent variables.

The results of the separate factor analyses of the two domains, reported in tables 3 and 4, were used to reduce the original twenty-four domestic and external indicators to a smaller number of intradomain composite indices. To do this, factor scores for each four-week interval were computed for each of the domestic and external dimensions.[18] This set of nine composite

[18]The FACTAN program in the University of Michigan's OSIRIS package was used to compute the factor scores. Unlike the factor scores computed by Rummel, which were based on only those indicators with loadings of .50 or higher on a factor, the scores used in this study are computed on the basis of the loadings of all the indicators on a factor. Since they

indices—three domestic and six external—were then used to determine the degree to which knowledge of the three domestic dimensions of Syria's politics could statistically predict the condition of each of her six external political dimensions, and vice versa. The nine composite indices, as defined by the nine domestic and external dimensions, are:

Domestic

1. Mass conflict
2. Elite conflict
3. Government cooperation

External

1. Indirect conflict
2. Direct conflict
3. High-level cooperation
4. Minor agreements
5. Unilateral friendly statements
6. Low-level cooperation

Table 7 suggests[19] that the scores on the three domestic dimensions were

**Table 7.   Multiple Regression of Six External Dimensions
on Three Domestic Dimensions**

Dependent Variable	Standard Deviation	Standard Error	Multiple R	R^2 (Percent)
Indirect conflict	1.00	.93	.41	17
Direct conflict	1.00	1.00	.21	4
High-level cooperation	1.00	1.00	.12	1
Minor agreements	1.00	.95	.38	15
Unilateral friendly statements	1.00	.99	.27	7
Low-level cooperation	1.00	.99	.25	6

Note: N = 74.

not good predictors; that is, variations in the several dimensions of external politics were not strongly dependent upon variations in domestic politics. The three domestic dimensions in combination explained only 17 percent and 15 percent of the variance (R^2) in the dimensions indirect external conflict and minor agreements, respectively; they explained considerably less of the variance in each of the other external dimensions. In short, the

---

are computed for factors in an orthogonally rotated solution, the factor scores on a dimension are uncorrelated with the factor scores on all other dimensions in that domain. This property allows us to use uncorrelated independent variables in our regression models.

[19]Since the regression analysis does not yield impressive results, we have decided not to report the cumulative regression, partial correlation coefficients and prediction equations.

results of the regression analysis do not support the notion that knowledge of Syria's domestic politics would have permitted accurate predictions about her external politics between 1961 and 1967.

The predictors and predictands were then reversed in order to test suggestions in the traditional literature of international politics that the external politics of a nation influences its domestic politics. Table 8 indicates

Table 8. Multiple Regression of Three Domestic Dimensions on Six External Dimensions

Dependent Variable	Standard Deviation	Standard Error	Multiple R	R^2 (Percent)
Mass conflict	1.00	.99	.32	10
Elite conflict	1.00	.93	.46	21
Government cooperation	1.00	.94	.45	20

Note: N = 74.

that the external dimensions are better predictors of the domestic dimensions than vice versa. In absolute terms, however, the several dimensions of Syria's external politics are not potent predictors of her domestic politics. They collectively explain 21 percent and 20 percent of the variance in domestic elite conflict and government cooperation, respectively; they explain considerably less of the variance in the major domestic domain dimension, mass conflict. According to these results, Syria's volatile domestic politics during the period of this study were quite independent of her equally volatile relations with the rest of the world.

Interdomain Time-Lagged Regression Analysis. Up to this point, the search for relationships between Syria's domestic and external politics has proceeded under the assumption that whatever relations existed were simultaneous—that is, they operated within rather than across the time intervals. In the final stage of the analysis, the dependent variable in each of the nine regression models was lagged one and two intervals on each of the independent variables in the model. The temporal structure which optimized the predictive power of each of the models was estimated through a careful inspection of the simple correlation matrix of the lagged and unlagged factor scores. For example, this rather impressionistic empirical procedure led us to conclude that indirect external conflict at time t might best be predicted by domestic nonelite conflict at $t - 1$, government cooperation at $t - 2$, and domestic elite conflict at t. The goal in each case was to find a sequential pattern among the dependent and independent variables which both increased the amount of variance explained and lent itself to a meaningful interpretation.

Table 9 shows that the introduction of time lags did not change the re-

Table 9.   Time-Lagged Multiple Regression of Six External Dimensions
on Three Domestic Dimensions

Dependent Variable	Standard Deviation	Standard Error	Multiple R	R^2 (Percent)
Indirect conflict	.90	.83	.46	21
Direct conflict	1.01	.98	.31	10
High-level cooperation	.99	1.00	.17	3
Minor agreements	.99	.90	.47	22
Unilateral friendly statements	1.00	.99	.28	8
Low-level cooperation	.99	.98	.27	7

Note: N = 72.

sults to a considerable degree.[20] Lags of one or two intervals—that is, four or eight weeks—only slightly increased the ability to predict from the domestic dimensions to indirect external conflict, direct external conflict, and minor agreements; in the cases of high-level cooperation, low-level cooperation, and unilateral friendly statements, the increase was imperceptible. Similarly, table 10 indicates that the introduction of lags does not greatly

Table 10.   Time-Lagged Multiple Regression of Three Domestic Dimensions
on Six External Dimensions

Dependent Variable	Standard Deviation	Standard Error	Multiple R	R^2 (Percent)
Mass conflict	1.00	.94	.45	20
Elite conflict	1.00	.94	.45	20
Government cooperation	.99	.89	.52	27

Note: N = 72.

improve the ability to predict from the external dimensions to the domestic dimensions. The results confirm only modest increases in the variance explained in the domestic nonelite conflict and government cooperation dimensions. In the former case, the variance explained rose from 10 percent to 20 percent; in the latter case, it rose from 20 percent to 27 percent. On the basis of the results reported in tables 9 and 10, it is difficult to maintain that the use of time lags holds the key to the discovery of strong linkages between the domestic and external politics of Syria.

As a final point, what tables 7–10 do not show is that the relatively weak lagged or unlagged relationships between the dimensions of Syria's domestic politics and those of her external politics tended to be negative during

[20]Since the attempt to introduce lags did not greatly change the results, we have decided not to report the temporal structure that was built into each of the nine regression equations.

the period from 1961 to 1967—that is, they had an inverse relationship with one another. As in the case of the interdomain correlations of the original domestic and external indicators, both the correlations of the lagged and unlagged dimensions and the coefficients in the lagged and unlagged regression models usually were negatively signed. In other words, to the extent that increases in the scores on the domestic dimensions did predict the scores on the external dimension, they predicted a decrease in those scores. This same negative relationship prevailed in the case of the slightly greater ability of the external dimensions to predict each of the domestic dimensions.

CONCLUSIONS AND DISCUSSION

This study has used a variety of data-making and data-analysis techniques to determine the strength and direction of relationships between the domestic and external politics of Syria during the period from the breakup of the U.A.R. in 1961 to the outbreak of the Six-Day War in June 1967. Though conceived to prove the contrary, the study basically confirms the finding of R. J. Rummel and Raymond Tanter that the domestic and external politics of nations are largely independent of one another. Our results differ from their results only in the details. As in their studies, the results of correlational analysis, factor analysis, and multiple regression analysis uniformly brought into serious question the commonly held notion that the two domains are strongly related.

These similar findings emerged despite basic differences in research design. The longitudinal analysis of a single nation did not uncover the relationships which Rummel and Tanter failed to find in their cross-sectional analyses of many nations—and this despite the fact that the nation chosen was selected because its politics often has been characterized in terms of the interdependence of the two domains. The use of shorter time intervals, intervals which seemed intuitively to be more suited to the subject of study than three-year intervals, and the lagging of indices one or more intervals, also failed to yield appreciably different results. Finally, the use of a different category scheme, one which included domestic and external cooperation as well as conflict, served only to confirm the findings of Rummel and Tanter.

This study is not the final chapter in the search for relationships between the domestic and external politics of nations. It is still quite probable that the failure to find these relationships is due less to their absence then to the crudeness of the various designs used to study them. If important relationships between the two political domains exist, they are probably of a rather complex nature. If so, then the failure of this study and others to isolate them should not be surprising. Despite its several refinements, the design of this study is quite naive. A major weakness it shares with the designs of Rummel and Tanter is its monolithic treatment of a nation's external environment; relationships are sought between a nation's domestic politics and the external environment as a whole. Quite probably, however, the relationships between the domestic and external politics of any given nation will vary considerably depending on the target of its external conflict and cooperation. It may be that political elites regularly use external conflict to cope with or manage domestic unrest only in the case of certain external targets—for example, traditional enemies, smaller nations, more remote nations, and so on. If so, then the treatment of the external environment as a single entity can only serve to confound the search for relationships between the two domains. In short, the most elementary knowledge of international politics suggests the need to use targeted external data. Preliminary analysis of targeted Syrian data points rather clearly to differences in the relationship between Syria's domestic politics and her external acts toward the U.A.R., Israel, and the United States.

Another weakness in the design of this study lies in the decision to test for relationships between domestic and external politics over the entire set of time intervals. The implicit assumption that relationships hold over all time periods, which is equivalent to Rummel's and Tanter's assumption that they hold over all nations, may have led to confounding results. It may be that relationships between domestic and external politics which exist during one period do not exist at another period. Indeed, some preliminary correlational analysis and an O-factor analysis[21] suggest that the relationship between Syria's domestic and external politics did undergo a fundamental change in early 1964. Relationships that prevailed before this time do not seem to prevail thereafter. Future designs will have to allow for the analysis of temporal subsets in which different relationships between domestic and external politics are suspected to prevail.

Finally, the designs used in this study and those of Rummel and Tanter were restricted to an unmediated relationship between domestic and external politics. No attempt was made to build even simple psychological or "state of mind" variables into the hypothetical relationships, much less to collect data on such variables. In the same sense, no attempt was made to control for possibly important situational factors which might have conditioned the relationships between the two domains.

The search for relationships in nature requires designs which best cap-

[21]O-factor analysis is the longitudinal equivalent of the more widely used cross-sectional Q-factor analysis. For an example of the use of this technique to find a cutting-point in a set of time series, see Robert Burrowes and José Garriga-Picó, "The Road to the Six Day War: A Relational Analysis of Conflict and Cooperation Within and Between the Arab-Israeli and Inter-Arab Political Domains," in *Methodologies in Search of Relevance: Assessing Arab-Israeli Relations,* ed. Joseph D. Ben-Dak (New York: Gordon and Breach, forthcoming).

ture the complexities of those relationships. If relationships exist between the domestic and external politics of nations, they probably do so only for certain types of nations, at certain times, and under certain circumstances. Further inquiry in this area will require that these and other conditions be identified and built into our theoretical frameworks and research designs.

APPENDIX
Coding Category Decisions and the Definitions of the Final Set of Twenty-four Indicators

The external and domestic data were originally coded into an inclusive set of forty-eight mutually exclusive categories. These categories were first intercorrelated to determine the strength of both the intradomain and interdomain correlations. At this time, frequency distributions of each of the indicators were examined to determine the mean frequency and the presence of such distributional irregularities as zero entries and extreme values.

Next, the original forty-eight indicators were aggregated (summed) in such a way as to form all of the conceptually justifiable combinations of indicators. Each of the resulting aggregate indicators was intercorrelated with every other one and with the original unaggregated set of indicators. Frequency distributions of the newly formed aggregations were inspected and compared with the original indicators.

Finally, the set of mutually exclusive aggregated and unaggregated indicators to be used in the analysis was selected on the basis of the interplay of the following two criteria: (1) the correlations of the indicator with other indicators within its own domain and with indicators in the other domain, and (2) the distributional characteristics of the indicator.

This decision process led us to eliminate many categories, among them attempted coups, acts of terrorism, and implementation of agreements. The extremely low frequencies of coup attempts ($N = 9$) and acts of terrorism ($N = 29$), and the unstable correlations they produced, led us to deny them separate status in the final set of indicators. The attempt to aggregate them together or with other indicators also proved unsatisfactory. As a result, these data were deleted altogether.

The reasoning behind the elimination of implementations of external agreements was based less on distributional irregularities than on its "fit" within the correlation matrix. By itself, this indicator correlated at very low levels with each of the other indicators. When it was aggregated with external acts of support, the strength of many of the correlations between external acts of support and other measures decreased. On this basis, we decided to exclude implementation of agreements from this analysis.

The definitions of the final set of twenty-four indicators are:

1. *Informal protests or accusations:* public statements by the incumbent political leaders of a country or their spokesmen that contain a charge, protest, accusation, or slur against another country or countries which are not formally lodged with the subject country, countries, or an international body. Editorials in or broadcasts on controlled mass media are counted as informal protests or accusations if they are of this nature.

2. *Informal threats or warnings:* public but not formally lodged statements by the incumbent political leaders of a country or their spokesmen that state or imply that a country or countries will be subjected to certain deprivations if they act or fail to act in a specified way. Such threats may include the negative sanctions listed below in item 4, as well as threats of war, military action, or diplomatic sanctions. Statements containing such threats in state-controlled mass media are counted.

3. *Formal protests or warnings:* official spoken or written diplomatic communications of the above nature (items 1 and 2) that are formally lodged with the subject country, countries, or an international body. Public statements made in connection with a formal protest are counted as informal protests (e.g., speeches or press statements at the U.N.).

4. *Negative sanctions or other minor unfriendly acts:* hostile acts such as official boycotts, diplomatic sanctions, granting asylum, nurturing dissident nationalists, deportations, warning of foreigners, breaking off or postponing talks, refusal to apologize or accept guilt, rejecting offers, withdrawal of military or economic aid, freezing of assets, embargoes, or official acts against the life, property, or freedom of movement of foreign nationals. Troop movements or mobilizations are included, as are government sponsored or tolerated antiforeign demonstrations and anti-foreign statements by public figures outside the government.

5. *Isolated border skirmishes:* Incidents of short duration (less than one hour) that involve small arms fire and/or incursions over the borders of a nation. They often involve border guards or civilians and often are accidental and nonreciprocal in nature.

6. *Sustained military actions:* long-term and major military battles involving the regular forces of a country directed against the territory, property, or citizens of another country. Included are sustained air attacks, tank and artillery bombardments, and assaults or invasions.

7. *Guerrilla actions:* skirmishes, exchanges of gunfire, and acts of terror-

ism and sabotage attributed to independent guerrilla commando units or individual members of guerrilla organizations. During the period from 1961 to 1967, the guerrilla movement was almost exclusively supported and controlled by the Syrian government leaders.

8. *Low-level visits:* visits to or from a country by lesser governmental, political, or quasi-public figures such as members of economic, trade-union, or cultural delegations. The publicized meeting of an ambassador with the leader of the country to which he is assigned is counted in this category.

9. *High-level visits:* visits to or from a country by top governmental, military, or political figures. Heads of state, premiers, chiefs of staff, important cabinet members (defense, economic, and foreign ministers), and top leaders of the ruling party are included.

10. *Unilateral statements of friendship or common cause:* statements or declarations by the incumbent political leaders of a country of friendship for or common cause with another country or group of countries.

11. *Joint statements of friendship or common cause:* verbal or written communiques or declarations of friendship and/or common cause issued jointly by the executive leaders of two or more countries. Such statements often follow important visits, and are counted separately.

12. *Acts of support or other minor friendly acts:* offer or use of "good offices," transfer or unblocking of funds, easing of trade and exchange controls; apologies, acceptance of offers, invitations, exchange or repatriation of personnel, opening borders, presentation or acceptance of credentials, arrival of ambassador, signing of protocols, ratification of agreement, exchange of ratification agreement, and establishment or elevation of diplomatic relations.

13. *Cultural, social, or minor economic agreements:* agreements that provide for the flow over a specified time period of specified amounts of money, credit, goods, technical assistance, cultural items, or persons from one country to another.

14. *Major economic, political, or military agreements:* alliances, defense pacts, treaties, political-economic agreements of a general, long-term nature that are formally signed by the executive leaders of two or more countries. These agreements often provide the framework within which the more specific, short-term agreements (item 13) are reached and executed.

15. *Demonstrations or strikes against the government:* nonviolent, nonverbal behavior in which the nonelite are participants. Included are public gatherings or meetings designed to express hostility toward other political groups or the authority, leaders, or policies of the government, and withdrawals of labor from places of private or public employment regardless of whether the action is actually work-related.

The closing of shops by merchants and the withdrawal of services by the self-employed are counted. Demonstrations and strikes in different cities are counted as separate events.

16. *Riots against the government:* violent, nonverbal behavior in which the nonelite are participants. Included are public manifestations involving violence, regardless of the initiator or user of violent actions. Incidents between rival military garrisons are counted if they are not part of a concerted, immediate effort to overthrow the government.

17. *Verbal and nonverbal acts by the counterelite against the government:* nonviolent behavior including petitions, manifestos, declarations, or ultimatums that contain an implicit or explicit warning, threat, accusation or criticism of the government, its leaders, or policies. Resignations by cabinet ministers or other high-ranking government officials are included. Strike threats are also included, as are statements that explain voluntary resignations or refusals to participate in a government or governmental program. Ultimatums by mutinous garrisons are included if they are not a part of a concerted effort to overthrow the government.

18. *Verbal conflict by the government:* nonviolent behavior in which both the counterelite and nonelite are targets. Includes spoken or written statements or declarations by incumbent political leaders or their spokesmen that contain implicit or explicit warnings, threats, accusations or criticisms of opposition groups or leaders. Statements of punitive or hostile intent are included (e.g., the announcement that wrongdoers will be tried).

19. *Government imposition of restrictions:* nonviolent, nonverbal behavior in which both the counterelite and nonelite are targets. Includes actions designed to maintain or restore order in periods of domestic turmoil; declaration of emergency, state of seige, or martial law; suspension of constitution or executive assumption of legislative power; closing of schools, roads, borders, or airports; imposition of curfew or censorship; ban on partisan activity, demonstration, or bearing of arms; creation of special tribunals; mobilization or movement of military or police for reasons of internal security.

20. *Government punitive acts against the nonelite:* violent and nonviolent nonverbal behavior. Includes arrest, detainment, trial, imprisonment, execution, retirement, pensioning off, transfer, demotion, or other deprivation or punishment of citizens and lesser officials or military personnel (NCO's). The closing or seizure of shops, small businesses, and other private property is included. Arrested demonstrators, strikers, or terrorists are assumed to be nonelite unless otherwise identified.

21. *Government punitive acts against the counterelite:* nonviolent nonverbal behavior. Includes dismissal, purges, demotion, arrest, de-

tention, trial, imprisonment or exile of top officials, politicians, military officers, or other leaders of society. Banning of a particular party, newspaper, trade union, or any political organization. Seizure or nationalization of property of economic and social elites.

22. *Verbal and nonverbal support for the government:* behavior in which both the counterelite and nonelite are participants. Includes statements or declarations by groups or leaders outside the incumbent government that pledge support or endorse the government and/or its policies. Also, pro-government demonstrations or rallies.

23. *Government requests for support:* verbal behavior in which both the nonelite and counterelite are targets. Includes statements or delarations by the incumbent political elite or its spokesman that call for national unity, support, or sacrifice to defeat common enemies or achieve common goals.

24. *Government acts designed to win support:* nonverbal behavior in which both the nonelite and counterlite are targets. Includes acts or statements of friendship by the government designed to generate support, lessen opposition, or allay fears within the citizenry. Acts freeing prisoners, dropping of charges, waiving tuition, raising pensions, and distributions of land are counted.

PART III

DOMESTIC CONFLICT BEHAVIOR LINKAGES

.11. A Linkage Model of Domestic Conflict Behavior

JONATHAN WILKENFELD
and
DINA A. ZINNES

THE RELATIONSHIP between aspects of a nation's domestic situation and its foreign policy outputs has received considerable attention in recent years. The bulk of these studies have dealt with foreign conflict behavior as one form of policy outcome. While one group of studies has been concerned with attribute and behavior variables as contributors to foreign policy outcomes,[1] a second group has dealt specifically with conflict behavior as one aspect of foreign policy behavior in general, and has attempted to specify the variables that may be important in explaining the extent, as well as the timing, of such behavior.[2]

A much less frequently dealt with notion is that involving the domestic consequences of foreign policy actions. In particular, our concern here is with the extent to which external events can predict to domestic conflict behavior. While little empirical work has been done on this important question, we must agree with Kelly and Miller:

---

[1] R. J. Rummel, "The Relationship Between National Attributes and Foreign Conflict Behavior," in *Quantitative International Politics*, ed. J. David Singer (New York: Free Press, 1968), pp. 187–214; Michael Haas, "Societal Approaches to the Study of War," *Journal of Peace Research* 2 (1965): 308–23; idem, "Social Change and National Aggressiveness, 1900–1960," in Singer, ed., *Quantitative International Politics*. See also papers by Haas (chap. 7), Leo A. Hazlewood (chap. 6), and Richard H. Van Atta (chap. 8), this volume.

[2] R. J. Rummel, "Dimensions of Conflict Behavior Within and Between Nations," chap. 3, this volume; Raymond Tanter, "Dimensions of Conflict Behavior Within and Between Nations, 1958–1960," *Journal of Conflict Resolution* 10 (March 1966): 41–64; Jonathan Wilkenfeld, "Domestic and Foreign Conflict," chap. 4, this volume; idem, "Models for the Analysis of Foreign Conflict Behavior of States," in *Peace, War, and Numbers*, ed. Bruce M. Russett (Beverly Hills, Calif.: Sage Publications, 1972); Dina A. Zinnes and Jonathan Wilkenfeld, "An Analysis of Foreign Conflict Behavior of Nations," in *Comparative Foreign Policy*, ed. Wolfram F. Hanrieder (New York: David McKay Co., 1971), pp. 167–213; Robert Burrowes and Bertram Spector, "The Strength and Direction of Relationships Between Domestic Conflict and External Conflict and Cooperation: Syria, 1961–67," chap. 10, this volume.

From the perspective of the performance of domestic systems, we can scarcely neglect impinging international forces, in the great states because they are intimately involved in critical transactions, in the small states because they are weak and dependent.[3]

Perhaps the classic empirical study on this phenomenon is that of Pitirim A. Sorokin.[4] The following constitutes a listing of Sorokin's major conclusions:

1. Most of the internal crises ... come and pass their acute stage within a period of a few weeks.
2. There is hardly any periodicity in the ups and downs of internal disturbances.
3. There may be a very slight tendency for disturbances to occur more frequently in a period of (international) war and in the years nearest wars; but the tendency is neither strong, consistent, nor quite tangible.
4. Disturbances have occurred not only in the periods of the decay and decline of society, but in its periods of blossoming and healthy growth.
5. The forces generating disturbances rarely, if ever, work in one country only.[5]

Thus, Sorokin is forced to conclude that war, whether successful or unsuccessful, is neither a necessary nor a sufficient condition for starting or reinforcing internal disturbances.[6] Kelly and Miller, while rejecting the notion of a direct relationship between external and internal conflict behavior, maintain that there are nevertheless certain linkage patterns within specific civilizations.

"Civilizations" contain motives or factors of revolutionary disturbance which either transcend the authority problems of the individual political units included or else may be regarded as pertinent to other, more osmotic and extensive "systems," cultural or economic. Unlike an international "war system," which must be described in terms of the component political units, the idea of generalized "civilizational" disturbance describes antagonisms carried by the printed page, trade, disease, or religion that do not, so to speak, stop at the *douane*.[7]

The specific focus of the present study will be the extent to which we may explain a portion of the domestic conflict behavior of nations as a

---

[3]George A. Kelly and Linda B. Miller, "Internal War and International Systems: Perspectives on Method," in *Struggles in the State,* ed. George A. Kelly and Clifford W. Brown, Jr. (New York: John Wiley and Sons, 1970), p. 230.

[4]Pitirim A. Sorokin, *Social and Cultural Dynamics*, abridged (Boston: Porter Sargent, 1957).

[5]Quoted in Kelly and Miller, "Internal War," p. 239.

[6]Pitirim A. Sorokin, "Quantitative Measurement of Internal Disturbances," in Kelly and Brown, eds., *Struggles in the State,* p. 141.

[7]Kelly and Miller, "Internal War," pp. 239–40.

consequence of the type and degree of foreign conflict behavior the nation has experienced. Several recent studies have used correlation and regression models with and without time lags to investigate this relationship.[8] The question asked in these studies is whether the amount of domestic conflict at one point in time is linearly associated with the amount of foreign conflict at a specified point in time. In most instances, only very weak relationships were found. But the scarcity of studies devoted to this relationship and the similarity in the research designs of these studies leads not to the conclusion that no relationship exists, but rather to the suggestion that another research strategy should be adopted. The present study proposes a different conceptualization of the relationship between the variables, utilizing a nonlinear model.

THE MODEL

In the earlier studies the basic relationship examined was between foreign conflict behavior as the independent variable, and domestic conflict behavior as the dependent variable. Thus, it was speculated that under certain circumstances there may be domestic reaction to foreign involvement. Overextension abroad, with the consequent neglect of domestic problems, may lead to domestic repercussions. Perhaps, however, foreign conflict behavior is a "mediating" or "intervening" variable that affects or tempers a more basic relationship between domestic conflict behavior at one point in time and domestic conflict behavior at another point in time. Or to state it somewhat differently, perhaps foreign conflict behavior affects *changes* in domestic conflict behavior rather than the absolute amounts of domestic conflict at a given point in time. Thus we will examine the following two ingredients of this proposed process: (1) Holding the level of foreign conflict behavior constant, is there a relationship between domestic conflict behavior at one point in time and domestic conflict behavior at the next point in time? Having determined this answer, we can then ask (2) whether the level of foreign conflict behavior affects the changes or transitions over time between levels of domestic conflict behavior.

The analyses proposed in (1) and (2) are in effect a Markovian interpretation of the relationship between foreign and domestic conflict behavior: a prior level of domestic conflict behavior affects a subsequent level of domestic conflict behavior and foreign conflict behavior affects these transitions. Accordingly, we will analyze transition matrices that describe changes in the level of a state's domestic conflict behavior over time. The

[8]Wilkenfeld, "Domestic and Foreign Conflict"; Leo A. Hazlewood, "Political Violence and the Political System" (Ph.D. diss., University of Pennsylvania, 1969); Michael Stohl, "The Study of Conflict Behavior Within and Between Nations: Some New Evidence" (Paper delivered at the Midwest Political Science Association Meetings, Chicago, 1971).

construction of these matrices and the analyses performed on them make no assumptions about linearity. A description of the construction of these matrices and the types of analyses performed will be presented after a brief review of the data.

In several of the more recent studies,[9] it has been noted that more relationships are uncovered by controlling for the type of state. Consequently, the analyses will first be done for all states combined, and then separately for three groups of states. The grouping of states is explained below and generally corresponds to the classification of states used in the earlier studies.

THE DATA

The data for the present study were collected by R. J. Rummel and Raymond Tanter in connection with the Dimensionality of Nations Project. Specifically, the data were collected for seventy-four nations for the period between 1955 and 1960. There are nine measures of domestic conflict and thirteen measures of foreign conflict. The exact nature of these data has been adequately described elsewhere.[10] (For the list of nations included in the study, and for the definitions of conflict variables, see appendices 1 and 2 of the Rummel study.)[11]

Factor analysis was employed in order to identify the specific dimensions of domestic and foreign conflict behavior. These analyses resulted in two domestic factors—turmoil and internal war—and three foreign factors—war, belligerency, and diplomatic conflict. The results of these factor analyses are discussed elsewhere,[12] and are summarized in tables 1 and 2.

The data for the Markov analysis proper are the factor scores that emerged from these factor analyses. These factor scores allow us to define three levels of intensity of conflict behavior: 0, 1, and 2. The $D = 0$ or $F = 0$ levels were those in which, for a given year, the factor scores indicated that there was either no domestic or no foreign conflict behavior of that type. It was less easy to determine the proper cutoff points between the $D = 1$ and $D = 2$ levels, and between the $F = 1$ and $F = 2$ levels. The factors scores for each factor were plotted. An inspection of these plots indicated an appropriate point at which the intensity of conflict became quite high, while the number of cases dropped sharply. It was this point which was chosen to differentiate between levels 1 and 2.

[9]See Wilkenfeld, "Domestic and Foreign Conflict"; Hazlewood, "Political Violence"; Stohl, "Study of Conflict Behavior."

[10]Rummel, "Dimensions of Conflict Behavior"; Tanter, "Dimensions of Conflict Behavior"; Wilkenfeld, "Domestic and Foreign Conflict."

[11]Rummel, "Dimensions of Conflict Behavior."

[12]See Wilkenfeld, "Domestic and Foreign Conflict."

Table 1.   Factor Analysis of Domestic Conflict Behavior Variables, 1955–60
Orthogonal Rotation

Variables	Internal War	Turmoil	h^2
Assassinations	.30	.47	.31
Guerrilla warfare	(.72)	.09	.52
Government crises	(.53)	.35	.40
Revolutions	(.80)	.12	.65
Strikes	.25	(.62)	.44
Purges	(.53)	.15	.30
Riots	.23	(.81)	.71
Demonstrations	.02	(.85)	.72
Domestic killed	(.67)	.42	.63
Percent Common Variance	50.6	49.4	100.0
Percent Total Variance	26.3	25.7	52.0

Note: Parenthesis indicates loading ≥ .50.

Table 2.   Factor Analysis of Foreign Conflict Behavior Variables, 1955–60
Orthogonal Rotation

Variables	War	Belligerency	Diplomatic	h^2
Severence of diplomatic relations	.14	(.64)	−.32	.54
Expulsions and recalls– ambassadors	.09	−.03	(.55)	.31
Military actions	(.62)	.17	.18	.45
Wars	(.80)	−.04	.16	.67
Troop movements	.08	.09	(.62)	.40
Mobilizations	(.56)	.25	−.05	.38
Antiforeign demonstrations	.21	(.56)	.13	.38
Negative sanctions	.16	(.64)	.21	.48
Protests	.34	.26	(.66)	.62
Expulsions and recalls– lesser officials	−.23	(.56)	.38	.51
Threats	.40	.48	(.51)	.66
Accusations	.47	.42	(.50)	.65
Foreign killed	(.77)	.09	.21	.65
Percent Common Variance	38.8	30.4	30.8	100.0
Percent Total Variance	20.0	15.7	15.9	51.6

Note: Parenthesis indicates loading ≥ .50.

THE ANALYSES

Each of the seventy-four states received a 0, 1, or 2 value for each of the years from 1955 to 1960 for each of the three foreign conflict factors and two domestic conflict factors.   For a given foreign or domestic factor, then, there are 74 states × 6 years or 444 data points. These data values (factor scores) are then transferred to transition matrices. The transition matrix is constructed for the transitions between D_n and D_{n+1} for a given level of F_n, where D_n is the level of domestic conflict at time n, D_{n+1} is the level of domestic conflict at time $n + 1$, and F_n is the level of foreign conflict at time n. If we ignore for the moment the variable F_n and consider only the transitions between D_n and D_{n+1}, the following matrix may be constructed:

$$D_{n+1}$$

A given state has six scores for one of the domestic conflict factors, one domestic conflict score for each year. These scores are either 0, 1, or 2. We now consider pairs of successive years and note the frequency with which certain transitions are made. Suppose the state's factor scores for the years 1955 to 1960, converted to levels of intensity are, in order: 0, 0, 1, 1, 1, 2. We note that there is one transition from 0 to 0, one transition from 0 to 1, two transitions from 1 to 1, and one transition from 1 to 2. A similar analysis is done for each of the seventy-four states and the resulting frequencies are entered in the above matrix. Transition probabilities are then obtained from this basic data matrix by dividing each cell entry by the sum of the frequencies in that row.[13]

The variable F_n is introduced by considering a slightly more complicated version of the above. Before the transitions between the various levels of domestic conflict behavior are considered, the years for a given level of foreign conflict are put into separate groups. For example, consider the following data for an arbitrary state for its corresponding D and F values for each of the six years. Before the transitions on the D variable are determined, the data are partitioned into sets on the basis of the value of the F variable. In this case the first set contains all the years for which F was 0, while the second set consists of all the years for which F was 2. The example gives no values for $F = 1$. A separate transition matrix is then constructed for each of the three F values, 0, 1, and 2.

[13]While there are six data points for each nation on each of the factors, there are only five transitions from one year to the next (1955–56, 1956–57, 1957–58, 1958–59, 1959–60). Thus, while we have a total of 444 data points, we have only 370 actual cases for analysis (5 × 74).

```
D:  +----+----+----+----+----+----+
    0    0    0    1    2    2

F:  +----+----+----+----+----+----+
    0    0    0    0    2    2

   1955  1956  1957  1958  1959  1960
```

The analyses are all based on transition matrices of the type described. Since there are two domestic factors and three foreign factors, every state has, in effect, five factor scores (two for domestic and three for foreign) for every year. It is thus possible to construct transition matrices of the type described above in 2 × 3 or six possible ways. Each domestic factor can be paired with each foreign factor to produce six total sets of transition matrices. In effect, then, all the analyses are performed six times, once for each possible pair between domestic and foreign factors.

The transition matrices for the domestic conflict behavior factors are presented in table 3. The entries within each matrix are proportions, and the values in any row of a matrix add to 1.00. These entries indicate the proportion of times that states made a transition from one level of domestic conflict to another in the following year. The matrices are arranged in columns on the basis of the level of foreign conflict in year n ($F_n = 0$, $F_n = 1$, $F_n = 2$). For example, the matrix in the top left-hand corner of table 3 gives the probabilities associated with transitions in domestic conflict of the turmoil type, when the level of foreign conflict of the war type is zero. The cells in each matrix indicate the proportion of times nations made a specific transition from one level of domestic conflict to another in the following year. Thus, the first matrix in the second row indicates that when internal war in year n is at level zero and war in year n is at level zero, in 76 percent of the cases the nations will continue to experience internal war at level zero in the following year. Similarly, when the level of internal war is one, and the level of war is zero, in 42 percent of the cases the nations will move down to internal war at level zero in the subsequent year. The transition probabilities are computed by determining the proportion of times domestic conflict at level i ($i = 0, 1, 2$) in year n is followed by domestic conflict at level j ($j = 0, 1, 2$) in the following ($n + 1$) year.

Three sets of analyses are performed. The first, known as the *order test*, examines the relationship between D_n and D_{n+1}. Each of the matrices for the $F_n = 0$, 1, and 2 conditions is separately analyzed to determine whether the level of domestic conflict in one year affects the level of domestic conflict in the succeeding year. This analysis in effect determines whether the transition process is a first rather than a zero order Markov chain.

Table 3. Total Transition Matrices

		$WAR_n = 0$ TUR_{n+1}				$WAR_n = 1$ TUR_{n+1}				$WAR_n = 2$ TUR_{n+1}			
		0	1	2		0	1	2		0	1	2	
TUR_n	0	.71	.24	.06	119	.74	.19	.07	70	.56	.44	.00	9
	1	.43	.42	.15	60	.19	.64	.17	47	.27	.53	.20	15
	2	.14	.39	.46	28	.13	.07	.80	15	.00	.71	.29	7
				$N = 207$				$N = 132$				$N = 31$	

		INT_{n+1}				INT_{n+1}				INT_{n+1}			
		0	1	2		0	1	2		0	1	2	
INT_n	0	.76	.21	.03	136	.84	.15	.01	81	.67	.33	.00	15
	1	.42	.34	.24	50	.41	.47	.12	34	.09	.73	.18	11
	2	.14	.33	.52	21	.18	.41	.41	17	.20	.60	.20	5
				$N = 207$				$N = 132$				$N = 31$	

		$BEL_n = 0$ TUR_{n+1}				$BEL_n = 1$ TUR_{n+1}				$BEL_n = 2$ TUR_{n+1}			
		0	1	2		0	1	2		0	1	2	
TUR_n	0	.70	.22	.08	97	.75	.22	.03	95	.33	.50	.17	6
	1	.49	.36	.16	45	.21	.63	.16	62	.27	.53	.20	15
	2	.16	.42	.42	19	.09	.30	.61	23	.13	.25	.63	8
				$N = 161$				$N = 180$				$N = 29$	

		INT_{n+1}				INT_{n+1}				INT_{n+1}			
		0	1	2		0	1	2		0	1	2	
INT_n	0	.74	.24	.02	103	.83	.15	.02	119	.70	.20	.10	10
	1	.43	.45	.12	42	.36	.39	.25	44	.22	.56	.22	9
	2	.25	.44	.31	16	.18	.29	.53	17	.00	.50	.50	10
				$N = 161$				$N = 180$				$N = 29$	

		$DIP_n = 0$ TUR_{n+1}				$DIP_n = 1$ TUR_{n+1}				$DIP_n = 2$ TUR_{n+1}			
		0	1	2		0	1	2		0	1	2	
TUR_n	0	.70	.25	.05	100	.74	.21	.05	86	.58	.17	.25	12
	1	.48	.39	.13	46	.22	.60	.18	68	.25	.50	.25	8
	2	.15	.35	.50	20	.13	.35	.52	23	.00	.29	.71	7
				$N = 166$				$N = 177$				$N = 27$	

		INT_{n+1}				INT_{n+1}				INT_{n+1}			
		0	1	2		0	1	2		0	1	2	
INT_n	0	.76	.21	.03	103	.80	.19	.01	108	.86	.10	.05	21
	1	.36	.39	.25	44	.40	.45	.15	47	.25	.75	.00	4
	2	.16	.37	.47	19	.14	.41	.45	22	.50	.50	.00	2
				$N = 166$				$N = 177$				$N = 27$	

The second analysis, known as the *equality test*, centers around the basic question of the study: to what extent does the level of foreign conflict behavior affect the transitions in the level of domestic conflict behavior. The same transition matrices are used but the analysis requires that the matrices be rewritten. Corresponding rows, where the initial D_n is the same, are taken from each of the three F_n matrices, producing a new matrix of the following form:

$$D_{n+1}$$

	0	1	2
$F_n = 0, D_n = 0$			
$F_n = 1, D_n = 0$			
$F_n = 2, D_n = 0$			

This matrix is only for the $D_n = 0$ case. Similar matrices are constructed for $D_n = 1$ and $D_n = 2$. The analysis now determines whether F_n, the level of foreign conflict behavior, affects the transitions between D_n and D_{n+1}.

The final set of analyses searches for patterns. While the first and second analyses consider whether D_n has *any* affect on D_{n+1}, and whether F_n has *any* affect on the transitions between D_n and D_{n+1}, the last set of analyses examine the *pattern* of these relationships.

The three sets of analyses will be reported first for all states combined. Following a brief description of how the states were grouped, we will then present separate analyses for each of three groups of states.

1. The Order Test

As described above, the order test is performed on the basic transition matrices given in table 3. The chi-square test detects whether D_n affects D_{n+1}—whether a state's prior level of domestic conflict behavior influences its subsequent level of domestic conflict behavior—by determining whether the distributions in the rows are different. The results of a chi-square analysis are reported in table 4. The rows of table 4 represent the six different tests of the model with the various possible pairings between the two domestic and three foreign conflict factors. Individual chi-square results are given for each of the F_n conditions separately. The last columns of table 4 report the total chi-square result over all three F_n conditions. For each of the F_n and the total conditions the chi-square value (χ^2), the significance level (p), the degrees of freedom (df), and the number of cases in the analyzed matrix (N) are reported.

In general, table 4 shows that D_n has a striking effect on D_{n+1}. Almost

Table 4. Chi-Square Tests of the Order Properties of the Total Transition Matrices

	$F_n = 0$				$F_n = 1$				$F_n = 2$				Total			
	x^2	p	df	N	x^2	p	df	N	x^2	p	df	N	x^2	p	df	N
WAR-TUR	46.796	.000	4	207	77.759	.000	4	132	7.040	.133	4	31	131.595	.000	12	370
WAR-INT	58.972	.000	4	207	49.416	.000	4	132	10.787	.029	4	31	119.176	.000	12	370
BEL-TUR	25.456	.000	4	161	89.430	.000	4	180	5.218	.265	4	29	120.104	.000	12	370
BEL-INT	30.872	.000	4	161	65.504	.000	4	180	12.978	.012	4	29	109.355	.000	12	370
DIP-TUR	38.747	.000	4	166	70.544	.000	4	177	9.571	.048	4	27	118.863	.000	12	370
DIP-INT	47.067	.000	4	166	63.046	.000	4	177	9.359	.052	4	27	119.472	.000	12	370

all the p values are exceedingly small. The level of domestic conflict, at one point in time, then, is a very important factor in determining the level of domestic conflict at the next point in time. This result is an interesting corollary to one obtained earlier by Rummel.[14] Thus, Rummel, in one of the first quantitative studies devoted to the domestic conflict–foreign conflict relationship, found that domestic conflict variables were highly intercorrelated. The present analysis shows that a similar relationship also exists over time. Thus, not only is it the case that states experiencing one type of domestic conflict will also experience other forms of domestic conflict, but the level of domestic conflict in one year has an important effect on the level of domestic conflict in the following year.

2. The Equality Test

The equality test, as noted earlier, requires that the basic transition matrices be rewritten by taking corresponding rows from each of the original matrices. The same chi-square analysis is performed on these new matrices. We are now, in effect, examining the same transitions, but under different levels of foreign conflict behavior. By asking whether the distributions in the rows are the same, the chi-square analysis determines in this case whether the level of foreign conflict behavior has any effect on the transitions in domestic conflict behavior.

The results of the tests are presented in table 5. The results in this case are considerably less startling than in the order analysis. If we require that $p \leq .05$, there is in effect only one total chi square that emerges as significant: the war-turmoil pair in the first row of table 5. If we relax the restriction on p somewhat and require that $p \leq .1$, then each of the turmoil factors provides some results as seen in rows one, three, and five. It is disturbing, however, that these total results are primarily a function of only one or two significant D_n matrices. Thus, the war-turmoil total result is principally due to the $D_n = 2$ matrix. This means the foreign conflict behavior "war" as measured by the variables loading most highly on this factor (military actions, wars, mobilizations, and foreign killed) affects transitions in domestic conflict behavior as captured by the "turmoil" factor (strikes, riots, demonstrations) primarily when domestic conflict behavior is at a very high level, $D_n = 2$. When there are few strikes, riots, or demonstrations, then military actions, wars, mobilizations, and foreign killed do not have much effect on the level of this type of domestic conflict behavior. Similarly, an examination of the third and fifth rows shows that the foreign conflict behavior "belligerency" affects domestic conflict behavior "turmoil" only when turmoil is initially at level 1, while "diplomatic" foreign conflict behavior affects turmoil only when $D_n = 0$ and 1.

---

[14] Rummel, "Dimensions of Conflict Behavior."

Table 5. Chi-Square Tests of the Equality Properties of the Total Transition Matrices

	D = 0				D = 1				D = 2				Total			
	χ^2	p	df	N	χ^2	p	df	N	χ^2	p	df	N	χ^2	p	df	N
WAR-TUR	3.529	.525	4	198	7.690	.102	4	122	10.408	.034	4	50	21.627	.042	12	370
WAR-INT	4.156	.386	4	232	7.650	.104	4	95	1.875	.762	4	43	13.681	.321	12	370
BEL-TUR	6.621	.156	4	198	10.436	.033	4	122	1.888	.759	4	50	18.944	.090	12	370
BEL-INT	6.102	.190	4	232	3.456	.513	4	95	4.162	.385	4	43	13.720	.318	12	370
DIP-TUR	8.537	.073	4	198	8.955	.061	4	122	1.549	.820	4	50	19.041	.087	12	370
DIP-INT	3.211	.525	4	232	3.472	.516	4	95	2.530	.643	4	43	9.213	.686	12	370

Two characteristics of the results in table 5 are, however, interesting if not dramatic. Of the two domestic conflict factors, turmoil and internal war, the variables loading on the turmoil factor are of a considerably lower magnitude. Thus strikes, riots, and demonstrations are certainly less severe forms of domestic conflict than are guerrilla warfare, governmental crises, revolutions, purges, or domestic killed. Thus, when foreign conflict has any effect, meager though the effect is, it only affects the lesser forms of domestic conflict behavior. A society so torn apart by guerrilla warfare and revolutions is apparently incapable of feeling the effects of foreign conflict behavior.

The pattern with which foreign conflict behavior affects the turmoil factor is also interesting. Once again the factors "war," "belligerency," and "diplomatic" can probably be ranked from more to less extreme measures of foreign conflict behavior on the basis of the variables loading on these factors (see table 2). We note, then, that as we move from the first to the third to the fifth rows of table 5 for the individual D matrices we pick up significant values for lower and lower D values. Thus, war, the most extreme of the foreign conflict factors, affects turmoil only when turmoil is at a high level, $D_n = 2$. Belligerency, however, a somewhat less intense mode of foreign conflict behavior, principally affects transitions in turmoil when turmoil is at a medium level, i.e., $D_n = 1$. Finally, the diplomatic dimension of foreign conflict behavior affects turmoil transitions when $D_n = 0$ or 1. Since D_n represents the level *from which* the transitions are made there appears to be a matching between the *starting level* of the transition in domestic conflict and the effect of the severity of foreign conflict behavior. The more severe forms of foreign conflict behavior affect transitions from the more intense levels of turmoil, while the less intense levels of foreign conflict behavior affect transitions from the less intense levels of the turmoil type of domestic conflict behavior. As we have already noted, the more intense forms of domestic conflict behavior are unaffected by foreign conflict behavior.

3. Patterns: The Matching Phenomenon

We have seen, then, that a strong relationship exists between transitions in domestic conflict behavior; the amount of domestic conflict behavior a state experiences at one point in time is an important factor in determining how much domestic conflict it will experience at the next point in time. Further, foreign conflict behavior only affects the less intense types of domestic conflict behavior, i.e., the turmoil factor, and it only affects this factor at certain levels. We now need to explore the direction of these effects. We principally wish to discern *how* foreign conflict behavior affects the transitions in domestic conflict behavior.

Let $p(D_{ij}/F_k)$ be the probability of a transition between domestic conflict behavior at level i and domestic conflict behavior at level j given foreign conflict behavior at level k. For example, $p(D_{01}/F_1)$ is the probability of a transition from $D_n = 0$ to $D_{n+1} = 1$ when foreign conflict behavior is at level one, $F_n = 1$. We will assume that the pattern in the relationship D_n and D_{n+1} can be described by a *matching rule* and is a direct function of F_n. Specifically, the matching rule argues that all transitions D_{ij} under conditions F_k should be transitions D_{ik}, viz., $j = k$. In other words, it argues that the second point in time of all domestic conflict transitions must match the foreign conflict level at the previous (nth) point in time. Thus, the matching rule says that foreign conflict behavior affects domestic conflict transitions by forcing the change in the level of domestic conflict to match the level of foreign conflict behavior. This analysis is comparable to but *not* identical with the assumption of linearity employed in the earlier studies. The idea here, as in the earlier studies, is that as foreign conflict increases it should raise the level of domestic conflict behavior, or as foreign conflict behavior diminishes it should produce a corresponding decrease in domestic conflict. Thus, D_{n+1}, domestic conflict behavior at the second point in time, should roughly be at the same level, i.e., match, foreign conflict at time n, F_n.

The matching assumption leads to two sets of predictions concerning the relative probabilities of certain transitions. The first and most obvious prediction is that $p(D_{kk}F_k) > p(D_{kj}F_k)$. If domestic conflict behavior is at level k and foreign conflict behavior is also at level k, then the most probable transition, if foreign conflict is to have any affect on domestic conflict, is for domestic conflict to remain at the same k level. In effect, the level of domestic conflict behavior has been "reinforced" by the same level of foreign conflict behavior and should thus remain constant. Specifically, we make the following predictions:

$$p(D_{00}/F_0) > p(D_{01}/F_0) \text{ and } p(D_{02}/F_0) \tag{1}$$

$$p(D_{11}/F_1) > p(D_{10}/F_1) \text{ and } p(D_{12}/F_1) \tag{2}$$

$$p(D_{22}/F_2) > p(D_{21}/F_2) \text{ and } p(D_{20}/F_2) \tag{3}$$

$$p(D_{00}/F_0) > p(D_{00}/F_1) \text{ and } p(D_{00}/F_2) \tag{4}$$

$$p(D_{11}/F_1) > p(D_{11}/F_0) \text{ and } p(D_{11}/F_2) \tag{5}$$

$$p(D_{22}/F_2) > p(D_{22}/F_1) \text{ and } p(D_{22}/F_0) \tag{6}$$

As can be seen, the predicted most probable transition is always the one in which the transition in the level of domestic conflict matches the level of foreign conflict behavior at the previous time point. The first three inequalities correspond to a comparison of the cells across the rows of the original matrices given in table 3, though only one row from each of the F_n matrices is being examined (the other rows present more difficult

Table 6. Predicted and Observed Inequalities (1), (2), and (3)

	(1) $p(D_{00}/F_0) > p(D_{01}/F_0)$ and $p(D_{02}/F_0)$			(2) $p(D_{11}/F_1) > p(D_{10}/F_1)$ and $p(D_{12}/F_1)$			(3) $p(D_{22}/F_2) > p(D_{21}/F_2)$ and $p(D_{20}/F_2)$		
WAR-TUR	.71	.24	.06[a][b]	.64	.19	.17[a][b]	.29	.71	.00
WAR-INT	.76	.21	.03[a][b]	.47	.41	.12[a][b]	.20	.60	.20
BEL-TUR	.70	.22	.08[a][b]	.63	.21	.16[a][b]	.63	.25	.13[a]
BEL-INT	.74	.24	.02[a][b]	.39	.36	.25[a]	.50	.50	.00
DIP-TUR	.70	.25	.05[a][b]	.60	.22	.18[a][b]	.71	.29	.00[a]
DIP-INT	.76	.21	.03[a][b]	.45	.40	.15[a][b]	.00	.50	.50

[a] Data conform to prediction.

[b] $p < 0.5$ In this case, a test of significance was performed, based on a modification of the Fisher Exact Test. The probability of the 1×3 matrix is computed by adding the probability of the particular matrix to the probabilities of all matrices which are less or equally probable given the same row marginals.

interpretative problems). The last three inequalities are comparisons of the cells of columns of the rewritten matrices used in the equality analysis.

The results for the first three inequality predictions (1), (2), and (3) are given in table 6. We note that 14 out of the possible 18 predictions hold. The four inequalities that do not hold occur when $F_n = 2$. It thus appears that when foreign conflict is very intense there is a greater probability of making a transition on the domestic level to *less* intense domestic conflict behavior levels. When foreign conflict is high there is a decrease in the intensity of domestic conflict. Note that this latter statement is particularly true with respect to the effects of the war factor on the two domestic factors.

In connection with inequalities (1) through (3) it is also interesting to note that of the four cases that do not conform to our predictions, three involve the internal war factor, i.e., the more intense type of domestic conflict behavior. Furthermore, even when the internal war transitions conform to the predictions, the associated probabilities are lower than those for the turmoil transitions. This appears to add additional weight to the earlier finding that the turmoil type of domestic conflict behavior is more sensitive to foreign conflict behavior than is the internal war type of domestic conflict.

The results for inequalities (4), (5), and (6) are given in table 7. Since these inequalities come directly from the rewritten matrices on which the equality test was performed, it is not surprising to find that most of the inequalities are not supported by the data. The chi-square analysis, after all, compared the distributions involving all three cells of the rows in a matrix. To test these inequalities we are, in effect, just comparing one cell of each of the three rows. Thus, it is not surprising that we again find that the only relationships to hold involve the turmoil factor. It is interesting, however, that these relationships primarily hold only for medium and high levels of domestic conflict, i.e., D_{11} and D_{22}.

The second set of predictions that emerge from the matching rule predict that $p(D_{kk}F_k) > p(D_{ik}F_k)$. Unlike the above inequalities where comparisons were made between correct transitions (i.e., transitions in D which matched the F value) and incorrect transitions (i.e., transitions in D which did not match the F values), the present set of inequalities make comparisons between different types of "correct" transitions. Thus, in the above inequality the transition in D on *both* sides of the inequality moves *to* the value k which matches the value of the F variable. The argument here is that it is easier to *stay* at the correct value, D_{kk}, than it is to move from an "incorrect" value i to a correct one, k, vis. D_{ik}. Specifically, the predicted inequalities are:

$$p(D_{00}/F_0) > p(D_{10}/F_0) \text{ and } p(D_{20}/F_0) \tag{7}$$

$$p(D_{11}/F_1) > p(D_{01}/F_1) \text{ and } p(D_{21}/F_1) \tag{8}$$

$$p(D_{22}/F_2) > p(D_{12}/F_2) \text{ and } p(D_{02}/F_2) \tag{9}$$

Table 7. Predicted and Observed Inequalities (4), (5), and (6)

	(4) $p(D_{00}/F_0) > p(D_{00}/F_1)$ and $p(D_{00}/F_2)$			(5) $p(D_{11}/F_1) > p(D_{11}/F_0)$ and $p(D_{11}/F_2)$			(6) $p(D_{22}/F_2) > p(D_{22}/F_1)$ and $p(D_{22}/F_0)$		
WAR-TUR	.71	.74	.56	.64	.42	.53[a]	.29	.80	.46
WAR-INT	.76	.84	.67	.47	.34	.73	.20	.41	.52
BEL-TUR	.70	.75	.33	.63	.36	.53[a]	.63	.61	.42[a]
BEL-INT	.74	.83	.70	.39	.45	.56	.50	.53	.31
DIP-TUR	.70	.74	.58	.60	.39	.50[a]	.71	.52	.50[a]
DIP-INT	.76	.80	.86	.45	.39	.75	.00	.45	.47

[a] Data conform to prediction.

The results for this set of inequalities are presented in table 8. With 17 of 18 cases conforming to the predictions, there appears to be a definite tendency for the probability of correctly maintaining the prior level of domestic conflict to be greater than that associated with a correct change in levels.

To summarize the results to this point, we have found a very strong relationship between the level of domestic conflict at one point in time and its level at the next point in time. Foreign conflict behavior appears to only affect those transitions involving the lesser of the two domestic conflict factors, turmoil, and even here the evidence is that the effect is minimal. The examination of the inequalities shows further that under the condition of F_k the transitions D_{kk} are more probable than either incorrect transitions D_{kj} or other correct transitions D_{ik}. Thus, a comparison of the D transitions under the same F_k condition seems to suggest that F reinforces a correct-to-correct response. However, for the most part, it is not the case that the same transition D_{kk} compared under different values of F conforms to the matching rule. A correct-to-correct response is thus not more probable when F matches the level of domestic conflict behavior than when F does not match the D transitions.

ANALYSIS BY NATION TYPE

In earlier studies it was found that a number of relationships were obscured by combining all nations in a single analysis.[15] It is thus important to consider whether the above findings are primarily an artifact of not discriminating between very different sorts of entities. Thus, the seventy-four nations in the above analysis were classified into types using a factor analysis performed by Banks and Gregg.[16] In that study, a Q-factor analysis was performed on the political variables included in *A Cross-Polity Survey*.[17] Of the five groups identified in that analysis, the three labeled *personalist*, *centrist*, and *polyarchic* were found to be useful in the present study. The personalist group is composed of 15 states, most of which are Latin American dictatorships. The centrist nations, numbering 26, are characterized by a high degree of political centralization. The Soviet Union and its Eastern European allies load highly on this factor. The polyarchic group is composed of 33 states, most of which are economically developed and Western.[18]

It is interesting to note the ranking of these three groupings on factors

[15] See Wilkenfeld, "Domestic and Foreign Conflict."

[16] Arthur S. Banks and Phillip M. Gregg, "Grouping Political Systems: Q-Factor Analysis of *A Cross-Polity Survey*," *The American Behavioral Scientist* 9 (November 1965): 3–6.

[17] Arthur S. Banks and Robert B. Textor, *A Cross-Polity Survey* (Cambridge, Mass: MIT Press, 1963).

[18] For a more extensive discussion of the nature of these groups, see Wilkenfeld, "Domestic and Foreign Conflict."

Table 8. Predicted and Observed Inequalities (7), (8), and (9)

	(7) $p(D_{00}/F_0) > p(D_{10}/F_0)$ and $p(D_{20}/F_0)$			(8) $p(D_{11}/F_1) > p(D_{01}/F_1)$ and $p(D_{21}/F_1)$			(9) $p(D_{22}/F_2) > p(D_{12}/F_2)$ and $p(D_{02}/F_2)$		
WAR-TUR	.71	.43	.14[a]	.64	.19	.07[a]	.29	.20	.00[a]
WAR-INT	.76	.42	.14[a]	.47	.15	.41[a]	.20	.18	.00[a]
BEL-TUR	.70	.49	.16[a]	.63	.22	.30[a]	.63	.20	.17[a]
BEL-INT	.74	.43	.25[a]	.39	.15	.29[a]	.50	.22	.10[a]
DIP-TUR	.70	.48	.15[a]	.60	.21	.35[a]	.71	.25	.25[a]
DIP-INT	.76	.36	.16[a]	.45	.19	.41[a]	.00	.00	.05

[a] Data conform to prediction.

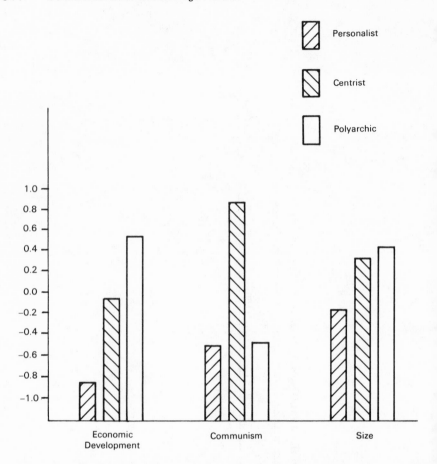

Figure 1.   Group Means of Factor Scores on Russett Factors

extracted by Russett from a different set of data.[19]   Figure 1 indicates the mean of the factor scores for the personalist, centrist, and polyarchic nations on three central factors extracted by Russett: economic development, communism, and size.   These are fairly central attribute groupings, having been identified theoretically by Rosenau,[20] and empirically by Sawyer[21] and Rummel.[22]   It will be noted that there are rather sharp

[19] Bruce M. Russett, *International Regions and the International System* (Chicago: Rand McNally and Co., 1967).

[20] James N. Rosenau, "Pre-Theories and Theories of Foreign Policy," in *Approaches to Comparative and International Politics*, ed. R. Barry Farrell (Evanston, Ill.: Northwestern University Press, 1966), pp. 27–92.

[21] Jack Sawyer, "Dimensions of Nations: Size, Wealth, and Politics," *American Journal of Sociology* (September 1967): 145–72.

[22] R. J. Rummel, "Indicators of Cross-National and International Patterns," *American Political Science Review* 63 (March 1969): 127–47.

differences between the three types of states on these factors. These differences may be helpful in explaining the different patterns of conflict behavior exhibited by these groups.

The conflict behavior data are again arranged in transition matrices but we now have three sets of matrices, one each for the personalist, centrist, and polyarchic groups. These matrices are presented in tables 9, 10, and 11. It will be noted that the earlier N of 370 for the total group has been broken down to 75 for the personalist group, 130 for the centrist group, and 165 for the polyarchic group. As before, each case is one nation-year.

When we perform the same order test on each of the matrices of tables 9, 10, and 11 we obtain the results given in tables 12, 13, and 14 for the personalist, centrist, and polyarchic groups, respectively. Once again we original results obtained for all the states combined were indeed specific to only certain types of states. Thus, the level of domestic conflict at one point in time affects the level at the next point in time only for centrist and polyarchic states, but not for personalist states. The personalist states exhibit only a slight tendency to perpetuate from year to year domestic conflict behavior levels. This finding was clearly obscured in the total analysis reported earlier in table 4.

Rewriting the original matrices as was done before and performing the equality test we obtain the results shown in tables 15, 16, and 17 for the personalist, centrist, and polyarchic groups, respectively. Once again we find that the original results obtained for all the states are primarily a function of only certain groups of states. It will be recalled that the total group exhibited relationships only when the turmoil type of domestic conflict behavior was involved. We now note that this finding is primarily the product of the performance of the personalist and polyarchic groups. In the centrist group, with one slight exception, transitions in domestic conflict behavior appear to be immune from the effects of foreign conflict behavior. This finding parallels those reported earlier in the correlation studies, where it appeared that centrist nations apparently suffered little or no domestic repercussions arising from their involvement in foreign conflict behavior.[23]

A reexamination of each of the three sets of inequalities again shows that the type of nation has an important impact on the pattern of the relationship. The results for the first set of inequalities (1), (2), and (3) are given in table 18. It will be recalled that when all the states were combined, these three inequality predictions were primarily supported. We now see in table 18 that the support comes principally from the personalist and polyarchic states. The matching behavior occurs much less frequently for the centrist states.

[23] Wilkenfeld, "Domestic and Foreign Conflict."

Table 9. Personalist Transition Matrices

		$WAR_n = 0$ TUR_{n+1}				$WAR_n = 1$ TUR_{n+1}				$WAR_n = 2$ TUR_{n+1}			
		0	1	2		0	1	2		0	1	2	
TUR_n	0	.13	.67	.20	15	.29	.57	.14	7	1.00	.00	.00	1
	1	.38	.48	.14	21	.24	.71	.06	17	.00	1.00	.00	2
	2	.20	.40	.40	10	.50	.00	.50	2	.00	.00	.00	0
				$N = 46$				$N = 26$				$N = 3$	

		INT_{n+1}				INT_{n+1}				INT_{n+1}			
		0	1	2		0	1	2		0	1	2	
INT_n	0	.53	.42	.05	19	.50	.42	.08	12	.50	.50	.00	2
	1	.36	.21	.43	14	.14	.57	.29	7	.00	1.00	.00	1
	2	.23	.23	.54	13	.29	.43	.29	7	.00	.00	.00	0
				$N = 46$				$N = 26$				$N = 3$	

		$BEL_n = 0$ TUR_{n+1}				$BEL_n = 1$ TUR_{n+1}				$BEL_n = 2$ TUR_{n+1}			
		0	1	2		0	1	2		0	1	2	
TUR_n	0	.25	.50	.25	12	.22	.78	.00	9	.00	.50	.50	2
	1	.75	.17	.08	12	.09	.82	.09	22	.17	.67	.17	6
	2	.50	.25	.25	4	.17	.50	.33	6	.00	.00	1.00	2
				$N = 28$				$N = 37$				$N = 10$	

		INT_{n+1}				INT_{n+1}				INT_{n+1}			
		0	1	2		0	1	2		0	1	2	
INT_n	0	.60	.40	.00	15	.50	.44	.06	16	.00	.50	.50	2
	1	.63	.25	.13	8	.09	.36	.55	11	.00	.67	.33	3
	2	.40	.20	.40	5	.30	.30	.40	10	.00	.40	.60	5
				$N = 28$				$N = 37$				$N = 10$	

		$DIP_n = 0$ TUR_{n+1}				$DIP_n = 1$ TUR_{n+1}				$DIP_n = 2$ TUR_{n+1}			
		0	1	2		0	1	2		0	1	2	
TUR_n	0	.25	.50	.25	12	.18	.73	.09	11	.00	.00	.00	0
	1	.56	.39	.06	18	.09	.77	.14	22	.00	.00	.00	0
	2	.20	.20	.60	5	.33	.50	.17	6	.00	.00	1.00	1
				$N = 35$				$N = 39$				$N = 1$	

		INT_{n+1}				INT_{n+1}				INT_{n+1}			
		0	1	2		0	1	2		0	1	2	
INT_n	0	.50	.44	.06	16	.53	.41	.06	17	.00	.00	.00	0
	1	.33	.25	.42	12	.20	.50	.30	10	.00	.00	.00	0
	2	.43	.00	.57	7	.17	.42	.42	12	.00	1.00	.00	1
				$N = 35$				$N = 39$				$N = 1$	

Table 10. Centrist Transition Matrices

WAR$_n$ = 0 / WAR$_n$ = 1 / WAR$_n$ = 2, TUR$_{n+1}$

		WAR$_n$ = 0 TUR$_{n+1}$				WAR$_n$ = 1 TUR$_{n+1}$				WAR$_n$ = 2 TUR$_{n+1}$			
		0	1	2		0	1	2		0	1	2	
TUR$_n$	0	.77	.13	.10	39	.86	.09	.05	43	.67	.33	.00	6
	1	.82	.18	.00	11	.36	.55	.09	11	.38	.50	.13	8
	2	.33	.33	.33	6	.33	.33	.33	3	.00	.67	.33	3
					N = 56				N = 57				N = 17

INT$_{n+1}$

		INT$_{n+1}$				INT$_{n+1}$				INT$_{n+1}$			
		0	1	2		0	1	2		0	1	2	
INT$_n$	0	.84	.14	.02	44	.95	.05	.00	38	.80	.20	.00	5
	1	.64	.18	.18	11	.64	.18	.18	11	.14	.57	.29	7
	2	.00	.00	1.00	1	.00	.50	.50	8	.20	.60	.20	5
					N = 56				N = 57				N = 17

BEL$_n$ = 0 / BEL$_n$ = 1 / BEL$_n$ = 2, TUR$_{n+1}$

		BEL$_n$ = 0 TUR$_{n+1}$				BEL$_n$ = 1 TUR$_{n+1}$				BEL$_n$ = 2 TUR$_{n+1}$			
		0	1	2		0	1	2		0	1	2	
TUR$_n$	0	.78	.12	.10	41	.86	.09	.05	43	.50	.50	.00	4
	1	.64	.36	.00	11	.43	.43	.14	14	.60	.40	.00	5
	2	.17	.50	.33	6	.33	.33	.33	3	.33	.33	.33	3
					N = 58				N = 60				N = 12

INT$_{n+1}$

		INT$_{n+1}$				INT$_{n+1}$				INT$_{n+1}$			
		0	1	2		0	1	2		0	1	2	
INT$_n$	0	.85	.13	.03	39	.93	.07	.00	44	.75	.25	.00	4
	1	.80	.33	.17	12	.54	.23	.23	13	.50	.25	.25	4
	2	.14	.43	.43	7	.00	.33	.67	3	.00	.75	.25	4
					N = 58				N = 60				N = 12

DIP$_n$ = 0 / DIP$_n$ = 1 / DIP$_n$ = 2, TUR$_{n+1}$

		DIP$_n$ = 0 TUR$_{n+1}$				DIP$_n$ = 1 TUR$_{n+1}$				DIP$_n$ = 2 TUR$_{n+1}$			
		0	1	2		0	1	2		0	1	2	
TUR$_n$	0	.77	.17	.06	35	.87	.09	.04	45	.63	.13	.25	8
	1	.60	.30	.10	10	.47	.47	.06	17	.67	.33	.00	3
	2	.29	.29	.43	7	.25	.50	.25	4	.00	1.00	.00	1
					N = 52				N = 66				N = 12

INT$_{n+1}$

		INT$_{n+1}$				INT$_{n+1}$				INT$_{n+1}$			
		0	1	2		0	1	2		0	1	2	
INT$_n$	0	.80	.17	.03	35	.93	.07	.00	43	1.00	.00	.00	9
	1	.40	.30	.30	10	.59	.24	.18	17	.50	.50	.00	2
	2	.00	.43	.57	7	.00	.67	.33	6	1.00	.00	.00	1
					N = 52				N = 66				N = 12

Table 11. Polyarchic Transition Matrices

$WAR_n = 0$ / $WAR_n = 1$ / $WAR_n = 2$ — TUR_{n+1}

		$WAR_n = 0$, TUR_{n+1} 0	1	2		$WAR_n = 1$, TUR_{n+1} 0	1	2		$WAR_n = 2$, TUR_{n+1} 0	1	2	
TUR_n	0	.80	.20	.00	65	.65	.25	.10	20	.00	1.00	.00	2
	1	.32	.46	.21	28	.05	.63	.32	19	.20	.40	.40	5
	2	.00	.42	.58	12	.00	.00	1.00	10	.00	.75	.25	4
				$N = 105$				$N = 49$				$N = 11$	

INT_{n+1}

		0	1	2		0	1	2		0	1	2	
INT_n	0	.78	.19	.03	73	.84	.16	.00	31	.63	.38	.00	8
	1	.36	.48	.16	25	.38	.63	.00	16	.00	1.00	.00	3
	2	.00	.57	.43	7	.50	.00	.50	2	.00	.00	.00	0
				$N = 105$				$N = 49$				$N = 11$	

$BEL_n = 0$ / $BEL_n = 1$ / $BEL_n = 2$ — TUR_{n+1}

		0	1	2		0	1	2		0	1	2	
TUR_n	0	.75	.23	.02	44	.74	.23	.02	43	.00	.00	.00	0
	1	.27	.45	.27	22	.19	.58	.23	26	.00	.50	.50	4
	2	.00	.44	.56	9	.00	.21	.79	14	.00	.33	.67	3
				$N = 75$				$N = 83$				$N = 7$	

INT_{n+1}

		0	1	2		0	1	2		0	1	2	
INT_n	0	.69	.29	.02	49	.85	.14	.02	59	1.00	.00	.00	4
	1	.32	.59	.09	22	.40	.50	.10	20	.00	1.00	.00	2
	2	.25	.75	.00	4	.00	.25	.75	4	.00	.00	1.00	1
				$N = 75$				$N = 83$				$N = 7$	

$DIP_n = 0$ / $DIP_n = 1$ / $DIP_n = 2$ — TUR_{n+1}

		0	1	2		0	1	2		0	1	2	
TUR_n	0	.75	.25	.00	53	.77	.20	.03	30	.50	.25	.25	4
	1	.33	.44	.22	18	.17	.55	.28	29	.00	.60	.40	5
	2	.00	.50	.50	8	.00	.23	.77	13	.00	.20	.80	5
				$N = 79$				$N = 72$				$N = 14$	

INT_{n+1}

		0	1	2		0	1	2		0	1	2	
INT_n	0	.81	.17	.02	52	.77	.23	.00	48	.75	.17	.08	12
	1	.36	.50	.14	22	.35	.60	.05	20	.00	1.00	.00	2
	2	.00	.80	.20	5	.25	.00	.75	4	.00	.00	.00	0
				$N = 79$				$N = 72$				$N = 14$	

Table 12. Chi-Square Tests of the Order Properties of the Personalist Transition Matrices

	F = 0				F = 1				F = 2				Total			
	x^2	p	df	N	x^2	p	df	N	x^2	p	df	N	x^2	p	df	N
WAR-TUR	5.301	.257	4	46	5.036	.283	4	26	3.000	.079	1	3	13.337	.147	9	75
WAR-INT	10.244	.036	4	46	3.358	.502	4	26	0.750	.609	1	3	14.353	.110	9	75
BEL-TUR	6.215	.182	4	28	5.354	.252	4	37	4.667	.323	4	10	16.235	.180	12	75
BEL-INT	6.597	.158	4	28	9.305	.053	4	37	0.533	.769	2	10	16.435	.087	10	75
DIP-TUR	9.097	.058	4	35	2.569	.636	4	39	—	—	0	1	11.666	.166	8	75
DIP-INT	9.299	.053	4	35	7.804	.098	4	39	—	—	0	1	17.103	.029	8	75

Table 13. Chi-Square Tests of the Order Properties of the Centrist Transition Matrices

	F = 0				F = 1				F = 2				Total			
	x^2	p	df	N	x^2	p	df	N	x^2	p	df	N	x^2	p	df	N
WAR-TUR	6.939	.138	4	56	16.619	.003	4	57	4.604	.330	4	17	28.162	.006	12	130
WAR-INT	16.950	.002	4	56	34.160	.000	4	57	6.517	.162	4	17	57.627	.000	12	130
BEL-TUR	12.360	.015	4	58	13.794	.008	4	60	3.387	.503	4	12	29.540	.004	12	130
BEL-INT	18.701	.001	4	58	27.319	.000	4	60	5.400	.248	4	12	51.421	.000	12	130
DIP-TUR	9.961	.040	4	52	16.696	.003	4	66	4.476	.345	4	12	31.133	.002	12	130
DIP-INT	21.821	.000	4	52	29.572	.000	4	66	5.455	.064	2	12	56.848	.000	10	130

Table 14.   Chi-Square Tests of the Order Properties of the Polyarchic Transition Matrices

	F = 0				F = 1				F = 2				Total			
	χ^2	p	df	N	χ^2	p	df	N	χ^2	p	df	N	χ^2	p	df	N
WAR-TUR	51.258	.000	4	105	39.132	.000	4	49	2.986	.563	4	11	93.376	.000	12	165
WAR-INT	31.624	.000	4	105	35.014	.000	4	49	3.438	.060	1	11	70.075	.000	9	165
BEL-TUR	30.336	.000	4	75	53.374	.000	4	83	0.194	.663	1	7	83.905	.000	9	165
BEL-INT	11.437	.022	4	75	44.015	.000	4	83	14.000	.008	4	7	69.453	.000	12	165
DIP-TUR	32.440	.000	4	79	44.072	.000	4	72	7.800	.098	4	14	84.312	.000	12	165
DIP-INT	22.887	.000	4	79	49.784	.000	4	72	5.833	.052	2	14	78.504	.000	10	165

Table 15.   Chi-Square Tests of the Equality Properties of the Personalist Transition Matrices

	D = 0				D = 1				D = 2				Total			
	χ^2	p	df	N	χ^2	p	df	N	χ^2	p	df	N	χ^2	p	df	N
WAR-TUR	4.434	.350	4	23	3.557	.529	4	40	1.440	.509	2	12	9.432	.508	10	75
WAR-INT	0.283	.988	4	33	4.518	.340	4	22	1.294	.528	2	20	6.096	.808	10	75
BEL-TUR	4.376	.358	4	23	17.525	.002	4	40	4.917	.295	4	12	26.818	.008	12	75
BEL-INT	8.583	.071	4	33	9.094	.058	4	22	2.467	.654	4	20	20.143	.064	12	75
DIP-TUR	1.445	.510	2	23	10.202	.006	2	40	3.687	.548	4	12	15.334	.052	8	75
DIP-INT	0.029	.974	2	33	1.497	.523	2	22	6.463	.166	4	20	7.989	.565	8	75

Table 16. Chi-Square Tests of the Equality Properties of the Centrist Transition Matrices

	D = 0				D = 1				D = 2				Total			
	χ^2	p	df	N	χ^2	p	df	N	χ^2	p	df	N	χ^2	p	df	N
WAR-TUR	4.187	.382	4	88	5.973	.200	4	30	1.600	.811	4	12	11.760	.534	12	130
WAR-INT	3.142	.537	4	87	5.700	.222	4	29	3.867	.574	4	14	12.708	.391	12	130
BEL-TUR	6.598	.157	4	88	2.899	.578	4	30	0.533	.967	4	12	10.031	.614	12	130
BEL-INT	3.079	.547	4	87	0.435	.976	4	29	2.433	.660	4	14	5.947	.919	12	130
DIP-TUR	5.968	.200	4	88	1.186	.880	4	30	2.064	.727	4	12	9.219	.685	12	130
DIP-INT	4.971	.289	4	87	1.828	.770	4	29	14.794	.006	4	14	21.593	.042	12	130

Table 17. Chi-Square Tests of the Equality Properties of the Polyarchic Transition Matrices

	D = 0				D = 1				D = 2				Total			
	χ^2	p	df	N	χ^2	p	df	N	χ^2	p	df	N	χ^2	p	df	N
WAR-TUR	14.137	.007	4	87	5.416	.246	4	52	8.787	.012	2	26	28.340	.002	10	165
WAR-INT	2.946	.570	4	112	5.562	.233	4	44	4.661	.095	2	9	13.168	.214	10	165
BEL-TUR	0.004	.989	2	87	2.563	.637	4	52	1.373	.508	2	26	3.940	.863	8	165
BEL-INT	5.024	.284	4	112	1.960	.746	4	44	6.187	.184	4	9	13.171	.356	12	165
DIP-TUR	10.850	.028	4	87	3.316	.508	4	52	2.022	.365	2	26	16.187	.094	10	165
DIP-INT	4.269	.371	4	112	2.642	.623	4	44	5.962	.049	2	9	12.873	.230	10	165

Table 18. Predicted and Observed Inequalities (1), (2) and (3)

	(1) $p(D_{00}/F_0) > p(D_{01}/F_0)$ and $p(D_{02}/F_0)$			(2) $p(D_{11}/F_1) > p(D_{10}/F_1)$ and $p(D_{12}/F_1)$			(3) $p(D_{22}/F_2) > p(D_{21}/F_2)$ and $p(D_{20}/F_2)$		
Personalist									
WAR-TUR	.13	.67	.20[b]	.71	.24	.06[ab]	.00	.00	.00
WAR-INT	.53	.42	.05[ab]	.57	.14	.29[a]	.00	.00	.00
BEL-TUR	.25	.50	.25	.82	.09	.09[ab]	1.00	.00	.00[a]
BEL-INT	.60	.40	.00[ab]	.36	.09	.55	.60	.40	.00[a]
DIP-TUR	.25	.50	.25	.77	.09	.14[ab]	1.00	.00	.00[a]
DIP-INT	.50	.44	.06[ab]	.50	.20	.30[a]	.00	1.00	.00
Centrist									
WAR-TUR	.77	.13	.10[ab]	.55	.36	.09[a]	.33	.67	.00
WAR-INT	.84	.14	.02[ab]	.18	.64	.18	.20	.60	.20
BEL-TUR	.78	.12	.10[ab]	.43	.43	.14	.33	.33	.33
BEL-INT	.85	.13	.03[ab]	.23	.54	.23	.25	.75	.00
DIP-TUR	.77	.17	.06[ab]	.47	.47	.06[b]	.00	1.00	.00
DIP-INT	.80	.17	.03[ab]	.24	.59	.18	.00	.00	1.00
Polyarchic									
WAR-TUR	.80	.20	.00[ab]	.63	.05	.32[ab]	.25	.75	.00
WAR-INT	.78	.19	.03[ab]	.63	.38	.00[ab]	.00	.00	.00
BEL-TUR	.75	.23	.02[ab]	.58	.19	.23[ab]	.67	.33	.00[a]
BEL-INT	.69	.29	.02[ab]	.50	.40	.10[a]	1.00	.00	.00[a]
DIP-TUR	.75	.25	.00[ab]	.55	.17	.28[ab]	.80	.20	.00[a]
DIP-INT	.81	.17	.02[ab]	.60	.35	.05[ab]	.00	.00	.00

[a] Data conform to prediction.
[b] $p < .05$ (see note in table 6).

Table 19. Predicted and Observed Inequalities (4), (5) and (6)

	(4) $p(D_{00}/F_0) > p(D_{00}/F_1)$ and $p(D_{00}/F_2)$			(5) $p(D_{11}/F_1) > p(D_{11}/F_0)$ and $p(D_{11}/F_2)$			(6) $p(D_{22}/F_2) > p(D_{22}/F_1)$ and $p(D_{22}/F_0)$		
Personalist									
WAR-TUR	.13	.29	1.00	.71	.48	1.00	.00	.50	.40
WAR-INT	.53	.50	.50[a]	.57	.21	1.00	.00	.29	.54
BEL-TUR	.25	.22	.00[a]	.82	.17	.67[a]	1.00	.33	.25[a]
BEL-INT	.60	.50	.00[a]	.36	.25	.67	.60	.40	.40[a]
DIP-TUR	.25	.18	.00[a]	.77	.39	.00[a]	1.00	.17	.60[a]
DIP-INT	.50	.53	.00	.50	.25	.00[a]	.00	.42	.57
Centrist									
WAR-TUR	.77	.86	.67	.55	.18	.50[a]	.33	.33	.33
WAR-INT	.84	.95	.80	.18	.18	.57	.20	.50	1.00
BEL-TUR	.78	.86	.50	.43	.36	.40[a]	.33	.33	.33
BEL-INT	.85	.93	.75	.23	.33	.25	.25	.67	.43
DIP-TUR	.77	.87	.63	.47	.30	.33[a]	.00	.25	.43
DIP-INT	.80	.93	1.00	.24	.30	.50	.00	.33	.57
Polyarchic									
WAR-TUR	.80	.65	.00[a]	.63	.46	.40[a]	.25	1.00	.58
WAR-INT	.78	.84	.63	.63	.48	1.00	.00	.50	.43
BEL-TUR	.75	.74	.00[a]	.58	.45	.50[a]	.67	.79	.56[a]
BEL-INT	.69	.85	1.00	.50	.59	1.00	1.00	.75	.00[a]
DIP-TUR	.75	.77	.50	.55	.44	.60	.80	.77	.50[a]
DIP-INT	.81	.77	.75[a]	.60	.50	1.00	.00	.75	.20

[a] Data conform to prediction.

Table 20. Predicted and Observed Inequalities (7), (8) and (9)

	(7) $p(D_{00}/F_0) >$	$p(D_{10}/F_0)$ and	$p(D_{20}/F_0)$	(8) $p(D_{11}/F_1) >$	$p(D_{01}/F_1)$ and	$p(D_{21}/F_1)$	(9) $p(D_{22}/F_2) >$	$p(D_{12}/F_2)$ and	$p(D_{02}/F_2)$
Personalist									
WAR-TUR	.13	.38	.20	.71	.57	.00[a]	.00	.00	.00
WAR-INT	.53	.36	.23[a]	.57	.42	.43[a]	.00	.00	.00
BEL-TUR	.25	.75	.50	.82	.78	.50[a]	1.00	.17	.50[a]
BEL-INT	.60	.63	.40	.36	.44	.30	.60	.33	.50[a]
DIP-TUR	.25	.56	.20	.77	.73	.50[a]	1.00	.00	.00[a]
DIP-INT	.50	.33	.43[a]	.50	.41	.42[a]	.00	.00	.00
Centrist									
WAR-TUR	.77	.82	.33	.55	.09	.33[a]	.33	.13	.00[a]
WAR-INT	.84	.64	.00[a]	.18	.05	.50	.20	.29	.00
BEL-TUR	.78	.64	.17[a]	.43	.09	.33[a]	.33	.00	.00[a]
BEL-INT	.85	.50	.14[a]	.23	.07	.33	.25	.25	.00
DIP-TUR	.77	.60	.29[a]	.47	.09	.50	.00	.00	.25
DIP-INT	.80	.40	.00[a]	.24	.07	.67	.00	.00	.00
Polyarchic									
WAR-TUR	.80	.32	.00[a]	.63	.25	.00[a]	.25	.40	.00
WAR-INT	.78	.36	.00[a]	.63	.16	.00[a]	.00	.00	.00
BEL-TUR	.75	.27	.00[a]	.58	.23	.21[a]	.67	.50	.00[a]
BEL-INT	.69	.32	.25[a]	.50	.14	.25[a]	1.00	.00	.00[a]
DIP-TUR	.75	.33	.00[a]	.55	.20	.23[a]	.80	.40	.25[a]
DIP-INT	.81	.36	.00[a]	.60	.23	.00[a]	.00	.00	.08

[a] Data conform to prediction.

The results for the second set of inequalities, (4), (5), and (6) are given in table 19. Here the results are surprising. It will be recalled that for all states combined these inequalities were only supported in a few cases. We now find considerably greater support for the inequalities given specific types of nations. Thus, the matching prediction *is supported to a large extent* by the personalist and somewhat less so by the polyarchic states. Once again, the inequalities are unsupported by the data for the centrist group of nations. That is, while the personalist and polyarchic groups exhibit situations in which transitions in domestic conflict behavior correctly match previous levels of foreign conflict, this is not an attribute of the centrist group.

The final set of inequalities, (7), (8), and (9) are reported in table 20. Once again, important differences arise between the states. In the original analysis most of the inequalities were supported. Now we discover that while inequality (7) is supported by all three groups, inequalities (8) and (9) are supported only by the personalist and polyarchic groups.

SUMMARY AND CONCLUSIONS

In reviewing the analyses performed in the study, it appears to us that four findings are of particular interest.

1. It is noteworthy that the level of domestic conflict behavior can be best predicted from knowledge of the level of prior domestic conflict; there is considerable evidence that domestic conflict behavior is a first-order Markov chain. Drastic changes do not often occur in the level of violence which a nation is experiencing.

2. We find that foreign conflict behavior affects these transitions only under very special conditions, namely when domestic conflict behavior is of a less intense variety. That is, the turmoil type of domestic conflict behavior, composed of demonstrations, riots, and strikes, is much more likely to exhibit the effects of foreign conflict behavior on its transitions from year to year, than is internal war, composed of the more violent forms of domestic conflict, such as revolutions, guerrilla warfare, domestic killed, purges, and government crises.

3. We have found that these two relationships are specific to particular types of states. It is principally in centrist and polyarchic states that we find the relationship over time between levels of domestic conflict behavior, while foreign conflict behavior primarily affects transitions in domestic conflict behavior for the personalist and polyarchic states. Thus, the domestic conflict behavior of the centrist states appears to be principally a function of prior domestic conflict behavior, while changes in domestic conflict behavior for the personalist and polyarchic states are more heavily influenced by foreign conflict behavior.

4. We have found that the transitions in domestic conflict behavior follow a matching pattern largely influenced by foreign conflict behavior. But again, the results are specific to only certain types of states. For the most part, the matching phenomenon occurs in the polyarchic and personalist states.

 **BIBLIOGRAPHY**

Bibliography

Abel, T. "The Element of Decision in the Pattern of War." *American Sociological Review* 6 (1941): 853–59.

Adelman, Irma, and Morris, Cynthia Taft. *Society, Politics and Economic Development.* Baltimore: Johns Hopkins University Press, 1967.

Adorno, T. W., et al. *The Authoritative Personality.* New York: Harper & Brothers, 1950.

Ahmavaara, Yrjo. "Transformation Analysis of Factorial Data." *Annales Academiae Scientiarum Fennicae* 88 (1954): 1–150.

Alker, Hayward. "The Long Road to Theory: Problems of Statistical Non-Additivity." In *New Approaches to International Relations,* edited by Morton A. Kaplan. New York: St. Martin's Press, 1968.

Allison, Graham; May, Ernest; and Yarmolinsky, Adam. "Limits to Intervention." *Foreign Affairs* 48 (January 1970): 245–61.

Allport, Gordon W. *The Nature of Prejudice.* Cambridge, Mass.: Addison-Wesley, 1954.

_____. *Personality.* New York: Henry Holt & Co., 1937.

Anderson, T. W. *Introduction to Multivariate Statistical Analysis.* New York: John Wiley, 1958.

Angell, Robert. *The Family Encounters the Depression: A Re-Analysis of Documents Bearing on the Family Encountering the Depression.* New York: Social Science Research Council, 1942.

Apter, David E. *The Politics of Modernization.* Chicago: University of Chicago Press, 1965.

Ashby, W. Ross. *An Introduction to Cybernetics.* Science ed. New York: John Wiley, 1963.

Banks, Arthur S., and Gregg, Phillip M. "Grouping Political Systems: Q-Factor Analysis of *A Cross Polity Survey.*" *The American Behavioral Scientist* 9 (November 1965): 3–6.

Banks, Arthur S., and Textor, Robert B. *A Cross Polity Survey.* Cambridge, Mass.: MIT Press, 1963.

Barnard, Chester. *The Functions of the Executive.* Cambridge, Mass.: Harvard University Press, 1950.

Bechtoldt, Harold P.; Benton, Arthur L.; and Fogel, Max L. "An Application of Factor Analysis in Neuropsychology." *Psychological Record* 12 (1962): 147–56.

Bedeski, Robert E. "The Prospects of Crisis in East Asia: Dimensions and Approaches." Mimeographed. Columbus, Ohio: Ohio State University, 1971.

Beloff, Max. "Reflections on Intervention." *Journal of International Affairs* 22, no. 2 (1968): 198–207.

Benda, J. A. "Revolutions and Nationalism in the Non-Western World." In *New Era in the Non-Western World,* edited by W. S. Hunsberger. Ithaca, N.Y.: Cornell University Press, 1957.

Bendix, Reinhard. *Nation-Building and Citizenship.* New York: John Wiley, 1964.

Berkowitz, Leonard. *Aggression: A Social Psychological Analysis.* New York: McGraw-Hill, 1962.

Bernard, Jessie. "The Sociological Study of Conflict." In *The Nature of Conflict,* edited by the International Sociological Association. Paris: UNESCO, 1957.

Berrien, Kenneth F. *General and Social Systems.* New Brunswick, N.J.: Rutgers University Press, 1968.

Berry, Brian J. L. "Basic Patterns of Economic Development." In *Atlas of Economic Development,* edited by Norton Ginsburg, pp. 110–19. Chicago: University of Chicago Press, 1961.

_____. "An Inductive Approach to the Regionalization of Economic Development." In *Essays on Geography and Economic Development,* edited by Norton Ginsburg. Chicago: University of Chicago Press, 1960.

Black, C. E. *The Dynamics of Modernization.* New York: Harper & Row, 1966.

Blalock, Hubert M., Jr. *Causal Inferences in Nonexperimental Research.* Chapel Hill: University of North Carolina Press, 1964.

_____. "Theory Building and Causal Inferences." In *Methodology in Social Research,* edited by Hubert M. and Ann B. Blalock. New York: McGraw-Hill, 1968.

_____. *Theory Construction: From Verbal to Mathematical Formulation.* Englewood Cliffs, N.J.: Prentice-Hall, 1969.

Blau, Peter M. *Exchange and Power in Social Life.* New York: John Wiley, 1964.

Bliss, Chester I. *Statistics in Biology, II.* New York: McGraw-Hill, 1970.

Blong, Clair Karl. "A Comparative Study of the Foreign Policy Behavior of Political Systems Exhibiting High Versus Low Levels of External Penetration." Mimeographed. Ph.D. dissertation prospectus, University of Maryland, 1971.

Bobrow, Davis. "Ecology of International Games: Requirements for a Model of the International System." *Peace Research Society Papers* 9 (1969): 67–87.

Bodurt, G. *Losses of Life in Modern Wars.* Oxford: Clarendon Press, 1916.

Borgatta, E. F., and Cottrell, L. S., Jr. "On the Classification of Groups." *Sociometry* 18 (1955): 665–78.

———, and Meyer, H. J. "On the Dimensions of Group Behavior." *Sociometry* 19 (1956): 223–40.

Bornstein, Joseph. *The Politics of Murder.* New York: Sloane, 1958.

Boulding, Kenneth E. *Conflict and Defense.* New York: Harper & Row, 1962.

Brinton, Crane, et al. *The History of Civilization,* Vol. 1. Englewood Cliffs, N.J.: Prentice-Hall, 1967.

Brogan, Denis Wm. *The Price of Revolution.* New York: Harper & Brothers, 1952.

Buchatzsch, E. J. "The Influence of Social Conditions on Mortality Rates." *Population Studies* 1 (1947): 229–48.

Buckley, Walter. "Society as a Complex Adaptive System." In *Modern Systems Research for the Behavioral Scientist,*" edited by Walter Buckley. Chicago: Aldine, 1968.

———. *Sociology and Modern Systems Theory.* Englewood Cliffs, N.J.: Prentice-Hall, 1967.

Bunker, Rod. "Linkages and the Foreign Policy of Peru, 1958–1966." *Western Political Quarterly* 22 (June 1969): 280–97.

Burton, John W. *Conflict and Communication: The Use of Controlled Communication in International Relations.* New York: Free Press, 1969.

———. *Systems, States, Diplomacy and Rules.* London and New York: Cambridge University Press, 1968.

Bwy, Douglas. "Dimensions of Social Conflict in Latin America." *American Behavioral Scientist* 11 (1968): 39–50.

Campbell, Donald T. "Evolutionary Theory in Social Science: A Reappraisal." Paper read at the conference on Social Science and the Underdeveloped Areas: A Revival of Evolutionary Theory, June 1961, at Northwestern University.

———, and LeVine, Robert. "Propositions about Ethnocentrism from Social Science Theories." Mimeographed. Evanston, Ill.: Northwestern University, 1965.

Cantril, H., and Buchanan, W. *How Nations See Each Other: A Study of Public Opinion.* Urbana, Ill.: University of Illinois Press, 1953.

Carr, L. J. "A Situational Approach to Conflict and War." *Social Forces* 24 (1946): 300–3.

Carroll, J. B. "The Nature of the Data or How to Choose a Correlation Coefficient." *Psychometrika* 26 (1961): 347–71.

Casanova, Pablo Gonzales. "Internal and External Politics of Underdeveloped Countries." In *Approaches to Comparative and Inter-*

national Politics, edited by R. Barry Farrell. Evanston, Ill.: Northwestern University Press, 1966.

Cattell, Raymond. "The Dimensions of Culture Patterns of Factorization of National Characters." *Journal of Abnormal and Social Psychology* 44 (1949): 443–69.

_____. *Factor Analysis*. New York: Harper & Brothers, 1952.

_____. "The Principal Culture Patterns Discoverable in the Syntal Dimensions of Existing Nations." *Journal of Social Psychology* 32 (1950): 215–53.

_____; Breul, H.; and Hartman, H. Parker. "An Attempt at More Refined Definition of the Cultural Dimensions of Syntality in Modern Nations." *American Sociological Review* 17 (1951): 408–21.

Childers, Erskine B. *The Road to Suez*. London: Macgibbon & Kee, 1962.

Choucri, Nazli, and North, Robert C. "The Determinants of International Violence." *Peace Research Society Papers* (1968): 33–63.

_____, "Pressure, Competition, Tension, Threat: Toward a Theory of International Conflict." Paper read at the annual meeting, American Political Science Association, 1969, at New York.

Christ, Carl. *Econometric Models and Methods*. New York: John Wiley, 1966.

Clark, Robert P., Jr. "Economic Integration and the Political Process: Linkage Politics in Venezuela." Mimeographed. 1969.

Cobb, Roger W., and Elder, Charles. *International Community: A Regional and Global Study*. New York: Holt, Rinehart & Winston, 1970.

Coleman, James S. *Community Conflict*. Glencoe, Ill.: Free Press, 1957.

Collins, John N. "Factor Analysis and the Grouping of Events Data: Problems and Possible Solutions." Paper read at the First Annual Events Data Conference, 1969, at Michigan State University.

_____. "Foreign Conflict Behavior and Domestic Disorders in Africa." Paper read at the annual meeting, American Political Science Association, 1969, at New York. Mimeographed.

Comrey, Andrew L., and Levonian E. "A Comparison of Three Point Coefficients in Factor Analysis of MMPI Items." *Educational and Psychological Measurements* 18 (1958): 739–55.

Cooley, William, and Lohnes, Paul. *Multivariate Procedures for the Behavioral Sciences*. New York: John Wiley, 1962.

Corning, Peter A. "The Biological Bases of Behavior and Some Implications for Political Science." *World Politics* 23 (April 1971): 321–70.

_____. "Toward an Evolutionary-Adaptive Theory of Politics." Paper read at the annual meeting of the Midwest Political Science Association, 1971, at Chicago. Mimeographed.

Coser, Lewis. *The Functions of Social Conflict*. New York: Free Press, 1956.

Couloumbis, Theodore A. "The Foreign Factor in Greek Politics." Mimeographed. 1971.

――――. *Greek Political Reaction to American and NATO Influences.* New Haven: Yale University Press, 1966.

Coyle, Grace. *Social Process in Organized Groups.* New York: Richard R. Smith, 1930.

Crozier, Brian. *The Rebels: A Study of Post-War Insurrections.* Boston: Beacon Press, 1960.

Dahlke, H. O., "Race and Minority Riots: A Study in the Typology of Violence." *Social Forces* 30 (1952): 419–25.

Denton, Frank. "Some Regularities in International Conflict, 1820–1949." *Background* 9 (1966): 283–96.

――――, and Phillips, Warren R. "Some Patterns in the History of Violence." *Journal of Conflict Resolution* 12 (1968): 182–95.

Deutsch, Karl W. *The Analysis of International Relations.* Englewood Cliffs, N. J.: Prentice-Hall, 1968.

――――. "External Influences on the Internal Behavior of States." In *Approaches to Comparative and International Politics,* edited by R. Barry Farrell, pp. 5–26. Evanston, Ill.: Northwestern University Press, 1966.

――――. *Nationalism and Social Communication.* New York: Technology Press, MIT, 1953.

――――, and Foltz, William J., eds. *Nation-Building.* New York: Atherton, 1963.

――――, and Senghaas, Dieter. "Toward a Theory of War and Peace: Propositions, Simulations, and Reality." Paper read at the annual meeting, American Political Science Association, 1969, at New York.

Diamant, Alfred. "Is There a Non-Western Political Process?" *Journal of Politics* 21 (1959): 123–27.

Dollard, J. *Frustration and Aggression.* New Haven: Yale University Press, 1939.

Dominguez, Jorge I. "Mice That Do Not Roar: Some Aspects of International Politics in the World's Peripheries." *International Organization* 25 (Spring 1971): 175–208.

Drake, St. Clair. "Some Observations in Interethnic Conflict as One Type of Intergroup Conflict." *Journal of Conflict Resolution* 1 (1957): 155–78.

Draper, N. R., and Smith, H. *Applied Regression Analysis.* New York: John Wiley, 1968.

Dumas, Samuel, and Vedel-Petersen, K. O. *Losses of Life Caused by War.* Oxford: Clarenden Press, 1923.

Duncan, Otis Dudley. "Path Analysis: Sociological Examples." *American Journal of Sociology* 72 (1966): 1–16.

Dunn, Fredrick S. *War and the Minds of Men.* New York: Harper & Brothers, 1950.

Eckstein, Harry. "On the Etiology of Internal Wars." *History and Theory* 4 (1965): 133–62.

_____ , ed. *Internal War.* New York: Free Press, 1964.

Edmondson, Locksley. "Africa and the African Diaspora: Interactions, Linkages, and Racial Challenges in the Future World Order." Mimeographed, n.d.

Eisenstadt, S. N. *Essays on Comparative Institutions.* New York: John Wiley, 1965.

Eley, John W. "Internal Wars and International Events: An Analysis of the Internationalization of Internal Wars." Ph.D. dissertation, University of Maryland, 1969.

_____. "The International Dimensions of Internal Wars: A Preliminary Analysis." Paper read at the annual meeting of the Southern Political Science Association, 1970. Mimeographed.

_____. "Toward a Theory of Intervention: The Limitations and Advantages of a Transnational Perspective." *International Studies Quarterly* 16 (June 1972): 245–56.

Etzioni, Amitai. *The Active Society.* New York: Free Press, 1968.

Ezekiel, Mordecai, and Fox, Karl A. *Methods of Correlation and Regression Analysis.* 3rd ed. New York: John Wiley, 1959.

Farrell, R. Barry. "Foreign Politics of Open and Closed Political Societies." In *Approaches to Comparative and International Politics,* edited by R. Barry Farrell. Evanston, Ill.: Northwestern University Press, 1966.

Feierabend, Ivo, and Feierabend, R. L. "The Relationship of Systemic Frustration, Political Coercion, International Tension and Political Instability: A Cross-National Study." Paper read at the American Psychological Association Meetings, 1966, at New York.

Feld, Werner J. "National-International Linkage Theory: The East European Communist System and the EEC." *Journal of International Affairs* 22, no. 1 (1968): 107–20.

Fenichel, Otto. "Elements of a Psychoanalytic Theory of Antisemitism." In *Antisemitism, A Social Disease,* edited by Ernst Simmel. New York: International Universities Press, 1946.

Fink, Clinton F. "Some Conceptual Difficulties in the Theory of Social Conflict." *Journal of Conflict Resolution* (December 1968): 412–60.

Fisher, R. A. "The Use of Multiple Measurement in Taxonomic Problems." *Annuals of Eugenics* 7 (1936): 179–88.

Fitzgibbon, R. H. "Revolutions: Western Hemisphere." *South Atlantic Quarterly* 55 (1956): 263–79.

Fox, Karl A. *Intermediate Economic Statistics.* New York: John Wiley, 1968.

Frankel, Joseph. *International Relations.* New York: Oxford University Press, 1964.

Freymond, Jacques. *The Saar Conflict 1945–1955.* New York: Praeger, 1960.

Fruchter, Benjamin. *Introduction to Factor Analysis.* Princeton, N. J.: D. Van Nostrand, 1954.

Galtung, Johan. "A Structural Theory of Aggression." *Journal of Peace Research,* no. 2 (1964): 15–38.

―――. "A Structural Theory of Imperialism. "*Journal of Peace Research,* no. 2 (1971): 81–117.

―――. "A Structural Theory of Integration." *Journal of Peace Research,* no. 4 (1968): 375–95.

George, Alexander L.; Hall, David K.; and Simons, William R. *The Limits of Coercive Diplomacy: Laos-Cuba-Vietnam.* Boston: Little, Brown, 1971.

Gerth, Hans, and Mills, C. Wright. *From Max Weber.* New York: Oxford University Press, 1946.

Gluckman, Max. *Custom and Conflict in Africa.* Oxford: Blackwell, 1955.

Godfrey, E. P., Fiedler, Fred E., and Hall, D. M. *Boards, Management, and Company Success.* Danville, Ill.: Interstate, 1959.

Gold, David. "Some Problems in Generalizing Aggregate Associations." *American Behavioral Scientist* 8 (1964): 16–18.

Goldberger, Arthur S. *Econometric Theory.* New York: John Wiley, 1964.

Good, Robert C. "State Building as a Determinant of Foreign Policy in the New States." In *Neutralism and Nonalignment,* edited by Lawrence W. Martin. New York: Praeger, 1962.

Grace, H. A., and Neuhaus, J. O. "Information and Social Distance as Predictors of Hostility Toward Nations." *Journal of Abnormal and Social Psychology* 47 (1952): 540–45.

Gregg, Phillip M., and Banks, Arthur S. "Dimensions of Political Systems: Factor Analysis of *A Cross Polity Survey.*" *American Political Science Review* 59 (September 1965): 602–14.

Gross, Feliks. *The Seizure of Political Power.* New York: Philosophical Library, 1958.

Grundy, Kenneth W. "The Foreign Policies of Black Southern Africa." Paper read at the Symposium on International Law and National Development in Southern Africa, 1970, at Los Angeles. Mimeographed.

―――. "Host States and the Southern African Liberation Struggle." *Africa Quarterly* 10 (April–June 1970): 15–24.

Gulliver, P. H. "Land Shortage, Social Change, and Social Conflict in East Africa." *Journal of Conflict Resolution* 5 (1961): 16–26.

Gurr, Ted R. "A Causal Model of Civil Strife: A Comparative Analysis

Using New Indices." *American Political Science Review* 62, no. 4 (1968): 1104–24.

———. *New Error Compensated Measures for Comparing Nations: Some Correlates of Civil Violence*. Princeton: Center for International Studies, Research Monograph No. 26, 1966.

Haas, Ernst B. "The Study of Regional Integration: Reflections on the Joy and Anguish of Pretheorizing." In "Regional Integration: Theory and Research," edited by Leon N. Lindberg and Stuart A. Scheingold. *International Organization* 24 (Autumn 1970): 607–46.

———, and Whiting, Allen S. *Dynamics of International Relations*. New York: McGraw-Hill, 1956.

Haas, Michael. "Dimensional Analysis in Cross-National Research." *Comparative Political Studies* 3 (1970): 3–35.

———. *International Conflict*. Indianapolis: Bobbs-Merrill, forthcoming.

———. "Regional Cooperation for What?" Paper read at the Southeast Asia Development Advisory Group Regional Development Seminar, 1970, at Honolulu.

———. "Social Change and National Aggressiveness, 1900–60." In *Quantitative International Politics*, edited by J. David Singer. New York: Free Press, 1968.

———. "Societal Approaches to the Study of War." *Journal of Peace Research* (1965): 308–23.

———. "Types of Asymmetry in Social and Political Systems." *General Systems Yearbook* 12 (1967): 69–79.

Hanrieder, Wolfram F. "Actor Objectives and International Systems." *Journal of Politics* (February 1965): 109–32.

———. "Compatibility and Consensus: A Proposal for the Conceptual Linkage of External and Internal Dimensions of Foreign Policy." *American Political Science Review* 61, no. 4 (1967): 971–82.

Harman, Harry H. *Modern Factor Analysis*. 2nd ed. Chicago: University of Chicago Press, 1967.

Harrington, Michael. *The Accidental Century*. New York: Macmillan, 1965.

Hart, Hornell. "Depression, War, and Logistic Trends." *American Journal of Sociology* (September 1946): 112–22.

Hazlewood, Leo A. "Informal Penetration, Systemic Constraints, and Political Violence." Mimeographed, 1971.

———. "Political Violence and the Political System." Ph.D. dissertation, University of Pennsylvania, 1969.

Heise, David. "Problems in Path Analysis and Causal Inference." In *Sociological Methodology*, edited by Edgar F. Borgatta. San Francisco: Jossey-Bass, 1968.

Henrysson, Sten. *Applicability of Factor Analysis in the Behavior Studies: A Methodological Study.* Stockholm: Almquist and Wiksell, 1957.

Hoadley, J. Stephen, and Hasegawa, Sukehiro. "Sino-Japanese Relations 1950–1970: An Application of the Linkage Model of International Politics." *International Studies Quarterly* 15 (June 1971): 131–57.

Hobsbawm, E. J. *Primitive Rebels.* Glencoe, Ill.: Free Press, 1960.

Hodnett, Grey, and Potichnyj, Peter J. *The Ukraine and the Czechoslovak Crisis.* Canberra: Australian National University, 1970.

Hoffman, Stanley. "International Organization and the International System." *International Organization* 24 (Summer 1970): 389.

Hofstaetter, P. R. "A Factorial Study of Culture Patterns in the U.S." *Journal of Psychology* 32 (1951): 99–113.

Holsti, Ole R.; North, Robert C.; and Brody, Richard. "Perception and Action in the 1914 Crisis." in *Quantitative International Politics,* edited by J. David Singer, pp. 123–58. New York: Free Press, 1968.

Holt, Robert T., and Turner, John E. *The Political Basis of Economic Development.* Princeton, N.J.: D. Van Nostrand, 1966.

Hooper, J. W. "Simultaneous Equations and Canonical Correlation Theory." *Econometrica* 27 (1959): 245–56.

Hopper, R. D. "Revolutionary Process, A Frame of Reference for the Study of Revolutionary Movements." *Social Forces* 28 (1950): 270–79.

Horowitz, Donald L. "Multi-Racial Politics in New States: Toward a Theory of Conflict." In *Issues in Comparative Politics,* edited by Robert L. Jackson and Michael B. Stein. New York: St. Martin's Press, 1971.

Huff, Curtis E., Jr. "Regional Patterns and Changes after Military Coups D'Etat: The Foreign Relations of African States." Paper read at the annual meeting, American Political Science Association, 1971, at Chicago.

Huntington, Samuel P. *Political Order in Changing Societies.* New Haven: Yale University Press, 1968.

Hurley, John R., and Cattell, Raymond B. "The Procrustes Program: Producing Direct Rotation to Test a Hypothesized Factor Structure." *Behavioral Science* 7 (1962): 258–62.

Ilchman, Warren F., and Uphoff, Norman T. *The Political Economy of Change.* Berkeley: University of California Press, 1969.

Jackson, D. "The Trigonometry of Correlation." *American Mathematical Monthly* 31 (1924): 275–80.

Janowitz, Morris. "Military Elites and The Study of War." *Journal of Conflict Resolution* 1 (1957): 9–18.

Jonassen, Christen T., and Peres, Sherwood H., *Interrelationships of Dimensions of Community Systems.* Columbus: Ohio State University Press, 1960.

Jowitt, Kenneth. "The Romanian Communist Party and the World Socialist System: A Redefinition." *World Politics* 23 (October 1970): 38–60.

Kaiser, Henry F. "The Application of Electronic Computers to Factor Analysis." *Educational and Psychological Measurements* 20 (1960): 141–51.

————. "Computer Program for Verimax Rotation in Factor Analysis." *Educational and Psychological Measurements* 19 (1959): 413–20.

Kaplan, Morton A. *System and Process in International Politics.* New York: John Wiley, 1957.

Kelly, George A., and Brown, Clifford W., eds. *Struggles in the State: Sources and Patterns of World Revolution.* New York: John Wiley, 1970.

————, and Miller, Linda B. "Internal War and International Systems: Perspectives on Method." In *Struggles in the State,* edited by George A. Kelly and Clifford W. Brown, Jr. New York: John Wiley, 1970.

Kerr, C., and Siegel A. "The Isolated Mass and the Integrated Individual —An International Analysis of the Inter-Industry Propensity to Strike." In *Industrial Conflict,* edited by A. Kornhauser et al. New York: McGraw-Hill, 1954.

Kerr, Malcolm. *The Arab Cold War, 1958–67.* New York: Oxford University Press, 1967.

Klineberg, Otto. *Tensions Affecting International Understanding: A Survey of Research.* New York: Social Science Research Council, 1950.

Korbonski, Andrzej. "Theory and Practice of Regional Integration: The Case of COMECON." *International Organization* 24 (Autumn 1970): 942–77.

Kornhauser, A.; Dubin R.; and Ross, A. M., eds. *Industrial Conflict.* New York: McGraw-Hill, 1954.

Land, Kenneth C. "Principles of Path Analysis." In *Sociological Methodology,* edited by Edgar F. Borgatta. San Francisco: Jossey-Bass, 1968.

LaPalombara, Joseph, ed. *Bureaucracy and Political Development.* Princeton, N. J.: Princeton University Press, 1963.

————, and Weiner, Myron, eds. *Political Parties and Political Development.* Princeton, N.J.: Princeton University Press, 1966.

Laqueur, Walter. *The Road to Jerusalem.* New York: Macmillan, 1968.

Laub, Rose. "An Analysis of the Early German Socialist Movement." Master's thesis, Columbia University, 1951.

Leites, Nathan, and Wolfe, Charles, Jr. *Rebellion and Authority.* Chicago: Markham, 1970.

Lenin, Vladimir I. *Imperialism.* New York: International Publishers, 1939.

Lerner, Daniel. "Some Comments on Center-Periphery Relations." In *Comparing Nations,* edited by Richard Merritt and Stein Rokkan. New Haven: Yale University Press, 1966.

LeVine, Robert A. "Anti-European Violence in Africa: A Comparative Analysis." *Journal of Conflict Resolution* 3 (1959): 420–29.

Levy, Marion J. " 'Does It Matter if He's Naked' Bawled the Child." In *Contending Approaches to International Politics,* edited by Klaus Knorr and James N. Rosenau, pp. 87–109. Princeton, N.J.: Princeton University Press, 1969.

Lewin, Kurt, and Loppitt, R. "An Experimental Study of the Effect of Democratic and Authoritarian Group Atmospheres." *University of Iowa Studies in Child Welfare* 16, no. 3 (1940): 45–198.

Lewis, Vaughan A. "The Structure of Small State Behavior in Contemporary International Politics." Ph.D. dissertation, Jamaica, W.I., 1971.

Lindberg, Leon N. "Political Integration as a Multidimensional Phenomenon Requiring Multivariate Measurement." *International Organization* 24 (Autumn 1970): 649–731.

————, and Scheingold, Stuart A. *Europe's Would-Be Polity: Patterns of Change in the European Community.* Englewood Cliffs, N.J.: Prentice-Hall, 1970.

Lipset, Seymour M. *Agrarian Socialism.* Berkeley: University of California Press, 1950.

————, and Rokkan, Stein, eds. *Party Systems and Voter Alignments.* New York: Free Press, 1967.

Lowenthal, Leo, and Guterman, Norbert. *Prophets of Deceit,* Vol. 5. *Studies of Prejudice.* New York: Harper & Brothers, 1950–51.

McClelland, Charles A. "Access to Berlin: The Quantity and Variety of Events, 1948–1963." In *Quantitative International Politics,* edited by J. David Singer, pp. 159–86. New York: Free Press, 1968.

————. "The Acute International Crisis." In *The International System,* edited by Klaus Knorr and Sidney Verba. Princeton, N.J.: Princeton University Press, 1961.

————. *Theory and the International System.* New York: Macmillan, 1966.

————; Harrison, Daniel; Martin, Wayne; Phillips, Warren; and Young, Robert. "The Communist Chinese Performance in Crisis and Non-Crisis: Quantitative Studies of the Taiwan Straits Confrontation." China Lake, Calif.: Behavioral Sciences Group, Naval Ordinance Test Station, 1965.

McClelland, David C. *The Achieving Society.* Princeton, N.J.: D. Van Nostrand, 1961.

McCoy, Terry L. "External Outputs and Population Policy Making in

Latin America." Paper read at the annual meeting, American Political Science Association, 1971, at Chicago.

———. "A Functional Taxonomy of International Population Programs." Paper read at the American Society of International Law Regional Meeting, 1971, at Charlottesville, Virginia. Mimeographed.

MacCrone, Ian Douglas. *Race Attitudes in South Africa: Historical, Experimental and Psychological Studies.* Johannesburg: Witwatersrand University Press, 1937 (1957).

McGowan, Patrick J. "A Formal Theory of Foreign Policy as Adaptive Behavior." Paper read at the annual meeting of the American Political Science Association, 1970, at Los Angeles. Mimeographed.

McHale, John. *The Future of the Future.* New York: Braziller, 1969.

Mack, Raymond W., and Snyder, Richard C. "The Analysis of Social Conflict—Toward an Overview and Synthesis." *Journal of Conflict Resolution* 1 (1957): 212–48.

Manley, Robert H. "Linkage Politics: The Organization Environment for Guyanese Nation-Building." Paper read at the annual meeting of the International Studies Association, 1971, at San Juan, P.R. Mimeographed.

Maruyama, Magorah. "The Second Cybernetics: Deviation Amplifying Mutual Causal Processes." In *Modern Systems Research for the Behavioral Scientist,* edited by Walter Buckley. Chicago: Aldine, 1968.

Marx, Karl, and Engels, Friedrich. *Manifesto of the Communist Party.* New York: International Publishers, 1948.

Meadows, Martin. "Theories of External-Internal Political Relationships: A Case Study of Indonesia and the Philippines." *Asian Studies* 6 (December 1968): 297–324.

Meadows, P. "Town and Country in Revolution." *Sociology and Social Research* 31 (1947): 273–78.

Merton, Robert K. "Discrimination and the American Creed." In *Discrimination and National Welfare,* edited by Robert K. Merton. New York: Harper & Brothers, 1948.

———. *Social Theory and Social Structure.* Glencoe, Ill.: Free Press, 1949.

———, and Kitt, Alice S. "Contributions to the Theory of Reference Group Behavior." In *Studies in the Scope and Method of "The American Soldier,"* edited by Robert K. Merton and Paul Lazarsfeld. Glencoe, Ill.: Free Press, 1950.

Michael, Donald N. *The Unprepared Society.* New York: Basic Books, 1968.

Michels, Robert. *Political Parties.* Glencoe, Ill.: Free Press, 1949.

Miller, James G. "Living Systems: Basic Concepts; Structure and Process; Cross-Level Hypotheses." *Behavioral Science* 10 (1965).

Millis, Walter. "A World Without War." In *A World Without War*, edited by Walter Millis et al., pp. 53–106. New York: Washington Square Press, 1961.

Mills, C. Wright. *The Causes of World War Three*. New York: Simon & Schuster, 1958.

Mitchell, C. R. "Civil Strife and the Involvement of External Parties." *International Studies Quarterly* 14 (June 1970): 166–94.

Modelski, George. *A Theory of Foreign Policy*. New York: Praeger, 1962.

Moore, John Norton. "The Control of Foreign Intervention in Internal Conflict." *Virginia Journal of International Law* 9 (May 1969): 209–342.

Morgenthau, Hans J. *Politics Among Nations*. New York: Alfred A. Knopf, 1967.

Morris, Charles. *Varieties of Human Value*. Chicago: University of Chicago Press, 1956.

Morrison, Denton, and Henkel, Ramon E., eds. *The Significance Test Controversy: A Reader*. Chicago: Aldine, 1970.

Mosier, Charles I. "Influence of Chance Error on Sample Structure: An Empirical Investigation of the Effect of Chance Error and Estimated Communalities on Simple Structure in Factorial Analysis." *Psychometrika* 4 (1939): 33–44.

Moyal, J. E. "The Distribution of Wars in Time." *Journal of the Royal Statistical Society* 112 (1949): 446–49.

Nef, John U. *War and Human Progress*. Cambridge, Mass.: Harvard University Press, 1950.

Nettl, J. P. *Political Mobilization*. New York: Basic Books, 1967.

Oliva, Gary, and Rummel, R. J. "Foreign Conflict Patterns and Types for 1963." Research Report No. 22, Dimensionality of Nations Project, University of Hawaii, 1969.

Olson, Mancur. "Rapid Growth as a Destabilizing Force." *Journal of Economic History* 27 (1963): 529–52.

Osgood, Charles. "Behavior Theory and the Social Sciences." In *Approaches to the Study of Politics*, edited by Roland Young. Evanston, Ill.: Northwestern University Press, 1958.

Park, Tong-Whan. "The Role of Distance in International Relations: A New Look at the Social Field Theory." Paper read at the International Studies Association, South-Southwest Regional Meetings, 1970, at New Orleans.

Parsons, T. "Certain Primary Sources of Aggression in the Social Structure of the Western World." In *Conflicts of Power in Modern Culture*, edited by L. Bryson et al., pp. 29–48. New York: Harper & Brothers, 1946.

_____. *Religious Perspectives of College Teaching in Sociology and Social Psychology.* New Haven: Edward W. Hagen Foundation, n.d.

Paul, David W. "Soviet Foreign Policy and the Invasion of Czechoslovakia: A Theory and a Case Study." *International Studies Quarterly* 15 (June 1971): 159–202.

Pear, T. H. *Psychological Factors of Peace and War.* New York: Philosophical Library, 1950.

Phillips, Warren R. "The Conflict Environment of Nations: A Study of Conflict Inputs to Nations in 1963." Paper read at the annual meeting, American Political Science Association, 1970, at Los Angeles.

_____. "The Dynamics of Behavioral Action and Reaction in International Conflict." Paper read at the Peace Research Society (International) Meetings, 1970, at Philadelphia.

_____. "Dynamic Patterns of International Conflict." Ph.D. dissertation, University of Hawaii, 1969.

_____, and Hall, Dennis R. "The Importance of Governmental Structure as a Taxonomic Scheme for Nations." *Comparative Political Studies* 3 (1970): 63–89.

Pierson, D. "Race Prejudice as Revealed in the Study of Racial Situations." *International Social Science Bulletin* 2 (1950): 467–78.

Pike, F. B. "Sources of Revolution: Their Impact on Freedom and Reform in Latin America." In *Freedom and Reform in Latin America,* edited by F. B. Pike, pp. 28–58. South Bend, Ind.: Notre Dame Press, 1959.

Plato. *The Republic.* Translated by Benjamin Jowett. Garden City, N.Y.: Doubleday, n.d.

Pool, Ithiel de Sola. *Symbols of Internationalism.* Hoover Institute Studies, Series C, No. 3. Stanford, Calif.: Stanford University Press, 1951.

Przeworski, Adam, and Teune, Henry. *The Logic of Comparative Social Inquiry.* New York: John Wiley, 1970.

Pye, Lucian W. *Aspects of Political Development.* Boston: Little, Brown, 1963.

_____. "The Non-Western Political Process." *Journal of Politics* 20 (1958): 468–86.

Quigley, Carroll. *The Evolution of Civilizations.* New York: Macmillan, 1961.

Rae, Douglas, and Taylor, Michael. *The Analysis of Political Cleavages.* New Haven: Yale University Press, 1970.

Rapoport, Anatol. *Fights, Games and Debates.* Ann Arbor: University of Michigan Press, 1960.

_____. "Lewis Fry Richardson's Mathematical Theory of War." *Journal of Conflict Resolution* 1 (1957): 249–99.

Rashevsky, N. *Mathematical Biology of Social Behavior.* Chicago: University of Chicago Press, 1951.

_____. *Mathematical Theory and Human Relations; An Approach to a Mathematical Biology of Social Phenomena.* Bloomington, Ind.: Principia Press, 1947.

Reid, George L. "Linkage Theory in Application to Micro-States." Mimeographed. Ph.D. dissertation prospectus, South Hampton, 1970.

Reves, Emery. *The Anatomy of Peace.* New York: Harper & Brothers, 1946.

Rhee, S. "Communist China's Foreign Behavior: An Application of Field Theory Model II." Research Report No. 57, Dimensionality of Nations Project, University of Hawaii, 1971.

Rhodes, E. C. "Construction of an Index of Business Activity." *Journal of the Royal Statistical Society* 100 (1937): 18–39.

Richardson, Lewis Fry. *Arms and Insecurity.* Pittsburgh: Boxwood Press, 1960.

_____. "Contiguity and Deadly Quarrels: The Local Pacifying Influence." *Journal of the Royal Statistical Society* 115 (1952): 219–31.

_____. *Statistics of Deadly Quarrels.* Pittsburgh: Boxwood Press, 1960.

Riggs, Fred W. *Administration in Developing Countries.* Boston: Houghton Mifflin, 1964.

_____. "The Dialectics of Developmental Conflict." *Comparative Political Studies* 1 (1968): 197–226.

_____. "International Relations as a Prismatic System." In *The International System,* edited by Klaus Knorr and Sidney Verba. Princeton, N.J.: Princeton University Press, 1961.

Rosecrance, Richard N. *Action and Reaction in World Politics: International Systems in Perspective.* Boston: Little, Brown, 1963.

Rosenau, James N. *The Adaptation of National Societies: A Theory of Political System Behavior and Transformation.* New York: McCaleb-Seiler, 1970.

_____. "Adaptive Strategies for Research and Practice in Foreign Policy." In *International Studies: Present Status and Future Prospects,* edited by Fred Riggs. Philadelphia: American Academy of Political and Social Science, 1971.

_____. *Of Bridges and Boundaries: A Report on a Conference on the Interdependencies of National and International Political Systems.* Princeton: Center for International Studies, Research Monograph No. 27, 1967.

_____. *Calculated Control as a Unifying Concept in the Study of International Politics and Foreign Policy.* Princeton, N.J.: Center for International Studies, Research Report No. 15, 1963.

_____. "Compatibility, Consensus, and an Emerging Political Science of

Adaptation." *American Political Science Review* 61, no. 4 (1967): 983–988.

———. "The Concept of Intervention." *Journal of International Affairs* 22, no. 2 (1968): 165–76.

———. *Domestic Sources of Foreign Policy.* New York: Free Press, 1967.

———. "Foreign Intervention as Adaptive Behavior." In *Law and Civil War in the Modern World,* edited by John Norton Moore.

———, ed. *International Aspects of Civil Strife.* Princeton, N.J.: Princeton University Press, 1964.

———. *International Studies and the Social Sciences.* Minneapolis: International Studies Association, 1971.

———. "Intervention as a Scientific Concept." *Journal of Conflict Resolution* 13 (June 1969): 149–71.

———, ed. *Linkage Politics: Essays on the Convergence of National and International Systems.* New York: Free Press, 1969.

———. "Pre-Theories and Theories of Foreign Policy." In *Approaches to Comparative and International Politics,* edited by R. Barry Farrell. Evanston, Ill.: Northwestern University Press, 1966.

———. "Toward the Study of National-International Linkages." *Linkage Politics,* edited by James N. Rosenau. New York: Free Press, 1969.

———, and McGowan, Patrick J. "Toward a Dynamic Theory of Foreign Policy." Mimeographed. Syracuse, 1971.

Rosenberg, Milton J. "Attitude Change and Foreign Policy in the Cold War Era." In *Domestic Sources of Foreign Policy,* edited by James N. Rosenau. New York: Free Press, 1967.

Rosenblatt, P. C. "Origins and Effects of Group Ethnocentrism and Nationalism." *Journal of Conflict Resolution* 8 (June 1964).

Ross, A. M., and Irwin, D. "Strike Experience in Five Countries 1927–1947: An Interpretation." *Industrial and Labor Relations Review* 4 (1951): 323–42.

Rostow, Walt W. *Politics and the Stages of Growth.* London and New York: Cambridge University Press, 1971.

———. *The Stages of Economic Growth.* London and New York: Cambridge University Press, 1960.

Rummel, R. J. *Applied Factor Analysis.* Evanston, Ill.: Northwestern University Press, 1970.

———. "Dimensions of Conflict Behavior Within and Between Nations." *General Systems Yearbook* 8 (1963): 1–50.

———. "Field Theory and the 1963 Behavior Space of Nations." Research Report No. 44, Dimensionality of Nations Project. University of Hawaii, 1970.

———. "Field Theory and Indicators of International Behavior." Paper read at the annual meeting, American Political Science Association, 1969, at New York.

————. "A Field Theory of Social Action with Application to Conflict Within Nations." *General Systems Yearbook* 10 (1965): 183–211.

————. "A Foreign Conflict Behavior Code Sheet." *World Politics* 18 (1966): 283–96.

————. "Indicators of Cross-National and International Patterns." *American Political Science Review* 63 (1969): 127–47.

————. "International Patterns and National Profile Delineation." In *Computers and the Policy Making Community: Applications to International Relations,* edited by Davis Bobrow and Judah L. Schwartz. Englewood Cliffs, N.J.: Prentice-Hall, 1968.

————. "The Relationship Between National Attributes and Foreign Conflict Behavior." In *Quantitative International Politics,* edited by J. David Singer, pp. 187–214. New York: Free Press, 1968.

————. "A Social Field Theory of Foreign Conflict Behavior." *Peace Research Society Papers* 5 (1965).

————. "Some Attribute and Behavioral Patterns of Nations." *Journal of Peace Research,* no. 2 (1967): 196–206.

————. "Some Dimensions in the Foreign Behavior of Nations," *Journal of Peace Research,* no. 3 (1966): 201–24.

————. "Status, Field Theory and International Relations." Research Report No. 50, Dimensionality of Nations Project, University of Hawaii, 1971.

————. "Testing Some Possible Predictors of Conflict Behavior Within and Between Nations." *Peace Research Society Papers,* no. 1 (1963): 79–111.

————. "Understanding Factor Analysis." *Journal of Conflict Resolution* 11 (1967): 444–80.

————. "U.S. Foreign Relations: Conflict, Cooperation, and Attribute Distances." In *Peace, War, and Numbers,* edited by Bruce M. Russett. Beverly Hills, Calif.: Sage Publications, 1972.

Russett, Bruce M. "Indicators for America's Linkages with the Changing World Environment." *The Annals* 388 (March 1970): 82–96.

————. *International Regions and the International System.* Chicago: Rand McNally, 1967.

————. *What Price Vigilance?* New Haven: Yale University Press, 1970.

————, et al. *World Handbook of Political and Social Indicators.* New Haven: Yale University Press, 1964.

Rustow, Dankwart. *A World of Nations.* Washington, D.C.: Brookings Institution, 1967.

Safran, Nadav. *From War to War: The Arab-Israeli Confrontation.* New York: Pegasus, 1969.

Sartre, Jean Paul. *Commentary.* Vol. 5 (1946).

Sawyer, Jack. "Dimensions of Nations: Size, Wealth, and Politics." *American Journal of Sociology* (1967): 145-72.

Schelling, T. C. *The Strategy of Conflict.* Cambridge, Mass.: Harvard University Press, 1960.

Schnore, Leo F. "The Statistical Measurement of Urbanization and Economic Development." *Land Economics* 37 (1961): 229-45.

Schubert, Glendon. "The 1960 Term of the Supreme Court: A Psychological Analysis." *American Political Science Review* 56 (1962): 90-113.

Scott, Andrew M. "Military Intervention by the Great Powers: The Rules of the Game." Mimeographed. New York, 1968.

————. *The Revolution in Statecraft: Informal Penetration.* New York: Macmillan, 1967.

Seale, Patrick. *The Struggle for Syria.* London: Oxford University Press, 1965.

Selznick, Philip. "Foundations of the Theory of Organizations." *American Journal of Sociology* 13 (1948): 25-35.

Seton-Watson, H. "Twentieth Century Revolutions." *Political Quarterly* 22 (1951): 251-65.

Sherif, Muzafer, et al. *Intergroup Conflict and Cooperation.* Norman, Okla.: University of Oklahoma, Institute of Group Relations, 1961.

Shibutani, Tamotsu, and Kwan, Kian M. *Ethnic Stratification: Comparative Approaches.* New York: Macmillan, 1965.

Shils, Edward A. "Primary Groups in the American Army." In *Studies in the Scope and Method of "The American Soldier,"* edited by Robert K. Merton and Paul Lazarsfeld. Glencoe, Ill.: Free Press, 1950.

Sidman, Murray. *Tactics of Scientific Research.* New York: Basic Books, 1960.

Silberner, Edmund. *The Problem of War in Nineteenth Century Economic Thought.* Translated by Alexander H. Krappe. Princeton, N.J.: Princeton University Press, 1946.

Simmel, Georg. *Conflict and the Web of Group-Affiliations.* Glencoe, Ill.: Free Press, 1955.

Simon, Sheldon W. "Further Reflections on a Systems Approach to Security in the Indian Ocean Arc." Paper read at the annual meeting, American Political Science Association, 1971, at Chicago.

Simpson, George E., and Yinger, Milton J. *Racial and Cultural Minorities.* 3rd ed. New York: Harper & Row, 1965.

Singer, J. David. "The Level-of-Analysis Problem in International Relations." *World Politics* 14 (October 1961): 77–92.

———, and Small, Melvin. "Alliance Aggregation and the Onset of War, 1815–1945." In *Quantitative International Politics*, edited by J. David Singer, pp. 247–86. New York: Free Press, 1968.

Smelser, Neil J. "Mechanisms of Change and Adjustment to Change." In *Industrialization and Society*, edited by B. F. Hoselitz and W. E. Moore. The Hague: UNESCO–Mouton, 1963.

Smoker, Paul. "A Time Series Analysis of Sino-Indian Relations." *Journal of Conflict Resolution* 8 (1969): 172–91.

Snyder, Richard C. *Decision Making or an Approach to the Study of International Relations*. Princeton, N.J.: Foreign Policy Analysis Project, 1964.

Snyder, Richard C., and Paige, Glenn D. "The United States Decision to Resist Aggression in Korea." *Administrative Science Quarterly* 3 (1958): 341–78.

Sondermann, Fred A. "The Linkage Between Foreign Policy and International Politics." In *International Politics and Foreign Policy*, edited by James N. Rosenau. New York: Free Press, 1961.

Sorokin, Pitirim A. "Quantitative Measurement of Internal Disturbances." In *Struggles in the State*, edited by George A. Kelly and Clifford W. Brown, Jr. New York: John Wiley, 1970.

———. *Social and Cultural Dynamics*, Vol. 3, New York: American Book Co., 1937.

Stohl, Michael. "The Study of Conflict Behavior Within and Between Nations: Some New Evidence." Paper read at the annual meeting, Midwest Political Science Association, 1971, at Chicago.

Strachey, Alex. *The Unconscious Motives of War: A Psycho-Analytical Contribution*. London: Allen & Urwin, 1957.

Sullivan, John D. "International Consequences of Domestic Violence." Paper read at the annual meeting, American Political Science Association, 1969, at New York. Mimeographed.

Sumner, William A. *Folkways*. Boston: Ginn, 1906.

Tamkoc, Metin. *International Civil War*. Ankara: Middle East Technical University, 1967.

Tannenbaum, Frank. *Darker Phases of the South*. New York: G. P. Putnam's, 1924.

———. "On Political Stability." *Political Science Quarterly* 75 (1960): 161–80.

Tanter, Raymond. "Dimensions of Conflict Behavior Within and Between Nations, 1958–1960." *Journal of Conflict Resolution* 10 (March 1966): 41–64.

————. "Dimensions of Conflict Behavior Within Nations, 1955–1960: Turmoil and Internal War." *Peace Research Society (International) Papers* 3 (1965): 159–83.

Thiam, Doudou. *The Foreign Policy of African States.* New York: Praeger, 1965.

Thibaut, John W., and Kelly, Harold. *The Social Psychology of Groups.* New York: John Wiley, 1959.

Thurstone, L. L. *Multiple Factor Analysis.* Chicago: University of Chicago Press, 1947.

Tilly, Charles. "Research on the Relations Between Conflict Within Polities and Conflict Among Polities." Mimeographed. Ann Arbor, 1970.

Tischendorf, A. "Assassination of Chief Executives in Latin America." *South Atlantic Quarterly* 60 (1961): 80–88.

Tsao, L. E. "Chronological Table of Major Wars in Europe and Asia in the Last One Hundred and Fifty Years." *Chinese Social and Political Science Review* 20 (1936): 393.

Tukey, John. "Causation, Regression and Path Analysis." In *Statistics and Mathematics in Biology*, edited by Oscar Kempthorne et al. Ames: Iowa State Press, 1954.

Turney-High, Harry Holbert. *Primitive Wars, Its Practices and Concepts.* Columbia, S.C.: University of South Carolina Press, 1949.

Van Atta, Richard H., and Rummel, R. J. "Testing Field Theory on the 1963 Behavior Space of Nations." Research Report No. 43, Dimensionality of Nations Project, University of Hawaii, 1970.

Wahlback, Krister. "Finnish Foreign Policy: Some Comparative Perspectives." *Cooperation and Conflict* 4 (1969): 282–98.

Wall, Charles, and Rummel, R. J. "Estimating Missing Data." Research Report No. 20, Dimensionality of Nations Project, University of Hawaii, 1969.

Wallace, Victor H. *Paths to Peace.* New York: Cambridge University Press, 1957.

Waltz, Kenneth. *Man, the State, and War.* New York: Columbia University Press, 1959.

Weede, Erich. "Conflict Behavior of Nation-States." *Journal of Peace Research*, no. 3 (1970): 229–35.

Whiting, Allen S. *China Crosses the Yalu.* New York: Macmillan, 1960.

Wilkenfeld, Jonathan. "Domestic and Foreign Conflict Behavior of Nations." *Journal of Peace Research*, no. 1 (1968): 56–69.

————. "Models for the Analysis of Foreign Conflict Behavior of States." In *Peace, War, and Numbers*, edited by Bruce M. Russett. Beverly Hills, Calif: Sage Publications, 1972.

————. "Some Further Findings Regarding the Domestic and Foreign Conflict Behavior of Nations." *Journal of Peace Research*, no. 2 (1969): 147–56.

Williams, R. M., Jr. *The Reduction of Intergroup Tensions*, New York: Social Science Research Council, No. 57, 1947.

Winch, Robert F., and Campbell, Donald T. "Proof? No. Evidence? Yes. The Significance of Tests of Significance." *American Sociologist* 4 (1969): 140–43.

Withey, Steven, and Katz, Daniel. "The Social Psychology of Human Conflict." In *The Nature of Human Conflict*, edited by Elton McNeil. Englewood Cliffs, N.J.: Prentice-Hall, 1965.

Wolff, Kurt H., trans. and ed. *The Sociology of Georg Simmel*. Glencoe, Ill.: Free Press, 1948.

Wood, Robert C. *1400 Governments*. Cambridge, Mass.: Harvard University Press, 1961.

Wright, Quincy. "The Nature of Conflict." *Western Political Quarterly* 4 (1951): 193–209.

_____. *Problems of Stability and Progress in International Relations*. Berkeley and Los Angeles: University of California Press, 1954.

_____. *The Study of International Relations*. New York: Appleton-Century Crofts, 1955.

_____. *A Study of War*, Vols. 1 and 2. Chicago: University of Chicago Press, 1942 and 1965.

Wright, Sewell. "The Interpretation of Multivariate Systems." In *Statistics and Methamatics in Biology*, edited by Oscar Kempthorne et al. Ames: Iowa State Press, 1954.

Zartman, William. *International Relations in the New Africa*. Englewood Cliffs, N.J.: Prentice-Hall, 1966.

_____. "National Interest and Ideology." In *African Diplomacy: Studies in the Determinants of Foreign Policy*, edited by Vernon McKay. New York: Praeger, 1966.

Zawodny, J. K. "Unexplained Realms of Underground Strife." *American Behavioral Scientist* 4 (1960): 3–5.

Zinnes, Dina A. "Hostility in International Decision-Making." *Journal of Conflict Resolution* 6 (1962): 236–43.

_____. "Review of James N. Rosenau, *Linkage Politics*." *Midwest Journal of Political Science* 14 (May 1970): 344–47.

_____, and Wilkenfeld, Jonathan. "An Analysis of Foreign Conflict Behavior of Nations." In *Comparative Foreign Policy: Theoretical Essays*, edited by Wolfram F. Hanrieder. New York: David McKay, 1971.

Zolberg, Aristide. "The Structure of Political Conflict in the New States of Tropical Africa." *American Political Science Review* 52, no. 1 (March 1968): 70–87.

 INDEX

Index